Avant-Garde Magazines

CITY LIGHTS

1952 - 1955

Edited by
PETER MARTIN

Five issues complete in one volume

A GOTHAM BOOK MART SELECTION

ARNO PRESS
A New York Times Company
1974

Reprinted by permission of Peter Martin

ISBN 0-405-01758-8

Manufactured in the United States of America

35 cents

Film Criticism

Short Stories

Poems

CITY LIGHTS

Number One ■ San Francisco   July 1952

SUMMER SERIES

berkeley cinema guild

LE CONTE SCHOOL AUDITORIUM
... Russell at Ellsworth ...
FRIDAYS AND SATURDAYS — 7:30 AND 9:30 P.M.

JULY 11 & 12 — **CHARLIE CHAPLIN in**
The Cure   The Floorwalker   The Fireman   The Pawnshop (1917)
THE GOOD OLD DAYS (short)

JULY 18 & 19 — **CHARLIE CHAPLIN in**
The Rink   The Vagabond   The Adventurer   Easy Street (1917)
MARCH OF THE MOVIES (short)

JULY 25 & 26 — **CHARLIE CHAPLIN in A BURLESQUE ON CARMEN** (1915)
His first feature-length film

TIME IN THE SUN by Sergei Eisenstein
(1939) (feature—one hour)

AUG. 8 & 9 — **CHARLIE CHAPLIN in TILLIE'S PUNCTURED ROMANCE** (1915)
An early feature-length comedy co-starring Marie Dressler

MAN OF ARAN
by Robert Flaherty (1934) (feature—one hour)

AUG. 15 & 16 — **CRIME AND PUNISHMENT** - Pierre Blanchar and Harry Baur
(1935)
THE LOON'S NECKLACE (short in color)

AUG. 22 & 23 — **THE LADY VANISHES**
starring Margaret Lockwood, Michael Redgrave, Paul Lukas (1938)
THE NIGHT MAIL — Verse commentary by W. H. Auden. Music by
Benjamin Britten (short)

AUG. 29 & 30 — **CHEKHOV FILM FESTIVAL** - The Moscow Art Theatre (1946)
JUBILEE. Based on Chekhov's "The Anniversary."
MARRIAGE. Based on Chekhov's "The Wedding."
Norman McLaren's LA POULETTE GRISE (short in color)

SEPT. 5 & 6 — **DR. KNOCK** starring Louis Jouvet (1936)
Pare Lorentz's classic THE RIVER
Music by Virgil Thompson (short)

Patrons who wish to be notified of future programs are urged to add their
names to the Cinema Guild's mailing list by filling in the coupon below.
This should be sent to the Director, Berkeley Cinema Guild, 2609 Hillegass
Avenue, Berkeley 4, California, or handed to an usher at the door. For
information please call AShberry 3-1886 or BErkeley 7-8571.

BERKELEY CINEMA GUILD
2609 HILLEGASS AVE.   BERKELEY, 4, CALIF.

Name ....

Address .... Tel. ....
            (street)   (city)   (zone)

What type of film interests you most? ....

San Francisco   July, 1952   No. 1

Editor   PETER MARTIN

Assistant Editor   NORMA SWAIN

Editorial Assistant   JEAN TAYLOR

Contributing Editors

> ARTHUR FOFF
> HERBERT KAUFFMAN
> WILDER BENTLEY
> ANTOINETTE WILLSON
> M.W.F. POLLACK

Managing Editor   RICHARD MILLER

Presswork
> by Richard Pool

Lithographed
> by Alan's at 46 Kearny Street

Process photography
> by David Leong

Advertising copy
> by Mary Laage and
> Daphne MacMasters

Cover design
> by Don Smith

In Future Issues of
CITY LIGHTS

A NEW MAGAZINE

IN SAN FRANCISCO

Behold now this vast City;
a City of refuge, the man-
sion house of liberty...
should ye suppress all this
flowery crop of knowledge
and new light sprung up and
yet springing daily in
this City?

                    -Milton

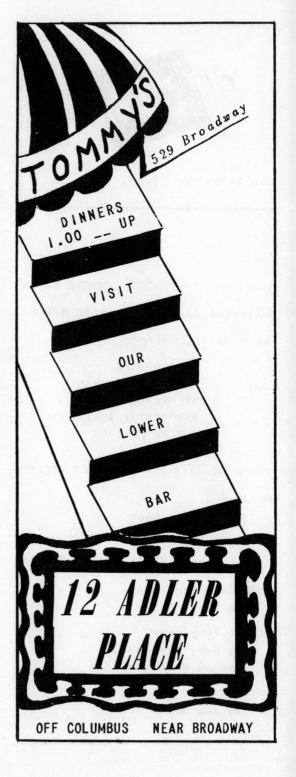

An Open Letter to CITY LIGHTS

From ROBERT DUNCAN

This is a tricky idea, a City. At its very worst possibility, it is civic-mindedness, a cultural busybody-dom, to pull oneself up by one's own city bootstraps. It is my own very worst impossibility; I am always becoming engaged in it with an enthusiasm that trickles out and a sense of the wrongness that grows——in plans for civic improvement, poetry concerts, art festivals, how to make the city about us conscious of "art", meaning us. I like the idea of being very important if it meant only the kingdom, the power, and the glory; but in reality it means a digression of forces, a confusion of interests. As a poet, am I interested in the City's consciousness of me or am I interested in my consciousness of the city? When I am in my right mind, the challenge is not to cónquer the City, but to know it. And so I look forward to a CITY LIGHTS that will not be civic-minded, that will not seek to educate the city but to be a journal of our education in the city. Not to reform, but to know what we are.

At its next to worst possibility, the City is San Franciscoism, "Bagdad-by-the-Bay", etc. To become another NEW YORKER? The danger I have in mind is for all of us the same danger of civic-mindedness as above. Here we proceed to make the city conscious of itself instead of conscious of art or or culture or us. All these endeavers stand between the writer and the exploration and articulation of human experience.

To translate the alien into the human. To see the city in which we live, not in the terms of civic concern, not in the terms of American culture. But to see it in the terms of our humanity, this quickens the imagination.

Now what I thoroughly like about the idea of CITY LIGHTS at this point is that it invites us all to turn from the manufacture of culture or the exploration of traditions, from the advance-guard of revolution or the rear-guard of values, from the elevation or salvation of man, back to the field of experience. What we ought to be or ought not to be will still loom large— we have been steeped in the business of the apocalypse. But it is a real possibility in art, a promise of freshening sources for the writer, to turn to the exploration of the life we live, our city living. Editorially, this doesn't mean, as your prospectus hints, the exclusion of manifestoes or of culture or of controversy. Even when these are not explorations of what we are, they are always evidence of what we are. What tells is the editorial focus.

I am all for that conversation you propose when I imagine it as the daily liveliness of the city. Alive with issues, with observations, with personalities, with pleasures, with contesting and corresponding interests, elective affinities, with visions, and with experience.

1

CONTENTS

City Lights is published at 580 Washington Street, San Francisco.
Telephone DOuglas 2-8193. Copyright, 1952, by City Lights for
its contributors.

The Bronze Moment

by JANE BOBBA

Eleanor walked her salmon tweed out of the door of the American Express Agency into the brittle snow brightness of Mozartplatz. It was serious to be putting the fifty dollars worth of Austrian shillings away in her best brown handbag, to smell face powder and unused taffeta. She had wanted to keep that last blue folder, but since there had been no more checks the teller had said, 'Please?' in that European way Eleanor didn't·like and had torn it in two with a little snap. So now, in Salzburg, there were no more. There were, in fact, no more anywhere. A small woman in one of those great shaggy fur coats the Europeans affected said, 'Please?' in that way again so Eleanor stepped a little from the doorway into the square ('Platz, in Austria a square is a platz.') and finally looked at Mozart.

He leaned in bronze, his legs curved tight with metal, and Eleanor was frightened again, as she had expected to be, standing in the melting snow and. seeing the young man dark against the winter sky. It had been most frightening that morning when she had first seen him and when seeing him had made

JANE BOBBA, who wrote *The Bronze Moment* in Zurich, was born in New York City, is 24, and now lives and works in San Francisco.

her think a terrible thought. She had thought then that one could climb up on that pedestal ('if I wore a full skirt') and lean against Wolfgang Mozart, push against the sky. ('People would notice but I'd press hard against him and he'd be wonderfully cool and say nothing so the people would finally go away and I would kiss his fingers and his lace ruff till the moon came up.') That was all she had thought; she hadn't even walked any nearer, but now she felt flushed even to be in the platz. It was too warm now with the sun attacking from all the crystals of snow--too warm, so she turned away from the slender metal man balancing on the sheet of music he held in his young hand.

Eleanor walked her brown suede shoes into one of the narrow streets that led to the bridge. These European streets, she thought, as a wagon rolled so close that the long crusted eyelashes of the horse brushed before her face. Nothing was ever Austrian or French or Italian to her-- simply European. She always knew which country she was in as it was her custom to sit right down at the first stop and make herself fluent with the rate of exchange, buy a guidebook to the principal cities, and learn from a waitress how one asked for the toilette. So it was damen toiletten in Austria, where she had stayed for the past month for it was the cheapest country in Europe ('but still clean'); and her money had been going, now was gone save for the fifty dollars.

Half way across the bridge she stopped to watch the little river squeezed between the bergs, poured under the foot bridges and auto bridges. It was still, she thought, picturesque. Eleanor mourned what Europe had been more intensely than any European. She had first seen it when she was forty-three, which was a year ago, but she knew that it was all spoiled now. Except, possibly, for the cathedrals. Music, violin music something like the Third Man Theme one heard everywhere, added to her mood and thrilled her--made her feel picturesque, too—(well-dressed, mature woman finding time to stop her rushing to enjoy the beauty of ancient Salzburg.) The music stopped and she saw the empty white eye of the violinist, saw into it, and it made her sick like escargots in Paris. Afraid of looking sick, afraid of the silence on the bridge after the Third Man Theme, she opened her bag and gave him some shillings. Too much, for he said, 'Danke' and then 'Please?' in a loud voice and smiled. It was one of Eleanor's convictions that unfortunates should not be hypocritical and smile. He did not play again until she was off the bridge. She knew he wanted to watch her with his one good eye.

She was grateful for the heavy odor of the Cafe Sohr, for the thick green felt winter drapes that held to her topcoat before they released her into the three o'clock suspension of the cafe. The table where she had sat most of the morning was free, and the waiter near it smiled vaguely above his black coat so she supposed she couldn't really change though sitting too near the herren toiletten displeased her. Austrian men were too fat ('even after the terrible war') and they never looked so fat as when they arose from their beer and apfelsaft to squeeze green trousered thighs between the marble table tops. But on this side of the room the ivory net draperies had been drawn and Eleanor liked the way the sunlight was filtered into cream. She felt that it was becoming to her, who was, she always said, one of those brown-haired women who could wear browns and golds.

The waiter reappeared with a four day old Herald Tribune which she had read that morning and a Viennese Illustrated Weekly. 'Bitte, one large cup of coffee and no sugar, keine sugar.' She enunciated this very clearly for him, then closed her eyes, let her hands fall limp, and looked composed until he returned with the oval silver tray--one glass of water, one small cup of very black coffee, one dish of three cubes of sugar and a precise pitcher of cream.

For an hour she sat and tried to feel like everyone else but the loss of the little blue check book made the pretense difficult. She was not just like everyone else. She had, at forty-three, left her job and her brother and his family back home and gone off to Europe. For no reason. She had never known any Europeans nor had she wanted to until that summer.

With a thirty day vacation and two thousand dollars saved outside of her insurance, she had simply thought one day--Europe! Paris. Rome. Vienna. That was fourteen months ago, and she had never since been able to think of a reason for going home. But there was no reason for staying either, for she did not really like Europe. Well, she was now out of money and this would force a decision. Tomorrow, she would cable her brother. Tomorrow, she would say in a wire 'am coming home.'

He had been in the herren toiletten and was now coming out but she had not been aware as he was small, quite thin, and hadn't jogged the chairs with his walking. Now she was aware of him, for he wore a heavy, musky perfume like sour, over-scented soap from gift boxes of three or four cakes. He returned to his place facing her across the room, startling her with a gaily white smile before opening his foreign newspaper. ('I suppose I have been staring.') Eleanor was amused as she personally hated the European custom of staring at people, in cafes, on the streets, everywhere. Always staring to see whether you've money or whether you're respectable or what. He was not respectable, she decided, as he read his paper and sipped his little black coffee with tiny, absentminded sips. Neatly dressed, though, in a sport jacket and slacks which she liked even on an older man. But perfume! She reached for the four day old Herald Tribune and tried to read about Senator Taft, a man she admired. He reached for the crotch of his blue

slacks and raising himsllf gracefully-smoothed the wrinkles and settled comfortably. She saw this and colored. ('Why I am <u>coloring</u>.')

Her eyes were very still. ('What would a man like that do? If one spent all day with him where would he go, what would he see? What would he do to me?') She daydreamed, her face suspended above the oval tray, through a drink in a dim American bar, a hotel room overheated against the winter, a struggle without form, the musk and the Yardley's she wore, an attack, painstaking and bitter, ('Wolfgang, No, Wolfgang!') and his awful, pointed orange shoes. The man stood in his pointed orange shoes and said, 'Might I borrow the Tribune?' He tilted toward her. 'I like very much to read English frequently.' 'Certainly,' Eleanor said because her breasts were hurting.

'Oh,' his mouth a little pink hole in his face, 'your sugar!' 'What?' 'Your sugar, might I have it?' 'Of course, do.' And she watched as he sat carefully on the chair opposite, took one cube of sugar and dipped it into her cup of coffee standing cold and untouched, dipped it saying 'May I really,' and making the over-sized wristwatch on his small wrist gleam with the silver pitcher. He first made the coffee creep into the little cube grain by grain ('He made me go with him.') and then he sucked the moisture from the still firm cube. ('Me too, me too.') 'You are an American, correct, I am Hungarian.' And he did it twice again with the cubes, the little pink mouth, the sucking noise, the sucking up of the brown stain and the crunching of the sugar in his even, yellow teeth. 'But, we both love Austria, so surely?'

No, I'm an American. I am going home tomorrow. I'm so glad I'm going home.' He had finished with the crunching and dipping and sucking and was standing, slapping his thigh with the Tribune, in his pointed orange shoes. 'So?' And then to thank her and say goodbye and because he was an Hungarian, he clicked his heels. 'Please?' He had not understood that she was going home.

Let Me Put You STRAIT

By FREDERICK ANDREWS

Trust plain talk to make it all plain.
Dead of night is plain as day.
The open is the hiding place.

You saw a moon? That mistake
More light will clear away.
The open is the hiding place.

Any may learn which words to say.
The hush--all speak as none!--is deafening.
The open is the hiding place.

So this terror of, for, and by
Ourselves ensures its reign:
The open is the hiding place.

An American In New York

By WALTER GLASER

IT WAS VERY LATE AT NIGHT AND IT WAS snowing outside. There were only three of us left in the bar and I didn't feel like leaving because there wasn't any place to go. There wasn't any place to go because I'd never been to New York before and I didn't know anybody to call and I'd already been in this bar for three hours. Sometimes when you sit in a strange bar in a strange town for three hours you get a feeling that even though the place is really dead, and even though you don't like anything about the place, you nevertheless can't leave. Because dead as it might be, and strange as it might be, it still remains the only place you know and that in itself makes you feel a little bit safe. Anyway that's why I didn't feel like leaving.

So the three of us sat there.

There were really four of us, but I didn't feel like counting the bartender because he didn't have to sit on our side of the bar and pretend that at any moment he was going to leave to do something important. Something that he'd luckily just remembered. He was a very small man

Walter Glaser was born in San Francisco in 1926 and has studied New York and Los Angeles closely. He now lives in Mill Valley.

with a bald, bullet shaped head and a mouth with a kind of built-in contemptuous sneer. His whole person seemed to give you the feeling that he was annoyed with the three of us. That's the last reason. I didn't feel like counting him in. That, and those big hairy arms of his.

Sitting two stools down from me was a plain but rather nice looking girl. She was a brunette and she had on a gray tailored suit that looked nice although you could tell it wasn't very expensive as far as women's clothes go. She looked lonely and uneasy and like she might be stuck with the place the same way I was. I watched her in the mirror behind the bar but she kept her eyes down most of the time.

Two more stools from her sat this big guy with a crew haircut. He had on a dark blue suit with a white shirt that was open at the collar and enough of his necktie was sticking out of his coat pocket so that you had the feeling he wanted people to know that he always wore a tie with a suit, but that now he was tired and it was late so he had taken the tie off. You were just positive that he never wore that tie but always carried it in his pocket like that. His face was that good looking square type you might see on a navy recruiting poster or maybe on a magazine ad for a new cheap shaving lotion. He appeared to be lonely too, and he kept his eyes down about the same way as the girl did.

I suddenly had this feeling that aside from our mutual loneliness, the three of us had to stay because of the bartender. I couldn't stand the idea of a guy like the bartender thinking that any of us would leave on his account.

The drinks that I had been having were finally catching up with me and the anxious feeling that I had been carrying around in my stomach was beginning to evaporate. I was becoming certain that I would have to speak to the other two. The more I drank and the more I watched the man and woman, and the bartender, who was doing us a big favor by selling us liquor, the closer I got to the point when I knew I would get up and say something.

I drank down the last of the rye and soda in my glass, and then I was standing up and walking over to a place between the man and woman. It was like I was watching myself, because although I felt fairly confident, I was very nervous.

'Look,' I heard myself saying to both of them, 'I don't know a soul in this town and it's late and snowing out, and I know this kind of thing can be offensive and embarrassing, but I really feel like I know you people and if you would join me I would like very much to buy the three of us a drink.' I caught a glimpse of the bartender watching me and frowning and shaking his head, and I never hated anyone like that in my life.

The man and girl had both turned and the man was smiling and saying that he thought it would be a fine idea and then the man and I and that damn bartender were all waiting to see what the girl would say.

She hesitated and I watched the moment of indecision in the green eyes and then they got very green and I could see she had made up her mind, and she said yes, that she would be happy to have a drink with the man and I. The bartender shook his head again like he had just witnessed a final validating example of the wretchedness of human behavior. I'm telling you I hated him.

We introduced ourselves and I told them I was from Sacramento, California, and they told me they were both living in New York and as it happened they both turned out to be from Chicago originally.

We talked very pleasantly and they told me some of the things I should see while I was in New York. I told them that I was leaving the next day but that the next time I was in New York I would take in all the places they suggested.

We finished our first drinks and then a strange thing happened. No one said anything about another drink and so I asked them if they would like to have another round. There wasn't a moment's hesitation. They both readily agreed that it would be fine. The man didn't make any attempt to pay for the round, but I was so thankful to be talking to people that I didn't think anything about it. I was so pleased about bringing three strangers together in this big city.

From there on in I paid for all the rounds as though it was simply understood, although I didn't understand it, and the conversation at all times was pleasant and interesting. We talked a great deal about New York but I kept noticing that the man and woman were always talking to me and never to each other.

After the fourth round of drinks I excused myself to go to the men's room. I doused my face with cold water and for a second I had a good glimpse of myself as a real hick. A sucker. I tried to tell myself it didn't make any difference about my paying for all the drinks since I wasn't alone anymore.

I came out of the men's room and our table was empty. The man and woman were gone. For a moment I couldn't believe it, and then I had a terrible rush of feeling for Sacramento, California.

I went to the table and got my hat and coat. The bartender was busy setting glasses on the shelf and his back was towards me, so I hurried on out.

Hippocampus

By GUY WERNAM

Winged in water, gravely slow,
Pygmy dignitaries go:
Hoofless coursers, roaming free—
Eohippus of the sea—
Bustling through brine to secret places:
Chess knights with poker faces.

Two Stories on a Single Theme

By STUART VIBERT

1. Scully

THE SCREEN DOOR BANGED AND THE sound echoed down the valley through the hot moist air. Then the labored rattle of the pickup truck followed and obliterated the door sound as the truck headed down the road, the wheels throwing dust behind them that settled in little pats and whorls on the roadway. High above a lone buzzard swung in wide lazy circles hunting for some death that might lie in the parched summer grasses in the valley, or in the saged hills.

Scully waited until the sounds died away and the hum of summer insects became the only thing audible. He rose from his comfortable position beside the stream and walked up toward the house through the prune

---

These two stories are printed together because they concern the same characters and situation, for they are so strikingly different in treatment and form that they provide a valuable insight into the processes of writing. *A Cool Place* was written in 1950, while *Scully*, which is the opening chapter of a forthcoming novel, was written early this year. STUART VIBERT is a young San Francisco writer at present working on a novel.

orchard. He heard a noise come from the direction of the house and looked up through the neatly rowed trees. It was Ryka Johnson going out to give grain to the chickens. He looked up and saw the buzzard making tight circles now, over the gabled house.

'Mornin' Ryka,' Scully greeted the dumpy figure in the chicken yard.

'There's hot coffee in the kitchen,' Ryka answered without turning to face him. 'I'll be in presently.'

Scully banged through the door and poured himself a cup of coffee, then slouched into a kitchen chair as if it were an overstuffed couch. The house had some remnants of morning coolness left, but Scully didn't notice or care as he stared at a spot on the stained wallpaper, waiting for Ryka to come in.

'It's going to be another scorcher today, Scully,' she said as she entered. She seemed to be smiling at him and he realized that she rarely smiled. 'If only the fog would come in from the ocean in the morning it wouldn't get so hot in the daytime.'

'I guess,' Scully said, and somewhere in the dimness of the house he heard a thin cry.

10

'That'll be the baby,' said Ryka. 'I guess she's hungry again.'

Scully shifted a bit in his chair and watched Ryka leave the kitchen already unbuttoning the top of her faded cotton dress. She returned with the infant sucking comfortably from one of her striated breasts, and sat down across the table from Scully.

'This one's really a feeder,' she said proudly. 'Neither of the boys ever ate like this near as I can recall.'

'They're both pretty thin alright.'

'Not thin, Scully, lean; those boys are strong.'

'I guess.'

'They wouldn't have been drafted if they weren't strong.'

'What about the Limos kid? He couldn't weigh more than a hundred pound an' they took him.'

'He weighed more than that!' said Ryka, shifting the child to the other breast and watching Scully as he eyed the moist vacated nipple.

'He couldn't more'n hold his ground in a light wind.'

'Oh, Scully!...have some more coffee. It's still warm.'

'Thanks.' Scully removed his train engineer's cap and poured the coffee. 'You not havin' any?'

'No, I've had enough this morning thanks. Looks like this baby is finished eating already, she's getting sleepy, see?'

Scully looked at the child as her mouth sloughed off the leathery nipple and her head cradled into the crevice between Ryka's breasts.

'I guess it's about time for the mail,' Ryka went on. 'I haven't heard from either of the boys for a long time. Maybe something'll come today.'

'I saw that girl Charlie was sweet on in town yesterday; she was with a couple of sailors.'

'Sailors!' Ryka said, 'With some sailors?' Scully nodded and sipped some coffee, and watched the half smile creep onto Ryka's face and then disappear. 'I guess I'd better not tell Charlie about that when I write him,' she went on, 'I don't suppose he'd like that any too well.'

'I don't suppose.'

'He was mighty sweet on Billie, though.'

'He's likely forgotten her by now,' Scully grinned, 'bein' away and all for so long.'

'Still I'd best not to tell him; he's got enough worrying just staying alive.'

'I guess.'

'I wish the boys were home,' said Ryka, blankly staring through Scully, 'why do we have to have wars?'

'There's always wars.'

'Yes, that's true I suppose,' Ryka looked down at the baby, 'but this one won't ever have to go to war.'

'I guess she'll be havin' kids who will though...same as you an' everyone else.'

'No, not her. Maybe this is going to be the last one.'

'Could be, I guess.'

The bright foreign sound of an auto horn broke in upon them in the hotness of the room. Ryka started, looked anxiously at Scully and then got up and carried the baby up to the bedroom. 'That'll be the mailman, it's a package I suppose, from the way he's blowing that horn; but who'd be sendin' a package?'

Ryka returned quickly to the kitchen, buttoning the top of her dress as Scully followed the movements closely from button to button. 'I'll go down and pick it up; I sure hope it's something from one of the boys.' Scully watched the shapeless cotton-dressed Ryka disappear and went over to the icebox and got out a bottle of beer. From behind the icebox, through the doorway to the small laundry room, there came the damp clammy smell of wet wash. Scully went into the room and stood in its coolness, pulling now and then on the bottle as he looked into the hamper heaped with diapers and faded under-wear. He was there when Ryka came back; he heard her come in through the door, and then only sensed her presence in the kitchen as she stood there motionless beside the screen.

'Scully, where are you?' Her voice was small, distant.

'Only here... in the laundry.'

'Oh, I thought you'd gone,' he came out into the kitchen and faced her, 'I thought you'd gone.'

'Somethin' the matter Ryka?' Scully's stolid face almost changed expression.

'I don't know. I'm afraid.' She held up a telegram envelope. 'Fred got a telegram. We never got one before, what do you suppose it is?'

'I guess you could open it and see.'

'No, it's for Fred, I never open his mail. He never liked for me to open his mail. I'm afraid, Scully, I'm afraid; I know it's one of the boys, I can tell it.'

'I wouldn't worry... it's probably nothin'.' Scully could feel cold sweat coming from his armpits and tickling its way down his flanks. He thought of taking another pull at the beer, but it didn't seem right to him that he should be drinking beer with Ryka feeling the way she did.

'Maybe I'd better go and come back tomorrow,' Scully offered, 'It's probably nothin' anyways.'

Ryka didn't answer, but simply stared down at the table as she leaned her bulk against the door jamb. Scully felt a wriggly worm of discomfort wriggle in his bowels now that the subject of her sons had been broached in this way. He didn't like to picture himself and Ryka in the bedroom, and the things they did there while her husband worked and her sons were in distant foreign places.

She looked at him, through him, 'No, don't go,' she begged, 'Come and sit with me a while.' Why did she have to look like that, Scully thought, why did she have to?

He sat on the bed and watched Ryka shading the light from her eyes with her thick forearm. She wasn't crying or about to, as near as he could tell. She simply lay there lumped up, sagging the mattress into the center and breathing heavily of the close air that crowded hotly into the upper part of the house. He could feel the sweat start on his forehead and see her sweat running down her ruddy stump neck.

'Ryka, why don't you open it. At least you'd know. It's not knowin' that's the worst.'

The arm came away from her eyes and

she looked at him this time.

'Sometimes,' she was saying hoarsely, 'sometimes you remind me of Charlie.' She sat up and kissed him hard, not like usually, not distant or sloppy or indifferent; in the heat with the sweat sliding their faces, they embraced and Ryka clasped the straps of his overalls in her hands and seemed to want to tear them off. 'Scully, Scully!'

—SCULLY, SCULLY! out through the great screened porch he could see the glistening from the pale gold spume of straw that blew from the thresher, and all around the great machine, standing rusty red on the prairie, the men feeding the bundled wheat onto the endless belt, vaulting the bundles up and in. There was the smell of food in the kitchen where women prepared the mountains of food for the hands at mealtime. He could feel the muscles beginning to bunch hard and big around his shoulders and up along his neck where there hadn't been any before.

—SCULLY, you'd better be gettin' on to work out with the men or they'll be handin' you an apron and we'll put you to work in here.

There was the chaff itching its way down his spine, the sun boiling the water out of his body, and his father standing down on the field below the machine ladling some of the cool spring water into his mouth, then the silvery arc of it as he spat to the ground and drew his strong brown forearm over his mouth and looked up at him. There were the big meals on the oak table out under the trees with the women running

back and forth with pitchers, bowls, and plates. He would sit next to Laura Belsen's brother and ask him about the war and every so often he'd slip in a question about Laura and Lang would laugh and stuff a potato into his mouth and still be laughing with the veins on his neck standing out like thick blue worms. Then there was the waning afternoon sun and the wheat pouring like gold into the hoppers as the heat haze began to obscure the horizon and the great billowing thunderheads threatened and waned. Later when the work ended the men grouped around the water trough washing the itchy chaff and red dust from their bodies because Scully's mother didn't want her immaculate house looking like a stubbled wheatfield. And he would hitch up the team and go over to Laura Belsen's early, even though it seemed he didn't have a chance with all the veterans from France hanging around with their cars or with their suits and straw hats and bragging about the war or about how much money they made in town; but she always seemed to be there when he arrived and they went out with the team clopping slowly along the dirt road and looked at the gigantic orange thing that was the moon rising through the haze. He'd tie the reins and give the horses leave to go where they wanted because he loved Laura so much and wanted both hands to touch her and feel her and tell her how much he loved her without saying it, because he couldn't say it, he'd never be able to say that or much of anything. Laura's face, framed in her short bobbed hair would laugh and she

would love him back in the same way.
She loved him into things he never
dreamed possible, even though he'd
heard it talked about by the men and
the older boys. It never seemed real
to him, it wasn't happening to him
until one night she said she was late
and when he didn't understand she
told him that she was going to have
his baby, but he didn't say anything.
He didn't say anything about the
searing pain he'd first felt that
morning, nor the running; so he didn't
say anything except that it was too
bad, it was certainly too bad. Now
he saw why the veterans kept coming
back in their cars, so the next
morning after dawn he stood at the
farmgate looking down the dirt road
that ran sloping up to the long
rounded hill that ran from horizon to
horizon. He always told himself that
this was the curve of the earth and
that road ran up and over the curve of
the earth. But he had never been
there; the ridge was a couple of
miles off and he had never had call
to go that way. He was sure there
were many wonderful things there,
past the curve of the earth, where the
sun set. He walked east, away from
the curve, and kept on until he was
at the railway station and there was
Lang Belsen looking mean and saying
something about marrying his sister,
and it looked like he was going to
have to do it until he discovered the
use of his great ham fists and with a
single blow knocked Lang off the
station platform and into the dust.

He stayed on the train through all
the stops, looking out at the monotonous plains sweeping by, his head

on his fist and letting the sight
filter through him. Then there seemed
to be endless miles of some dank grey
city and it seemed to him that it was
as vast as the plains and as the train
bore through to the city's center he
felt more and more lost at the piles of
filthy brick. Then the train stopped
and the man said it was Chicago, so
he looked at his ticket and that said
Chicago too, so he got off and walked
around in the chill winds that blew
off the lake, feeling the knifepain
cutting his crotch, and he looked in
amazement as he watched the big ships
angle warily through the narrow
river. Scully found a room, and the
landlord got him a job where he
worked because as he said he didn't
want any big young bucks hanging
around all day with nothing to do
while his wife was so hot for it.
And Mr. Cason, the landlord, sent him
to a man who stopped the burning and
running, for most of the time at
least, and he worked in the steel mill
with Mr. Cason, and sweated in the
heat of the incandescent molten stuff
instead of the hot brightness of the
sun. And instead of the smell of
earth and air his nostrils became
clogged with the gummy smell of coke;
and great clanging noises echoing
about all the time. He didn't take
notice of them, but in the night he'd
lie in his bed and think of the plains
and the wheat and Laura and then his
bowels seemed to knot up, but after
many months of nights there wasn't
even this. Then on Saturday nights
Bertie took care of him at a dollar a
throw as he'd try not to notice her
flaccid breasts or the mottled sagfat

of her belly. After a time he got used to it, and used to the stale sooty air and seeing the smutty clouds on the urban horizon at sunset. He stopped missing the great moons that came up out on the plains and shone big through the dust of the harvest. Then one day Mr. Cason fell into a ladle full of molten steel and Scully stood there for a minute and waited for him to come up to the surface until he remembered what it was Mr. Cason had fallen into, glowing hot below him——so he went home and told Mrs. Cason and she carried on for a while in a frightening manner and at the bodiless wake she got very drunk on beer and so did Scully and the next thing he knew he was married to Mr. Cason's old woman and he owned a boarding house and suddenly seemed to have a lot of extra money which really didn't seem to mean much to him. He kept going to Bertie's every Saturday night out of sheer habit, but one night there was some kind of scuffling in the dark hall and he threw a man down the splintered stairs and there was all sorts of noise and screaming whores and Bertie standing there with her sag visible through her open wrapper screaming at him that he'd killed a man and now she'd get closed up.

——SCULLY, He turned and there on a corner in the loop where he'd flown from the sight of the crumbled man limp and quite dead at the bottom of the whore's staircase, through neon flecked night, over the dense dark of tenements on the stilted El to stand on street corners and watch people laugh past him——there on this corner

at the foot of the groaning el the man spoke....

——SCULLY, And it was someone from home, someone he knew but couldn't remember after the years, and the man told him about his father going into the thrash machine with the bundled wheat and moaning for someone to kill him and how all the girls had grown up and been married and now there was just his brother there on the farm, and his mother looking poorly with a yellow cast to her skin. Scully thought of the big farmhouse there on the plains and how he had watched the trains go by on the bluff far off with the smoke streaking out across the sky and the sound of the whistle at night, when he lay in bed, calling long and low in the distance. And he asked about Laura Belsen and heard about all the children she had but how the first one had been born blind. She had married one of the Edson boys in town, but her brother Lang was still single and seemed to be getting old before his time all gnarled with rheumatism. So Scully thought of home again and the big curving place on the horizon to the west that looked like the curve of the earth and he remembered that he hadn't thought of it for a long time and he walked away from the familiar person, leaving him to the crowd of intense young people in the Saturday night loop. He walked along the nighted streets and noticed the slinking rats crawling in and out of sewers and saw how lonely the dim light of a pool hall was far down the bleak canyoned street. As he walked he heard soft low woman laugh coming faintly to him through the open slit of a darkened window. There was the river misting in the night and the distant hollow noise of the loop coming out to him on the chill wind as if he were standing on the rim of some vast chasm hearing the din and cry of immense nocturnal struggles.

Then there was the train leaving Chicago and he was home again with the dawn as he had left and he saw an old wizened woman come out and look toward him momentarily, but she couldn't see that far. He stood in the fresh morning and watched her go to the water pump and then he walked west toward the place where the earth curved.

SCULLY, SCULLY, And he looked and saw Ryka's daughter staring at him, at them, as they lay sweated in the bed. Scully tried to move, to rise and buckle his overalls and go back across the creek to the Redland place where he worked and where Ryka couldn't clutch at him that way, couldn't seem to start crying like that and dig her fingers into his shoulders; he didn't want to have to look into her eyes as they clouded and became blank.

'Ryka, I got to go now, you know that.'

'Go? Scully, no. Don't go...'

'I've got my noon chores.'

'Chores? Yes, the chores. I forgot about the chores.'

'An' don't worry about the telegram, it's probably nothin'.'

'No.'

Scully stood by the bed and looked down at her as she lay with her clothes all askew and staring at the place in the wall where the plaster was falling from the lathes.

'I'll be goin' now, Ryka.'

She didn't answer and he clumped heavily down the stairs and out of the house. He didn't feel the hot sun on his back as he walked slowly down through the orchard and crossed the creek to the path that led to the Redland place, nor did he look back to where Ryka Johnson lay in her house that sat up against the sage line in the foothills, although you could see the house from the Redland place. He neither looked back nor wondered, but went about his chores. Above him, the buzzard was still circling and screeching impatiently at the immortal day.

2. A Cool Place

NEAR THE STREAM, MOTIONLESS AND clear in the hazy summer days, and protected by the abundant profusion of green willows and leafy sycamores, there was coolness—relief from the encompassing heat of July. But on higher ground, across the orchard at the base of the sage covered foothills, the house of the Johnson family stands shimmering in the heat. Standing at the road one can hear the flat sound of the screen door banging into place. The sound echoes down the small valley, attenuating the hum of pestful insects and the high pitched cry of the buzzard circling interminably overhead, his flawless eye searching for carrion.

If one had lived close by it would have been possible for him to set his watch by that sound. It indicated that Fred Johnson was leaving for work. Where he worked does not matter; work is work. He was one of many in a long line who added little parts together with other little parts until they became great sulking monsters out of his sight and hearing, in some other space and time. Daily without stint he plied his newly learned trade at the distant factory, and brought home to Ryka Johnson more money than either of them had ever known. The two Johnson boys worked also, but they did not come home every day tired and hungry. They had been fitted out in uniforms and sent away to fight in some distant place.

When the dust that was stirred by Mr. Johnson's small pickup truck had settled in little pats and whorls on the powdered clay on the road, a figure could always be seen between the neatly rowed trees of the orchard, trudging slowly up toward the house...

Scully

Ryka Johnson's lover

Once again the bang of the screen door would echo down the valley, and in the darkened interiors of the old house, Scully, big Scully, inarticulate and unthinking, would, for reasons known to all but Ryka, fill the place of the two boys who no longer fished and trapped by the stream, or hunted in the fields and foothills. In the draftless heat of the bedroom, between its crumbling plaster walls, the dumpy figure of Ryka Johnson and the hulk of Scully would grind feverishly together. Bathed in sweat.

Fred Johnson could not know of this. He was tired at the end of the day, and slept the sleep that was due his honest fatigue. The boys could not know, for they were far away; their sister in the cradle was too young to know even when she saw. Only the oppressive heat could know, and the carrion-seeking buzzard, and the invisible insects that talk endlessly in the heat.

One day Ryka Johnson learned that her youngest son had died... in the usual manner that insignificant people participate in world events. Far from home, in a foreign and distant land, he lay rotting in the damp earth.

17

Ryka Johnson did not seem to break down. Mr. Johnson was of course very kind; he mumbled something appropriate and patted her shoulder gently.

But Scully in his expressionless way realized more. He saw in her face, in her eyes, but mostly in her deep vacuous smile, something that gripped him with a deep fear. Scully was dumb and unemotional--even fear was rare to him. In the heat of the day he ambled down the dusty road and went far away, trying to forget that he had ever known Ryka Johnson.

She did not count the days; they were endless and without meaning. She did not number the times that she padded down the dusty road to the mailbox. Looking fruitlessly for the impossible, Ryka Johnson became giddy and paralyzed in a moil of grief.

One day Fred Johnson came home and found the dumpy figure of his wife sprawled stiffly across the tattered sofa. Her body felt cold in the hot stuffy room. In the next room the baby cried lustily for nourishment, but Ryka Johnson was dead.

Mr. Johnson felt a twinge of understanding nagging him. He felt hot, feverish, as he stared at the motionless form of his dead spouse. He tried to regard her differently, but it remained the same as when she had lived. Mr. Johnson wanted to go where it was cool, where he could breathe, where he could escape the crying child. He did not think of the stream--the cool green places where a small trap lies forgotten under the rustling willows and the lush grasses.

Tokyo Rose—

Folklore And Justice

by GEORGE OLSHOUSEN

NATIONAL FOLKLORE DID NOT CEASE with King Arthur's Knights or Robin Hood. Modern times have made their contribution to the body of popular myths, and the American people spun a goodly quota of them as recently as World War II. One of the most curious of these contemporary folk tales was the myth of "Tokyo Rose"— a story that came to an unhappy denouement here in San Francisco only a few years ago.

Everyone knew about "Tokyo Rose". She was a woman who broadcast seductive and seditious programs to the American troops in the Pacific. No one knew who she was, but everyone felt sure that she was an American of Japanese descent gone over to the enemy. Moreover she had uncanny powers that far outdistanced the pedestrian competence of an ordinary radio broadcaster. She was not merely a broadcaster but a spy and a clairvoyant as well. Had she not on repeated occasions told American troops precisely where they were going even though future troop movements were kept

Iva Toguri d'Aquino has been in the Federal Women's Reformatory in Alderson, West Virginia since December, 1949. Here GEORGE OLSHAUSEN, one of Mrs. d'Aquino's attorneys, discusses some of the implications of the disturbing case of Tokyo Rose.

secret from the men themselves? Was she not able to pin point an individual soldier on an island in the Pacific and recall to him the delights of the particular American town from which he hailed? And so insidiously effective was Tokyo Rose that "some of our boys committed suicide over her ".*

All this and the famous seductive voice made her a fitting successor to Lilith, Circe, the Sirens, Cleopatra, Salammbo, and others--a Twentieth Century femme fatale. National myths not only go on forever, but tend to repeat themselves. The fatal woman holding a warrior in thrall is Keat's "La Belle Dame Sans Merci''; and Swinburne pointed out the recurring nature of this legend:

> Yea, I am famed the woman in
>   all tales,
> The face caught always in the
>   story's face:
> I, Helen, holding Paris by the
>   lips,
> Smote Hector through the head;
>   I, Cressida
> So kissed men's mouths that they
>   went mad or sick,
> Stung right at brain with me:
>   I Guenevere
> Made my Queen's eyes so precious
>   and my hair
> Delicate with such gold in its
>   soft ways
> And my mouth honied so for
>   Launcelot.

*As stated to the writer in conversation by a judge, who should have known better.

Contemporary literature has references such as John O'Hara's Butterfield 8: "For the first time he understood how these guys, these young subalterns, betray King and country for a woman. He even understood how they could do it while knowing that the woman was a spy, that she was not faithful to them..."

The radio-Siren with nearly super-human attributes, ensnaring men on distant islands of the Pacific and drawing them to surrender or death, differs only in detail from the Sirens of the Odyssey whose seductive music lures to destruction mariners voyaging far from home.

Since nothing was known about her, the country was fascinated by a tantalizing "whodunnit "--"who is Tokyo Rose?" Somehow Tokyo Rose was "known" to be a Nisei, who would pay the price of treason after America had won the war. The "knowledge" that Tokyo Rose was an American citizen of Japanese ancestry evidently justified what some persons felt about the Japanese-Americans. After all, there had to be some who were sabotaging the war effort or betraying their country to the Mikado. Blood tells--"A Jap is a Jap" and in a crisis these people would inevitably join Japan against the United States. It is true, when the war broke out none of the Nisei committed any acts of sabotage either in the continental United States or in Hawaii--but that proved all the more that they would do so in the future.

This type of emotional "thinking" affected the most responsible officials in government. Justice Murphy of the United States Supreme Court had this to say of the Army Commanders who ordered the Nisei internment on the American Continent:

Further evidence of the Commanding General's attitude toward the individuals of Japanese ancestry is revealed in his voluntary testimony on April 13, 1943, in San Francisco before the House Naval Affairs Subcommittee to Investigate Congested Areas, Part 3, pp. 739, 740 (78th Cong. 1st Sess): "I don't want any of them (persons of Japanese ancestry) here. They are a dangerous element. There is no way to determine their loyalty. The West Coast contains too many vital installations essential to the defense of the country to allow any Japanese on this coast....The danger of the Japanese was and is now--if they are permitted to come back—espionage and sabotage. It makes no difference whether he is an American Citizen, he is still a Japanese. American citizenship does not necessarily determine loyalty....But we must worry about the Japanese all the time until he is wiped off the map. Sabotage and espionage will make problems as long as he is allowed in this area."

The final report, p. 34, makes the amazing statement that as of February 14, 1942, "The very fact that no sabotage has taken place to date is a disturbing and confirming indication that such action will be taken." Apparently in the minds of the military leaders, there was no way in which the Japanese American could escape the suspicion of sabotage. (From Justice Murphy's dissenting opinion in Korematsu vs US 323 US. 214, 236, 241, footnotes 2 and 15.)

Furthermore, if traitors were not to be found in the United States and Hawaii they must be afoot elsewhere. On January 4, 1944, Marshall Hoot, a chief Boatswain's mate with the United States Navy in the Gilbert Islands wrote to his wife:

We have a radio now and we get Tokyo best. They have an American Jap girl who has turned down the United States for Japan. They call her Tokyo Rose and does she razz us fellows out here in the Pacific,, telling how well Japan is getting along and to hear her start out you would think that she were broadcasting from the US and sorry that we were loosing (sic) so many men and ships, it sure makes a fellow sore.

It never seems to have occurred to anyone that an English-language woman broadcaster in the Pacific might be other than an American citizen. Either our British and Australian allies were immune to such weaknesses, or no foreigner could possibly speak un-accented English. Still less was it thought that there might be several announcers. If a woman's voice came over the radio sixteen or eighteen hours a day, seven days a week, it must obviously belong always to the same person.

What were the facts? The Japanese had a staff of 15 or 20 English an-nouncers, including Japanese nationals, Germans, Swiss, Americans, Australians and Filipinos. About half a dozen were women--all potential "Tokyo Roses". Foumy Saisho, Ruth Hayakawa, Mieko Furuya Oki, Margaret Kato, and Mary Ishii were Japanese subjects who had either spent part of their childhood in the United States or had one English speaking parent and so were able to command unaccented English. June Suyama, since deceased, was a Canadian Nisei. Then there were Caucasians: Lillie Abegg was Swiss; a Miss Kramer, later Mrs. Reginald Hollingsworth (or Wollbauer) was German; Iva Toguri and Mrs. Genevieve Fayville Topping were American citizens. There were

also numerous men broadcasters, in-cluding American and Allied prisoners of war and a German named Wollbauer, who used the radio name of Reginald Hollingsworth.

Were any one or more of these women "Tokyo Rose'? When Japan surrendered American army authorities arrested Lillie Abegg, Iva Toguri, and one John Provoo. (The last named, an American Prisoner of War, has since been under prolonged psychiatric treatment.) Of the women Iva Toguri alone was singled out for a year's detention in Japan--six months by the United States Army and another six months by the Depart-ment of Justice.

Iva Toguri was an American Nisei born in Los Angeles on July 4, 1916; a registered Republican. After graduating from UCLA in 1941 she had sailed for Japan to visit a sick aunt on behalf of the family, or, as her prosecutors later hinted darkly, to study medicine. She received a Certificate of Identification rather than a passport, partly because she was in a hurry to leave, partly because the State Department had failed to issue her a passport since it "had publicly announced that travel abroad was not desirable". She lived in Japan with her aunt and uncle until December 1st, when her father cabled her from Los Angeles to board the Tatsuta Maru for the United States on the following day. But the red tape of Japanese currency regulation prevented her depar-ture, and she found herself still in Japan on the fatal December 7 of 1941. After the war broke out, Iva Toguri re-mained at her uncle's house, paying rent of 50 yen per month until June

1941. But the neighbors, the regular Japanese police, the Kampei-tai (secret police) agents made life so miserable because he harbored an American citizen that her uncle finally asked her to live elsewhere. For she had resisted—as she was to do throughout—all pressure from these agencies to make her abandon her American citizenship and become a Japanese subject. This loyalty would someday return to haunt her. Seven years afterwards the United States Government used witnesses who had changed from American to Japanese nationality in midst of war to testify that Iva Toguri d'Aquino had betrayed the United States.

Many American citizens caught in Japan when hostilities broke out were evacuated on exchange ships. Miss Toguri's efforts to get back to the United States, however, elicited the following notation by the American consul in Tokyo:

> April 4, 1942
> Records of the consulate general show that Miss Toguri applied for an American passport in September 1941.... Her application was referred to the Department of State, as are all cases of persons first applying for passport, and no reply was received up to the time the war broke out. Her American citizenship has not been proven, and it is not considered that her application for evacuation should receive any consideration other than that eventually to be accorded to other Nisei in Japan.

To say "Her American citizenship has not been proven" (though she had her birth certificate in Japan), was a subtle way of declaring that at this stage the United States refused to recognize the Nisei as citizens. Those on the continental United States were soon to be herded into concentration camps, delicately known as relocation centers". The phrase "consideration eventually to be accorded to other Nisei in Japan" must be read in the light of then current proposals that all Nisei should be deprived of their citizenship, by a constitutional amendment if necessary, and those in the United States should be shipped back to Japan after the war. (Cf. Carey McWilliams, Prejudice, p. 264.)

Five months later (September 7, 1941) she withdrew her application for repatriation, being without funds and both unwilling and unable to ask her parents, who were by that time in relocation centers, and according to one witness, in fear of being put into a relocation center herself. Having only fragmentary knowledge of Japanese she obtained such work as she could through her knowledge of English, being variously employed as monitor-typist at the Domei News Agency, at a private language school, and at the Danish consulate. In the summer of 1943, she secured a job as a typist in the accounts department of Radio Tokyo. At her trial she testified she had obtained it in a competitive examination, but one Edward Kuroishi, an otherwise undistinguished employee who had moved from Domei to Radio Tokyo, testified that his intercession got her this typing job. Three Allied Prisoners of War--an American, an Australian, and a Filipino--were then broadcasting over Radio Tokyo under duress of the Japanese Army. Early in

November of 1943, the Japanese conceived the idea of adding a woman's
voice to this prisoner of war program.
Upon learning of this plan the three
Allied prisoners succeeded in talking
their Japanese commandants into putting
Iva Toguri into the new spot for a
female voice.   She was duly directed
to broadcast by Shigechika Takano, head
of the Japanese overseas broadcasting
bureau, with the warning that "We
have received Army orders that you
have been selected by the prisoners
of war to be put on this new entertainment program--you have no choice.
You are living in a militaristic
country.   You take Army orders.   You
know what the consequences are.   I
don't have to tell you that."

Out of this was born Zero Hour,
broadcast seven days a week from
6-7 p.m., Tokyo Standard Time.   Miss
Toguri first appeared on it about
November 13, 1943, and worked six days
a week (Sundays off) until May, 1944;
five days a week (Saturdays and Sunday
off) from then until the end of the
war.   On the radio she was called
"Orphan Ann".   Her radio voice was
light and bantering--not that of the
legendary vamp.

Was Iva Toguri "Tokyo Rose" ?   The
answer is that she was one of several
broadcasters to whom the American
public had given this title without
realizing that more than one announcer
was on the air.   Records demonstrate
that the sobriquet "Tokyo Rose" cir-
culated in the United States before
November 1943—when Iva began broadcasting.   Mrs. Mae E. Hagedorn, of
Everett, Washington, was one of many
amateurs who listened to foreign

short wave broadcasts during the war
and logged all the messages they
received.   Her log reading for July
25, 1943, recited that she had heard
"Tokyo Rose" broadcast.   She stated
the announcer was identified as "a
Miss Ruth somebody.   I did not get the
Japanese name (Probably Ruth Hayakawa).
She interviewed a Mrs. Topping, an
American woman, before this time and
after this time."   "This time", remem-
ber, was more than three months before
Iva Toguri first appeared on the
Japanese or any radio.

Other persons were equally clear
that "Tokyo Rose" was a term circu-
lating long before November 1943.
Major Williston Cox, of the United
States Air Force, was shot down over
Mandang, New Guinea, on August 3, 1943,
and spent the rest of the war in a
Japanese prison camp.   He was familiar
with "Tokyo Rose" before being shot
down.   James Frank Whitten, chief petty
officer on the destroyer Gilmore, Sam
Stanley serving in the Seabeas, and
Nalini Gupta in the 27th Infantry
Division all had heard the expression
"Tokyo Rose" as early as 1942.

The United States government
operated a short wave monitoring
station at Portland, Oregon--"Portland Oregon Broadcast Receiving Unit"
(POBRU).   At its head was Amory
F. Penniwell.   When in the Spring of
1944, he was directed to record the
"Tokyo Rose" program, he did not know
to which broadcasts this order referred.   In his own words,

In early 1944 I received a
directive from my headquarters
to make a few permanent recordings

of the Tokyo Rose program. Well,
since we regularly listened to
Radio Tokyo, there was no program
announced as being Tokyo Rose, so
I asked for further clarification
from my headquarters. So in due
time I received notification from
them to record the Orphan Ann
portion of the Zero Hour as being
Tokyo Rose. So the recordings
taken by POBRU of Iva Toguri's
broadcasts were labelled "Tokyo
Rose".

Immediately after the surrender
of Japan, American newspaper correspondents made it their business to
solve the mystery of Tokyo Rose's
identity. Clark Lee and Harry Brundidge raced to Tokyo ahead of the Army
and commissioned one Leslie Nakashima
to find "Tokyo Rose" for them. Nakashima tells this story of what followed:

A. So I told Clark Lee that Radio
Tokyo had told us that there was
no single girl by the name of Tokyo
Rose, that there were five or
six girls and how about it?
Q. What did he tell you, or Brundidge?
A. Well, Lee did not give me any
immediate answer. He told me he
would think about it and later
on, I don't know how many hours
elapsed, either he called me or
I called him back, I don't remember, but he told me to go ahead
and get Iva Toguri anyway and to
offer her two thousand dollars
for an exclusive story.

Clark Lee himself testified at Iva's
trial: "I remember he came in the
hotel very hurriedly and we were in the
lobby and he said something to the
effect that he had found a Tokyo Rose
and I do not know whether he said a
Tokyo Rose or the 'Tokyo Rose'."

This was enough to satisfy Clark
Lee that Iva Toguri was "Tokyo Rose".
He thereupon offered her $2000.00

for an exclusive feature story for
Cosmopolitan Magazine. (The story was
never written and the money never
paid.) Thereafter Mrs. d'Aquino
(she had been married in April, 1945,
to Felipe d'Aquino, a lino-typist of
Portugese citizenship and mixed
Portugese and Japanese extraction)
signed herself "Tokyo Rose" whenever
soldiers in the Army of occupation
asked her to do so. Within three
after the surrender of Japan, Iva
d'Aquino was interviewed not only by
Lee and Brundidge but by a hundred odd
other correspondents, not to mention
Army Intelligence agents and members
of the F.B.I. The idea that she was
"Tokyo Rose" had caught on. Little if
any effort was made to interview other
announcers.

While most of the scripts of the
"Orphan Ann" program had been burned
in anticipation of the surrender, Iva
d'Aquino had saved some twenty or
thirty, and these she turned over to
American Army authorities. On October
17, 1945, she was arrested by the
U.S. Army for suspicion of treason and
held incomminicado until May 11, 1946
(except for visits from her husband
once a month for twenty minutes at
a time.) Deciding that she had committed no crime subject to military
jurisdiction, the Army turned her over
to the U.S. Department of Justice on
that date, which let her cool her heels
for another six months. Finally, on
October 6, 1946, after a year's
imprisonment, she was released. Army
records bear the notation, "Dept.
Justice no longer desires Iva Toguri
be retained in custody. No prosecution
contemplated at present."

The extant scripts, monitored recordings, and the testimony of available witnesses had convinced two departments of the United States government that "Tokyo Rose" had been a figment of popular imagination, and that Iva d'Aquino had broadcast nothing treasonable to the United States.

The case was apparently closed, and the government proceeded to destroy the recordings and transcripts which it had made of the Zero Hour program. At the receiving station in Hawaii, best located to monitor Tokyo broadcasts, almost everything was thrown away. A deceptive calm followed until the summer of 1947 when Iva d'Aquino applied for permission to reenter the United States in order to visit her father, now doing business in Chicago. Pressure was soon put on the Attorney General's office not only to bar her entry, but to reopen the treason prosecution against her.

In March, 1948, a Department of Justice attorney went to Japan to reinvestigate the case, accompanied by Harry Brundidge. This is the same Brundidge who in 1945 had raced ahead of the Army to Tokyo to get a story solving the "mystery" of Tokyo Rose. Brundidge was an employee of the Hearst press which had previously beat the drums for internment of the Nisei. (The Hearst papers, like all others, were later to give the trial substantially fair coverage. Mythology and logic are hard to reconcile.) He volunteered to "offer" his services to the Justice Department, "the Attorney General accepted his offer", and Brundidge flew to Tokyo in the same plane as the Department's Attor-

ney. Once these two were in Japan extraordinary happenings ensued. Brundidge, having "solved" the mystery of Tokyo Rose in 1945, appeared anxious to make his solution stick in 1948. He seems to have tampered with one witness and to have attempted to induce another to testify that they had heard Iva Toguri broadcast material over Radio Tokyo which they admittedly never heard her say at any time. One of these witnesses was Hiromu Yagi who testified for the government before the grand jury which indicted Mrs. d'Aquino. The other was Toshikatsu Kodaira who gave a deposition on Mrs. d'Aquino's behalf, which the jury, however, was not allowed to hear. The essentials of Kodaira's narrative may be given in his own words:

Q. Then, what was said by Brundidge, if anything.

A. Well, he suggested that "you and Yagi just saw and heard Tokyo Rose broadcasting".

Q. Did he suggest the time and the circumstances under which you heard her broadcast?

A. Yes, a little after the March bombing.

Q. Did he suggest that she might have broadcast on that occasion?

A. Yes.

Q. What was the suggestion?

A. That we heard Tokyo Rose broadcasting: "Soldiers, your wives are out with the war workers".

Q. Incidentally, when you left Brundidge's room, after the first meeting, what if anything did he give you?

A. Oh, he gave me a half finished bottle of whiskey. When I was going out he gave me a suit.

Q. Suit of clothing, you mean?

A. Suit of clothing.

In October, 1948, Yagi and others testified before the Federal Grand Jury in San Francisco, which thereupon indicted Iva d'Aquino, charging eight overt acts of treason. Before the trial Yagi confessed to Frederick G. Tillman, chief F.B.I. agent assigned to the case, that he had been bribed to come to San Francisco to testify falsely before the grand jury in the prosecution against Mrs. d'Aquino. Several months later, when Mrs. d'Aquino's lawyers learned of this episode, Tillman told them that he "had previously determined the situation to be as (they) outlined it."

As a Hearst correspondent worked to get the indictment, so before trial the Los Angeles Times carried advertisements for witnesses to help secure conviction. According to Carey McWilliams (Prejudice, pp. 107, 178, 252, 262, 266, 323.) the San Francisco and Los Angeles Examiners (both morning Hearst papers) and the Los Angeles Times were among the most vociferous promoters of Nisei evacuation and internment.

At the trial government attorneys challenged all jurors on a strictly racial basis. They excused all the non-whites called to the box—six or seven negroes and one Chinese American—and no one else. Furthermore, the evidence against Iva d'Aquino took on a curious pattern. On the one hand there were written or mechanical records of the Zero Hour; on the other there was the testimony of witnesses who claimed to remember what they had

heard Mrs. d'Aquino say. The records of her broadcasts uniformly showed no treason. Only the unsupported recollections testified to anything treasonable or even remotely political.

Thirty odd scripts which Mrs. d'Aquino had preserved and later handed to Army authorities and half a dozen recordings made by POBRU over a year's time constituted the documentary evidence which the United States produced on its case in chief. Why was there not more? Mrs. d'Aquino had broadcast about 340 programs, from November 13, 1943 to August 13, 1945. Photostats of two transcripts taken in Hawaii appeared in the government's rebuttal. But even so, there were less than 40 out of a total of 340. What had become of all the others?

Early in the trial, the Japanese witnesses whom the government had brought to the United States told about the destruction of papers in Japan. Not until the 51st day of testimony was it revealed that Hawaii had monitored the program for several months during 1945—and that the Hawaiian transcriptions no longer existed. Why?

We have already inferred that the Hawaiian records were destroyed after Iva d'Aquino was released from imprisonment in Japan, because they were then thought to be of no further value to anyone. The United States Court of Appeals observed "there is nothing to negative the Government's contention that the monitoring station records previously kept had been destroyed or lost in the process of the routine closing of such stations."

If so, the contents of the transcriptions must have been completely innocuous. On no other hypothesis is it reasonable that they should have been thrown out as a matter of routine.

Why did POBRU record only about half a dozen programs of the Zero Hour? Undoubtedly because they thought that these were typical and perhaps the most damaging they had heard. (They certainly heard everything; both the Japanese sending equipment and the American receiving equipment were of top quality. The reception was so good that at least one of these programs was picked up and recorded in Silver Hill, Md.)

The records produced at the trial underline the wholly apolitical character of Mrs. d'Aquino's broadcasts. Those made by POBRU and those contained in the scripts which she had succeeded in rescuing from the pre-surrender destruction were all of one piece. Mrs. d'Aquino introduced ordinary American musical recordings, and her introductory chatter did not vary from that of the Armed Forces Radio. None were more damaging than the following bit from the broadcast of September 15, 1944:

(Music "Day in Day Out") Ann (Mrs. d'Aquino): Yes, day in, day out. Coconuts and palm trees are all right for tourists, but a change of scenery won't hurt you boys any. I'm game, let's change our calling cards--While Sassy Sully Mason gets going with a little number entitled "Holy Smoke, Can't you take a Joke?" It all depends, Sully, what's tne Joke?

(Music "Holy Smoke, Can't you take a Joke?")

Two more typical examples of her authentic broadcasts:

February 22, 1944. "Hello, there, enemies. How's tricks? This is Ann of Radio Tokyo, and we're just going to begin our regular program of music, news, and the Zero Hour for our friends--I mean our enemies in Australia and the South Pacific. So be on your guard and mind the children don't hear. All set? O.K. here is the first blow to your morale, the Boston Pops playing "Strike up the Band"; and then into the theme piece....How is that for a start? Well, now, listen to me make subtle attacks on the orpahns of the South Pacific. Sergeant, where the hell's that orphan choir? Oh, there you are, boys. This is Ann here. How about singing with me tonight? You won't? All right, you thankless wretches, I'll enter-tain myself and you go play with the mosquitoes. Thank you, Mr. Payne, when you re ready. (selec-tion from "Love Parade") Yes, I thought that would start you singing. Well, you be good and we'll have some more, after which it will be time for your news from the American Home Front. Coming over." (The American Home Front" was broadcast by an American prisoner of war.)

August 14, 1944. Ann: Hello you orphans in the Pacific. How's trick's? This is after her week-end Annie back on the air strictly under union hours. Reception O.K.? Well, it better be because this is all request night and I've got a pretty nice program for my favorite little family--the wandering bone-heads of the Pacific Islands. The first request is made by none other than the Boss and guess what. He wants Bonnie Baker and "My Resis-tance is Low". My what taste you have sir, she said.

(Music--"My Resistance is Low")

Ann: The second request was sent in by a roving bonehead of an orphan, No. 29. He wants Tony Martin, of all people to help him forget the mosquitoes and dirty rifles. Well, you know--obliging Annie. Tony Martin and "Now it Can Be Told"

(Music--"Now it Can Be Told")

"Boneheads" was always spoken in a

jocular, bantering fashion—like Texas Guinan's "Hello Sucker" welcome to her patrons. A soldier who saw this script later testified at Mrs. d'Aquino's trial remarked that anyone in wartime would give military meanings to the titles, "My Resistance is Low" and "Now it Can Be Told".

Sam Stanley, a Seabea witness, introduced a significant slant when he said: "The only thing I was concerned with was the music and I was hoping that Tokyo Rose, like a lot of other people who hadn't heard her, that we would hear Tokyo Rose was witty and smutty and entertaining and telling dirty stories, but we never heard any of them."

This statement gives a glimpse of the contrast between myth and reality. Likewise the testimony of Robert Speed, an intelligence officer who listened to the Zero Hour:

> I was an intelligence interpreter in the regimental intelligence section. As such, one of my major jobs was to take prisoners, and one of our major methods of doing so was to make loudspeaker broadcasts. Now, we were always on the alert to find out better ways to do that, be more effective, and I felt that one way was to listen to Japanese broadcasts and see what they thought would be effective on us, possibly with the idea of using it back on the Japanese we were attempting to capture there or planned to capture later on also. But I listened to the Zero Hour originally with the specific purpose in mind and did not find propaganda. I did find propaganda on other broadcasts, so thereafter my chief motive in listening to the Zero Hour was just entertainment.

But at Mrs. d'Aquino's trial the "recollection" of witnesses fully made up for the lack of propaganda in any

authentic records of her broadcasts. They recalled that she had asked them what their wives and sweethearts were doing while they were in the foxholes; had said that their wives and sweethearts were running around with war workers; had asked them how they would like a cooling drink at the corner drug store in their home town which she always gave by name; how they would like dancing at a named night club with which the soldier was familiar; or how they would like a good thick steak. On the other hand, she had threatened that if they did not evacuate a certain island within a certain time they would all be blown to bits; and, last but not least, she predicted American troop movements. Not only did these broadcasts usually describe the details of the home town of the particular soldier who was listening, they also usually named the particular island on which he happened to be stationed. Some two months after the American conquest of Saipan she was "heard" to announce that all of Saipan was mined and the American troops would be blown sky-high if they did not leave within 48 hours.

Needless to say these "programs" were always exact reflections of the dreams, the hopes, the fears of the men on the Pacific Islands. Combined they make the folk story of the siren who tempts and destroys warriors swept into such situations—and so furnish a glimpse of the fable's psychological source.

James Frank Whitten, the chief petty officer referred to, remarked on this type of "broadcasts".

I heard the same type of scary

warning used on Nanomea nine months before, and the story there was that there wouldn't be a live marine left on Nanomea after the next full moon, and it was commonly used in the Pacific.

Q. But you never heard such a statement over Radio Tokyo, did you?

A. No, neither story did I ever hear.

The so-called predictions of American troop movements were introduced through a lone American Sergeant—though the United States had brought over and used as witness Major Shigetsugu Tsuneishi, the military head of the Japanese propaganda broadcasting system during the war. It is reported that after being dismissed from the stand he wondered out loud at not having been asked about this subject—saying that Japanese intelligence never got information of American troop movements early enough for Radio Tokyo to announce them beforehand and that no such announcements were ever made.

Several correspondents testified to statements Iva Toguri made when they interviewed her in September 1945. Clark Lee's is typical. He testified that she had said that the purpose of her program "was to make them homesick and unhappy about sitting in the mud." In 1948 however, he had published a book, entitled "One Last Look Around" in which, identifying Iva d'Aquino as "Tokyo Rose", he wrote: "Tokyo Rose's programs were at least entertaining to our troops". At the trial Mrs. d'Aquino's attorneys were not allowed to prove this latter statement to the jury, nor to cross-examine Lee upon it. The United States Court of Appeals

declared, "What Lee said in his book about the entertainment value of appellant's broadcast in no manner tended to contradict his direct testimony as to what appellant told him when he interviewed her."

While some of the "listeners" were clearly regurgitating rumors which they had swallowed, others must have heard different programs than the Zero Hour. For a while the Zero Hour went from 6-7 PM Tokyo time, several "listeners" claimed to have heard it at 6PM on Pacific Islands whose time differed by as much as three hours from that of Tokyo. Again, one man thought he heard the Zero Hour at 6PM in the Philippines and at 6PM in Eastern New Guinea—though during the war, with Eastern New Guinea on Australian daylight saving Time, there was a three hour time difference between it and the Philippine Islands.

The key to their testimony probably was that these witnesses had been allowed to hear a recorded Zero Hour broadcast as a means of identifying Mrs. d'Aquino's voice. This broadcast states that it went from 6-7 PM. So the witnesses, forgetting world time zones, promptly "remembered" that every broadcast which they had heard at 6 PM was the same voice. Several fixed on a program which by Tokyo time came on at three o'clock in the afternoon. This was the hour of Ruth Hayakawa's "Woman's Magazine of the Air".

One such was Marshall Hoot, (who listened at 6 PM in the Gilbert Islands). He undoubtedly heard the broadcast of Ruth Hayakawa, a Japanese subject, though he assumed out of hand that the broadcaster was " an American

Jap girl who has turned down the United States for Japan".

At Mrs. d'Aquino's trial, the United States prosecutor began his presentation by strikingly identifying Iva d'Aquino as "Tokyo Rose". The San Francisco Chronicle carried a day-to-day account of the proceedings captioned "Tokyo Rose on Trial". Yet in his argument to the jury the prosecutor declared "I don't think the element of 'Tokyo Rose' or who is 'Tokyo Rose' is of any importance in this case. Nobody broadcast from Radio Tokyo under the name of 'Tokyo Rose'. Apparently it was simply a name given facetiously by the GI's to some woman announcer of Radio Tokyo." The United States Court of Appeals for the Ninth Circuit later enriched American thought with the pronouncement that "It was hardly more significant that the records (taken at the Portland Oregon monitoring station) bore the notation "Tokyo Rose" than would have been the case had the recordings been painted a particular color or scratched in a peculiar manner."

Eight overt acts were charged against her—all based upon broadcasts or preparations for broadcasts on the Zero Hour. The witnesses to these acts were Mrs. d'Aquino's superiors at Radio Tokyo, some of whom were former American citizens who had adopted Japanese nationality in the middle of the war, and who were themselves perhaps in fear of the occupation authorities.

When the jury went into the jury room it stood 8-4 for acquittal. After two days it stood 9-3 for conviction and reported itself hopelessly dead-

locked. The judge sent the jurors back. The 9-3 division remained unchanged for two days more. Near the end of this period they made a last request for further instructions and half an hour later returned with a conviction—on one overt act—No. 6. Of the eight overt acts set forth in the indictment, only one—the eighth—was supported by any documentary evidence. But, like all other documentary evidence, it was innocuous, and the jury acquitted on that count. The sole act on which she was convicted charged that in October, 1944, she had broadcast after the battle of Leyte Gulf: "Now you fellows have lost all your ships. You really are orphans of the Pacific. Now, how do you, think you will ever get home?"

Nothing of the kind was picked up by any monitor. Mrs. d'Aquino denied having said anything like it. Even if taken at face value this incident was little enough to support a charge of treason. It was a mere three sentences, spoken in probably not over 10 seconds. Moreover, the men at Radio Tokyo who had exchanged American for Japanese nationality testified that they gave direct orders to make this broadcast—one of the few instances where they issued specific directions. In view of the dire consequences which the Japanese visited upon those who disobeyed orders coming from the army, the broadcast, if made, was hardly the product of voluntary choice.

The American authorities had reached strictly legal conclusions when two departments successively exonerated her in 1946. But "Tokyo Rose" was never purely a legal matter, but the final act in a folk myth created by the tensions, anxieties, and insecurities of the Second World War. It was the folk tale of the seductive Radio Siren in the Pacific, who, being an American citizen of Japanese descent, must be punished after the war.

Then the professional Jap-haters seized upon this legend, expanded it, promoted it, and climactically produced the victim in the person of Iva d'Aquino. What is quaintly termed the machinery of justice obliged with an execution.

HORSE

By JANE BOBBA

Unfettered, the horse heartless
And loving at once the heartsick hills,
Does leap to the recurring bluffs,
Each a segment of some old hurt beauty.
Eyes wounded with wonder of freedom,
With the imminence of captivity,
(For all golden-skinned and serenely shadowed things
  are everlastingly soon to be captive,
  soon to be rendered red dust and death.)
And the hope only is to go plunging,
Surging, into an intense and wooded nothingness.

    Place fields, heavy with warm beauty, around
The sadly arching neck
And sweep winds cool with clarity through
The thick sorrowing mane.
And still, in every wordless, speaking gesture
The horse tells the hills he knows. He knows.

20 – Cartoons – 20

By PETER MARTIN

Weekdays, San Francisco's *Newsvue* theatre, at Market and Mason streets, exhibits the most lavish technicolor westerns that money can buy. But every Saturday and Sunday this third-run movie house becomes the city's only theatre featuring that unique Hollywood institution, the Giant Cartoon Carnival, offering 20—(count them) Cartoons—20.

The Newsvue is a small house, and for 20 Cartoons it is invariably crowded, for these animated shorts from

© WARNER BROS. CARTOONS INC.

Warner Brothers((*Merry Melodies* and *Looney Tunes*), M.G.M. (*Tom and Jerry* and Tex Avery), U.P.A. (*Gerald McBoingboing* and *Mr. Magoo*,) and the Disney studios have attracted a devoted, if somewhat motley, audience. Surprisingly, there are few children; the Newsvue is no quiet neighborhood house, and when nice families do bring their children they soon realize that the Cartoon Carnival is essentially an adult affair.

Mostly, the weekend audience consists of drunks, servicemen (seldom drunk), old men, a sprinkling of effeminate young men, and a faithful contingent of young men, with or without horn-rimmed glasses, and young women, with or without abstract earrings. The drunks appear to find the roaring cartoons particularly soothing, while the sailors and soldiers seem to have a special feeling for this sort of thing. The old men are of that gentle kind you find sitting on park benches, walking in the zoo, and reflecting in Market Street movie houses. The effeminate young men hold hands and giggle and buy ice cream bars in an apparent attempt to recapture the imagined innocence of childhood. Sometimes they engage in a cautious game of "seat-hopping" that produces no resentments, no disturbance, only wordless understandings, one way or another. The intent contingent of young men and women consists of those who have dis-

covered in tne color cartoon the most
wildly imaginative, dizzily moving, and
psychologically insightful of contemporary cinematic forms.

Long stretches of uninspired imitations fill out the program of 20
Cartoons promised on the marquee, and
these have kept the band of aficio-
nadoes a small one. There are always
three or even four of Paul Terry's god-
awful Terrytoons, repetitive and tiresome, poorly drawn, weakly colored,
with an invariable squeaky musical
score. A considerable notch above
these are Paramount's *Popeye* and
Universal's *Woody Woodpecker*. Popeye
is crude and visually unimaginative,
but psychologically exciting because
of the insane, endless competition
between Popeye and his rival, Bluto,
for the rubbery charms of Olive Oyl.
Woody Woodpecker is much better, more
swiftly paced, and Woody's frenzied
materialism (he is outrageously greedy
and lazy) gives him a certain comic
force.

But all these are forgotten, and
even forgiven, when one of the true
comic figures of the color cartoon,
like Robert McKimson's immortal Bugs
Bunny, is flashed upon the screen.
Bugs, who is perhaps king of that
insane, free world created by the cartoon; Fred Quimby's Tom and Jerry; Tex
Avery's dogs, Droopy and Spike; UPA's
weakeyed Mr. Magoo; Charles M. Jones'
bears and cats and dogs—these provide
the mercilessly funny interludes that
make 20—Cartoons—20 an emotionally
and intellectually valuable experience.
The superb technical skill, the rest-
less and daring imagination, the penetrating social and psychological per-

© WARNER BROS. CARTOONS INC.

ceptions—often cruel, yet always
exhilarating—that these films display
explains the Cartoon Carnival's hold
on its audience. Brilliantly colored,
incredibly swift, savagely decisive,
they race across the screen to create
a movie experience that is unique and
powerful. Seeing these you realize
that the bold comic genius that characterized the movies of Chaplin, Buster
Keaton, Harold Loyd, and Laurel and
Hardy has not completely disappeared;
it has retreated before the wise-
cracking advance of the radio gag-
sters who captured the talking film
into the anonymity of the color cartoon.

But even more than most forms of the
movies, the art of the color cartoon
is an elusive one, difficult to observe
closely or to discuss critically. The
cartoon flashes before us for one
hallucinatory moment between the enormous double features, and then it is

almost irretrievably gone. Who are the men responsible for the best of them and what techniques they have employed are questions that are scarcely asked before the cartoon has raced through its allotted eight minutes and the Prevues of Coming Attractions are upon you. The strongest attraction of 20 Cartoons for the movie-lover is that there, with luck, a few of the great moments may be retrieved and, with perseverance, a few facts and general principles discerned.

Except for the recent U.P.A. productions, which depart somewhat from classical form, one theme persists through all the color cartoons. This is the theme of violence, a violence so obsessive, so unrestrained that it shatters the entire physical world, breaking physical laws as a matter of principle, distorting and fragmenting the cartoon characters themselves. Finally, it is this violence that justifies and creates the most advanced visual experience accepted by any *mass* audience today, one in which all the familiar objects and processes of daily life are attacked, destroyed, and then insanely reordered with the wholehearted participation of an audience that would indignantly reject the most reasonable of abstract paintings, the most cautious experimental films.

Fred Quimby's *Tom and Jerry* is a classical example. An eternal enmity links these two in a relationship of frenzied, compulsive destructiveness. Tom is dedicated, by the iron laws of his cathood, to the persistent destruction of Jerry. But Jerry invariably frustrates the cat by exploiting his smaller size, his superior intelligence (traditionally ascribed to the weak "victims" of every cartoon), and by manipulating an even deeper enmity between Tom and a particularly ferocious bulldog. In *That's My Boy* Jerry capitalizes upon the bulldog's excessive regard for his puppy-son to engineer one of Tom's most horrible defeats. The cartoon opens, of course, with Tom furiously pursuing a desperate Jerry; it ends eight minutes later with bulldog, puppy, and Jerry happily peering through the glass door of a Bendix washer at Tom, who is slowly whirling about in the soapy water. What occurred within that time is so vastly complicated, so dizzyingly paced and timed, that it could never be verbally described.

But the special genius of the cartoon world is still the immortal *Bugs*, created at Warners by Robert McKimson and Mel Blanc, who does the inspired vocal characterizations that liven the products of this studio. Note the name, *Bugs*, for this character started out to be crazy, screwy, like *Daffy Duck* or *Woody Woodpecker*. But somehow *Bugs* has evolved into a figure of great integrity and strength. He is the calm center of reason, stability, and order in a world that keeps going mad. Bugs is not himself aggressive or insane; on the contrary, he is the only real figure in an unreal world that is constantly trying to force its unreality upon Bugs. "Uh, what's up, Doc?" he always asks, innocently, mildly. "You know that this means war!" he proclaims when he discovers

(Continued on page 49)

De Sica, Dreams, and Dickens

By ARTHUR FOFF

DE SICA'S LATEST FILM, MIRACLE IN Milan, is a fantasy, replete with fakey montage, angelic acrobats, presumably fallen from God's—or perhaps Picasso's—trapeze, and gleaming police cars substituting for the now passé Dali-Cocteau motorcycle. Yet, thinking back to Shoe Shine and Bicycle Thief, we perceive a core of resemblance. In all three pictures our sensibilities were shocked with that bright wound of recognition which signs great art.

In evaluating De Sica's work we are confronted with two critical problems. We must discover what it is that wounds and heals, and we must indicate the cinematic techniques by which this is accomplished.

If, in memory, we follow the camera eye, we perform a visual and emotional exercise that has immediate rewards. De Sica's vision encompasses what all of us must see and feel who live here and now rather than in that 1790 rural society which our greeting card companies so slickly simulate in scenes of snowbound ranches and pastoral swimming holes. De Sica sees,

of course, the City—that gigantic, all-embracing behemoth of Western Civilization. Moreover, he has, through selective sight and deft direction, through lens and actor, created a poetry of the city.

This investment of value in the city is a rare, creative act. Not only must the poet overcome the crush of that vacuous retrospect which Ogburn termed 'cultural lag', but he must also shape the rough, chasmonic, and unwieldy complexity of the city to the pattern of his own insight. Only a few other artists have been able to accomplish this: one thinks at once of a few of Eliot's earlier poems, of Joyce's Dublin, Dickens' London, and of Chaplin's major films.

Technically, De Sica draws much from Chaplin and Dickens. He starts frequently with a mixture of pathos and comedy, but instead of dropping his situation *a la* Van Druten or Johnson he grimly presses it past the possibility of anxious laughter or hypocritical snuffling into its farthest limits—the silent and inner scream that marks the borderline between the genuinely comic and the genuinely tragic.

Like Chaplin and Dickens, he knows how to use the relationship between space and object. Characteristically,

ARTHUR FOFF has published a number of short stories and a novel, *Glorious in Another Day* (Lippincott, 1947). He teaches at San Francisco State College.

35

he poises the small, ragged human against the immensely indifferent bulk of the city. One recalls the solitary child following the hearse in Miracle in Milan; the fade-outs of Chaplin diminishing down the terrific perspective of a city street toward the country—a refuge which offers no real escape since it does not exist, has been lost in history rather than in space; and one remembers, too, the armies of homeless children who wander wearily through Dickens' London.

In his insistence on dislocation, De Sica is typical of the poets mentioned, for dislocation is the prime theme of urban culture. The psychic counterpart of physical dislocation is loneliness, and De Sica accents this loneliness by centering each film in the intelligence of a child. In this he is most like Dickens, that prodigious, almost Godlike, creator of battalions of newsies, orphans, bottle-blacks, and delinquents.

The homelessness of these children is recorded, or rather, rendered, by counterpoint. Like two other fine directors, Ford and Reed, De Sica is concerned with ruins, with the blast and shell of apartments and homes, with the psychological landscape of uprooted cobbles and polished junk heaps. He, as well as Dickens and Chaplin, often throws the essential loneliness of these wanderers from shantytown to St. James Infirmary into relief by juxtaposing their terrain with the industrial castles of the city, where flunkies understudy weathercocks and American jazz serves Italian tea.

De Sica also knows the use of symbol. He does not deal in the bogus mythology or abstract symbolism of Cocteau, but rather in that class of symbol which is bedded in reality, and which by its very skill and compression strikes us deeply and lastingly.

In each film the binding metaphor is the dream and wish of children. The two bootblacks in Shoe Shine, descendants of Caesar's Rome, have their dream of parading past the Colosseum on horseback. The son in Bicycle Thief wants to help his father; but his image is shattered by the brutal humiliation of his parent, and it is he, the child, who must, in a symbolic reversal, take his father's hand in his own and lead him off. Then, in Miracle in Milan, there is the archetypical dream, symbolized in the clean, well-ordered toy town that the old Dickensian woman builds for her foster son. 'Such a nice city!' she cries. And from that cry onward, the picture is obsessed with the boy's efforts to build a nice city—a kind of stone nursery—out of rubble and refuse.

This idée fixe, this struggle to find homes for the homeless and direction among derelicts, is also De Sica's obsession. In Shoe Shine the vision was destined for tragic crash. In Bicycle Thief the son lost his own identity when his father's role was destroyed. And in Miracle in Milan the dream never becomes more than dream; neither papal clouds nor happy masses mounted on broomsticks, nor even a gilded and dancing blonde, can gloss the futility of the search. Yet, this does not invalidate De Sica's art.

The search for love and the longing for home in themselves create communication. In this, De Sica's children are much like such other wanderers as Joyce's Bloom, Anatole Broyard's Hipster, and Chaplin's elegant and defeated tramp. All are modern counterparts of the classic and heroic Odysseus. Maybe all fail in their journey; they end up—Nowhere. But at least by their dream and by the dignity of their search they have made this vast, limitless concrete Nowhere, this city, into a place which we can inhabit with some comprehension and courage of our own.

Matisse's Wine

By RUTH RODRIGUEZ

All the joy of heart's desire
Clothes the sable brush
Telling, and telling
Of preposterous pots, and scented blue
And oblique flesh encircling you.

Dreams these are
That cannot listen
To your discussion
Of problems missing.

If your taut selves would play this tune,
If your many started thoughts would walk this rhyme,
If your turgid love would float this moon,
You could be the cup--Matisse the wine.

The Film HOWARD STREET

By LESLIE TURNER

HOWARD STREET IS A GREY, DIRTY street a few blocks to the South of Market in San Francisco and running parallel to it. It is a street of broken windows, rotten canvas awnings, rusting signs, dusty vacant shops, door-alleys filled with patterns of dust and wadded paper. A street of junk-filled shops (windows bulging with everything from gold mining pans through barber shears to melting phonograph records); and of slimy garbage cans;—misspelled signs in cafe windows in which no one could possibly eat with appetite and bars and stores selling cheap sweet wine for about 40¢ a bottle.

The traffic is heavy. Electric buses move up the street, with a hiss like steam engines. Trucks rumble and there is the constant clatter and ring of the street lights on the corners. And silently, almost every hour, the paddy wagon, blue and evil moves through the street—causing a flurry of excitement among the men...

This is the environment of Howard Street, San Francisco, both in actu-

LESLIE TURNER, who was born in Alabama, came to San Francisco in 1946. A painter and writer, as well as film-maker, he is now working on a new film, *Sea-story*, an collaboration with T.E.D. Oleshak, in addition to three short documentaries.

ality and in our film. Altogether it is a depressing area. A kind of still, whirling disk in the midst of the busy city. It is that one core, point of zero, that 'opposite' which it seems everything requires. The block between Third and Fourth Streets, in which the film was photographed, has grasped the name of the whole street, contracted it into something perhaps desperate, abstracted it and made the very name of the street have a special meaning, an evil meaning, to almost everyone who has ever heard the name of it. But the people there are not evil...

Howard Street is the Skid Row of San Francisco and is said to be the worst in the United States. Perhaps it is due to the U. S. Employment Bureau once having had an office there that it has become the hang out, home, of all the unemployed and psychologically unemployable, derelict men in San Francisco. These men stand in the sun hardly moving. They wear old gray sweat shirts, black with shiny dirt at the neck; they dress in black trousers, trousers left over from pin-striped suits, filthy yellow corduroy trousers. They are grey haired, yellowish grey haired, and they wear grey hats, shapeless and filthy with age. If they have a good coat or a good pair

38

of shoes they sell it for wine.

They are old. They love nothing but alcohol. They are young and their faces are red. Seeing man after man you can watch them grow old and lost before your eyes like Dorian's portrait. They are lost, like a leaf on the ocean or a word in a dictionary. But they are not evil—that is how they differ from Dorian's portrait.

And that is the men on Howard Street and the men in the film.

Howard Street was photographed by William R. Heick, edited by Leslie Turner, and produced by William R. Heick, Leslie Turner, and Bern Porter. It is, we believe, a new approach to documentary film making. All the documentary films we have seen or heard of so far have one thing in common—they tell how something is or was done, created, came about; or they investigate, from a purely physical point of view, some place or situation. This film does none of these.

It has no story, no plot, no apparent plan. It has no narrative continuity nor logical time sequence. All the things in it, all the images could be happening at once, at the same time, in the same place—or they could be happening in different years, in other centuries (as they have happened, and of course, will always happen, as long as there are people to make them happen or for them to happen to), or they could happen together so fast it would be impossible to understand them—or even to know they were happening. But they happen and happened. That is what we were

aware of in our first visualization of the film. And we were aware that these happenings were a part of a larger happening—the psychological world (reality) of the pressure of each of these men's compulsions, habits, results of habits, knowledge, talent, imagination, and lack of imagination.

Briefly this was the original idea: to photograph images which appealed to us, not because of their beauty, but because of their reality. To edit these images into one continuous whole in time in the almost unexplainable emotio-intellectual *grasp* of a completeness of form. Then to record sound in the same area with a tape recorder and edit the two together— shaping the whole into a form of its own. To contrast sound and image where that was best, to harmonize where that was best. And to work with our materials from the same point of view a modern painter does with his canvas, brushes, paints, pallet knife and turpentine—to force a new creation out of the materials of an old. To *create* instead of to copy. In Howard Street, the film, as well as in the street itself, nothing but Howard Street exists.

So with the visual image we contrasted, harmonized as our own psychological reality demanded we should. We exploded incidents, leaving them tailless, headless, and in reference (in a narrative sense) to their before and after, meaningless. But we kept the meaning of the place in which we worked.

We intended to do the same thing with the sound. It was discovered, however, that it would be best not to approach the sound in the way we had the image, It would, perhaps, destroy the true structure we were building and instead of letting our audience see all sides/things in our universe at once (as though he were a god) would shatter the whole; and it would no longer be like a bubble, a sphere, but would shatter and fly toward him in tiny pieces of glass like a nightmare, rather than like the dream we were trying to create. So we left the sound—of street noises, voices, buses, auto horns, whistles, foot-steps, wind, coughs, curses, four-letter words—as it was, just as we had recorded it on the street, taking out only a few squeaks of the tape when we stopped recording momentarily for some reason.

Films usually have a story; I mean a beginning, a middle, and an end. They progress, evolve. Howard Street does not. Except in places where we carried a fragment of an incident to near completion there is no progress along a narrative track. And even these fragments of what can only be called artificiality act as compound images which harmonize or contrast their surrounding images. The sound track is very monotonous (in the beginning, anyway) as was our intention, and it is this very quality we were striving for. It beats like a drum (I mean a steady rhythm) and lulls the audience into accepting, without intellectual evaluation, all the images (which could be called random) pearing before him on the screen.

That is why it is a psychological documentary. Time for it does not exist. It is, perhaps, all time—or a second—exploded and investigated in as many ways as you can think of. The audience is forced into being uncritical of what is happening (not of the film) and into accepting the things which happen in the way a lower type of animal perhaps accepts them: as happening—that is all.

The people we photographed were not always aware that they were being photographed—not because we hid the camera, nor because we cared—but because they were inside of themselves, not outside, and were looking back into the cave of themselves and not out at the world which surrounded them. They were, often, not aware of the reality of our camera. They would hear the insect-like whirr of it, but it was no more than a bus passing or the language they used. It was not imagination of a low order—but a sort of unawareness, of having given up, forced out, killed imagination, perhaps, before imagination killed them.

The audience is made aware of this when he sees the dream-like movement of some of the images, the obvious clowning of the men in some of the other images. And he sees, feels, the reality of the place that is Howard Street.

He sees people fighting, drinking, making obscene gestures; he sees a kind of beauty which is ugly and he sees the kind of ugliness which is very beautiful. (An old man with a face like a cancer who has been destroyed by his face...a man with no lower jaw, eating.) He sees a kindness in these men which comes not from understanding (which is really impossible) but from tolerance, acceptance. And he sees religion.

The missionaries of the district trying to make converts; the acceptance they are given—at least the interest. And the unacceptance they are given at the same time. For these men on Howard Street are aware that their reality has very little of religion in it. There is no hope in them—the basis of religion—only acceptance. So he sees the preachers waving their arms, persuading, promising things, trying to force their own reality onto people who cannot conceive of it.

And finally the audience hears a hymn on the sound track of the film which contrasts the images again and weaves them (at the same time) into a universal whole. Contrasting ironically and at the same time completing....

New Money

By FREDERICK ANDREWS

Let's throw all the words away,
The whole bolus, and in silence
'Mint again each clinking counter
Time's casuistry has stickied.

Bring bright meanings back,
Revivified, each one single.
The king in us is spent by coins
Cemented in chains and sinkers.

A Note on Robert Watson

By BEN ROSENBLUTH

It is a pleasure to re-discover, in seeing Robert Watson's paintings, how powerfully a dramatic imagination may inform the painter's art. Watson sees the playing out of human aspirations against the background of scenes that once loaned them strength and dignity but now offer them, at best, only a mocking nostalgic record of their former vitality. The scenes become the dramatic subjects of the paintings. They are studies of the various architectural structures that mark the boundary lines of a civilization: of sea walls and towers, of stranded jetties, bridges, ghost streets, isolated ruins, prisons, and boundless arid landscapes. Each painting (and most successfully the later ones which include "The Lighthouse") records the consequences of the impact of mindless forces of negation and neglect upon human efforts to create.

Watson re-creates a visually exciting impression of the original power and beauty of these architectural structures by representing their surface tones and textures as the very tissue of reality. Then in subtle compositional contrasts of shadow with substance, of infinite emptiness with heavy looming presence, of the fresh with the fading, of natural flow and freedom with forced halts and confinement, the drama of human resistance to negation and neglect assumes a kinaesthetic significance that transcends its own history.

Unlike the social realists and surrealists whose artistic (and political) failures were not a result of their lack of dramatic imagination but of their evasion of reality, Watson is a realist who takes the artist's responsibility for seeing life as it is lived and creating new realities that advise and enrich the living of it.

The Sea Journal

A similar prejudice exists against
persons frequenting the sea who, they
observe, can only be people of desperate
fortunes, and whose testimony, as such,
ought not to be admitted. They do not
hold fornication to be a crime.
—MARCO POLO

MARCH 3

I used to say to myself concerning
a voyage, to be taken that though I did
not look forward to it, loathed it,
this particular voyage in fact, yet I
would take it regardless in order to
see for myself what that voyage would
be like.

MARCH 4

This voyage a quest for youth,
inasmuch as I retrace the course of
an identical voyage made when seventeen. Yet fear I merely recapture for
a moment the insecurity and terror
of adolescence.

'On recontre sa destineé souvent
par des chemins qu'on prend pour
l'eviter.' (One finds his destiny
often by those roads he takes to avoid
it.) La Fontaine.

The ship is confined in the magic
circle of a fog. The air is cold and
windless, the water smooth and list-
less. Wetness clammily possesses all
surfaces. Daylight forces an opening
in the lid of fog; and with the en-
croaching pink of the sun it is slowly
drawn away. Thus it is in the Aleut-
ians--mother of fogs--in the summer.
the ghostly fog and furious typhoon
advance towards each other in mockery

of combat. Similarly warm north
flowing currents encounter south
floating icebergs. Meanwhile winds,
clouds, and birds make migratory
pilgrimages.

'Why must the sea be used for
trade--and for war as well? Why kill
and traffic on it, pursuing selfish
aims of no great importance after
all? It would have been so much
nicer just to sail about with here
and there a port and a bit of land
to stretch one's legs on, buy a few
books, and get a change of cooking
once in a while.' Conrad. A SMILE
OF FORTUNE

MARCH 4

Left over from the sailing ship
are four miserable belaying pins for
securing flag halyards and a small
blackboard, heir to the traverse board,
for recording courses; these and a
handful of ancient mariners.

Ship life offers an artificial
system of tensions which seem to
make life endurable. The alternative
is to have or create a situation in
which one may successfully cultivate
the arts of poetry and love, of food
and music.

Illustrative photographs:

1. Of the Northern Cross with framing porthole.
2. Of a Heath Sextant, a coffee mug, and a stopwatch.
3. The illuminated dial of a clock.
4. A quadruple exposure of compass, binoculars, flashlight and an eye.
5. Cumulus congestus in the trade wind.
6. Sea in force 8 wind, solus.
7. Rope.

MARCH 5

Similarity of a young storm, such as we pass through now, with its short heavy swell, heavy o' cast, rapidly declining barometer, gusty wind, uneven waves, with a young geological region with steep gorges, rapid descents of streams.

And similarity of an old storm with long heavy swells, rolling like wheatfields, broken clouds? etc.etc. to old geological region, etc. Consult geology text.

MARCH 5, LATER

Qualms, mirth, and curses accompany the approach of storm. Christ, what a stormy night with the sea sweating whitecaps, the wind beating and roaring.

The ship is a vector--an equal and opposite sum--to the forces of the storm. The wind makes its water mark--a finger riffle--which grows to a billow, yields to surf, and dissolves into a green white bruise--a patch-- through which a little of the interior of the ocean may be seen.

That part of the wind which is on our lee side, disengaged from the main current of the blast by reason of the ship's interposition, peels skims of foam and small fistulas of water from the exposed half round of the following part of the wave.

Everything moves at different--and unlikely--speeds. An eruption of sea, air, and cloud. Why do the words *orage* and tempest have peaceful connotations? Portholes are like coffin-lids. This is now, has become, the most furious storm, the ultimate Walpurgisnacht. The sea is polished and smoothed, has veins as in blue marble. Until now we were held steady by the constant, though unbelievably furious wind. Now we pitch and roll. Comforting glimpse of the North Star, *ago stella*.

At daylight, we emerge into an ocean glade. A black cigar of a cloud is poised overhead. The sun touches the upthrust tops of clouds with pink. Clouds stretch from sk to sea in patterns. Like the tempestuous marriage bed of wind and sea with sheets torn and scattered. Sun's disc even is fleetingly seen. Again a familiar comforting thing, a return of some slight continuity. Sledge hammer repeated blows from the northerly cross swell a return to reality. At last a partial adaptation to this new universe. Everything on the ship is either secure or already smashed.

No escape. This shuddering swinging steel thing must be for me, the world. The sea spits in my eye. The wind tears at my clothes. I hold fast lest I be hurled off balance and retire, not uncontent, to the half world of a mind shorn of images.

MARCH 5, AFTERNOON

En plein orage--I wish I could get my income--and this storm--pacified and controlled--so that I would have the leisure to worry about old age, death and eternity. The way things are I am condemned to perpetual youthfulness.

MARCH 6, 4 A.M.

Storm in full senseless career. A wanton tempest. We, the ship, like a berserk buzz saw burst foam in air. Stupid weather--that it is.

MARCH 14

Freud, in his 32nd and last lecture on psychoanalysis, says that therapy is the weakpoint. Of course, because the therapy must be magic--using my own definition of magic as that which empowers a change in an individual--it may be a word or a scent or a ritual or a pill through which the magic operates.

So that Freud's work viewed in this light seems to be an enormously long and skillful footnote--an erudite, closely reasoned examination of something already intuitively known. The next question is the form of magic to use. Poetry--yes. Music--yes. Art--yes, etc. And Marx a parallel footnote on social life.

MARCH 20

Going to sea is like running on the trail so that you can rest while the rest of the party catches up to you. Or like eating your spinach first to get it out of the way.

Buddhism (and existentialism which states the same badly) teach that man creates himself.

See to what extent at sea a man is held responsible to himself--for his character, his walk, his body. his soul. Here is a theme for a Henry James of the sea or a near Conrad.

MARCH 23

The whale shark with its four inch thick, rubbery skin and consequent imperviousness to attack, swims unperturbed on the surface of the water, straining algae and plankton through 3000 small teeth. It is like the Sequoia tree and the elephant whose bark and skin render them equally immune from fire and attack, and all are endowed with a similar longevity. Over-protected species. Man is over compensated rather than over protected.

APRIL 2

At sea. The bitch, ocean bitch. So many moods in a single day. Joy in morning with the watch done. Fatigue? Hope, home thoughts, a touch of malice passed like phlegm. A moment's heart break in the evening.

--Better be in first class spiritual shape—today—anything might happen. The fifth level of irony.

We live in the large angry shadow of our fate--and the only escape is to kill something--or even all--of ourself. Like D. who outsmarts marriage by remaining single.

By going to sea I do not seek to--nor do I—escape my fate—but meet it.

APRIL 3

Japan (A Modern Gulliver)

Your true medievalist or eighteenth centuryist would go live in Japan. Again I am reminded of curious a coincidence that land of Yamato, close to where Gulliver visited the Yahoos. And as a matter of fact not only have sections of Swift the peculiar flavor of Japan--but Japan itself has a pronounced Swiftian quality in the landscape.

Japanese Tea Shop

She say--bring peanuts? I point to my head and say 'Goku'(meaning thinker) and think heavily--for two minutes--'No peanuts.' Then she gives me a small slip of paper ceremoniously as though presenting some expensive gift and I as ceremoniously and graciously tear it in two and offer her one: Ha, ha.

Fifth Street. PX--beggars--sycophantic war veterans--dance hall--then store after store selling palpably fraudulent stuff. Fishing poles, binoculars, cameras, silk, jade, phonographs, records, canes...

On the train from Tokio to Nikko saw two butterfly hunters, fresh from the marshes, dressed in straw rain clothes, analogues of Marin County duck hunters.

APRIL 5

I'm not much of a story-teller and that's a fact. But one day at coffee time I was telling a story, one which amused me and I think the listeners too. I described seeing in Yokohama, the day before, a greasy looking, repulsive merchant seaman who had apparently been drunk for some days dickering with a Japanese shop keeper for a tea set--my point being that the whole thing hung together--the sobering seaman--the tea set--an institution in execrable taste that merchant seamen buy thinking this the

gift that their relatives or friends or whores want--too often being right.

I was somewhat disconcerted by someone saying that this showed that even in cups the man was thinking of someone else--someone at home.

This misconception of my intention somewhat startled and surprised me. I said, 'He was probably buying it for some big black nigger--' I was going to finish the sentence with the word 'whore' when I was conscious of sparks --an air of silence--from the corner-- where I, stunned, realized our negro messman was. I stopped in mid sentence and turned to Thomas. I apologized sincerely and deeply. But the damage was done--and Thomas' eyes glittered with hate--my apology made it worse. Could I explain that I intended 'black nigger whore' as a cliche--a melodramatic detail to emphasize the cheap taste, etc. Saying that I never used the word nigger just made it worse-- wide open.

Thos. without letting smoldering fire glinting through eyes diminish spoke softly saying it didn't sound as though I used the expression seldom. My admitting guilt, when should have, one would think, demonstrated that I agreed with Thos. word verboten--only laid me open to being by implication labelled some strange type of hypocrite. Impasse indeed.

APRIL 8

On the train from Hiroshima--fields encroach on hills terraced up to a planned left topknot--old curved lines destroyed and new ones made--junctions mortised with trees and tenoned by tombstones.

The purpose of Japanese history is that all of Japan be as perfect as Miya Jima and Nikko and graceful as Fujiyama.

Look at spring. Walk about growing old. Hiroshima. The town of the future. All suburbs. Heart bombed out.

APRIL 9

Sometimes, in fact, all of your thoughts and the experiencing of life takes the form of an interior conversation in which you tell things to yourself--a regular two sided conversation but one in which one party does all the talking and the other listens. Maybe this comes of living alone.

Anyway it seems likely that often when you talk to others it is not one of these two that is your true self (the listener) but rather the second party--that awful chatterbox--that speaks. People take a false view of you. Really you can't blame them for it.

WEDNESDAY

The sea is a purgative for the diabolic powers of nightmare. I feel the lurking presence of poisoners of wells in the shadows.

The Master sits in his office. Bottles, glasses and a kettle full of ice are on the table. He is but drunk North north west.

Distinguish between detachment, withdrawal, non-participation, non-resistance, irony, then let us consider the poise of the schizophrene, the detachment of the dead, the authority of the maniac.

APRIL 23, GUAM

Guam is an island with little human history; every two years on an average, a typhoon sweeps the island clean, uproots trees and houses, flattens the incipient jungle, rearranges the sand and shells.

...And coral gravel. So that the only human life is a thin geneological line of people going back to Magellan and Legaspi, the Spanish co-discoverers.

The only other life is snails and fungi and live mosquitoes and squid and shark and such. And cocoanut and taro in the low hills. So that with the influx of naval personnel, an American journalist, quite logically, began to invent new forms of life. He created a sea serpent scare, a brilliant hoax—and also started a story to the effect that a primordial man had emerged from the caves. But soon, he too, the journalist, became bored and left for more favorable lands.

...And sea shells which occupants have built from within their dwellings (coffins) —worked on in the littoral by the concussion of gravel and surf—colored by sun and bleached by rain—becoming finally found objects matched for the ears—notched for the catch—bored for the clasp.

APRIL 28, GUAM

From Guam Southwards--a highway by way of Yap (quote names in this region) to Pora Pora, the Marquesas and ultimately to the blessed isle of Tahiti.

MAY 30, HOMEWARD BOUND

The ultimate in boredom--time flops and droops like an oversize garment, or an unpegged tent or a flatulent elephant--time wags and whistles and waits for you by the side of the road--and one day even actually repeats itself as you cross the international date line.

JUNE 2

As your sailor nears home he figures taxes, wages, draws, slops, computing his payroll--as well as time and distance remaining till arrival--like a miser.

THE ISLES OF THE BLEST

It is natural that sailors who are in some new place should associate the idea of happiness (the most omnipotent idea of all) with some place: Guadalajara, where the women are docile, or the Canary Islands where the beer is cheap, or even be it a flat in Bloomsbury, an apartment on Russian Hill, or a walk-up in Greenwich Village.

JUNE 5

The archetypal returned wanderer, Ulysses, slays the wooers in slow sadistic melodrama. Homer spends six books on this part of the story. It tells of a triumphant and bloody destruction of the leeches that had

gathered round his home. It is like a sailor's dream.

JUNE 6

Shipboard life, especially is this so in regard to tedious periods, becomes a kind of externalized manic-depression. The true manic stage, however, does not arrive till the ship finally reaches home and is paid off. Then the world glows invitingly, pockets are full of money, and imagined freedom replaces the imagined servitude of ship life. The most unfortunate stage of this cycle comes when the life of imagined freedom begins to fail and money to dwindle. Then the depressive state overtakes its rival. It is like a stage in the cycle of a parasite. Earth is host. The sailor now imagines he needs the sea again and seeks new manacles.

'The unplumbed salt estranging sea.'

JUNE 8, FARALLONES

That these bleak rocks should be symbols of the warmth and joy of a sailor's returning; these bleak and craggy islets; these foggy, foggy islets which lie just athwart the delicate profile of heart's ease; is it not an irony? Yet it is here that the voyage (always, like the bed of Procrustes, too short or too long) terminates; here by an outcropping of the sea.

that what is up always threatens him. Only then does Bugs embark upon his purely private, defensive, and highly successful brand of warfare.

Charles M. Jones has created in *Tweedybird* and other cartoons a more subtle kind of violence based upon psychological frustration and defeat. *Tweedybird*, an outrageously plump and yellow canary, is the seemingly innocent object of relentless pursuit by an obscenely smirking, chop-licking cat named Sylvester. But the canary's repeated escapes from the cat's jaws, always in the shuddering nick of time, produce in Sylvester an hysterical determination that in the end becomes suicidal. In recent cartoons Jones has even more systematically driven his protagonists insane. In *Mouse-wreckers*, two chortling mice drive a cat mad by cruelly reordering his visual world until it is rendered totally meaningless. In *A Bear for Punishment,* an irritable, short-tempered bear (strongly reminiscent of Edgar Kennedy) is reduced to mumbling inanition by the relentless Fathers' Day attentions of his whining wife and moronic son. (Throbbing red veins criss-cross his eyes by the end of the day.)

But it is Tex Avery who has forced the violence theme to its extreme limits in his *Droopy* cartoons, and others. Droopy is a pathetically small, wistful dog, with a mournful expression and a slight lisp. The really central figure of these cartoons is an unusually villainous mastiff named Spike, who is the manly, upright Droopy's opposite (alter ego?) in every way. Vain, unprincipled, bullying, and stupid, he—never Droopy—is the per

petual victim, the astonished fall-guy, the colossal sucker, in the rapid-fire series of visual gags that Avery machine-guns at his audience. The situation is always the same; Spike, supremely confident, painstakingly devises a trap for the innocent Droopy; invariably, inexorably, the trap backfires; Droopy escapes or triumphs virtuously, and Spike is destroyed. Every time. Sometimes Spike is destroyed five or six times in a single cartoon, but he always returns, cocksure and undaunted. In *From Wag to Riches* Spike has his head blown completely off at least twice when plans to eliminate Droopy with cannon and boobytrap backfire. The first time he picks his head up and carries it in his arms while he leaves the scene. It has an extremely embarrassed expression on it. The next time he is so mortified that he conceals his head from the audience with a piece of cardboard while he tiptoes offstage. But at the last minute he turns his back to us, and we can see that his head is gone. In another cartoon Spike is propelled (somehow) with enormous force through a steel fence; the fence remains intact; for one single triumphant moment Spike emerges on its other side intact; then he dissolves into little square fragments the exact size of the divisions of the steel fence. Then there was the time Spike was flattened into a flat disc; all his features were discernible, but they were frozen into the proportions of a flat, round disc.

Many people object strongly to the insistent aggression and unrestrained violence of the color cartoon and react to Tex Avery's extremes with horror and disgust. If they acknowledge the cartoon at all, they are likely to approve the more restrained product supposedly emerging from the U.P.A. studio since the appearance of *Gerald Mc Boing-boing*. But that studio's *Frankie and Johnnie*, as well as its fascinating *Mr. Magoo* (he's *human*, went to Rutgers, and seems to be an old-fashioned liberal) hardly indicate any abondonment of the traditional basic themes...probably because the U.P.A. associates realize that they are the themes of all great comedy. But those who object are the same sort that sneered at the lusty Mack Sennet comedies, (though they are permissible now, from the Museum of Modern Art Film Library) they are the same who, learning their manners (never ideas) from the *New Yorker*, have always denied the powerful centrality of movies for our time, the same who fear and despise television today for the same reasons. What they really like about the U.P.A. cartoons is that they sometimes display that cozy modernity that seems to be prevailing in popular art today, a modernity that is based upon a "knowing" use of the post-impressionist art of this century, which means the bits and remnants of once vital forms with their original ideas and intentions carefully excised.

Finally, they forget that comedy, like tragedy, which dwells upon death and destruction in order to assert the values of living and creation, must look violence and disorder in the face, can only defeat those derangements— and then only provisionally,—by granting their existence—in the world and in our minds. Great comedy— Chaplin, Keaton's, and Field's comedy; McKimson's, Jones', and Tex Avery's comedy—creates a vision into reality that is steadier and more useful than our everyday vision because it includes, even insists upon, the fact of violence.

© WARNER BROS. CARTOONS INC.

FREDERICK ANDREWS, who wrote *New Money* and *Let Me Put You Straight*, is a young poet now living in San Francisco. More of his poems will appear in future issues.

RUTH RODRIGUEZ wrote *Matisse's Wine* after seeing the exhibit at the San Francisco Museum. She lives in Berkeley, is married and the mother of two children.

GUY WERNAM (*Hippocampus*) is a translator, occasional poet, a master of the limerick form. He lives here in San Francisco.

ROBERT WATSON, whose painting, *The Lighthouse*, is reproduced on page 42, is unique among Bay Area painters. He has recently had a show at the Kenneth Slaughter Gallery, and his painting, *The Bridge*, aroused considerable comment at the Annual exhibit of the Palace of the Legion of Honor.

FILM

The Berkeley Film Society

Summer Series
5 PROGRAMS

July 13   **The TRAGIC HUNT.** De Santis, Rome, 1946
The GOAT: Buster Keaton.

July 20   **VAMPYR.** Carl Dreyer, Danish, 1932
PICNIC: Curtis Harrington

July 27   **The GENERAL.** Buster Keaton.
The SALT OF THE EARTH. Rouquier.

Aug. 3   **DROLE DE DRAME.** Jouvet, Barrault. Dir. Carne
The STUDENT OF PRAGUE. 1913

Aug. 10   **HIMLASPELET.** Sjoberg, Stockholm, 1942
SUMMER INTERLUDE. Suchsdorff.

Series Ticket $4.50
Write P. O. Box 193. On Sale at U C Corner & Breuner's

Berkeley Little Theatre Allston Way

SUNDAY evenings at 8:15

* THE KINESIS GROUP

FILM

Films not available elsewhere may be obtained from KINESIS.

Group programs and series of recent experimental and abstract works are provided. Individual film makers' work is distributed. For information and catalogue write:

THE KINESIS GROUP   802 Montgomery Street   San Francisco II

Criticism

35 cents   Short Stories

Poems

CITY   LIGHTS

nber Two ■   San Francisco   October 1952

Little Symphony Society presents...

Little Symphony
of
San Francisco

GREGORY MILLAR, Conductor

BERKELEY
LITTLE
THEATER

October 22, 29 - November 5, 1952
WEDNESDAYS, 8:30 P.M.

Clip Along Dotted Line and Return to:

Series Tickets (3 concerts). All Seats Reserved.

Little Symphony Friends (Patron and Friend roster to appear on
  program) $6.50 plus $3.50 contribution.......................$10.00
General Admission 6.50
Student Admission.. 5.00

Little Symphony Society
c/o Radio Station KPFA
2207 Shattuck Ave.
Berkeley 4

☐ check
Enclosed is ☐ money order for_____

☐ Friend
☐ General
☐ Student ickets

quantity

Send to: Name_____

Address_____

City_____ Telephone_____

*KINESIS

Films not available elsewhere may be obtained from KINESIS.

Individual film makers' work is distributed.

Group programs and series of recent experimental and abstract works are provided.

For information and catalogue write:

THE KINESIS GROUP
556 COMMERCIAL
SAN FRANCISCO 11

THE ARTIST'S VIEW

The Artist's View is published by painters, poets, and sculptors here in San Francisco. Each issue is a four page monograph in which an individual artist presents his principal ideas and examples of his work. The first issue presented the paintings, poems, and working ideas of Hassell Smith. The second issue, recently released, is the product of Jeremy Anderson, sculptor. In time many different artists will be presented, many different points of view will be covered, and *The Artist's View* will become an important source of primary historical material for the art of our present period.

Since each issue is viewed as an individual monograph, a unique expression of the artist, no advertisements are accepted, and the magazine relies solely upon subscriptions and individual sales for its support.

Subscription rates are two dollars for eight numbers, or five dollars (patron subscription) for eight numbers signed by the artist. Individual copies may be purchased at Paul Elder's bookstore and at the San Francisco Museum of Art.

THE ARTIST'S VIEW
56 Magnolia Street
San Francisco 23

CITY LIGHTS

EDITOR:
    Peter Martin

ASSOCIATE EDITOR:
    Charles Polk

ASSISTANT EDITOR:
    Norma Swain

MANAGING EDITOR:
    Richard Miller

CONTRIBUTING EDITORS:
    Wilder Bentley
    Arthur Foff
    Herbert Kauffman
    Antoinette Willson
    M. F. W. Pollack

CIRCULATION:
    Jean Taylor

PRESSWORK:
    Richard Pool

LITHOGRAPHY:
    Alans, 46 Kearny Street

PROCESS PHOTOGRAPHY:
    David Leong

COVER AND DESIGN:
    Don Smith

ADVERTISING:
    Jerry Bowkett
    Mary Laage

CONTENTS

CITY LIGHTS is published at 580 Washington St., San Francisco, California. Telephone DOuglas 2-8193. Copyright, 1952, by CITY LIGHTS for its contributors. Manuscripts are invited, but no payment can be made at this time.

THE CHAPLIN CASE

When we first started this magazine last spring we wanted a name that would express our interest in films and at the same time convey our faith in the vitality and value of our urban American culture. A name, we thought, like *City Lights*, Charlie Chaplin's great movie. Now we discover, to our dismay, that this man, whom we consider a symbol of our affirmation, faces an official inquiry to determine his "desirability" as an "alien."

A few weeks ago, three days after Mr. Chaplin had sailed from New York for the London opening of his latest film, *Limelight,* the Justice Department announced that upon his return Chaplin would be examined as though he were an entering alien. Mr. Chaplin has greeted this news calmly, remarking mildly that he is sure the Government will honor the re-entry permit issued to him before his departure. But the newspapers have speculated that Chaplin's morals and his politics—both famous—may prove sufficient cause for his exclusion.

We think that Mr. Chaplin is right and that these speculations are mainly nonsense. We feel, on the good evidence of the movies he has made, that his morals are sounder than those of most men; and his politics during the past twenty years have not differed from the politics of most educated, liberal Americans. Furthermore, if the decision of the Immigration board should prove unfavorable, Mr. Chaplin can appeal to the American courts, where he should find a more sympathetic hearing, as well as a judicial review of certain portions of the new McCarran Act.

But some features of this emerging Chaplin Case still seem particularly disturbing. First is the mean animosity displayed by much of the press, revealing a curious hatred for Chaplin's lonely, individual role in the American film industry. Then there is the suggestion, chauvinistic and unhistorical, that a man cannot become an American without undergoing the legal processes of nationalization, even if he has lived and worked here for over forty years, pioneered our film industry, and carried the American movie into every remote corner of the world. Finally there is the implication that we cannot accept in this country a great world artist, "the first man of whom it can be...said that he is truly world famous." The same critic has observed that Chaplin, who belongs to the whole world, really lives forever in the small drab world of his childhood. How can we exclude this poet who, wherever he may be in actuality, will always, in his imagination, walk the same remembered side-streets of Cockney London?   P.M.

3

A NOTE ON THE POETRY

In *City Lights* we should like to publish poems that have to be re-read each time they are talked about, and at the same time have a way of insisting that they be talked about. We like poems that are pervaded with their author's love of words, a love of both their inherent capabilities of precision and of evocativeness. It is, however, not so much a point of trying to publish great or spectacular poems as it is a point of trying to publish poems that show the poet's awareness of the rigors of his craft and the traditions of the art of poetry. Rarely does a poem achieve eminence by virtue of its lonely uniqueness.

We like the poems we are printing and like the way they appear in the magazine's format. In the poem on the indictment of Kenneth Skinner, *V. M. di Suvero*, (a volume of whose verse will be published in November by the Greenwood Press,) expresses the indignation aroused by a contemporary and locally notorious event. It is a poem we admire to see attempted, and one that raises the question, "In what ways can a poem succeed in dealing with the phenomena of a city and with the anger and pity we feel at the tragedies described in our daily newspapers?"

In contrast, the poems of *Ruth Rodriguez* and *Joseph Kostolefsky* are in the lyric tradition of personal statement with a working toward a definition of feeling as the controlling intention; nevertheless, these poems allow, perhaps more than most lyric poems, inquiry into the conception implicit in the poem of the poet's idea of what verse is or should be. The question we are raising now is sharply defined by the presence here of the two poems of *Edgar Bowers,* whose idea of a lyric poem would seem to differ radically from those of Mrs. Rodriguez, Mr. Kostolefsky, and from the theory of verse implicit in the poems of *James Harmon*. Mr. Harmon's three poems, as those of Mrs. Rodriguez and Mr. Kostolefsky, are working in the tradition of what we can call, for want of a better name, the free verse tradition, whereas Mr. Bowers has availed himself of the traditional meters and stanzas of English poetry. The great majority of poems we receive turn away from metric and stanzaic norms, and if they have a norm it is an irregular rhythmic pattern that is unique to the poem in which it appears. Inquiry into the questions concerning the formal characteristics of verse lead to questions concerning the possible functions and uses of verse. We mention these matters to suggest to our readers a larger question, a question which includes that raised by the presence of Mr. di Suvero's poem, and that is, "In what ways can poetry best define the qualities of contemporary experience?" We think our poems suggest several possible answers. H. K.

4

Witness: to What?

The Meaning of Whittaker Chambers'
Action as a Counter-Revolutionist

MARJORIE FARBER

I. Introduction

IN TIMES when official corruption or mass complacency seems overpowering, a religious man may find no choice but to offer himself as a sacrifice: a witness to the truth. We understand this compulsion if an anarchist or Communist runs onto the floor of the Stock Exchange with a bomb hugged to his chest, or if a pacifist assassinates a warmonger in full view of the police. We can even understand the action of that Russian prisoner who, goaded by unanswerable brutality to his fellow-prisoners, is said to have poured a can of kerosene over himself and ignited his body as a torch.

It is harder, in the case of First-Century Christians and the later martyrs, to understand a like necessity. Their actions seem - without that political-economic background familiar to us - so needless or unmotivated that we fall back on a "psychological" explanation. They were "masochists," driven by the sin of pride. We do, however, understand that some sacrifice, of this First-Century kind, was chosen by Whittaker Chambers and by Alger Hiss when the Party sent them underground: moreover into the Soviet branch of the Underground. The rest of us were at that time standing enviously by, wishing that we too had a chance to become Robin Hoods of History. For we

Much has been written about Whittaker Chambers since the early days of the Hiss Case in 1948, and even more has been written recently, following the publication of his autobiography, *Witness*, early this year. MARJORIE FARBER'S analysis of Chambers' motives and the liberals' response is so individual and so challenging that we are devoting most of this second issue of *City Lights* to it.

5

had not yet grasped the religious nature of Communism.

The Party appeared to us then, as it appears to many still, in the melodramatic colors of Robin Hood, St. George and the Dragon, or David and Goliath. The meanings of Communism did not go beyond politics, on the one hand, and such *mythopoeic* elements of primitive religions, on the other hand, as may be incorporated in a boy's adventure tale. All such tales of chivalry represent the Individual against Society. Since the individual has become collectivized today, this rebel hero may appear to some as a merry band of warriors and to others as a sinister gang of cut-throats. But he remains the Communist, arrayed against Society. The liberals are in fact split here, into the anti-Communists and whatever we call the others (the newest term is *anti*-anti-Communist.) But what most liberals share is the belief that either a merry band or a sinister gang of Communists is fighting the (more or less overwhelming)Evil of (a more or less overpowering) Society.

IT HAS not occurred to many to reverse this picture, or to see the liberal himself mistakenly arrayed with Society, against the individual. Yet, as we shall later see, Society's prevailing philosophy today - whether called Naturalism or Scientific Materialism - is in large part a nonhuman Cosmology which, as something to live by, cannot help becoming an antihuman *mythos, ethos* or metaphysic.

For Hiss or Chambers, as for any underground revolutionist, his choice appears in far more serious or deadly terms than the mythic boyhood term described above. It partakes of true religious sacrifice: whether of the ancient Scapegoat, or of the Christian martyr. Today it is hard to grasp the fact that, within an incredibly short time, one of these two men was driven by the same necessity - official corruption and mass complacency - to make the same sacrifice again: this time in order to become a counter-revolutionary. Chambers may be right, of course, in his belief that no conservative liberalism, but only militant counter-faith, can defeat the Communist religion. So far, however, no militant counter-faith has appeared except the Catholic Church.

Thus many of us are groping at the moment for some third position: a humanism midway between the old Marxist- liberalism (now become the political "Right") and what seems to be an alliance of Churchmen, neo-Republicans and *avant-gardists* on the emerging "Left." To see the world through Chambers' eyes becomes a fascinating experience in itself. For here is a man who went directly from Communism, not into the Church but into some form of Christian humanism, bypassing the liberal position altogether. For those of us who had equated not only the Catholic Church, but all Christianity, with "Reaction," it may be a novel experience to realize that one does not need to be a "liberal" in order to hold humanitarian views.

Forced to look at the events of the Forties through the eyes of a religious man who is not a Churchman, we realize that we had taken off our Marxist spectacles for some things and not for others - thus achieving a somewhat bifocal vision. With no glasses on at all, certain "human" distinctions spring into focus which had been blurred before. For example, the members of that "Un-American Activities" Committee who had appeared to us indistinguishably as reactionaries—even "fascists"—now appear as individuals, whose motivation or moral characters are not identical with their political views.* We are surprised to learn that it was Rankin who at first refused to believe Hiss guilty: seeing that glittering appearance, he thought "This man cannot lie." Other committee-members, less bedazzled by appearances, heard the ring of untruth under the evasive speech and were thus forced to a decision which, at that time, involved considerable risk to their political careers.

To lose sight of all distinctions but the "Right" or "Left" may be inevitable during a presidential campaign, but to lose them from our liberal vocabulary is to live as though perpetually in an election year. Whatever political views the conservatives and reactionaries share in common they cannot all, certainly, share the same motives. Nor can we pin a common label on them unless we are willing to identify ourselves with Rankin and admit that we, too, are unable to look below the surface to find the quite un-fashionable and unwelcome truth.

LET'S look, first of all, head-on at that picture of 1948 as seen through Chambers' eyes. We must remember that the Communism of the Twenties, restricted to the intellectuals, had become a much larger "fellow-traveling" movement in the Thirties. Checked by the Nazi-Soviet Pact in 1939, Communism ceased to make new converts among the intellectuals, but passed instead into a prevailing "Popular-Front" psychology. No longer embraced by the liberals proper, this watered-down Communism continued to dominate the so-called "liberal" opinion of the educated masses. Not until the Hiss trials began in 1948 did this massed opinion receive its first serious blow; and by then Communism had had more than twenty years in which to disguise and spread its power.

During these nine years, from the Nazi Pact to the Hiss trials, Chambers had been (except for a few personal friends) alone. So far as he knew, he was almost alone in the world - fighting a single-handed battle which began, of all places, in the offices of TIME Magazine. Where were those great Reactionary Forces arrayed with, or behind, him? His co-workers at TIME (ca. 1940) received him joyously at first for, as the Party grapevine had informed them, he was a warrior fresh from Underground exploits. After he

*The presentday liberal, having rightly repudiated the social-political ethic which characterized the American scene from, say, 1870 to 1932, has come to identify the moral good with enlightened politics and to lump all conservative, reactionary or proto-fascist (but not necessarily Communist) politics together as immoral. This reduction of morality to politics on the one hand, or to sexual mores on the other, leaves us no word for all our remaining values—familial, friendly or erotic—beyond the scientific "interpersonal relations."

had undeceived them about his present
sympathies his door had often to be
locked against them. I think we all
remember those verbal lynching-bees
from our Marxist past - the shrill
voices: "We ought to frame *him*"
(i.e. Chambers) .. and (during the
Hiss trials) "How I'd like to get my
hands around his neck!" The fact that
Chambers describes, with humor, these
early and late stages of his unpopularity does not make them a less
embarrassing recollection for us.
For several years he worked against
a petty but thoroughly harassing
sabotage, which cost him many hours
of overwork and ended, finally, in an
enforced rest brought about by his
first attacks of *angina*. This sabotage - so repellent does the informer's job seem to the great informer
of our time - was never reported to
TIME's editors.

STILL there is a peculiar irony, un-
folding at several levels, about
Chambers' isolation from other anti-
Communist intellectuals working near

him at the time. For one thing, he is
not perhaps an "intellectual" in that
specialized, or gregarious, sense in
which most of the anti-Marxists, Soc-
ialists, or *literati* had become somewhat homogeneously allied. But if he
did not seek them out, neither did
they seek him out. Intellectuals, of
whatever opinion, would have found it
hard to accept anyone identified with
TIME's policy, and Chambers was working hard to change TIME's policy from
a confused liberalism to a consistently anti-Communist position. Today we
have to admit that, for all its obvious
limitations, TIME was more nearly correct about the important things than
the vast majority of liberal opinion.
Had we known earlier what Chambers'
motives were in working out the unique
salvation he found, even at TIME, I
hope we should have admired him as his
friends did. At any rate it was that
lonely road, partly self-imposed, which
brought him in the end to WITNESS: in
my opinion, one of the most profoundly
meaningful experiences recorded in our
generation.

II. The Political Necessity

BY 1948 a few individuals in the
Government had managed to convince themselves that Chambers'
incredible tales of espionage were
true. Had the Committee been ac-
tuated chiefly by personal or political motives, they would have dropped
the case as soon as the Hiss forces

began to show their power. Indeed
they were often tempted to do so,
from the moment when Hiss impress-
ively denied his old friend's story,
to the climactic moment in the hotel
room when Hiss had his friend stand
with his mouth hanging open, so that
he could examine his teeth. A mom-

ent of peak irony in this Case of cumulative horror did arrive, however, when the Committee nearly decided that Chambers was, after all, a psychopathic liar. This was when the Forces of Science, in the person of an expert from the Eastman Kodak Company, made a slight mistake in the date: Chambers' microfilm, the expert claimed, had not been manufactured at the time Chambers said he had received it. This occasion has become a favorite butt of ridicule, like the pumpkin itself, among the liberals. For this was when Chambers bought the can of cyanide gas and made what appears to many people a "phony" and rather comical attempt at suicide. To one reviewer of his book, I am sorry to say, the choice of insecticide seems only too appropriate a means of self-extermination. This review is titled *"I don't believe it"* and ends: "The Hiss case may yet prove that a monster with mysticism is still a monster." *

Chambers recovered from the expert's mistake, as he recovered physically from his suicide attempt. But, as I believe most readers of his book will agree, he never recovered totally or spiritually from this moment of crowning irony. The discovery that truth itself might depend, like his own fate and perhaps the fate of his country, on the word of an expert from the Eastman Kodak Company - this might have unhinged a less religious man than Chambers. It was around this time that he began to "pray": that is, to talk to his God in that personal way which seems most to have disgusted or amused

the reviewers. Such a phenomenon may come about when a man of religious temperament undergoes a suffering so intense that he must either cry out against God's injustice or, like Job, look within himself to find a crime equal to his punishment. But we have seen so many versions of mock-piety and mock-humility that this is one of the meanings of religion from which we have turned away in disgust.

Nevertheless it is interesting to note how "mysticism" is defined today. It seems to have been Chambers' habit of referring to his God as someone who took a personal interest in his fate, which all the reviewers agree is mysticism at its worst. (Part of the Naturalist credo, by the way, is that the only immanent god or goddess within Nature is Nature herself; *God* is defined as Descartes' transcendent Author, Architect or First Cause who created the Universe and then retired, having no further use for His creations). We may also note that the above-mentioned review based only its factual appeal to the reader on Chambers' perjury; its rhetorical appeal is squarely based on fifteen quotations from the book, all of which contain the word "God."

Perhaps this is the place to mention another favorite criticism, namely that Chambers' political views are "Manichaean": life seen as a conflict between the forces of Good and Evil. There is some comedy in this. How else are we to see the world in times of war and revolution? At least Chambers sees two somewhat equal forces

* By Vern Countryman, Associate professor of law at Yale University; *Frontier*, August, '52

arrayed against each other. The Mani-
chaeanism of the "Popular Front" or
"fellow-traveling" psychology sees, on
the other hand, only the 'Fascist" reactionary Enemy as powerful. It sees
oneself as the tiny harried liberal,
fighting bravely against a really *dirty*
Goliath - a Giant willing to use the
foulest means of warfare against the
little David. In such a case, it is not
of course unsporting for little David
to aim as many kicks below the belt as
his tiny foot can manage.

Moreover the modern Goliath is not
only a filthy bully: he is permanently
invincible. Long after the Communist
Underground had infiltrated every
branch of Government, we continued
to believe that the "Fascist" Conspiracy was invincible. Indeed, if
it were ever conquered, what Revolution
would be left? - what sport of war
could possibly replace the dignity of a
religious combat between David and Goliath, or give scope to our highest
aspirations toward heroism and self-
sacrifice?

RETURNING now to the early days of
the Hiss case: Before the documentary evidence of the microfilm
had forced the final decision—i.e.
to indict Hiss for perjury rather
than Chambers for espionage—the five
or six members of the "Un-American"
Committee had against them the entire
weight of the Administration, represented by the Justice Department, to
say nothing of the majority of the
press, radio, and public opinion.

The reason for this, as well as for
much of the bitterness aroused by the
Case, may be found in a fact suggested

earlier. By 1948 it had become impossible to distinguish a Communist from
a fellow-traveler, "dupe" or sympathizer - either by his public speech
or by his private opinions. Thus a
Party card became the all-important
criterion. But since the fellow-traveling "liberal" had no way of distinguishing himself from Hiss, except
through a Party membership, which Hiss
denied, the feeling grew that to single
out Hiss for punishment was a grave
miscarriage of justice. As indeed it
might have been, except for espionage.
And espionage was only implied, not
proved, by Hiss' conviction for perjury.
Moreover the Communist-sympathizer of
yesterday had become, by 1948, merely
a defender of himself, yesterday's
Communist sympathizer—a fellow-
traveler not of Communists but of
erstwhile Fellow Travelers. Such a
man could not believe that he himself
would ever have carried his fellow-
traveling (of whatever date) to the
logical extreme of espionage. Therefore Hiss was innocent, and remains innocent for many today.

Many people, even today, believe that
it is not we who, but for the grace of
God, might be in jail with Hiss - but
Chambers who ought to be in jail instead of Hiss. (However we arrange
this, it is somebody else who committed
the crimes and we who committed the
mistakes.) But, as any reader of his
book will understand, Chambers would
have been a relatively happy man if his
conscience had allowed him to choose
perjury and jail, instead of the sentence he imposed upon himself.

In 1948, at all events, it was hard
for most of us to believe that the

minority opinion for Chambers, against Hiss, could possibly be either correct or representative of a minority. For it was we, the liberals, who represented a tiny fighting minority against the whole "Reactionary" weight of opinion. The pro-Chambers people we regarded as a kind of Fascist mass, readers of the Hearst Press. Listen to Chambers' view of them:

> The contrast between them and the glittering Hiss forces is about the same as between the glittering French chivalry and the somewhat tattered English bowmen who won at Agincourt. Most of them ...came from the wrong side of the railroad tracks. I use the expression as the highest measure of praise, as Lincoln noted that God must love the common people..

At this date, Chambers apologizes for the term Common Man!

Now this picture will seem greatly exaggerated unless we keep in mind the date, 1948. This was the very peak of our liberalism, when we had come finally to ally ourselves with "the best people": the massed power of wealth, officialdom, press and State. Last of all the wealthy stars of sport and screen, and all the older wealth there was, came over to our side. We had converted them, by unceasing propaganda. Meanwhile there was stirring against us the blind resentment of those very people whose Savior we had determined to be: those whom we had educated, since only we knew what was good for them, to be our Proletariat and our Peasantry.

> No feature of the Hiss Case is more obvious, or more troubling

as history, than the jagged fissure, which it did not so much open as reveal, between the plain men and women of the nation, and those who affected to act, think, and speak for them. It was, not invariably, but in general, the "best people" who were for Alger Hiss and who were prepared to go to almost any length to protect and defend him. It was the enlightened and the powerful, the clamorous proponents of the open mind and the common man, who snapped their minds shut in a pro-Hiss psychosis, of a kind which, in an individual patient, means the simple failure of the ability to distinguish between reality and unreality, and, in a nation, is a warning of the end.

> It was the great body of the nation, which, not invariably, but in general, kept open its mind...waiting for the returns to come in.

We are beginning, without our Marxist glasses on, to get a glimpse of that great "Fascist Conspiracy" we saw everywhere in those days - running our schools and our government, stifling the press. When we look now at one of these 'plain men and women' sitting beside us in a movie, at a meeting fixing our car, collecting bus-fares, protecting our plumbing or our property - we can see how silly any American citizen would look, dressed up as a Peasant or a Proletarian. We get a whiff of that humorless arrogance underlying our Marxism, which erected economic Justice as its absolute and, by denying charity, compassion, love, humility, along with the related virtue - sense of humor - exposed itself as naked pride and power.

(Continued on page 38)

The New Yorker in Hollywood

HANS MEYERHOFF

NOBODY knew her before she came. Nobody would have paid the slightest attention to her had she come on her own. She was a pleasant and friendly person, to be sure, but not particularly decorative—something which ordinarily would have eliminated her immediately from circulation in Hollywood; she was not even what is known as an "interesting person." There was nothing in her present life that any columnist would have been interested in—except for the fame into which she was catapulted by writing a literary portrait of Hemingway. Nor did she have a "past": she came from a middle-class family, went to Hunter College, joined *The New Yorker* after graduation, and slowly worked herself up into the position of a regular staff writer. This is a perfectly honest and respectable background; from the Hollywood point of view, however, it was strictly dull— except for the fact that she had joined *The New Yorker* and not *Harper's*.

Now the girl from *The New Yorker* had come to Hollywood to do a full-length study of John Huston and the movie colony. For the assignment she had been equipped with a special wardrobe; she had brought along, as reading material, a complete set of bound volumes of *The New Yorker;* and she was preceded, upon her entry onto the stage of Hollywood, by the reputation she had earned from spending a week end in the company of Mr. Hemingway.

The piece on Hemingway was well written; it displayed all the finesse and transparent sophistication by which *The New Yorker* sets the style for those of us engaged in a harmless and vicarious flirtation with the "finer things" of life: imported perfumes and mink coats, a new showing of Modiglianis, cartoons by Charles Addams, or insights into the private lives of Hemingway and Toots Shor. There is something reassuringly democratic about these intimate glimpses of men of distinction: through the peep-hole we see them in the right context—Hemingway side by side with Toots Shor—and feel relieved. After all, they too are only human, all-too-human, that is, right there on our own level.

The portrait made Mr. Hemingway— one of the great writers of this country and the world—look like a retarded adolescent, or like a disgusting cross between an imbecile and a brute blabbering phony Indian baby talk and vulgarities; perhaps that's the way he is; then again, perhaps that's the way he chose to appear for the benefit of the girl from *The New Yorker*. Be that as it may, the reporter did her

12

job well: we certainly got Ernie's
number; we know that he begins his
day with a magnum of champagne; and we
know just how he feels about the *Kraut*,
Marlene Dietrich.

It used to be that these portraits
of distinguished contemporaries were
invariably drawn from representatives
within a certain radius of the great
city or, at least, from the Eastern
seaboard; but now it seems as if *The
New Yorker* has broken with this old
and firmly-established policy. What
is behind this change of policy (if it
be one), and what is the reason for
choosing Hollywood as the most logical
place for making the change, I am not
in a position to say.

Not that Mr. Huston doesn't deserve
to have a portrait written about him.
He is a prominent man in the movie
colony and a very good director of
motion pictures. He can certainly
hold his own with Toots. Of course,
Mr. Louis B. Mayer may tell you, in a
moment of desperation, that none of
Mr. Huston's pictures has made any
money; or he may buttonhole the producer
of Mr. Huston's latest opus, *The Red
Badge of Courage*, and ask some pertinent and embarrassing questions: to
wit, who knows anything today about
an "immortal classic" by Stephen
Crane (quite right, Mr. Mayer); the
Civil War was a long time ago, wasn't
it (right again, Mr. Mayer); besides,
it was simply kids' stuff in comparison with what audiences expect from a
war now (it sure was, Mr. Mayer);

those soldiers look awfully funny with
those visors on their military caps
(they sure do, Mr. Mayer); you like to
draw a fat pay check every week, don't
you; so why shouldn't I worry about
the box office returns (yes, why
shouldn't you, Mr. Mayer)——but this
is the other side of Hollywood perhaps
evoking the somber shades of Wall
Street, but not the light touch and
finesse of *The New Yorker;* and there
is no denying that Mr. Huston and his
producer have artistic ability——Mr.
Mayer's plaintive, paternal concern
notwithstanding. So there is no reason
why the girl from *The New Yorker* should
not have come to Hollywood to write a
portrait of John Huston.

As a matter of fact, on further
reflection, it appears that Hollywood
is quite the logical choice for setting
the precedent which will break with *The
New Yorker's* previous policy concerning
the geographical distribution of men
eligible for a literary portrait. For
I cannot imagine any community other
than Hollywood where the magazine is
held in higher esteem, approached with
more discerning appreciation, and
looked up to with a more bewildering
mixture of excitement, fear, trembling,
and respectful reverence.

It is not easy to account for these
sentiments; but it is likely that the
magic of expensive luxury goods deco-
rating the pages of *The New Yorker*——
by which Hollywood sets its standard
of *material* success—is only a surface
phenomenon. Underneath the surface
there are deeper roots. New York is
(or was) not only the physical home of

many who have made the long trek West
to dig the gold of Hollywood (and claim
to have regretted it ever since—a
pardonable form of human self-deception); but New York was, is, and perhaps always will be the spiritual home,
the level of the highest aspirations,
for the "better part" of Hollywood. And
The New Yorker is the symbol for this
spiritual home.

Thus to write for The New Yorker is
to have risen above "Hollywood" into a
different world, to an intellectual
level on and for which The New Yorker
is believed to be written; in short,
it is to have redeemed oneself from all
the power, glory—and failure which is
the better part of Hollywood. Any
producer's wife can drive a Jaguar or
wear a blue mink stole (but what is
that, alas, when anybody else can do
so, too?); anybody can peddle (yes,
that's the word for it in Hollywood)
a story for the movies if he drinks
cocktails with the right people, hangs
around long enough, has the right manners at gin rummy, and possibly a knack
for dialogue; but it is given only to
a few—ah, so few—to appear in the
pages of The New Yorker. This is more
than just to place a story in a respectable magazine, much more: it is an
act of self-realization.

Next to writing for The New Yorker
ranks being written up by The New
Yorker; for without some such theory
as this, I submit, it is difficult to
explain why and how Hollywood responded
to the challenge of the girl from The
New Yorker as it did. Arriving with
the imprimatur of The New Yorker she
had all the credentials she would ever

need to "crash" Hollywood.

She came, looked, and listened—
and for weeks and months she was the
center of attraction and worship. She
was a careful observer; she took
copious notes; she remembered my first
name after one casual meeting. But
she never seemed to say anything herself—except to ask questions.

These questions, however, were something else again. They were quite
deceptive in their sophomoric simplicity. Listening intently, and with
an air of an innocent child looking in
wonderment and rapture at a lighted
Christmas tree, she would occasionally
interrupt the speaker to ask: "What
makes you say that, John?" or, "Do you
really think so, dear?"; just like
that, as if it were the most natural
and the most sophisticated question in
the world. Perhaps more bewildering
and misleading, however, was another
set of questions she had at her disposal. She would simply ask for an
explanation of what is ordinarily taken
for granted, even in Hollywood. When
somebody mentioned B-girls, she would
ask innocently: "What are B-girls,
dear?"; and then, when this was explained, just for good measure, "Are
there really such people in the
world?"; when somebody else (just back
from Rome) held forth on the culture,
art, and beauty of Italy, she would
ask: "What's the quattrocento,
dear?"; or again, when somebody talked
about Dreiser's The American Tragedy
(another forthcoming movie), the girl
from The New Yorker, again listening
intently, would suddenly interrupt to
ask the momentous question: "What's

'The American Tragedy', Sam?"

Sometimes, if you didn't know that this was *The New Yorker,* these questions might be quite distracting. Thus they seem to have affected the Israeli Consul when, during a lively discussion of anti-Semitism throughout the world, she popped up with the question: "What is anti-Semitism, Mr. Dafni?" Mr. Dafni, the Consul, it seems, was quite upset. Perhaps he would have been even more bewildered if he had learned, a few nights later, that the same reporter reluctantly declined an invitation to a dinner party because it was the night for observing *jahrzeit.*

And thus she moved through an interminable succession of dinner parties—as if she didn't quite belong anywhere, just looking around and listening, and occasionally asking a few harmless, innocent questions. Ordinarily, as I was saying, she would have appeared strictly dull and "uninteresting"; and nobody in Hollywood would have had anything to do with her Yet, invariably she was the center of attention and attraction, for this was no ordinary situation.

Journalists are a mighty power anywhere, but especially in Hollywood where publicity is, as everybody knows, both a profitable business and a veritable mania. Reviews make and break contracts; and if Hedda Hopper has got something on you, you'd better go and see your chaplain. The press prospers and flourishes even if the movie industry doesn't. The journalists find open doors, glad handshakes, ready publicity handouts, free tickets

for Santa Anita, and a round of drinks anywhere along the regular beat.

But none of them ever became the center of the social life in Hollywood as did the girl from *The New Yorker.* Which isn't surprising since she was more than a journalist, much more. And the only time I ever heard her take a position on anything was to drive this point home, simply, but firmly and precisely. It happened when some assistant to the assistant director of "The American Tragedy" tried to find an excuse for not letting her see some of the rushes that were being shown the next day. It seems the press was excluded; and he was afraid if it became known that she had been present, the other journalists would resent this sort of favoritism. The girl from *The New Yorker,* listening intently and politely as always, straightened herself up just a little; then, looking directly at the man, she said quietly, yet almost curtly, like putting a little boy in his place: "Well, you know, dear, I am *not* a journalist."

She was, of course, right—absolutely right. She was not a journalist; and nobody treated her like a journalist. Hers was not a regular journalistic assignment at all; it was rather like a mission redeeming the better part of Hollywood for *The New Yorker.*

And thus she came to be the center of social life in Hollywood, the star performer in a grandiose show to redeem the better part of Hollywood. She was invited for breakfast, for lunch (Romanoff's, of course), for dinner, for afternoon parties and entertainment, at home, at the Mocambo, or the Colony Club. She was out on location; she went to every preview; she was flown to Las Vegas; she played baccarat and the slot machines; she was taken shopping on The Miracle Mile. She was always "booked" solidly; and wherever she went, she reigned supreme—although she didn't quite seem to belong anywhere.

She reigned supreme because Hollywood considered her the supreme test. Being weighed and found wanting by the girl from *The New Yorker* would be supreme failure; being weighed and found worthy, supreme achievement.

This is a hard test to be up against even with all the resources of Hollywood at one's disposal. For dinner parties and entertainment are one thing. But to prove oneself worthy of *The New Yorker* is still another: One must also be brilliant. One must have experiences that flash brilliantly against the screen of popular mediocrity; one must have ideas that are brilliant; and one must be able to express them brilliantly in punch-lines suitable for the end of each installment of the portrait in *The New Yorker*. Thus at every dinner party she was surrounded by men who were trying, gallantly, at times, desperately and frantically, for the most part, to outdo each other in manufacturing brilliant experiences or in generating brilliant ideas.

This is a hard test to impose on anybody. As time went on, a note of anxiety crept into Hollywood's worship

of the girl from *The New Yorker,* a gnawing suspicion that this was a game at which you couldn't win. This might do for a night at Las Vegas, but not for a spiritual test stretching over a period of months. As long as she was around collecting material (but not yet writing), it was easy enough to assuage this growing sense of anxiety by intensifying one's efforts of impressing her by giving bigger and better parties or by thinking harder and harder of more and more brilliant things to say. But, alas, the day would come when she would leave or withdraw to write her piece; and what then? Would anybody qualify for recognition by *The New Yorker?* Was it humanly possible to pass this sort of a test? Perhaps for a week end with the help of champagne and a hip flask of bourbon used by Mr. Hemingway to stimulate his reactions to the paintings in the Metropolitan Museum of Art; but for a period of three months or more, and in Hollywood? How long can anybody—even in Hollywood—go without saying something that is just ordinary and mediocre? And how could one ever be sure that whatever she wrote would elevate Hollywood to the intellectual level to which it aspired.

If she portrayed the movie colony as a harmless, average American community, it wouldn't be enough. If she let herself go and wrote as *The New Yorker* sometimes would write, it would be too much. It would just be another Hollywood expose. If she wrote "down" revealing the human-all-too-human stature of Hollywood—as she had

done in the case of Hemingway—
that would not do; for Hollywood, unlike Mr. Hemingway, cannot afford to
be written "down." If she wrote too
much about one person, this would make
everybody else angry and envious; if
she wrote nothing, the person would not
be recognized; if she wrote a little,
it might just be the wrong thing or
(God forbid) less than what she might
say about somebody else.

No, this was a game too much even
for the better part of Hollywood. Desperately and anxiously as its people
tried to win the pleasure, approval,
and recognition of the girl from *The
New Yorker,* they knew all along that
they were only her next victims.

Occasionally—at breakfast perhaps,
looking over the wreckage of last
night's effort to please her—they
might even admit to themselves what
and how they felt. They wished she had
never come; they hated her; they hated
themselves for submitting to the
indignity of this test; they wished
she were dead.

But, each time, someone would invariably reach for the phone and, with
a brave wan smile, set the stage for
another little surprise party for the
girl from *The New Yorker.*

The New Yorker in Hollywood is reprinted from the September 1951 issue
of *Partisan Review* through the courtesy
of the editors of *Partisan Review* and
Dr. Meyerhoff.

V. M. DI SUVERO

to san francisco on the indictment
of kenneth skinner aged 17

In the days of the Temple
It was enough that some of the sins remain
Unpublished and unopened.
It was enough that the lids on the coffins
Remain shut and that no pointing finger
Would rise to name and mark any.
It was enough, for
A scapegoat was brought
And all the unnamed sins were set on it
And the goat, rolling gaited and bleating,
Would be beaten out of the Temple,
Beaten out of the city of Jerusalem,
Beaten out beyond the oases,
And there perish in the deserts,
For the sins of Israel.

    You have done much, burnt much
    And much endured, San Francisco,
    Phoenix city tortured
    With the memory of regeneration.
    Fire strikes one terrible
    Shudder along the now straight streets.
    You cannot now remember how
    It was then, the people pushing
    And the swarms camping
    Out on the bare, rolling,
    California hills. The acrid stench
    Drifting through the tent flaps,
    The smell of burnt horsehair,
    The loud wailing, and those,
    The impromptu preachers,
    Who always arise at tragedy,
    Shouting in manic frenzy,
    " And thus was Sodom and
    Thus Gomorrah... "

Cry " Fire"
                         and the terror rises
          Out of the streets, halls
          And churches debouch with terror,
          If you cry it loud enough.

Fire starts in many places,
High roofs and low basements,
The beautiful orange flames
Licking upward, always upward.
The filth of the city is burnt
Consumed as in a sacrifice,
And the thick black billows
Of smoke rise and tower in air.
But since the Big Fire,
San Francisco, the Burn,
San Francisco, whenever
There is sacrifice, you
San Francisco, demand
Another sacrifice. Let one
Rathole of a hotel catch
The cleansing flame, clutch
It to its rickety heart and
There let the condemned burn, those
Condemned by poverty, by age,
Those body and pocket cripples,
Let those burn, and immediately
You take another to cap the list,
And let him be the seal,
Let him burn innocently,
And burn for years, slowly.
And this goat you take is
Alone, poor, a wanderer,
Defenseless in the city
And you take him for example,
All quietly inside saying well

          " This is what we would have done
          Had we caught the guy who done it. "
          The subjunctive is a tense
          Not much used in the vernacular,
          Conditionally speaking is a luxury,
          This must be so and is,
          " They caught someone, that's enough. "

No, not enough. What is enough
Is that dreams of you and I walking together
Need not extend the promenade
Through charred vistas and blackened
Boulevards. What sacrifices we make
San Francisco to the calm and order
And greenness of our dreams!

        The greater our dreams, the greater
        The sacrifice, at least so runs
        The theory—so, haunted city,
        Why take a twisted boy out
        As sacrifice to the security of the dream.
        To take the lowest is to confess
        The dream small, so petty
        It can ill afford the luxury
        Of not knowing who jarred it once.
        Grow, grow, San Francisco, grow up
        To the size of the dream, inquire
        Where the proper sacrifice can be found.

I have seen grown men in the mountains
Take flashlights and flush porcupines
Lumbering along their nightly trails
And club them again and again
Until the round ball of spines rolls over
And turns piteous eyes to the stars
While the clubs beat down and down
And finally one blade flashes in the
Ever ready rays and begins to cut
The fleshed nose off for the bounty
Of five .22 shells.
At least in the mountains
They did not go into the past and
Record of the spined animal.

        " This report shows that since early childhood
        Kenneth has been in conflict with society.
        His extreme poverty and failure to adjust
        Marked him early and continuously
        As a problem... "

                    Poor and weak,
And you stretched out your hand to help.
Kicked him out of the schools, beat him,
Starved him and his brothers, and then
Wondered why his work suffered
And he did not produce enough for admittance
To the select ranks of the beavers
And the boosters.
                    But the human animal,
Even the lowest, diseased, starved, beaten, blind
Animal is a wonderful thing. He is the image,
The infinite potential which will continue to grow
Towards godhead or perdition. The direction
Unfortunately depends on compassion
And the hearts it meets.

I have seen an unskilled craftsman
Take blocks of wood and gouge the grain
Out of use and out of beauty and curse
The wood and the grain and relegate
The splinters to the fire.

                "Teachers, social workers, psychiatrists,
                Physicians, Juvenile court attachés
                And counselors."
                            All you, and all you
                Others, San Francisco, who have dealt
                This half-blind, half-starved, half goat
                His hand of life, can you now point,
                Can you now say this world we live in,
                This most fair city has been besmirched
                By loud and terrifying soot
                Made by his hands. Relegate
                To the fire this life you shaped,
                This goat you moulded?
                                    "He can
be handled if we knew how!"
Your ignorance his damnation.

On April 25 of this year, Kenneth Skinner, 17, was convicted of eight counts of manslaughter, after a fire had destroyed the College Court Apartments on Haight Street on July 22, 1951, causing a loss of eight lives. While the jury recommended leniency, Skinner was denied probation and sentenced to serve one to ten years in San Quentin Prison.

GEORGE Herriman's *Krazy Kat* reminds us that *we* are the ones who make the classics, every bit as much as the original artist. The intensity of our response and our consequent demand that the work of art be returned to us, be "revived," creates a classic; the artist creates only his work of art. If Shakespeare's plays are classics today, it is because a minority agitated for their revival through

periods when the prevailing attitude was one of indifference and even dislike.

Nowhere is the nature of this process clearer than in our popular

arts, if they may indeed be called "popular." Our movies, songs, comic-strips, and radio and television entertainment seem only to be appreciated by a particular "mass" which, whatever the quality of its perceptions, is incapable of articulating its responses or making its demands known. But occasionally, reluctantly, the educated, articulate minority will recognize in one of the products of the popular arts that depth and intensity of perception and that mastery of the strategies of the medium that marks a true work of art. Then the process of classicization begins, for this active, vocal minority will demand that the particular work (a film like *City Lights,* a song like *Bye, Bye Blackbird,* a comic strip like *Krazy*) be brought back, again and again, until it has become what we call a classic.

Krazy Kat appeared daily and Sundays for over 30 years, from 1910 until Herriman's death in 1944. Gilbert Seldes first recognized *Krazy* in 1924 in his pioneering book *The Seven Lively Arts.* "America can pride itself on having produced," he said, "and can hastily set about to appreciate...(a) most amusing and fantastic and satisfactory work of art." A few years after Herriman's death and the subsequent disappearance of the strip (who

but Herriman could draw *Krazy?*) Henry Holt published in book form a wide selection of *Krazy* strips with an exciting, if somewhat obscure, introduction by E. E. Cummings. While the book was warmly received by the press and by reminiscent admirers of the strip, it apparently had a disappointing sale, for remaindered copies can can still be purchased occasionally for almost one quarter the original price.

None of the original *Krazy* has been made available since the Henry Holt book (1946), but the Kat has not been forgotten. His influence can be seen in strips like *Pogo* and *King Aroo*; and recently, too, a Dell Publication comic book of the same name has appeared. But if the characters and situations are superficially similar, the new strip is so slovenly drawn and simple-minded that it is an insult to Herriman's elaborate, complex genius.

Krazy Kat is our first comic-strip classic, and it is *Krazy*, the original

Krazy that we want—nothing else will do. For is this not how we create a classic?—We must have the original back, we demand that it be returned to us unchanged. We want Shakespeare's plays, not Johnson's "improvements."

So, as the 19th Century brought Shakespeare back, we will revive *Krazy*, again and again. Gilbert Seldes in 1924, the Henry Holt edition in 1946, even this little note in *City Lights*— are all incidents in this process. And someday soon some alert editor of a lively newspaper (the *Chronicle?*) will demand him—and then he will be back for sure...*Krazy* and *Ignatz* and *Offissa Pupp*. Because *Krazy* is a *Klassik*.

The *Laff* Movie

KEN KOLB

THE PLACE was squeezed in between two legitimate movie houses, and I might have missed it except for a sandwich board on the sidewalk which said → The Laff Movie. I sidled into the narrow alcove to look at the signs. There were four cartoon posters, some Laurel and Hardy stills, and another huge sign, white on blue, that said Three Hours of Laffs.

While I stood there indecisively, the single exit opened and a thin, middle-aged man came out, looking as though he were leaving his mother's funeral. While he limped slowly up the street I stepped over to the box office and put down my fifty cents. The girl looked up at me, so I smiled. She gave me the weary, sorrowful look worn by amusement operators the world over, then tore my ticket in half and handed me the stub. I walked through the untended door into a lobby slightly larger than a phone booth. There wasn't even room for a popcorn machine.

On the left wall a narrow door said Gentlemen. Opposite me a faded velvet curtain hung across the one entrance to the aisle. The right wall was

Every large city has its Laff Movie, devoted solely to comedies, color cartoons, and serials. KEN KOLB reports on San Francisco's, which is on Market next to the United Artists theatre.

blank, painted a dull grey. The management wasn't expecting any Ladies. I took three steps across the lobby and went through the curtain. The theatre was so long and narrow that the effect was like stepping into a railroad tunnel. On each side of the single aisle the narrow rows of seats ran into the distance like a double row of ties. From where I stood the screen was the size of a postage stamp, and because the floor was perfectly flat, it was suspended some fifteen or twenty feet above the audience.

I had come in between Laffs. The theatre was quiet as a mortuary. The crowd watched intently as a group of soldiers in World War I costume crawled over the silent screen in an epic filmed long before the invention of background music. In this eerie silence I took the long, long walk to the front of the theatre. When the screen had assumed normal size, I slipped in beside a little boy sitting on the edge of his upturned seat. He barely reached to my shoulder. Adjusting my head at a forty-five degree angle upward, I focused on the First World War. A volley of furious firing introduced an episode of intense confusion, many pratfalls, and no casualties. The audience maintained a perfect composure.

The War was followed by The Three Stooges in suits of armor. The suits of armor did not cover their heads, so the stooges were able to perform their one comic routine, namely, hitting each other in the face with a variety of props—in this case mostly blacksmith tools. The silence in the theatre deepened until the sound of metal on heads could be heard echoing painfully from the back wall.

The Three Stooges were followed by a Laurel and Hardy epic which featured an insane butler and a widow who wished to cut Hardy's throat. The widow was not insane. The high point of the picture arrived when Laurel was allowed to shoot Hardy in the toe with a shotgun. My own toes curled up in my shoes so tightly that I almost forgot the headache I had left from The Three Stooges.

A gentleman in white came up the aisle selling popcorn from a wooden hamper suspended around his shoulders, and for a dime I bought a temporary diversion. The popcorn was apparently made in a roomier building several blocks away. It was stone cold and rather salty. The boy next to me eyed the bag with a solemn stare, and I gladly gave it to him. He ate a small portion, chewing slowly through the gathering gloom, then, following the general precedent, dumped the rest on the floor.

There followed in rapid succession the four advertised cartoons. The first was organized around the famous and fatal train wreck of Casey Jones. The second involved a cat beating up on a mouse, and in turn being beaten up by a bulldog. The third pitted Donald Duck against two deranged woodpeckers in an all-out battle with knives, guns, ropes, and roasting ovens.

The fourth cartoon concerned the adventures of a Harvard geologist with Clementine and her father, the hard-rock miner. There were no fights, no chases, no falls, no head-bashes, and no explosions, but it still seemed funny.

With a feeling of blessed release I started to laugh. I laughed wholeheartedly, increasingly, with my head thrown back and my body shaking. Then, slowly, the horror dawned on me. Objectively, from somewhere outside myself, I heard my laughter echoing between those narrow walls. In that grief-stricken silence it was like the laugh of an idiot. My throat closed spasmodically and the back of my neck grew hot as I felt myself the focus of every eye in that long, dark tunnel. A feeling of shame rose in me, so strong that I could not sit still under it. I stood up and stepped into the aisle, turning to face the rows of silent watchers. One look made me realize the enormity of my blunder. I knew from every face that its owner was desperate; that the loneliness of the city had forced each of them into this dismal room in one last pitiful grasp at a straw. I hurried up the aisle and out into the neon glare of the street.

I, and the rest of us, are too lonely now
So alone we no longer look for a father
A kind one who might love us and show
The smile between us.
Even beauty is so far we hardly look
At the distant light yet lingering
And we grow cold and wish we could
Bear to give one cry or even admit
One whisper of the truth of the
Beauty and the father so far
Yet lingering slightly.
Lightly as the air goes
When we fall away
From the world of our knowledge
Goes the strength of our fathers
From us, and I, and all the rest of us,
Grow weak, slow-cold, and must die.

RUTH RODRIGUEZ

JOSEPH KOSTOLEFSKY

huzzahs for the heroine

Billie Dove-lovely is my fair lady.
Sparrows know her; flickers flare before
Her winging glance, so tinged is she with heaven.

Lady of all my matinees,
What screen could frame that sun-shot field
Wherein you move? What sound-track hum
That tango-timed companion of my pulse?

Through Saipan and Gallipolis,
All the black alleys of our dread,
In jungle damp or tempered ease,
Past monumental lowerings of the head,
You loom and linger.

If ripeness be all, so love is all,
And all my Pippin love I hold, yet give,
And, hat in hand, beg your heart's autograph,
An ancient music singing through my bones.

EDGAR BOWERS the snow man

Some boys rolled up a snow man in the yard
Whose idle face I watch these lunar nights;
His lack of something makes him prey to thaw,
Dumb show of nothing, to come and go with ice.

Yet in the night I start up with the crack
Of ice upon the dormant pool and range
From dreams of snow men melting on the grass,
Convulsed with frantic change and counter change.

He shall not be there when the summer spends
Its vegetable heat; but freeze will lurk
Behind each burning day, in steaming pool
And on the dusty law and range, to irk,

When lunar glare is falsely spread like snow,
My sleep with images of a snow man
Standing always in formulative cold,
In what must be perfect meridian.

on conversations with my grandmother

In latter day Vermont, when the holy season
Would press its cold mass on the hollied pane,
Then did the lurking blood of Christ give reason
To store up precept in the troubled brain.

And through His frosted breath upon the reason
Bright pictures of His passion and His pain
Drew the nerves that feasted on the season
And taught the cautious heart that stored the brain

That love from all the riches of the season
Will lay its issue in the measure of the brain
To feed the gradual weakness of the reason
When it has lost the idiom of His pain.

JAMES HARMON

a modern woman

As small child rejecting
the womb-winding comfort
slowly retreating
beyond touch of soft fingers.

As child the strong one
as child the hard
turning even child's back
on the love-flowing chalice.

Admiring in sheer adoration
the Roman-like maleness
retreating to the self-core
of stark isolation

There to build the walls
of your life's later prison:
man-mind in wife-body
in hard opposition.

But the core of a woman
is always volcanic
though gray ash lay dormant
on desolate mountain

The mind's triangles
built upon maleness
are crushed into dust
when the volcano erupts.

Power is the most evocative.
Do you mean the invasive, possessive
Power, now everywhere in sway:
The cheap battle of sex,
The thrusting dagger and the clawing trap?
That which made Aaron
Flee the chord, symbol of clang,
Flout family and seek the flute,
With its lilting alone line?
Or is it another thing:
Emanating, organic power-love,
Vegetable electric, alive
In ecstatic moments of life?
Lineament of fulfilled desire
Not a sentiment—a being:
Demon and possessor a fire
To burn the blood
Sear the bone
To fix the brood
Remove the bane?

for jaime d'angulo

Las Pesares, Big Sur
and sorrows
the infertile fruits
of your labor.
This year, 1949
for the first time
the grapes bore
but they are bitter.

Your plow lies idle and rusted
and you, an old man
need a gun
to kill the crows.

The Germans

PETER MARTIN

GERMANS and their Germany arouse in me even today feelings of fear, suspicion, and mistrust that not even my standard liberal mind can prevent from hardening into prejudice. The dark picture that the Thirties formed was stamped too deeply into my consciousness by the war years, far beyond the reach of that clean and orderly part of me that wants to be just and fair. Too many of those shouted speeches and throaty *sig heils;* too many newsreels of weeping women and happy children pelting the sleek limousines with flowers; too many banners, too many crowds, too much noise; too many shots of the curious, chortling little dance *he* executed at Compiegne; and then, later, when the war ended, too many charred bones. Now the language itself has taken on the harshness of those words, and of the static that seemed to convey, rather than interrupt, those screams; now the people themselves have been confused with the horrible events of all that time.

Yet it has not always been this way with me and the Germans. Once, when I was a child—no more than six or seven—their language seemed the sweetest I had ever heard, lovelier than my own; and the young immigrant couple who spoke it more beautiful and infinitely kinder than I had ever known people could be.

They were not the first Germans in my life, for both Olga and John Burcker, with whom I was "boarded," came from solid German families; and occasionally, in a spirit of unbuckled relaxation, they would even lapse into half-remembered German. But for me they were Americans; they were all the America I knew. They lived in one of those square, two-story clapboard houses, with the long, open front-porch and high stoop of the older Long Island suburbs. They had a lawn in front, boxed in by hedges that were clipped square; they even had a radio, and rich relatives—on John's side—who lived in Forest Hills, which was very nice. (And other relatives— on Olga's side—who lived in Jamaica in a dark apartment right *on* the El; and with these relatives they fought bitterly.) They voted for Alfred E. Smith because they were Catholics; they read the *N. Y. Daily News* and the *Graphic;* and they speculated knowingly about the motives of Ruth Snyder and Judd Gray.

Olga was fat, dutch-bobbed, and childlike; she wore vast cotton house dresses, polka-dotted or with tiny flowers; we children loved her, called her Mama, but we were afraid of her temper, too, which always brought terrible punishments and tears. Her husband was smaller, thin; he wore a suit into the city and clean

30

brown khakis on week-ends. He swore a lot, and worried about his job and his mortgage, and held fiercely a small number of loud opinions; we feared him, too—even more than Mama—and called him Uncle John. After a near-fatal mastoid infection had brought him close to yet larger worries we did not even call him Uncle John, nor Mr. Burcker, nor any name that I can remember.

Mama could never have children; I think we knew that even then, somehow. Probably that sad fact more than money worries led her to " boarding" other people's children. She was good with babies, every one said, and was never happier than in those exciting days when some new infant would be handed over to her by its frightened, wide-eyed young mother. Then we older children would have to watch out, for the babies came first always. We would play outside, in the yard, but not far away, for at any moment we might be called to the back door and told to run to the A&P for a can of Eagle Brand Condensed Milk, or up the block to Mrs. Sewell's to borrow a rubber sheet for the crib. But mostly we stayed out of the way until dark, when we would be called in to dinner at the big kitchen table—to soup with fat dumplings, round-steak and fried potatoes, string-beans or the hated "kale" which was so cheap; and finally to bed, which we hated most of all.

" We" were the two or three, some-times more, older kids who stayed on at the Burckers through all the babies' brief reigns. There was Charley, the little red-headed Swedish boy, whose father and mother were not married, and who was nervous, and cried easily. There was myself, a little ahead of Charley both in years and in time spent at the Burckers, whose parents may have been married but were separated. For a time there was Arthur, older than us but nice, and no bully, whose parents were married and living together, but were Jewish. Then there was Rita, whose mother smoked and had red hair, and who had no father. Finally there was Edith, who was only three, with her own red hair, who was everyone's favorite because she was the Burckers' adopted daughter.

Others came and left, but the day the Germans came is the day I remember more clearly than any other of all that time. Perhaps because they arrived so near the end of my stay with the Burckers, when I was older and could see more clearly about me. Perhaps because I had never seen a foreigner; had never heard a language other than John and Olga's English. Maybe I had never known adults so hesitant, so apologetically unsure, that they looked to us for assurance, for help, just as Charley had turned to me when he first came, and later Arthur and Rita in their turn. What-ever the reason, my memory of that German immigrant couple is the only one I have retained clear and sharp from a period in my childhood that I have almost completely discarded.

We knew in advance, of course, that a distant relative—some cousin of John's—was coming with his new wife all the way from Germany to the Burck-

er's house. Rita had been moved in
with Edith, and a bigger bed was
squeezed into her little room where
they were going to stay until they
got settled in a place of their own.
But we had seen relations before—
John's sister Emma, rich and happy,
whose husband owned a grocery store;
Olga's thin sister Minnie, who had
never left her father—and were completely unprepared for the astonishing
young couple that arrived at the
house one afternoon, "right from
the boat," as Mama excitedly informed
us.

First their clothes. He wore a
tight, skimpy grey suit of some heavy
cloth that made him sweat in the warm
afternoon sun. Yet he didn't take his
coat off as he tugged furiously (but
smiling) at the great wooden trunk
and heavy black valises that had been
strapped on the back of the car. He
was young, and he smiled at everyone,
even us, as he ran with the suitcases
up the front stoop to the porch. And
the girl! She was dressed in a long
blue dress that reached almost to her
ankles, and on top of her light hair
was an enormous black straw hat with
artificial flowers; a sort of hat I
had only seen old, old women wear.
Her face was burning red, from the
heat I supposed, and her eyes blazed
blue out of the dark back-seat of the
car. She was the youngest looking
adult I had ever seen; and in her
lap she clutched a curious suitcase
made of straw, that looked like a
basket. And then she would not get
out of the car, even though Olga and
Aunt Emma smiled at her and beckoned

and then reached in to her from the
sidewalk and urged her to join them.
She just sat there, holding her
basket-suitcase tightly to her, smiling
and smiling at them; until finally
he ran down the steps from the porch,
bowed quickly a couple of times to us
all, and sat down beside her in the
automobile. He held her hand and
talked to her for maybe a minute in a
low voice, and then she got out of the
car amid much laughter, and cries of
"There now!" and "That's right!"
and "Come up in the house and we'll
fix her something cool to drink!"

And that was the most astonishing
of all. His talking to her. Neither
of them spoke English, but they spoke
another language—low, murmurous,
and strange; a soft, gentle language that made one feel easy when
afraid, made everything all right
and happy again just when everyone was getting hot and irritable
and cross. *That* was German, then;
not just a few words for things to
eat—*sauerbrauten, strudel, schnappes*—
or a couple of phrases that made the
adults raise their eyebrows and glance
at us and snicker among themselves,
but another language, entirely. And
these were Germans, then, this smiling,
bowing couple, who had their own
secret language, and could neither
speak nor understand ours.

How wonderful to be a German, and
to speak the German language, I
thought, as I gaped at this extraordinary scene from my secure position
behind the square box-hedge. How
fine, how handsome they are! He
smiles at all of us, even me; he is
too polite to take off his heavy, odd

rey coat, even though he is sweating
o because he insists on carrying the
eavy trunk and the suitcases up the
stoop himself. How kind, how beautiful
she is! Her long blue dress and black
straw hat make her look like a nun;
she smiles and nods at us from her
seat in the car; her blue eyes blaze
kindly from her shining red face;
but she will not move until he comes
to hold her hand and speak to her in
their own soft, magical German!

Nothing ever happened during the
few weeks they stayed with us to
destroy my illusion about the Germans.
After the scene on the sidewalk, when
they had all gone up into the house,
we ran around the back and watched
them from the kitchen as they opened
bottles of cold beer and stirred
lemonade. Finally we were called
into the dining room and were laugh-
ingly presented to the still-perspir-
ing young man and his smiling wife.
He shook my hand vigorously and laughed
loudly with me, and said, "Good!
Good! Yes, yes!" She took my hand
for an instant, and spoke a few soft
words in her heavenly German, and
nodded sweetly. Later that night we
could hear them talking together,
just barely, and for the first time
we heard her laugh—very low, but you
knew it was laughter.

Once or twice I got to walk about
the neighborhood with them, and once,
after he had started working in the
piano factory, I went for a walk alone
with her. I remember it was a bright,
warm morning in summer, and we walked
along nodding and smiling as I happily
called off the names of the streets

we crossed. She repeated the names
slowly—they were common street
names like *Spruce, Poplar,* and *Spring,*
but I have never heard words sound
more beautiful. Once I pointed to a
tree and said the word "tree"; she
brightened and said the German word
for tree, which I have forgotten now,
but I repeated it after her then and
memorized it. Then I got excited and
began pointing to all sorts of objects,
far too rapidly for her to follow,
repeating the name of each in a loud,
happy voice. Lamp-post, sidewalk,
hedge, grass, front porch, front door,
house, roof—until she had to laugh,
and finally ended my outburst with one
of her own in German.

When they left, shortly after that,
in the same automobile, I cried.
The young man patted me nervous-
ly on the shoulder and leaned down
towards me and said, "No, no. That's
all right"; his young wife brought her
beautiful red face close to mine and
took my hand and said "Good-bye, good-
bye," just like that, perfectly.

I never saw the Germans again
because my own stay at the Burckers
ended soon after their departure. My
mother, who believed I was in a bad
environment, finally arranged for me
to live with her and her new husband.
He was an Italian and had many Italian
friends who spoke that language heat-
edly and at great length. Soon I
became a sophisticate and no longer
listened when they talked. Much
later, in school, I studied Spanish
and Italian, but I never took German.
Not German.

A NOTE ON Lorna Ferguson

THE FORCE in Lorna Ferguson's paintings comes from her pre-occupation with childhood, a feminine quality found frequently in the literature, but seldom in the paintings of women. It is the woman's mind, driven by the circumstances of our civilization *back* to her child-

the white cat

hood, where she may wander and perhaps re-discover the origins of free
perception and strength, the real or
imagined revelations of childhood,
and the lost self. This search,
which has impelled countless women
writers again and again to create
the child story, is strongly felt
in the poetic, almost "picture book,"
fantasies of Lorna Ferguson. Her
subjects—the stories, objects (animal
pets and toys) and festivities of
children—are usually projected in
simple, bold lines which evoke the
instructive quality of storybook
illustrations and the solid, black
A B C's. Her colors, cheery, bright,
and yet disturbing, work within
these lines to produce her fantasies.

From the stiffly-stuffed animals
of childhood emerges an owl who stares
from a bright orange light and who
is bigger and whiter than life*;
Halloween night is a haunted vision
of dour, costumed children who have
become the dark, spectral symbols
that their masks represent*; out of a
distant desert country come pale-
colored apparitions of people or
animals who ride floating horses
toward a destiny that, as in a dream,
is never revealed*. " The White
Cat," pictured here, who seems to have
attracted the mysterious people,
suggests some of the childlike belief
in the omnipotence of animals. Each

fantasy believes in itself, and in
taking form expresses things we knew
and felt before we were taught otherwise: faith in our power to talk
with animals, to change into something
other than ourselves, to cause things
to vanish. They express the feelings
that originally directed us to the
fairy tale.

In her fantasies there is also
an orderly, cheerful quality which
may account for her success in over-
coming the hopelessly buried, private
feelings so common to women's childhood stories.

> There is enough sadness and
> trouble in the world, so is it
> not right that the artist should
> choose a cheerful subject for his
> painting? Personally, I try for
> an interesting and yet simple
> composition. One that gives the
> effect of peace and quiet.

Perhaps she does aim for peace
and quiet, this woman who looks and
paints like a vigorous, Monday house-
wife, (she looks less like an artist
than the crowds that fill the North
Beach bars and restaurants where her
paintings are usually displayed)
but there are deeper meanings in her
paintings than she herself may be
aware of. In her peculiarly feminine
telling of the childhood story she
evokes the fantasies and half-for-
gotten magical notions inherited
from childhood by us all. E. M.

*Owls, on display at North Beach LOCAL COLOR shop.

*Children's Masquerade, prize painting in Art News National contest. Burned
in recent fire at the Iron Pot restaurant.

*Ghost Riders, second prize painting at the 1951 Palace of Fine Arts annual show.

The Sea Journal

The people of the ship are fouled
like jumbles of rain-soaked yarn.
The psychoanalytic spell of the
sea has but limited power to quiet
the devils that haunt souls at sea.
Peace visits them briefly during
night watches sensuously lovely,
or during furious storm. The Mid-
summer Night's Dream, and The Tempest.

Night Watch: twelve to four.

BROKEN from a dream wherein I
played the part of one menaced
by an overwhelming force—freed
of its suffocating grip—killed into
life without leisure for repentance—
the watch, a miniature voyage, begins.

A night watch is a spectacularly
difficult spiritual stunt. It is
formal in structure though satanic
forces move within its border.

A draught, a sneeze, a sniffle, a
wind.

At twelve-thirty the wheelhouse
clock goes once, and the lookout on
the bow, an invisible accomplice,
strikes an answering bell. Contracted
in torpor and darkness, the horizon,
like the rim of a black wall, is bound
round my forehead. Ample time now for
expiation. Guilt, remorse, and punishment, together with nostalgic images,
populate the masochistic-sadistic
rhythms of imagination. The complicity of ghosts.

The compass, a secret mirror of the
world.

A hunter's knowledge of sounds.
I hear the wash of waves on the ship's
flank, and the sound of receding foam,
the sound of the wind chaffing stays
and stanchions, and the sound of the

spinning wheel. Later come sounds
fashioned in the mind out of the low
amorphous noises of the night: a
hoarse rooster crowing; soft Chinese
music.

Stars and clouds and salt of the
sea.

The lights of knobs, and dials,
and buttons, and switches. The glow
from the binnacle.

Crazy Larsen, a spindly old man, is
at the wheel. He is a lank-shanked
child of seventy, a wobbly, a primitive human in the sense that a kind
of painting is called primitive. He
is a parcel of ironic laughter with
great style and in the night his voice
is my friend.

Sepulchrally—like Hamlet's father
in the cellarage—he speaks, saying,
"And they killed Lincoln." This is
his refrain, his fantasy. He chides
me for being responsible for the death
of Jerusalem Slim, saying that he was
tortured to death for my sins.

I ask him, casually, "Was Jerusalem
Slim a good carpenter?" He answers
with no hesitation. "Like all high
class Jews he didn't like to work.
That's why he became a hobo." After
a long silence, "How did Slim manage

36

to walk on the water?" "It was after he was re-erected from the dead. His bones was lighter then, having been fumigated, and he had his wings on." Then he tells this story: "Jerusalem Slim was on the bum near Jerusalem and he sees a mule tied to the fence. He took the rope and led the mule into the city. A man came and accused Slim of stealing the mule, but Slim, he said the animal had followed him—after he had taken the rope. Took a liking to me, he said. And that was the beginning of community property."

It ends on a long note of slow anticipation. The monastic discipline of the watch has slowly purged hate and oppression, and thoughts, precious as the love of God, or a coin at the bottom of a well, remain. Returned to the inner part of the ship, full as it is of the fetid perfume of the sleeping, I hold for a moment the thoughts of the watch. Then these that seem jewels of the night run quickly off.

I stumble sleepily down a ladder, feel my way along a companionway, and enter the chartroom. The gyrocompass, a hot, pulsating bake-oven wherein new directions are prepared, is in one corner. In another, limp charts are piled, smudged with the positions and courses of yesterday. The log book lies open under a desk light. I enter the barometer reading, the wind direction and force, the temperature, and other prescribed data, in the prescribed places.

Witness: to What Continued

Its Justice without mercy covers half the world.

There was indeed a Conspiracy, however, whose relation to Fascism soon became apparent. Chambers cannot tell us how many secret papers the Soviet Underground may have handed over to the Nazis during their brief alliance. He knew only that there was nothing to prevent such an exchange. Meanwhile, since these were still the Popular-Front days, most of us were hoping against hope that some right-thinking person in the State Department would succeed in sending a few of the papers, so conspiratorially labelled "Secret", to our faithful ally Soviet Russia.

THE DAY after the Nazi-Soviet Pact was announced, Cahmbers was out of the Party, trying to get in touch with Roosevelt. It would not have done us much good if he had, for those Popular-Front days lingered on in Government, as in public opinion, for another nine years. Popular opinion would not have allowed Roosevelt to act otherwise than he did, when he told Berle not to be a fool. The belief that Chambers is a psychopathic liar began then and there.

Chambers did, in fact, perjure himself more than once. And since most of the reviewers have used his self-confessed perjury to buttress their defense of our liberal past, we must look more closely (in Part III) at this perjury. But first: the reason why the book reviews are such an important part of this discussion. They are beginning to constitute, in themselves, an unplanned joint enterprise for defending all our liberal "mis-

takes." The chief defense seems to be that Chambers originally concealed the espionage of Hiss and himself and confessed only the Party membership. The implication here is that if Roosevelt had been told about espionage, he would have acted at once. And this in turn implies that our Administration lacked the wisdom to have heard about the Communist Underground, or to have any notion of what the stated aims and methods of the Communist Party were.

The fact is, however, that Chambers did tell Berle about such espionage agents as he knew to be most dangerous —those working in munitions factories or in the Military. And nine years later these agents were discovered by the F.B.I., still working there.

This does not excuse Chambers' concealment and subsequent perjury; nor does it accuse Roosevelt of more pro-Communism than any other liberal of the day. But the fact remains that in the year 1939, the Administration had already been successfully infiltrated. During the next nine years this nucleus, which Chambers had helped establish, apparently accomplished its objective. No one can read the recent testimony given to the Senate Judiciary Committee without marvelling at the way our Far Eastern policy was influenced, determined, and finally written by the same few men. One of these is now in jail for perjury, another has committed suicide, still others occupy influential posts. So far not one of them has confessed that he ever made so much as a mistake. The probability is that we shall never know which of these men were the Underground agents, which the sympa-

38

thizers and which the "dupes."*

All during the nine years, while this conspiracy in Government was accomplishing its objective, we were busy fighting that other Conspiracy called "Fascist" or "Reactionary." Thus it was no wonder that we saw conspirators everywhere during those years—— running the press, "selling out" to the Enemy, capturing our government and our schools. We had daily nightmares of Reactionary Powers, selling out our country to the Enemy. By the time the nightmare slowly lifted, we discovered that half the world belonged, for whatever reasons, to our old ally Soviet Russia.

If anything saved us, beyond sheer luck or power, from selling out ourselves, we may thank our great "Fascist Conspiracy"—that is, the handful of men in Congress who did finally commit themselves to a belated Witch Hunt against espionage and treason.

Chambers gives credit for this to the American people. Not to us, the self-appointed leaders of the people, but to the 'masses" whom we had failed to educate or who were beginning to stir resentfully against us. As an example of Chambers' "Messianic Complex" or of his 'still-Marxist" thinking, the following is often quoted:

From the very outset, I was in touch with that enormous force, for which I was making the effort, and from which I drew strength. Often I lost touch with it or doubted it, cut off from it in the cities, or plunged in the depths of the struggle. But when I came back to it, it was always there. It reached me in letters..of encouragement and solicitude; understanding, stirring, sometimes wringing the heart.

SO FAR we have discussed Chambers' "second sacrifice" only in terms of its political necessity. If this were the only meaning it had, it might indeed have been the overdone or futile sacrifice which the liberals seem to think it was. For it is not at all clear that it was Chambers himself who awakened us, if we are awakened, to the danger of destroying ourselves from within. It might have been the whole concert of ex-Communist and anti-Communist voices raised together which warned us of the danger. But out of all this chorus, it is Chambers' voice alone which may in time convince us of the more-than-political meaning of his sacrifice.

Still we cannot understand the nature of this sacrifice unless we can at least agree to some political necessity for it. Late as it was, and with much of the damage accomplished, a few individuals did finally awaken the nation to its danger. Nine years of silent espionage while we laughed at the Red Scare, excoriated the Witch Hunters, and pilloried such men as Chambers. We are saying now that we may have been in some respects mistaken.

The reader may take exception to the pronoun "we," covering so many dates

*The "dupe" is someone who can never be called a Communist. No matter how often he agrees with the Party Line, it is always for benevolent reasons of liberalism. The dupe is an "anti-Communist" who believes that Reaction or the Church is a worse enemy than Communism. And so we can distinguish him only by the primacy of his values: whether it seems more important to him to fight "witch-hunts" against Communists, or to fight Communism.

and degrees of complicity in these mistakes. But I have meant to address fellow liberals like myself: that is to say, erstwhile Marxists and (at some date) fellow-travelers, who lack as yet any other word - or much of any concept - for describing ourselves. It is bitter for us to accept our share, indeed any share, of guilt for the ruin we so very nearly succeeded in bringing to this nation. If not we, then who? Without the majority consent of the American people, led by liberals, how could any conspiracy have determined our foreign policy for so many years? I do not see how we can fail to admit that this was a conspiracy entered into by all of us together.

It is especially bitter to realize that the only people who have any reason for self-congratulation on this score are the "reactionaries"—including those pundits and politicos whose motives we have correctly discerned as anti-human, undemocratic or mock-pious. So it becomes more than ever important to distinguish a man's motives and character from his political opinions. A "liberal" may be no liberal at all; a "conservative" may be only timid; a "reactionary" may be a radical traditionalist. As it is, both Communism and liberalism are called "Left," revealing the fact that we have found no way to distinguish ourselves from Communists, except by degree. Many "anti-Communists" continue to believe that Stalin, or Lenin, merely "betrayed" that Higher Truth of liberalism, to which we still subscribe.

With this confusion of language, we are fearful of associating ourselves with anything traditionalist which might be called, by somebody, the "Right.' This leaves the lesser evil: we remain tied to Communism, as the far "Left." Many people find no solution to this dilemma, except to proclaim their dislike of the word "Communism," and to attack anyone who applies the word to them. But in our fear of being equated with the wrong people, we are trying to pretend that our mistakes were nothing - innocent liberal errors, benevolently motivated. And so we find no reason for examining the liberal philosophy itself, to discover what non-benevolence it may contain.

Under liberalism, men's highest values cannot transcend Morality. (We do not like this word, since the pious hypocrisies of the Nineteenth Century were largely committed in its name; nevertheless it was our moral sense which sickened us against these hypocrisies). In addition to our social-political Morality, we have achieved - with the help of the social sciences - some relative improvement in our private and domestic morality as well. Now I would argue that the vast public barbarisms of our time are not mere breaches of morality, to be explained in social-political or in psychological terms. They seem rather to be eruptions of some long-denied religious needs in men.

In our distaste for religious words or meanings, we kept our Marxist hopes on the Robin Hood or "little David' level of sportsmanship. This may be why no hero has yet arisen, out of the unthinkable clutter of senseless pain and cruelty of this century, to give our age any meaning. The only meanings we have bestowed, to date, on our military or "Resistance" heroes do not far transcend the meanings of a boy's adventure story. If any hero does arise, it will be left for the poets or the relatively uneducated masses of "reactionary" people to assign a religious value to his actions.

III. The Meaning of Perjury

SOME astonishing criticisms have been made of Chambers in the reviews of his book. And these all center, with a kind of politely disguised fury, on his religious beliefs. Yet Chambers is so far from being that "authoritarian character" who leaps from Communism to the Catholic Church, that he seems not to hold any dogmatic religious position at all. The picture we get from his book is rather of a gentle, and genuinely humble, man who might be described as a practising Christian. And there, I realize, I have not painted an attractive portrait. Indeed, we are forced to wonder if this is part of what has so enraged the liberal-minded reviewers: that Chambers does seem to be a practising Christian. It is a disturbing thought. Liberals are committed to the principles of religious tolerance - even as applied to Christians. Yet an old-fashioned anti-clericalism has made it hard to distinguish a Christian individual - even a Protestant - from the whole powerful institution of the Church.

Judging by the reviews, it is only Hiss' action which so far has had any meaning for the educated majority of liberal opinion. We can understand how a man like Hiss would choose to perjure himself, either from an unregenerate Communism or from a horror of "informing"; and also to protect others others higher up, perhaps, in the Administration. But we do not understand how a man like Chambers could choose the Informer's road, and still hold back evidence - perjuring himself in the hope of protecting others. Miss Rebecca West, one of the more "sympathetic" reviewers, finds it incomprehensible that Chambers (though not Hiss) could have rationalized his perjury on grounds of simple humanity or friendship, or could have placed any 'human' values above the Anglo-Saxon legality of Justice. She suggests that this was not the action of a civilized man.

Maybe not. It was one of those very "human" actions, as we call them, of a tormented and confused man not blessed with any divine certainties, who was trying to obey his divided conscience. Nine years earlier Chambers had thought it would be sufficient to reveal the Party Membership of Hiss and his other friends; it was not sufficient, as he discovered. But we can understand the kind of wreckage, both for his own family and for other families, which he was trying to avoid.

Small wonder, in these conflicting loyalties, if he lost sight of the simple legality of perjury and judicial truth. For Chambers is of that temperament which puts friendship very high on the scale of values. Probably no man who felt as he did about "informing" could have gone through with this betrayal from patriotic duty alone. Without his understanding of Communism as inhuman blasphemy, he would undoubtedly have accepted the easy way out. For, despite the reviewers, suicide was Chambers' greatest temptation. What restrained him, and what doubtless caused his one attempt to be so comically abortive, was the compelling duty he had chosen: to become a witness against Communism.

THERE is however, such a thing as spiritual death. And the fact that this may be chosen knowingly, for the sake of a higher duty, makes Chambers' sacrifice a rather appalling one to contemplate. Yet some form of spiritual death was unavoidable, if he was to accomplish merely his legal and patriotic duty. Chambers is one of those extremely "private" individuals, happy when alone or with his family, to whom it was an initial ordeal even to raise his voice in public.

He began to think of himself as a dead man when he first began his public confessions. He thinks of himself as a dead man now. And yet, in order to do what had to be done, he had day after day to kill off the suffering and protesting spirit, the humanity in himself. He

had explicitly, day after day, to put down the easy temptation of suicide, and to make himself as nearly like an animal as possible. An informer is required to keep his body alive for uncountable hours of testimony, repetitions, interviews, public and private hearings. For Chambers, these were uncountable hours of confession: confession of crimes which filled him with loathing, yet drew from the public complacent smiles of dislike and disbelief.

Now a man cannot try, day after day and for many months on end, to kill off the humanity in himself without to some extent succeeding. Yet this continued effort seems only to have made the suffering more intense. What Chambers was trying specifically to eradicate was one whole side of the conflict: namely, his ability to identify himself with his old friends and their families. This was almost as hard for a man of his temperament as the other necessity: to ignore self-interest, self-preservation and concern for his own family.

The more ludicrous the antics of Hiss became, the more shame and remorse was felt by his old friend. We have mentioned the moment of horrible comedy in a hotel room, with Hiss solemnly peering into Chambers' mouth. The fact that he had himself reduced his friend to such grotesque performance - this thought wiped out, for Chambers, any sense of the humiliating comedy of the scene from his own point of view. Only afterwards did he recall that he had been examined like a broken-down sheep for sale. Well, this is altruism: the real thing.

But even more important than the moral virtue here, though perhaps inseparable from it, is a most unusual intellectual virtue. That is, an honesty of logic operating even in extremity. Chambers reveals himself as a man who can keep in mind the logic of events - add up their cause and effect - even when the answer is most unflattering or painful to himself. Perhaps it is that altruistic sensibility itself which enables him to attain this objectivity under stress. A man identified with others is not occupied with self-deception.*

INDEED it is this capacity to share another's point of view, or another's suffering, which we call "humanitarian" and which does seem, most specifically, to distinguish the human from the animal. Such a person is slow to recognize malice or cruelty when it is directed against himself. Indeed he has no experience of malice or cruelty in himself by which to recognize it, and asks himself instead whether the seeming injustice against him has not been deserved. But such a person is also one (as Chambers describes his wife) who may be aroused to ferocity by the spectacle of cruelty or injustice to others.

In other words, Chambers was one of those revolutionists motivated less by abstract Justice than by an intensely personal identification with others: with the victims of pain, oppression or cruelty. We have in past times called such revolutionists "men of God." For it is impossible to separate, in our hearts or in our language, what is "human" from what is "religious." We have made the separation only in our educated thinking.

This capacity in Chambers caused intolerable pressure when his love for his own family, and his sympathy for others, came in conflict with a more abstract duty.—Especially since this higher or abstract duty is one for which our century has scarcely a name. We recognize it only in its Marxist or Socialist forms, as social-political brotherhood. But men's duty to humanity has, in the past, included many broader forms of brotherhood, based not on justice but on love.

IT IS time now to say why every word of Chambers' book may be accepted, or has been accepted by me, as the literal truth. If not the whole truth—who can give us that?—this is the astonishingly objective and altogether personal truth, as known to one man. It is the tone, especially in such a document, by which we judge a writer's character and his truthfulness. Whatever the style or content, whatever the outward facts of his life, there is a certain inner truth—an honesty or objectivity toward experience—which he cannot falsify and cannot help revealing.

We get no hint of the man Chambers from the opening chapters of his book, nor from the widely quoted

*A "masochist" would have reacted first of all to his own humiliation. Though he might have been too fearful to acknowledge anger, even to himself, he would certainly have felt no real compassion. For a man whose chronic dishonesty toward himself we call "neurotic" feels as little objectivity or compassion toward himself as he is able to feel for others: his "self-pity" is a concealed rage.

excerpts. Our knowledge of him unfolds with cumulative effect as we participate painfully in his experience; and as we think back later, to wonder how a man could achieve this tone after such an experience. And so the act of reading the book becomes, in itself, an astonishment, then a dawning revelation of what the meaning of our age is. Our feelings are complicated by admiration for the man who has shown us this meaning in his life and in his person.

We can not judge the book in purely aesthetic or rationalistic terms. The literary act, by which Chambers re-creates meaning for himself out of his own destruction, is fused with the moral acts which had first created those meanings. And so the book becomes what we call a "human" or a religious document, transcending art. And when we remember how much needless cruelty and insult was added to the necessary sacrifice, it is precisely the tone - of a transcendent objectivity, never judging or condemning - which most over-awes us. It is a tone which does not judge us, but may force us to judge ourselves.

IV. The Religious Necessity

WE HAVE seen that whatever meaning, beyond the political, lies in Chambers' action, this is not a moral one. There was no moral necessity, except the legal and patriotic duty which we are calling the *political*. Indeed the moral imperatives toward his friends and family only made his conflict more painful.

But Chambers saw the religious nature of Communism, and he saw the religious nature of the motives which have impelled nearly every man of "good will" in modern times to become either a Communist or a Communist-sympathizer. Worse than that, he refuses to call these motives "good" or even "well-meaning" in his own case. Instead he considers them to have been neither human nor truly religious, but motives of the most inhuman and blasphemous perversion of "religion" to have been seen on earth since ancient times.

It was for these blasphemous motives, and to this inhuman end, that Chambers felt he had tried to betray his country. He found no comfort in "good intentions" .To him the only fitting penalty for a treason which went beyond treachery to one's country and became a crime against the human spirit, was—of course—death. What Chambers means by "God" is the human spirit—the God in man. We might also call it the "humanity" in man. All the attacks by the reviewers have centered on these three points: first the use of the word "God" ("Absolutist".) Second, Chambers' feeling that his crimes involved a crime against God ("grandiose".) And third, the idea that a crime against God is not only worse than treason, but worse than a betrayal of one's friends

("mystic".)

SO FAR we have had a glimpse of Chambers' nature, and of his motives, and thence of the remorse and penitence which made his second sacrifice a true one. For him, the religious, or philosophical, necessity for it lies in the nature of Communism. But for us, his action takes on an additional religious meaning which we must try, in Part VI, to describe. This meaning resides in all the added cruelty and injustice we heaped upon him at the Trials, and are heaping on him still. By our own acts, Chambers acquires a very strange and intimate relation to ourselves. This partakes of an ancient ritual of purification by which men chose a Scapegoat and, in punishing him, cleansed themselves of impenitence and pride.

Some such catharsis may have been transmuted into the dramatic rituals and tragedies of early Greek culture, and again into the mediaeval "moralities" and pageants of our Western age. Since we have now come once more to the ending of a culture, we no longer possess either the aesthetic or the religious rites for the purging of pride "through pity and terror." We do what we can with the psychoanalytic purgings which, at best, cannot transcend the moral-interpersonal values. Or we take up some other substitute for religion. And the chief substitute in our time has, of course, been politics.

Since we believe the ancient rites to have been barbarous and superstitious, and believe that we have no superstition left in us, it is difficult to realize that the loss of faith in civilized religions may, in itself, make some more primitive faith inevitable. We had convinced ourselves that we, alone of all men in history, were getting along with no religion at all.

Nevertheless, it was not Chambers' decision to sacrifice himself, but our unwitting relation to him as our Scapegoat, which has transformed a patriotic duty into a true religious Ordeal. Let us describe this first in more familiar terms. When a man of Chambers' temperament takes up the public burden of confessing what he believes to be loathsome crimes, there is no room in his heart for self-pity or complacency. But for us to hear a man confessing our own benevolent mistakes and the logical results of these as "crimes" — and confessing them in this spirit of humility, neither excusing himself nor blaming others—his example becomes in itself an intolerable accusation.

You may be saying "But I committed no crimes!" No, and this is the crux of our confusion today. The liberal has no blood on his hands and did not knowingly incite other men to espionage and treason. He may have done so unknowingly, but more often he merely hoped that other men would commit the revolutionary deeds after he himself had helped to set the revolutionary force in motion. For we can now see that the worldwide Revolution of this century is no spontaneous combustion of economic-political forces, like a localized peasant revolt. It is on the contrary an immense conflict between two faiths, two sets of values - definitions of the *human* - old and new.

The liberal, upon discovering that you

cannot make a revolution without breaking eggs, retired: like Descartes' God,
he took no further responsibility for
his creations. It seems to me that we
became a nation of conspirators who
wanted all the glory and the fun of
revolution, with none of the murders,
treason or responsibility of revolution.
This makes it easier for us to identify
with the man like ourselves, who got
caught, than with the man who - unlike
ourselves - voluntarily confessed his
crimes, not blaming others. But both
Hiss and Chambers have been far more
logical about this than we. Hiss refuses
to consider his actions treasonable:
for him they were courageous revolutionary deeds, undertaken for a Higher
Truth. Chambers, on the other hand - who
ought to represent ourselves - takes
the view that treason, for whatever
Cause, is treason.

So it is much easier to call Chambers' attitude the fake humility of
masochism, or the arrogance of the martyr who sets himself up as Christ,
than to find any meaning in it for ourselves. Today his long sacrifice has no
meaning; it remains a futile self-
destruction. You will notice hints,
even in supposedly sympathetic reviews,
that the whole thing was over-done,
unnecessary, unbalanced. No reviewer
can fail to be moved by such a record
of suffering, unless he is totally
blinded by the Marxist faith. But he
can be exasperated by the very intensity
of a suffering which seems to him pointless. He can analyze the sin of pride,
the arrogance involved in this particular example of First-Century martyrdom. He can criticize Chambers' terminology in describing the worldwide
conflict between two faiths.

In fairness to the reviewers, it can
be admitted that Chambers often does
fall into a terminology we associate
with churches or with the reactionary
press. But the meanings of his experience exist independently of his explicit
views on religion: indeed these are
very nearly irrelevant. It is doubtful
whether Chambers himself believes that
the only alternative to Communism resides in some existing Church.

THE alternatives "between Man and
God", as seen by Chambers, are accurate enough in one sense, but
the metaphor is misleading. It
implies that our secular scientific philosophy has been a humanism, dedicated to Man. On the
contrary, a special set of men's interests and values has been elevated at the
expense of what we call our "human"
side: "human" values. If you stop to
ask yourself what, exactly, is the
human "side" of a human being, you see
how non-human our values have become.
The present war of faiths - which
divides us internally, in our common-
sense beliefs, as it divides us on the
political front—is a conflict of
the human *and* religious needs in man
against his more boyish technological
and scientific interests.

Miss West is one of the few reviewers
who has been willing to call Chambers a
religious man at all, without implying
that he is a pious fraud. But she calls
him a "mystic" and deduces from this
adjective, rather than his book, that
he must be a very difficult man to live
with. Ignoring, like all the reviewers,
any internal evidence of the book which

might contradict a prior theory, she decides that Chambers' wife and children were deluding themselves with their notion of being an unusually happy and devoted family.

Miss West agrees also, with the other reviewers, that Chambers has greatly over-estimated the religious nature of Communism: in two ways. He sees it as a blasphemous parody of religion, anti-human and irreligious, yet powerful enough to win half the world from older religions. Secondly, he sees that men were attracted to it precisely for those reasons of old religion, too long denied under the modern scientific faith.

The liberal anti-Communist has learned, of course, that the dedicated Party Member feels only contempt for the innocent idealism of Fellow Travelers. And so the liberal tends now to think of Communists as though they were power-driven gangsters, separated from his own idealism by an absolute gulf of quality. He interprets his own ideals as a secular humanitarianism, having no motives behind it of any long-denied religious needs in man. But, as Chambers knows very well, we shall never understand the Communist faith if we interpret it as the self-interest of political gangsters. Self-interest, in the authoritarian caste-society of Com-

munism, is in fact a highly dangerous motive to have: punishable by death.

If the Communist end is cynically justified by any means whatever, this is only because the end is a Higher Truth - a parody of the Kingdom of Heaven - embodied in the Soviet Union. It is a Mystery, like the Catholic Mass, of the Spirit embodied in the flesh and blood, and thence embodied in the sacramental bread and wine. The Soviet Union is the symbolic bread and wine of the Marxist communion.

The fact that Communism is profoundly "irreligious," in its hatred of Christianity, does not make it therefore an un-religious or secular movement. Like the mediaeval Black Mass, through which men celebrated ancient matriarchal rites long banned from the patriarchal church, Communism also contains some very exact parodies, or inversions, of Christian practices and beliefs. But it has even closer parallels with certain pre-Christian faiths described by anthropologists. A bloody spirit of communal sacrifice, requiring cruel self-mutilations, characterized many of the ancient matriarchies. At the opposite extreme stand the Western democracies, founded on one God and the inviolable spirit of Man: the unique value of the individual transcending the value of Society.

V. The Mystique of Naturalism

UNDOUBTEDLY the most dangerous result of our willful ignorance, or forgetfulness, of religious values is our present incapacity to distinguish a true or useful religion from a false or inhuman one. If we cannot discern the non-human values underlying our scientific faith, neither can we discover any part of Christianity which might be psychologically true, morally useful, or "humanly" necessary. (We do not hold the same bias against Judaism as we do against the Church).

Our distaste for the meanings of "religion" has left us no word but "instinct" to describe any prime necessity or motivation in man. The rationalist liberal cannot understand, therefore, that his own faith in liberalism is any faith at all; nor that it is related to his faith in that larger mystique, known as Scientific Materialism or philosophic Naturalism.

This makes it easy for him to call people of other faiths "mystics." The reviewers seem not to have recognized that Chambers' actions were founded on perfectly ordinary Judaeo-Christian thought and practice - although these were carried out with a singular intensity and courage. Or if they did recognize a Christian motive in his behavior this seems only to have been equated with "Reaction," putting Chambers in a class with the Catholic Church itself.

Since the liberal can scarcely distinguish a Christian value from a Christian institution, he finds it nearly impossible to take seriously the Judaeo-Christian values underlying the democracies. In fact, the liberal credo on Religion was set down one hundred and fifty years ago by Tom Paine, in "The Age of Reason." It remains intact today. Religion cannot be more than that physical idolatry of the suffering Christ which the Eighteenth Century (with some justification) felt it to be. Thus religion is a body of superstition contradicted by the "scientific rules of evidence."

Yet today the scientific rules of evidence are beginning to show us - through an anthropology deducible also from psychoanalysis - that modern man is not qualitatively different from all his forbears but is motivated, like them, primarily by some reason (or inversion) of religious faith. The Nineteenth Century, far from becoming irreligious, simply transferred its faith in a patriarchal God to a biological Matriarch called "Nature." Out of the Naturalist faith came Scientific Materialism, modern liberalism, and a new Science of Man. Nature, as a hostile or indifferent Life Force, has many parallels with ancient goddesses of fertility. But She is perhaps unique in having created no human beings, but only animals and "organisms."

So men became collective "human organisms," dedicated to Nature's "biological" values, and humbly collecting the scientific "facts" about Her nature. Equally unknowable "facts" about our own nature were deduced from our unknowable origins in Nature. It was not a long step from this to the elevation of that larger organism, "Society," over the individual organism, Man. Long before this philosophic collectivism had advanced, with sickening logic, to the totalitarian Society, we had learned to think of ourselves as "social animals"—more precisely a kind of insect, living in a communal bee-hive.

Thus the Christian or "Jeffersonian" elevation of the individual, over his society, came utterly to be perverted. Yet we reveal how much we still cherish the old Christian 'individual," whenever the nation's work is suspended in order to extricate one miner from a cave-in, save one child from drowning, keep one man from jumping off a building. Compared to the expenditure of men in war, this popular concern for the individual is admittedly illogical and inconsistent. Yet it is for a principle like this one - like the principle of anti-slavery - that wars are nevertheless fought. The values necessary to fight Communism reside, as everyone knows, in the Christian-democratic principles. This is a truism - meaning, perhaps, that it is too true to be believed. Certainly we lack all faith in this truism as the truth.

It may be that our own liberal principles have been repeated so often by Republicans or reactionaries that we no longer recognize them as democratic. But I think the faith of the Enlighten-

ment was overthrown by nineteenth-century Materialism to a greater extent than we realize. Our views on the Christian Church remain intact, but in other respects we gave up Paine's individualism in favor of more collective faiths. Hence it is easier for a Christian than for a liberal to see that Scientific Materialism led straight to Communism, whereas Fascism was, in large part, a nihilist reaction against Scientific Materialism. This may largely account for the liberal prejudice that one totalitarian state is 'better" than another.*

THOSE inhuman experiments on human flesh, which so horrified us in the Nazis, have now been duplicated and carried further: they have become quite inhuman successes on the human spirit. A new type of man has been successfully created, using chiefly 'spiritual' or psychological means. Now surely we can agree with Hawthorne (to name one moralist): that the only supreme or unforgivable Sin is the human effort to transcend humanity and become superhuman. And perhaps we can agree that it is precisely this effort which characterizes the modern temper.

Yet we are haunted more by the physical tortures, and the quantitative enslavement or obliteration of peoples, than we are by the successful obliteration of the human spirit. Humanity,

---

* As for religious persecution, it was only an accident of ideology which led one State to begin with the Jews and proceed next to the Christians, while the other State has reversed the procedure. Indeed this accident of selection provides a culminating horror to the murder of six million Jews. This remains one of the monster Facts of all time, never to be explained by Reason. But some effort of imagination is required here to remember that we saw the Jews murdered almost "with our own eyes." The mass murders of Communism have not yet been demonstrated with the same immediacy to our imaginations.

humanitarianism - all concept of the 'human' as an ideal norm - have vanished behind the Iron Curtain, along with the concepts of Justice, Love, history, Truth and every other specifically "human" meaning or value developed through ten thousand years of history. People are treated as though they were nothing but animals, organisms, neuter objects or machines.

And yet it was Science which first defined us as neuter objects and "human machines": as "it," the human organism. Scientific values cannot, by definition, be 'human values." The aim of Science had been defined originally as the "control and manipulation of natural objects in man's physical environment." It was man who then defined himself, under Naturalism, as a "natural object" included or (as Dewey calls it) "implicated" in his own physical environment. With the loss of all subjective definitions, these "natural objects" and organisms came to be our only true or "objective" definition of Man.

Now the scientific control and manipulation of these natural objects, ourselves, has in our country been largely benevolent. But there is nothing in the Naturalist philosophy itself, to prevent a more literal or widespread manipulation of human beings. We have seen this fear of inhuman "scientism" mythologized in popular culture as the "Mad Scientist"; we have seen its actuality abroad. The frightening thing is that *there is nothing in our philosophy* to prevent it here. All the preventives lie in those older values, prior to the Nineteenth Century, which do exist - though in very unclear and con-

flicting form - in our unexamined "common sense." What stands between us and the full logic of Scientific Materialism seems therefore to be the Illogic and Inconsistency by which we keep our practice separate from our beliefs.

> *By "we" I mean that majority opinion which liberals, collectively, set in motion and which lingers on destructively long after we, as individuals, have "seen the light." But this light we have seen has enabled us so far only to criticize certain political portions of our prevailing philosophy. What led most directly and immediately to Communism seems to us wrong, but our reasons for being so misled seem to us no more wrong than the prevailing sum of Scientific Materialism.*

Against this background of Naturalism then, which impedes our freedom and beclouds our thought, and suffocates us with its idolatry of the animal, the physical, the bodily and the numerical, we can understand how Tom Paine felt when he wanted all the windows of Nature opened on a similar idolatry - the same mass weight of superstition - hanging over his day. Nature liberated men for a very short time, then Herself became a new enslavement. What we need now is to close the windows on Nature for a while, and look within ourselves to find the truth.

We do not need the misleading term "godless," as applied to our philosophy by the Church. The term "inhuman" is enough. It would be enough to recognize the non-human cosmology of

Naturalism, and the inhuman mythology of ourselves as neuter "human organisms." This was a false psychology and a false religion, which did not set up Man as God - except in a few scientific or scientismic respects. It set up "Nature" as a biological Goddess. Man, debased as a "natural object," came inevitably to be an object of social and political manipulation.

WHAT we have had is an anti-humanist religion, phrased in secular terms. And since the human needs and impulses toward religion do not die, even in the most "irreligious" times, we can now see in our motives of the Thirties a kind of parody, or garbling, of ancient rituals. We chose not one savior-hero as a Victim who might afterwards be venerated; a few of us chose ourselves, collectively, to be the Saviors of mankind. The "masses" were then educated to venerate those chosen few.

A "hero" (so the historians of myth and language tell us) was once a sacrificial victim to the matriarchal goddess Hera. But we do not need the historians to see, everywhere we look, that the old patriarchal God of Jews and Christians has been replaced by a goddess: "Nature." It seems futile to find psychological motives for this in the relations between the sexes. Our philosophy has been worshipping the "values" of a biological Matriarch for nearly a hundred years.

Now some matriarchal principle is doubtless needed for any "true" or useful faith. The old Goddess represented poetry, as she represented life, growth, fertility of nature. A too-patriarchal faith becomes one-sided. Moreover her rites - when they were knowingly performed - were not so barbarous as we imagine. Many of them were, in fact, apt and necessary social expressions of psychological or spiritual needs in men. It is when we lack all appropriate expression for these needs, as the past century has lacked them, that primitive outbreaks and mass bloodlettings may occur. The term "blood-thirsty" itself refers to a barbarous practice, repudiated by civilized men. The blood of the Victim which had once been drunk, in orderly and reverential fashion, became the sacramental wine of Jews and Christians. But now we have to ask ourselves: was this early practice really more barbarous than the meaningless, accidental, sacrifice of six million Jewish Victims - to say nothing of the countless other Sacrifices of our day?

SEEN only in social-political terms, the whole mass horror remains totally without meaning. Its motive is inexplicable in rational terms, whether as an Instinct of Aggression or as original sin. No inherent evil in man includes the organized, "scientific," extermination of whole peoples. What we have overlooked is the fact that churches are civilizing agencies, which give men wine to drink instead of blood. And men, lacking sacramental wine, will eventually be "thirsty"; blind thirst for ancient meanings may lead them, finally, to drink the ancient blood.

We, who have believed ourselves too civilized to need religion, have believed this only because our philosophy told us, in the Eighteenth Century, that men of Reason do not need a church and, in the Nineteenth Century, that animals do not have a church. So the rational and civilized 'human organism," doing its best to get along with no religion, has got rid of the civilized words and meanings of religion and kept only the primitive attitudes and practices.

The Jews are already turning from the rationalism of their "reformed" church to more radical and traditional forms of worship. Insofar as mass-exterminations are an incentive to the radical examination of tradition, Christians have only to use their imaginations a little to find the same incentive. But for those of us who belong to no church, no radical Christianity has appeared. Some Judaeo-Christian synthesis can be created privately, of course, and - as the widely private circulation of Martin Buber's pamphlet *I and Thou* would indicate - may be in process of formation. On the other hand what we have just had, under Marxism, was a secular Judaeo-Christian synthesis: rebels of both faiths seeking a communal church.

VI. The Scapegoat

RETURNING now to Whittaker Chambers: here is a man who, in his "second choice," did not set himself up as anything. He offered only to ruin himself as a man: partly as a simple patriotic duty, partly as an expiation of past crimes. Because he understands what Communism is, however, he confessed not only those logical results of our "mistakes" which the law considers crimes: i.e. espionage and treason.

He was confessing, in his own past, those even greater sins or crimes against the human spirit, which we consider our "mistakes." And we cannot, apparently, tolerate this confusion of the "crime" with the "mistake." Indeed this is the dilemma which the German people have had to face: where did their own mistakes end, and the Nazi crimes begin? Here again the criterion based on Party Membership proved very shifting and uncertain. Yet we have bestowed a generous amount of our righteous indignation upon the whole German people, not distinguishing the Nazi-sympathizers very clearly from the "dupes." This is not altogether our fault: the sympathizer, as we said before, cannot be clearly distinguished from the dupe. Each is hoping for the benefits and glory of a revolution, dissociated from its unpleasantness.

Chambers submitted voluntarily to the necessary ruin entailed by his confessions. He did not ask for the gratuitous insult, disbelief and hatred he received and is receiving still. Since he was, in a sense, trying to save Our People from us, their Chosen Saviors, we repaid his act with a hatred of a peculiarly intense and intimate variety. We flayed him with insult, as though he were our Scapegoat. And in so doing, it was we ourselves who invested his Sacrifice with some very ancient meanings. Yet paradoxically, it is our continued refusal to invest this sacrifice with any conscious meaning, which causes our curiously intimate relationship with Chambers to continue.

WHITTAKER and Esther Chambers were indeed treated to a public flaying—a spiritual hanging, quartering and disembowelling - accomplished entirely by words. In such non-physical torture, no merciful oblivion overtakes the sufferer; he must stay alive and answer questions. Had we known what this kind of torture is, or what it does to gentle spirits like the Chambers', the Inquisition would have satisfied our cruellest hopes in full.

If we want to be honest with ourselves, I think we know well enough why Chambers came so close to being indicted in Hiss' stead, and for what crime. Many of us wanted Chambers cruelly punished, not as a traitor against the State but as a traitor and Informer against the New Deal, against Yalta, against our liberal faith. We feared his wish to save us from ourselves, and to save the country from us, as a demand that we betray our faith. The whole Higher Truth of liberalism was at stake, for Communism, as we said, has been differentiated from us only by degree.

Without these hidden fears or confusions of values, the curiously intimate hatred we felt for Chambers cannot be explained by the whispering-campaign alone. Vicious as it was - and only partially inspired by Communists - the picture of Chambers as a dirty-minded

psychopath, liar, masochist, repressed homosexual who "loved' his dead brother with some peculiarly modern combination of necrophilia and incest: these filthy stories were a measure of the fear that grew among us, when Hiss' guilt became too obvious to be denied. Beginning with the fact that Hiss had only one legal defense - namely, the defamation of Chambers' character - these tales have left Chambers permanently branded as a, to say the least, very queer fish indeed. A "monster with mysticism."

Still, these stories might explain some dislike or contempt: they do not explain our hatred. For hatred is not a clear emotion, like rage or anger; it has been well defined as a "confusion." Such confusion generally betrays divided values, putting forth a conflicting self-defense. We must remember that all the book reviews under discussion here have been written by liberals or by liberal-minded literary critics. I cannot believe that an unprejudiced reader could fail to see that this picture of Chambers is utterly contradicted by his tone. For our ability to judge a man's truthfulness is not restricted to literary critics. On the contrary: the general public, often deceived by a writer's ideas or his aesthetic merit, is almost never deceived by his tone.

Yet many people do believe, even after reading his book, that Chambers has not been sufficiently punished: or that going to jail would have been a greater punishment. So far Chambers has been the only critic to have understood our motives, in making him our Scapegoat. Understanding them, he does not blame us too heavily: he feels that his sins at least outweigh our punishment of him. But this charity of the victim, directed against his persecutors, becomes still another arrogance and accusation. The man not only pities us—he understands us!

I THINK we cannot otherwise explain the reviews which have all found an opportunity, in one form or another, to suggest that Chambers is both masochistic and arrogant: sets himself up as Christ, suffers from the sin of pride. Yet I have never been forced before, by any book, to participate in a suffering of such intensity and such awareness - a suffering borne with quite this patience, compassion and understanding - nor have I encountered often a tone of such transcendent objectivity as to suggest a dead man, creating meaning for himself out of the wreckage of his death. This book is written from an agony of penitence, incomprehensible to us, but it is an agony long past and dead. In this realm of the dead, compassion comes in the end to cover everything - including oneself. We cannot fail to believe a man who takes a tone of undeceived wry charity, *even toward himself.*

At the opposite extreme from charity stands fear, or maybe it is pride. An impenitent pride of righteousness and moral indignation wants "justice," not mercy. As ex-Marxists, we are still haggling over justice in its lowest legalistic terms - dupe or sympathizer? establishing our legal innocence by dates and degrees of complicity. "Did you join the Party of your own free will?" or were you forced, by public opinion, to become a sympathizer merely?

A man who had done nothing more than admit his own guilt, not blaming others, would have been a Witness to the truth we lack. But in heaping insult and disbelief upon him, we laid religious garlands on his neck. By forcing him to forgive us, we are adding still more crimes for which we can revile him once again. It would seem that the least we could do, in face of such a document as his, would be to bow the head or bend the stiff neck a trifle. But no, it is Chambers who is stiff-necked, arrogant, proud--sets himself up as a Savior to take Our People from us; now condescends, as a final insult, to forgive us our insults.

In our curiously illogical hatred of Chambers, we wish him punished for accepting the consequences of a faith shared by all of us; punished for being the spy and traitor which we, happily, were not; punished too, for confessing to the very crimes we wanted most of all to hide. Now this punishment of the Scapegoat resembles, in all but one respect, a very salutary, needful, ancient rite. The one respect is our denial of its meaning or necessity. And so our crowning punishment of Chambers is to withhold all meaning from his sacrifice.

AND yet we dreadfully reveal our need to find some meaning in it. This present blindness, which accuses only others of a greater or a later blindness, and never looks within--we are groping in this blindness, like the Germans, for a villain to blame ourselves upon; hoping our sins of conscience will be expiated by merely staying out of jail. We need, like the German people, to recognize our guilt in a way that goes beyond mere guilty denials and achieves understanding: a change of heart.

In ancient times if men hung a scape-goat from a cross, in order knowingly to revile him for their sins, it was this realization alone by which they saved themselves from the blind suffer-ing of impenitence, hatred, and dis-honest pride. It was this realization which allowed the chosen victim, too, to suffer and die in the full honest pride of meaning and accomplishment. So these victims came to be revered as savior-heroes, then as gods: thus "re-ducing" gods to mortal men or casting that physical-material interpretation on religion which our generation has rightly learned to dread. Yet the spiritual needs for such religious cleansing do not die.

Here is the Either/Or of *Witness*. Not a choice between Church and Com-munism; not a choice between "Man and God." Either we discover that some re-ligious necessity exists, for liberals as for all other men/Or we deny that life has any meaning beyond the moral-political, the moral-domestic, and the moral-aesthetic. To all these values we must add the "human," and the *human* always has a larger standard for its definition. Men first imagined Nature as their goddess, then imagined God; then we imagined the goddess again as "Nature." It is time now that we im-agined ourselves as the creators of our gods.

CITY LIGHTS

IN THE NEXT ISSUE

HOW TO SOLVE THE MYSTERY OF THE FILM *RASHOMON* bv Parker Tyler. (Reprinted through the courtesy of the cinema 16 society of New York and Mr. Tyler.)

ENTERTAINMENT, ART and MAGIC. Marjorie Farber finds that a confusion between art and entertainment on the "high-brow" level may be preventing a just evaluation of our "popular" arts and entertainments.

THE GREAT TENOR MAN. A short story by Leslie Smith.

IN FUTURE ISSUES

INDIVIDUALISM RECONSIDERED. David Riesman, brilliant sociologist and author of *The Lonely Crowd* and *Faces in the Crowd,* contributes a provocative description of the survival of individualism in unrecognized and even scorned forms.

A SPECIAL TELEVISION ISSUE is planned for the 4th number of CITY LIGHTS. Some of the country's most astute critics of popular culture will join this first comprehensive study of the impact of television on American life. See the next issue for a complete announcement of contributors and articles.

MORE SPECIAL NUMBERS dealing with other portions of our popular culture are planned for future issues. Watch for a detailed announcement of future issues on:

POPULAR MUSIC: jazz and Bop

THE FUNNIES: From Dick Tracy to Pogo

Subscription Blank

City Lights
580 Washington Street
San Francisco 11, California

six issues for $2.00.
twelve issues for $4.00.
Bill me.
Check, cash, or money
order enclosed.

Send City Lights to:

Name - Please Print

Address

City   Zone

A NEW MAGAZINE

IN SAN FRANCISCO

Behold now this vast City;
a City of refuge, the man-
sion house of liberty...
should ye suppress all this
flowery crop of knowledge
and new light sprung up and
yet springing daily in
this City?

                    Milton

Criticism

35 cents   Short Stories

Poems

CITY   LIGHTS

...mber Three ■   San Francisco   Spring 1953

DON SMITH

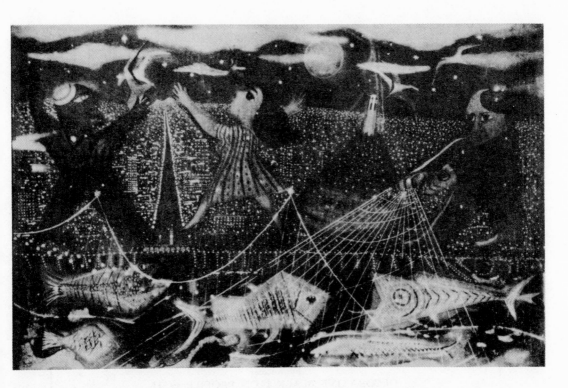

from Emmy Lou Packard's City Lights window at the Paper Doll

the Paper Doll

524 UNION STREET
SAN FRANCISCO

CITY LIGHTS

SAN FRANCISCO   SPRING 1953

CONTENTS

CITY LIGHTS is published at 580 Washington St., San Francisco, California. Telephone DOuglas 2-8193. Copyright, 1952, by CITY LIGHTS for its contributors. Manuscripts are invited, but no payment can be made at this time. Rates: thirty-five cents an issue; two dollars for six issues. Advertising rates upon request.

Editors, Peter Martin, Norma Bowkett, Wilder Bentley, Herbert Kauffman, Joseph Kostolefsky, Charles Polk. Managing editor, Richard Miller.* Business manager, Raymond Davidson. Editorial assistants, Mary Laage, Jean Taylor, Edith Weinberg. Presswork, Richard Pool. Process photography, David Leong. Lithography by Alan's at 46 Kearny St. Cover and design, Don Smith.

*Late publication of this third issue is due primarily to Richard Miller's induction into the U.S. Army.

INDIVIDUALISM RECONSIDERED

DAVID RIESMAN

I

OUR KNOWLEDGE of the existence of diverse cultures (including the stratified or ethnic sub-cultures within a single sizeable country), our preoccupation with semantics, our increasing awareness that emotion and character structure inevitably distort and guide perception, these give the writer in our day an ambiguous relation to his potential audiences. Occasionally, he makes the futile attempt to flee from ambiguity into a supposedly emotion-free terminology or jargon; but his newly laundered vocabulary will remain such about as long as a window curtain will remain white in Pittsburgh or Chicago. Occasionally the writer tries, by employing a private language, to cut down his audience to one he "knows," but even this does not last long: the "obscure" poets of a generation back are the textbook staples of today. It would seem that only by taking full account of ambiguity, by

Printed in *City Lights* through the courtesy of the author and of Prentice-Hall. From *Religious Faith and World Culture*, a symposium edited by A. William Loos. Prentice-Hall, Inc., 1951, 5.00.

recognizing that one always writes in a given context, can these limitations of discourse be turned into stimulation for writer and reader alike.

Since such terms as "society" and "individual" tend to pose a false as well as a shifting dichotomy, we must anticipate misunderstanding; if we succeed in being suggestive to at least a few, we shall be satisfied. We live in a social climate in which, in many parts of the world and of the United States, the older brands of ruthless individualism are still a social danger, while in other parts of the world and of the United States, the newer varieties of what we may term "groupism" become increasingly menacing. Actually, we can distinguish conceptually between the needs of society (as a system of social organization) and those of the environing group (as a system of psychological ties and expectations). As so defined, society, the larger territorial organization, often provides the mechanisms by which the individual can be protected against the group, both by such formal legal procedures as bills of rights, and by the fact that large-scale organization may permit the social mobility by which individuals can escape from any particular group. Prior to the rise of passports and totalitarianism, the modern Western city provided such an asylum and opportunity for many, while the existence of this safety-valve helped alleviate the pressure of "groupism" everywhere.

2

JUST AS a self-proclaimed "realist" is a different fellow in the Middle Ages, in the Enlightenment, and in modern America, so also the meaning of "individualism" depends on the historical setting. And it is worth tracing here the paradoxical development which, in the course of the modern era, freed Western men progressively from many previous restraints while at the same time developing a seemingly individualistic character-type enclosed within new psychological restraints. Men of the emerging middle classes, after the Renaissance, were turned loose in an economic order freed from the supervision of mercantilism, in a political order freed from the supervision of an hereditary aristocracy, in a religious order freed from the supervision of ecclesiastical hierarchy. To many observers of this process, whether radical or reactionary, these men who were freed of external restraints under the slogans of laissez-faire economics, utilitarian philosophy, and so on, appeared fiercely and viciously individualistic and competitive.* But if we look at these new men from the inside, so to speak, we can see that it was precisely their internalization of a great deal of restraint that allowed them to become free of the group sanctions that might have been arrayed against their "individualism." They could disregard the religious anti-money-making attitudes that had survived from the medieval and early Reformation period only because (as Max Weber pointed out) their Puritan religious ethics provided them with stern justification and with a shell of protection against the shocked attitudes of their contemporaries.

Today, with some old evils behind us, we can admit that the hardy men who pioneered on the frontiers of production, exploration, and colonization in the last three hundred years were usually men who acted according to a code and who, though of course there were many pirates like Daniel Drew and the slave traders among them, were more likely to subscribe to high moral principles (e.g. the elder Rockefeller). These men were bound by a character orientation I have termed inner-direction: they were guided by internalized goals and ideals which made them appear to be more individualistic than they actually were. Often, they were men

---

* To Werner Sombart, these men appeared free of "scruples"—that is, free from such traditional obligations as those of guild morality. The fighting slogans were, of course, often blatantly individualistic.

who walked in the imagined footsteps of idealized parents--and this gave them their seven-league boots, and their feeling of having a personal destiny. And since the ideals that were internalized included many vestiges of older traditions, they were frequently paternalistic men, who, despite nominal belief in free enterprise, helped ameliorate the worst abuses brought about by their innovations. They shared, then, more than appears of the ethics of their anti-individualistic critics, from Owen and Marx to Karl Mannheim and R.H.Tawney. Proof of this may be found in comparing these Western enterprisers with their counterparts in other countries, such as South America or China or the Soviet Union, where when traditional restraints on ruthlessness broke down, fewer internalized restraints were available to take their place. In sum, it proved possible in the West in early modern times to carry individualism to its limits of usefulness--and, in some cases far beyond these limits-- because a fair amount of social cohesiveness was taken for granted both as part of the traditional social order and as part of men's internal character structure.

Moreover, the same sort of moral compulsions which many of these "freedmen" carried within themselves, as the result of their socialization in a patriarchal family, were also turned loose upon the society at large. Individualistic "promoters" turned up not only in business and colonization, but in the many zealous reform movements of the last several hundred years. These movements fastened new restraints on a

society that was shaking loose from old ones—how effectively, we can see by contrasting the attitudes towards law and society in India today, as the legacy of British rule, with the attitudes in neighboring countries which were not compelled to internalize the "white man's burden." In the West, the nineteenth century witnessed the triumph of the Victorian way: a triumph of legal and orderly justice, of honesty in business and government, of greater concern for women and children, and so on. (Inclined as we are today to patronize the Victorians, we generally see the seamy side of their attainments and emphasize their hypocrisy, failing to observe that this hypocrisy was itself some evidence of their success in driving corruption, vice, and social sadism underground.) In the eighteenth century it was impossible to walk unarmed in many English cities, let alone in the country; public and private violence abounded; corruption was taken for granted; the slave trade was thriving. By the middle of the nineteenth century, the lower orders had been freed, the lower impulses (as well as some higher ones) subdued. The development in America ran parallel, but was never, of course, as complete,or as spectacular; as we all know, lawlessness reigns in many areas of American life today.

Nevertheless, anti-individualist writers such as Tawney, while they may have neglected the dangers of collectivism out of their disgust with their acquisitive society (and their failure to appreciate that medieval society, was if anything, more acquisitive still), do express a very common mood of dislike for the cash nexus—a mood which appears in more astringent form in Veblen. It is hard for people to find satisfaction in a society whose best defense is that it is a lesser evil than some other social form. People can become greatly attached only to a society which takes account of their longings for connection with each other, and they may even opt for totalitarianism because it pretends to satisfy these longings and to get rid of the felt indecency of the cash nexus. To the degree that capitalist individualism has fostered an ethic of callousness, the result has been to undermine all forms of individualism, good or bad.

3

IN THE perspective of hindsight, we can see how Darwin's Origin of Species came to be so completely misinterpreted when it first appeared, as a brief for struggle to-death *among individuals*. We can see, as the pendulum has swung towards groupism, that Darwin's book might just as well be interpreted as demonstrating the need for social solidarity or symbiosis within and among given species in order to achieve survival; thus (as Kropotkin pointed out) the book has much to say about cooperation as a technique of competition.

But the hardy Victorians, who had freed themselves from external restraints on economic competition and who were at the same time still sensitive, as I have indicated, to anti-moneymaking ethics, welcomed their interpretation of Darwin as a support in their continuing polemic against restraints—a polemic carried out also within themselves. One can, for instance, almost watch William Graham Sumner trying to stamp out, with the aid of Darwin, any softness and tenderness towards those who were pushed aside in the competitive struggle; he would have been less violent towards "do-gooders" if he had not feared their echo inside himself.

Today the argument against Sumner, and against this nineteenth century variety of individualism, seems very dated. We have come to realize that men who compete primarily for wealth are relatively harmless as compared with men who compete primarily for power (though, to be sure, there are violent, even totalitarian, implications in the treatment of labor, at home and abroad, as a commodity). Nevertheless, we are still inclined to use the word "bourgeois" as an epithet; we are well aware of the vices of the money-grubber, and perhaps less sensitive to the meannesses of spirit that develop in a monastery or a university where wealth as a goal is minimized. Even so, the centuries-old campaign against the middle class should not have hidden from us the advantages of a social system in which some men seek wealth (including wealth through power), pretty much for its own sake, and others seek power (including power through wealth), pretty much for its own sake, thus establishing a dichotomy of drives in which protective separation of specifically political powers can take its stand.

I recall Walter Duranty talking some twenty years ago about the Soviet abandonment of the "New Economic Policy," the policy by which, in the early twenties, a moderate capitalism had been encouraged in Russia. He spoke of the horror with which the ascetic Communists had reacted to the champagne parties and lovely ladies of the burgeoning NEP-men who were speculating in commodities, and making fortunes overnight by methods hard to distinguish from black-marketing. I felt then, and still feel, that if these Communists had been more historically minded and less morally

indignant they might have seen that the NEP policy offered the only chance of curbing the totalitarianism which sets in when only power, and not money, talks. (The Communists were like those farmers who, in their hatred of varmints, get rid of the very creatures on whom the natural ecology of the soil depends.) At the same time, we can see that if the Russian capitalists had not allowed moral restraint to be monopolized by the Communists, they might have aroused less of this sort of antagonism. (Today, it is the top party functionaries—and occupation troops—who have access to champagne and ladies!) And we also see that economic control through the "impersonal" market mechanism (Adam Smith's "invisible hand"), where this is possible, is decidedly preferable to the all too visible and personal hand of the state or private monopolist.

4

IN THE epoch when "money talked," the conception of human nature underwent a series of changes quite as ironical as the social developments themselves. The view of man as naturally cooperative runs through the writings of a number of otherwise quite diverse nineteenth century thinkers: St. Simon and Comte, Kingsley and Marx, Durkheim and Bellamy, Kropotkin and Ruskin. All these writers, more or less explicitly, reject competitive capitalism in favor of a medieval type of guild harmony and order, while differing in their

attitudes towards the machine and in their remedies for the diseases of industrialization.

Likewise, the view of man as naturally antagonistic has given rise to a number of diverse solutions to the problem of the social order thus presented. Freud, for example, finding men innately aggressive, thought that a strong elite, with a monopoly on the capacity for being reasonable, would have to compel the majority to cooperate in the tasks of civilization, at once demanding submission from the

masses and providing them with con-
solation. In Elton Mayo and in other
recent writers, one can find a similar
elitism and a similar concern with the
formation of group concensus through
strong leadership.

All these writers thus arrive at
positions in which they become advocates of what I have labelled "groupism," whether they start from reactionary or revolutionary political
positions, or from Rousseauistic or
Freudian and even Hobbesian views of
human nature. That is, whether one
begins with the assumption that cooperation is man's natural state, which
he is prevented from attaining by a
reactionary social order, or with the
assumption that the "state of nature"
is one of war of all against all, one
can readily end by focussing on forcing
or allowing men to define themselves
entirely as social animals. (To be
sure, in the early Marx, and even in
Bellamy, one finds more anarchistic
strains; and some thinkers of the last
century and of this one, such as John
Stuart Mill and Bertrand Russell, have
worried less about order than about
liberty.)

Obviously, the preoccupation with
the desires and needs of men for group
affiliation testifies, often enough,
to the actual presence of disorder in
the society. But it often testifies
also to the obsessive feeling on the
part of some intellectuals that disorder in itself is a terrible thing.
Furthermore, one of the themes that
unifies many of these writers is their
attitude towards the disorderly trait
of "selfishness" ; in true medieval
fashion, they denounce it and welcome,

if not always altruism as such, then
at least a class or national consciousness that submerges individual self-
interest. The confidence in self-
interest that ran from Mandeville
through Smith to Sumner, seems to have
been almost utterly defeated among influential thinkers by the end of World
War I; it is still assumed that self-
interest is natural—and sometimes,
indeed, that an "enlightened" self-
interest is called for—but on the
whole, reliance is placed on concern
for the needs of the group.

This altruism might have worked
during the 1900-1950 shift toward
emphasis on the group, if those group
needs had themselves been clear. In
that case, people might have developed
a pattern of obedience to the group
in certain limited spheres (regarding
the group demands as a kind of tax collection), while retaining individuality
in other spheres. If this had happened,
the shift from the preceding attitudes
of subtly socialized individualism
would hardly have been noticeable. But
in fact, the group needs have not been
clear; moreover, they have been constantly changing. There has developed
today a great preoccupation, less with
specific group needs, than with group
mood—a feeling on the part of individuals that they wanted or felt they
had to spend their energies, first in
making a group, and second, in attending to and improving its morale.

This groupism, which rests not on
obvious group emergencies but on the
vague disquietude of lonely individuals, is probably strongest in
America, where people appear to be
most vocally concerned about the prob-

lems of group participation and belongingness. Americans have devoted less
scientific attention to the measurement
of group needs and potential wants
through market research techniques
(save in the most obvious commercial
forms) than to what we might term "mood
engineering" in work, play, and politics. Mood engineering leads not so
much to specific "altruistic" behavior
as to a general readiness to participate in the given group activities of
the moment, even if their only purpose
is to help other people pass the
evening. As Margaret Mead has pointed
out, Americans feel selfish if they
stay at home when they might be amusing
people who are "under-privileged" in
the skills of self-amusement.

It would take us too far afield
even to begin to try to explain the
reasons for the psychological changes
which have occurred at least as rapidly
as those in social and political
organization. For example, shifting
patterns of child socialization are
important: among other things, parents
today face the responsibility of
" making a group" with their children—are on the defensive vis-a-vis
their children's moods—in a way quite
different from the attitude of parents
in an earlier day. Not all the developments towards groupism are to be
deplored. Groupism rests in part on
an increasing sensitivity to subtle
states of feeling, and this is an
advance. Only, as always, such ad-
vances bring with them a dialectical
train of new perplexities and limit-

ations. We must skeptically question
the demands for greater social participation and belongingness among
the group-minded while, on another
front, opposing the claims of those
who for outworn reasons cling to
individualism as a (largely economic)
shibboleth.

5

It is not easy, for obvious reasons,
to discover the actual state of this
conflict in Soviet Russia today. We
do not know, for instance, to what
extent people have become cynical and
apathetic as a way of resisting an
enforced group belongingness. However, occasional arguments appear in
the press which, by claiming that the
issue is settled, show that it is not
settled. Thus, in 1948 there was a
discussion of a psychology textbook
which was attacked, not only for its
" objectivity," but for its failure
to realize that the whole science had
undergone a profound change in the
Soviet Union. " The tragedy of the
loneliness of the individual," it
was asserted, " which characterizes
a society founded on classes, has
been liquidated. The conflict between
the individual and the community has
disappeared. The interests of the
Soviet people are harmoniously identified with the interests of Soviet
society." Furthermore, theories
about " unchanging human nature" are
damned as bourgeois (an issue not
absent from American social science
polemics)—it would seem that Lysenko-
ism operates in the field of human

beings too.*

To be sure, it is no adequate answer to Western advocates of group-ism to show how the idea has fitted so well into the totalitarian pattern (which eventually serves to destroy all local groupings). In fact, the advocates of an anti-individualist position use the seeming success of the dictatorships to buttress their views (not seeing to what extent the dictatorships, beneath their ideology, are seeking to imitate us), pointing out that men welcome social solidarity even if they must pay, in the loss of freedom, a high and terrible price for it; and that actually they want demands made on them—a point to which much war experience also testifies—rather than to be left alone and forced to direct their own efforts. Still other voices argue that, in crder to defeat the USSR, we must evoke our own spirit of sacrifice and devotion to the group: our alleged anarchy will be our undoing in the war of the two worlds. And still other, though few, voices would like to see international anarchy put down by an all-powerful world state.

What strikes me in many of these proposals is an ascetic uninventiveness reminiscent of the discussions which bored the Polish letter-writer quoted in the footnote. We assume that all possible forms of human relatedness have already been experienced, so that if present forms are unsatisfying, then better ones must be looked for in our own past, in wartime comradeship, or in the grisly present of the Soviet Union. Ironically, the very people who extol groupism, whether as an inexorable necessity or as desirable in its own right, usually do not themselves lead parochial and "groupy" lives; they draw sustenance from all the continents and all of history; they have friends everywhere, just as their material needs, through the modern division of labor, are met from everywhere. But like Plato and many other unhappy intellectuals since, they believe that those others, the masses (obviously, the very term "masses," is heavily value-loaded) can be saved from a Durkheimian anomie only by an enforced groupism and its concomitant ideology.

We can see, moreover, other forces

---

*A poignant newspaper story from Warsaw indicates that the Poles may be maintaining some resistance to the Stalinist extremes of groupism. A young Polish girl loosed a flood of abuse and correction on herself by writing a letter to the newspaper Standard of Youth declaring that "my private life does not concern anyone." She continued that the ideal member of the Union of Polish Youth was a "creature with wings...wearing a long and clean cloak of sackcloth. When it meets a pal it discusses only Marxism. It does not push in tramways nor spit on the floor and walks only on the right side of the street... According to you we should wear only a spotless uniform of our organization, straight hair and, of course, no trace of makeup...—all, in order to discuss the development of education in the New China!...I am young and lucky enough to have survived the war and have a right to live as I like. Z.M.P. meetings, discussions and some artistic shows are not enough for me." For this display of "selfishness," the writer was termed demoralized by war and occupation, said to "almost sanction(s) debauchery," and informed that "exceeding the pro-duction target...is happiness. Work in the organization provides happiness certainly greater than that gotten out of dancing or making up.''

than a simple nostalgia, or even simple elitism, at work. Anti-urbanites, for example, argue among themselves, in the guise of instructing the "masses." Unable to stand alone, lacking the "nerve of failure," they tend to project onto others their own uneasiness and frequently their own contempt for intellectuality. I do not mean, of course, that there is no malaise in our great middle and working classes in urban life; but rather, on the one hand, that the intellectuals greatly underestimate the terror, anxiety, and disorder of the "statue society" of the past which they so much admire, while underestimating, on the other hand, the tremendous achievements of modern men in making themselves comfortable in the face of the novelty of a fluid industrial society.

Americans of the more mobile classes have not only adapted themselves to a fluid society, but have also begun to adapt the society to their own needs. They have achieved an extraordinary ability to make judgments about, and friends with, a great variety of humankind. Whereas more traditional societies have an etiquette to govern the relation between people of different age, class, and sex groups, these Americans have abandoned etiquette for a more individualized and personalized approach. And while we are familiar with the negative aspects of this development—its enforced joviality of the "greeter" and gladhander, its enforced politeness of the Helen Hokinson type—we may in our self-contempt be less ready to see its great adventurousness: the liberation of people and their movements from the chain mail of etiquette.

In the arts of consumption as well as in the arts of production, Americans have moved so fast that, in architecture and design, in moving pictures and in poetry and criticism, we are living in what I believe to be one of the great cultures of history. It is not fashionable to say this. Yet we may ask, as Crane Brinton does in *Ideas and Men*: What is there in Pericles' famous praise of Athens that does not apply to us, in some or even in extended measure?

Sensitive Americans—and they are more in number than each individually is apt to think—have become exceedingly allergic to anything that smacks of chauvinism. Vis-a-vis Europe, we have lost the defensive aggression of Mark Twain, though his was a needed corrective; vis-a-vis Asia, we were until recently taken in by the image of the peaceable, unaggressive, technologically-unseduced Chinese. It now seems likely that we shall fall for the idea that the Russians have more to offer the Far East than we; and that they have unequivocally convinced the peasants that this is so. While this attitude stems in part from our disenchantment with machine civilization and our failure to use machinery as a means to greater, more creative, leisure, it would appear ludicrous to that part of the world, which needs machines before it can realize the possibility of becoming disenchanted with them!

One of the interesting semantic expressions of our own disenchantment

is that of bewailing our society as
" impersonal. "   What would the member
of the village group or small town
not give at times for an impersonal
setting where he was not constantly
part of a web of gossip and sur-
veillance? Furthermore, this use of
the term " impersonal " is a way of
deprecating our great human achievement
of turning over productive routines to
machinery and to formal organization.
One result of this attitude is clear
enough: the sphere of work tends to
come increasingly under the supervision
of the engineers whose concern is less
to reduce the time and strain of the
worker, than to render the workaday
world "meaningful" in terms of shared
emotions reminiscent of the guilds, or
rather of our nostalgic image of the
guilds.

A contrary attitude would assume
that we should be grateful to find, in
our work, areas of freedom from people,
where the necessary minimum of productive activity could be accomplished
without the strain and waste of time
involved in continuous concern for the
morale of the working group. If men
were not compelled to be sociable at
work, they could enjoy sociability in

their leisure much more than they often
do now.   In fact, while men in the
nineteenth century may have under-
estimated their satisfactions from
solitary occupations, hobbies and other
pursuits, we tend today to reverse
these extremes and to forget that men
can enjoy, let us say, the physical
rhythms of work or the private fantasies of leisure even when they are
for long periods deprived of social
comradeship at work and play. What is
necessary is some sort of balance which
will find room for quite idiosyncratic
individual desires to be, variously,
alone and with others. The flexibility
of modern industrial organization, no
longer bound geographically to rail
lines and power sites, the steady decrease of hours of compulsory work
which our abundance allows, and our
increasing sensitivity to the psychic
as well as physical hazards of the different occupations——these developments
permit us to move towards the reorgan-
ization of work so that it can offer a
greater variety of physical and social
challenges and stimulations. But work
should never be allowed to become an
end in itself simply out of a need to
keep ourselves busy.

6

APART from the everpresent threat
of war—not seldom used as a rationalization to sop up our "excessive"
comforts, leisures, and painfully-
attained easygoingness—most of our
social critics cannot imagine a society
being held together without putting

organized work in the forefront of its
goals and agendas. Their efforts to
restore the participative significance
of work, allegedly enjoyed in earlier
social stages, show the same poverty of
imagination as their belief in the inevitable need for the parochial group

as the only conceivable building block of society. When we turn to formal politics, we see that the same fundamentally reactionary ideology leads to a demand for national unity and a distrust of the chaos of democratic politics and of the war among the so-called "special interests."

The notion that there must be "agreement on fundamentals" in order that democratic politics may go on is an illusion. Carl J. Friedrich, in *The New Image of the Common Man,* provides a discriminatory critique. While it is true that people must be prepared to accept the fact of a vote or election going against them, and to accept certain legal and juridicial minima of the same sort, this is not what is meant when agreement on fundamentals is asked as the price of national unity and survival. What is meant is actually a surrender of special interest claims, whether these grow out of ethnic loyalties, church affiliation, regional, occupational, or other ties. What is meant is agreement that democracy itself (defined to mean more, much more, than the legal minimum) is a good thing; agreement on equality of races; agreement to put American needs ahead of any foreign loyalty. Yet the fact is that our democracy, like that of Switzerland, has survived without securing such agreements. In our country, this has been attained by a party system that serves as broker among the special interest groups: the parties do not ask for agreement on fundamentals—certainly, not on ideological fundamentals—but for much more mundane and workable concessions. At the same time, our expanding economy (and concomitantly expanding state services) has made these concessions possible without bankruptcy and, on the whole, with a steady reduction in hardship and injustice.

Those who would like to see the parties "stand for something," and those who have framed their own image of the future in terms of some Armageddon of proletarian revolution or overthrow of the "interests," feel unhappy and misgoverned under such a system. To them it seems simply a lack of system. Thus, we are in part the victims of ideals of polity which turn our virtues into vices and which have confused the Western world since Plato's *Republic,* if not before. What we need are new ideals, framed with the future rather than the past in mind— ideals closer to the potentialities actually realizable under the impetus of industrialization.

One of the elements in such a new ideal would seem to me to be a relaxation of the demand for political dutifulness now made by many citizens who are worried about apathy. Apathy has many meanings. Its expression today may be one of the ways the individual— in the Soviet zone or Franco's Spain, no less than here—hides from ideological pressures, hides from "groupism". Lacking an active counterfaith in individualism, or any way of meeting up with others who share his resentments, he falls back on apathy as a mask behind which he can protect the remnants of his privacy. If it were widely recognized that not all people in a democracy need concern them-

selves continuously with public affairs
(or with the union, or with the PTA,
or what not), but that all should have
a " right of veto" of which to make
sparing, residual exercise, they might
more readily agree to comply with the
minimal demands for information and
participation that such a veto would
need for its effectiveness. And with
politics no. longer regarded as a continuous duty, people might feel less
resistance to participation.

7

IF THE international (and hence
domestic) outlook continues to be as
grim as during recent years, readers
may wonder whether this advocacy of
" irresponsible" individualism is
not sheer escapism. It would be
insufficient to answer that " escape,"
like ''compromise,'' or ''appeasement,''
has become a bad word to the crusaders
for political and group commitment.
It would perhaps be a better answer
to observe that if America is to be
saved from destruction or self-de-
struction, it will be by preserving,
as part of our armory of significant
escapes, our humor and creativity
and sense of perspective.

I recognize, of course, that many
Americans feel guilty about their
" luxuries" if others are forced to
fight and suffer, and so would welcome
a kind of edited hardship as an alle-
viation of their guilt. But though
this is understandable, and in many
ways, desirable, it provides the
privileged countries and groups with
much too limited and hence too easy a
morality. The present international
dangers menacing America (real enough
in the view I hold of Stalinism) can
obviously be used by many people in
America to rationalize their partiality
for the shared hardships of war against
the solitary hardships of developing
their individuality in time of peace.

Again, it should be obvious to the
reader that I speak in a social context
in which anarchy and " unbridled"
individuality are much less likely
prospects (except on the international
scene) than the all-too-evident danger
of the " garrison state. " This
danger must make us particularly
sensitive to the fact that we depend
for advance, in morals no less than in
physical science, on individuals who
have developed their individuality to
a notable degree. We must give every
encouragement to people to develop
their private selves—to escape from
groupism—while realizing that, in
many cases, they will use their freedom in unattractive or ''idle'' ways.
Our very abundance makes it possible
for us, even in the midst of war, to
take the minor risks and losses involved in such encouragement as against
the absolutely certain risks involved
in a total mobilization of intellect
and imagination.

Yet in these remarks I find myself,
as a final irony, addressing the

defense of individualism to some presumed director of unselective service: I am using, Adam Smith style, group-survival arguments to justify the "selfish" living of an individual life. (Much the same irony overtakes many devout people who "sell" religion as a variety of group therapy—because it is good for morale rather than for morals.) Possibly I am thereby revealing my own arguments against my own guilts. But I think more is involved. I am trying to answer Dostoevsky's Grand Inquisitor in terms that he would understand, as well as in the transcendent terms that his interlocutor, Jesus, understands. I am insisting that no ideology, however noble, can justify the sacrifice of an individual to the needs of the group. Whenever this occurs, it is the starkest tragedy, hardly less so if the individual consents (because he accepts the ideology) to the instrumental use of himself. But I am also insisting that ethics must eventually be grounded on the experience of the human enterprise; that it need not and cannot rest on authoritative "revelation"; and that human experience, over the long pull, shows that we depend on such moral teachers as Jesus to cut through the rationalizations by which the grand inquisitors would bind us to our misery.

This, it should be plain, is no plea for "great men." on the Nietzschean mold, though it is a plea on his mold, against "little men." Since Nietzsche's time, through our increased knowledge of psychology and anthropology, we have become fully aware of the extent to which individuals, great and little, are the creatures of their cultural conditioning; and so we neither blame the little nor exalt the great. But the same wisdom has sometimes led us to the fallacy that, since all men have their being in culture and as the result of culture, they owe a debt to that culture which even a lifetime of altruism could not repay. (One might as well argue, and in fact many societies in effect do, that since we are born of parents, we must feel guilt whenever we transcend their limitations!) Sometimes the point is pushed to the virtual denial of individuality: since we arise in society, it is assumed with a ferocious determinism that we can never transcend it. All such concepts are useful correctives of an earlier solipsism. But if they are extended to hold that conformity with society is not only a necessity but also a duty, they destroy that margin of freedom which gives life its savor and its endless possibility for advance.

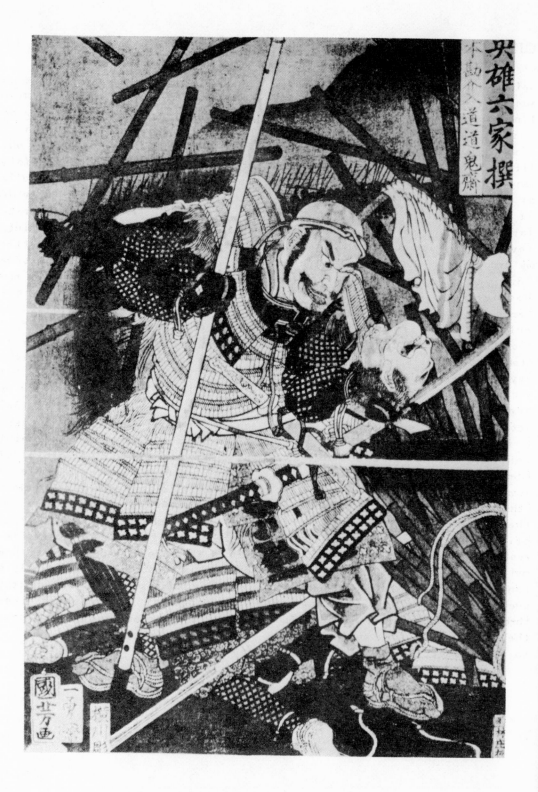

Rashomon as Modern Art

how to solve the mystery

of the film *Rashomon*

PARKER TYLER

R ASHOMON, the new Japanese film masterpiece, is a story about a double crime: rape and homicide (or possibly suicide). The time is the Eighth Century A.D. It is told in retrospect, and in successive layers, by the three participants, the dead warrior (through a mediumistic priestess), his raped wife, and a notorious bandit perhaps responsible for the warrior's death as well as for his wife's violation, and by a woodcutter who alleges himself to have witnessed, accidentally, the whole episode. The quality of the film narrative is so fine that an astonishingly unified effect emerges from the conflicting stories furnished by the three principals and (following the inquest) by the lone witness. The bandit and the woman have separately fled the scene of the crimes, where the woodcutter claims, at first, to have arrived only in time to find the warrior's corpse. Nominally, the film comes under the familiar heading of stories that reconstruct crimes. How-

ever, this story does not go much beyond the presentation of each person's testimony.

The woman claims to have killed her husband in an irresponsible fit of horror after the rape took place; her husband claims to have committed hari-kiri out of grief and humiliation; the bandit claims to have killed him in honorable combat; and the woodcutter confirms the bandit's story while picturing the conduct of all participants quite differently from the ways they respectively describe it. As no trial of either of the living participants is shown, and as no consequent action reveals anything conclusive as to the crime, the decision as to the actual truth of the whole affair falls to the spectator's option. Since technically the woodcutter is the only "objective" witness, he might seem the most reliable of the four testifiers. But his integrity is *not* beyond question; the version by the warrior's ghost has contradicted his version in an incortant detail—one inadvertently confirmed by the woodcutter's implicit admission (in an incident following the inquest) that he stole a dagger at the scene of the crime. The ghost has testified that he felt "someone" draw from his breast the dagger with which he alleges he committed hari-kiri.

Logically, if one's aim be to establish in theory the "legal" truth of the affair, the only obvious method is to correlate all the admissible facts of the action with the four persons involved in order to determine their relative integrity as individuals—a procedure complicated necessarily not merely by the given criminal status of one participant but by the fact that all but the woodcutter have willingly assumed guilt. A further difficulty, in general, is that nothing of the background of any character is given beyond what can be assumed from his visible behaviour and his social status; for example, there is only the merest hint of something unusual in the journey of the warrior and his lady through the forest. Again, even from direct observation, we have to depend on these persons as seen through the eyes of each other. So, unless one be prejudiced for one sex or another, one social class or another, it seems almost impossible to make a really plausible choice of the truth-teller (if any). Are we to conclude, in this dilemma, that *Rashomon* amounts to no more than a trick piece, a conventional mystery-melodrama, left hanging? My answer is *No*. There are several things about the movie which argue it as a unique and conscious art, the opposite

of a puzzle; or at least, no more of a puzzle than those modern paintings of which a spectator may be heard to say: "But what is it? What is it supposed to mean?"

Perhaps more than one profane critic has wisecracked of a Picasso, a Dali, or an Ernst, that it demands, a posteriori, the method described by the police as "the reconstruction of the crime." My opinion is that the last thing required for the elucidation of *Rashomon's* mystery is something corresponding to a jury's verdict. Such a judgment, esthetically speaking, is as inutile for appreciating the substance of this movie as for appreciating the art of Picasso. In *Rashomon*, there is no strategic effort to conceal any more than a modern painter's purpose is to conceal instead of reveal. The basic issue, in art, must always be *what* the creator desires to reveal. Of such a painting as Picasso's *Girl Before Mirror*, it may be said that it contains an "enigma". But this enigma is merely one specific aspect of the whole mystery of being, a particular insight into human consciousness in terms of the individual, and so has that complex poetry of which all profound art partakes. So with the enigma of *Rashomon*. This great Japanese film is a "mystery story" to the extent that existence itself is a mystery as conceived in the deepest psychological and esthetic senses. As applied to a movie of this class, however, such a theory is certainly unfamiliar and therefore has to be explained.

CHAGALL with his levitated fantasy-world and childhood symbols, Picasso with his creative analysis of psychological movements translated into pictorial vision—such painters set forth *nude* mysteries of human experience; each, in the static field of the painting, reveals multiple aspects of a single reality, whether literally or in symbols. *Rashomon*, as a time art, cinema, corresponds with multiple-image painting as a space art. The simplest rendering of time-phases in an object within the unilateral space of a single picture is, of course, in Futurist painting, such as Balla's famous dog, ambling by the moving skirts of its owner; the dachshund's legs are portrayed multiply with a fanlike, flickering kind of image similar to images as seen in the old-fashioned "bioscope" movie machine. The same dynamic principle was illustrated by Dr. Marey's original time-photography of a running horse, except that the register there was not instantaneous but successive; at least, the photographer had the cinematic idea of keeping pace with a running horse to show the pendulum-like span of its front and hind legs while its body seemed to stay in the same place (treadmill dynamics). Even in the contemporary movie camera, some movements may be so fast that one gets the sort of blur shown in Futurist images. The analogy of *Rashomon* with such procedures of stating physical movement is that, for the single action photographed, a complex action (or "episode") is substituted, and for the single viewpoint toward this action, multiple (and successive) viewpoints. The camera in this movie is actually trained four times on what

theoretically is the same episode; if the results are different each time, it is because each time the camera represents the viewpoint of a different person; a viewpoint mainly different, of course, not because of the physical angle (the camera is never meant to substitute for subjective vision) but because of the psychological angle.

"Simultaneous montage" in cinema is the double-exposure of two views so that multiple actions occur in a *unilateral space visually* while existing in *separate spaces literally* and possibly—as when a person and his visual recollection are superimposed on the same film-frame—also in separate times. A remarkable aspect of the method of depicting memory in Rashomon is its simplicity: each person, squatting in Japanese fashion as he testifies, squarely faces the camera and speaks; then, rather than simultaneous montage, a flashback takes place: the scene shifts wholly to the fatal spot in the forest. The police magistrate is never shown and no questions addressed to the witnesses are heard. When it is the dead man's turn to testify, the priestess performs the required rite, becomes possessed by his spirit, speaks in his voice, and the scene shifts back as in the other cases. Thus we receive the successive versions of the action with little intervention between them and with the minimum of "courtroom action."

Of course, there is a framing story, which retrospectively reveals the inquest itself. The action literally begins at the Rashomon Gate, a great ruin where the woodcutter and the priest, who has brought the woman and been present at the inquest, are sheltered during a rainstorm; joined by a tramp, these two gradually reveal everything that has taken place according to the several versions. What is important is the inherent value of the way the technique of the flashback has been variously used. The separate stories are equally straightforward, equally forceful; no matter which version is being related, his own or another's, every participant behaves with the same conviction. As a result (it was certainly this spectator's experience) one is compelled to believe each story implicitly as it unfolds, and oddly none seems to cancel another out. Therefore it would be only from the policeman's viewpoint of wanting to pin guilt on one of the persons that, ultimately, any obligation would be felt to sift the conflicting evidence and render a formal verdict. Despite the incidental category of its form, *Rashomon* as a work of art naturally seems to call for a response having nothing to do with a courtroom.

Of an event less significant, less stark and rudimentary in terms of human behavior, the technical question of "the truth" might prove insistent enough to embarrass one's judgment. The inevitable impulse, at first sight, is to speculate on which of those who claim guilt is really guilty of the warrior's death. But whatever conclusion be tentatively reached, what eventually slips back into the spectator's mind and possesses it, is the traumatic violence

of the basic pattern: that violence that is the heart of the enigma. The civilization of this medieval period is turned topsy-turvy by the bandit's strategy, in which he tricks the man, ties him up, and forces him to witness his wife's violation. It is only from this point forward that the stories differ: the woman's reaction to the bandit's assault, the husband's behavior after being freed from his bonds—everything is disputed by one version or another. But is not the heart of the confusion *within the event itself*? Is this happening not one so frightfully destructive of human poise and ethical custom that it breeds its own ambiguity, and that this ambiguity infects the minds of these people?

ALL THE participants are suffering from shock: the warrior's agonized ghost, his hysterical wife, the bandit when caught, seized with mad bravado. Unexpectedly—for the paths of the couple and the bandit have crossed purely by accident—three lives have been irretrievably altered after being reduced to the most primitive condition conceivable. Two men (in a manner in which, at best, etiquette has only a vestigial role) have risked death for the possession of a woman. Basically, it is a pattern that was born with the beginnings of mankind. Such an event, in civilized times of high culture, would of itself contain something opaque and even incredible. What matters morally is not how, from moment to moment, the affair was played out by its actors but that it

should have been played *at all*. The
illicit impulse springing up in the
bandit's breast as the lady's long
veil blows aside, is so violent that
its consequences attack the sense of
reality at its moral root. Regardless
of what literally took place in the
forest's depths that mild summer day,
each participant is justified in
reconstructing it in a manner to
redeem the prestige of the moral
sense, which, consciously or not, is a
civilized person's most precious possession. It should be emphasized that
it is the Japanese people who are
involved, and that to them honor is of
peculiarly paramount value; even the
bandit is quick to seize the opportunity to maintain—truthfully or not—
that he behaved like a man of caste
rather than an outlaw; he has testified that following the rape (to
which he says, the woman yielded
willingly) he untied the husband and
worsted him in fair swordplay.

Hence, a psychologically unilateral, indisputable perspective
exists in which the tragic episode can
be viewed *by the spectator*: a perspective contrary to that in which
one of the persons appears technically
guilty of the warrior's death. This
perspective is simply the catastrophe
as a single movement which temporarily
annihilated the moral reality on which
civilized human consciousness is
based. The "legal" or objective
reality of the affair (what might be
called its *statistics*) is exactly what
cannot be recovered because the
physical episode, as human action, has
been *self-annihilating*. Of course,

then, it might be claimed that the
woodcutter, not being involved except
as a spectator, is a disinterested
witness of the episode, and accord-
ingly his story that the three actors
in the tragedy really played a grim
farce, in which two cowards were the
heroes and a shrew the heroine, is the
correct version. But the opening
scene of the framing story makes it
plain that the woodcutter's mind is
in a state similar to that of the
participants themselves; indeed, he is
evidently dismayed and apparently by
the fact that all their testimony
belies what he proceeds to reveal to
the priest and the tramp as "the
truth." However, as the shocked witness of such a debacle of the social
order—in any case a victory of evil
over good—this peasant may have withheld his testimony out of superstitious timidity. If, in fact, he saw
all that took place, then the added
confusion that the participants
contradict each other may raise
bewilderment in his simple mind—may
even tempt him to exploit his sub-
conscious envy and resentment against
his betters by imagining their behavior as disgraceful and ludicrous.
It seems within *Rashomon*'s subtle
pattern to suggest that even a simple,
disinterested witness should be
drawn psychologically into the chaos
of this incident; after all, there is
no proof that he did not invent his
own account in competition with the
others'. This assumption would lend
credit to the conclusion that the
real function of each witness's story
is to salvage his own sense of
reality, however close his version to

the event as it took place. Perhaps it would be accurate to add that the facts themselves have no true legal status since each witness is forced to draw on his subjective imagination rather than on his capacity to observe. In this case, each is in the position of the proto-artist. who uses reality only as a crude form the sense of invention enters *into* reality. On the other hand, there is the literal truth of the denouement, the climax of the framing story, in which the woodcutter adopts a foundling baby who has been left in the Gate's interior. The relation of this incident to the story proper strikes me as the most problematical element of all, if only because the film would have remained intact without it.

Morally, of course, this incident functions as a reinstatement of human values in the sense of good. But the specifically religious view that humanity has hopelessly degraded itself in the forest episode (the view represented by the priest) is more external than essential to the whole conception. The priest thinks in terms equivalent, logically, to the law's terms: truth or falsehood. Since some lying is self-evident, the sin of concealment is added to crime; i.e., concealment of the truth, not of the crime, for all profess crime. Ironically enough, confession has become a sin. What seems significant to the whole is the collective nature of the liars: they literally outnumber the truth-teller (whichever he may be.) The "sin" involved has gone

beyond individual performance and exists objectively as would a natural cataclysm such as a volcanic eruption. That each participant assumes guilt, including the dead man, reveals the comprehensiveness and irresistibility of the disorder. A lie, then, actually becomes the symbol of the operation by which these people mutually regain their moral identities. These identities having been destroyed as though by an objective force beyond anyone's control, any means seems fair to regain them. Since, however, they cannot separate themselves from the sense of *tragedy*, they prefer to be tragedy's heroes—its animating will rather than its passive objects. But why should the three tragedies seem as one?

TO REVERT to our analogy with the visual media of painting and still photography, the plastic reality with which we have to deal in *Rashomon* is multiform rather than uniform. Within one span of time-and-space, reality (the episode in the forest) has been disintegrated. While the witnesses' stories accomplish its reintegration, they do not do so in terms of the *physically unilateral* except in the final esthetic sense in which the totality of a work exists all at once in a spectator's mind. The analogy is complex, but literally it is with the Futuristic image of the walking dog; like this image, the total image of *Rashomon* varies only in detail and degree. There is no variation on the background and origin of the tragedy; no contradiction as to the main physical patterns of the rape and the death of the warrior by a blade wound. So the main visual aspect is held firmly, unilaterally, in place. Another image of Futurist painting renders the angles of air-displacement caused by the nose of a racing auto. Such "displacements" exist in *Rashomon* severally in the respective accounts of a physical action deriving from one main impetus: the desire to possess a woman.

The total psychological space in this movie, because of its complexity, is rendered in literal time as is music. A similar psychological space is rendered *simultaneously* in Picasso's "Girl Before Mirror" by the device of the mirror as well as by the double image of profile-and-fullface on the girl. Her moonlike face has a symbolic integralness as different "phases" of the same person; that is, her fullface denotes her personality as it confronts the world and her profile her personality as it confronts itself: the mirror image in which the fullface character of her is diminished. To Meyer Schapiro we owe a basic observation as to this painting: it plays specifically on the body-image which each individual has of himself and others, and which is distinct from the anatomical image peculiarly available to photography. The mirror-image in Picasso's work thus asserts a psychological datum parallel with the dominantly subjective testimony of each witness in Rashomon's tragedy. The mirror of the movie screen is like the mirror in the painting as telescoped within the image of the total painting; successively, we see people as they think of themselves and as they are to others; for example, at one point during the woman's story, the camera substitutes for the viewpoint of her husband toward whom she lifts a dagger: we see her as conceived by herself but also as she would have been in her husband's eyes. In revealing, with such expressiveness and conviction, what novels have often revealed through first-person narratives or the interior-monologue, the film necessarily emphasizes its *visual* significance. The sum of these narratives in *Rashomon* rests on the elements of the tragedy in which all agree: one raped, one was raped, one killed, one was killed. The "variations" are accountable through something which I would place parallel with Schapiro's body-image concept: the psychic image that would apply especially to the memory of a past event in which the body-image is charged with maintaining, above all, its moral integrity, its ideal dignity. In a sense, Picasso's girl reconstructs and synthesizes her outer self-division within the depths of the mirror; so in the depths of each person's memory, in *Rashomon*, is recreated the image of what took place far away in the forest as consistent with his ideal image of himself.

In modern times, the human personality—as outstandingly demonstrated in the tragi-comedies of Pirandello—is easily divided against itself. But what makes a technically schizo-

phrenic situation important and dramatically interesting is, paradoxically, the individual's sense of his
former or possible unity, for without
this sense he would not struggle
morally against division: he would be
satisfied to be "more than one person." In analytical cubism, we have a
pictorial style expressing an ironic
situation within the human individual's total physique, including his
clothes; we do not perceive, within
an individual portrayed by Picasso in
this manner, a moral "split" or psychological "confusion"; rather we see the
subject's phenomenal appearance portrayed formalistically in terms of its
internal or "depth" elements, its
overlaid facets, or complex layers of
being, which— though presumably not
meant to signify a conflict in the
personality—correspond logically,
nevertheless, to the moral dialectic
within all consciousness (subjective/
objective, personal/social, and so
on). The same logical correspondence
is seen even more plainly in the anatomical dialectic of Tchelitchew's
recent paintings, where the separate
inner systems are seen in labyrinthine
relation to the skin-surface. Indeed,
man as an internal labyrinth is common
to diverse styles of modern painting,
all such styles neccessarily implying,
as human statements, the sometimes
bewildering complexity of man's spiritual being. Great beauty is justi-
fiably found in such esthetic forms,
which indirectly symbolize an ultimate
mystery: that *human* mystery to which
Rashomon so eloquently testifies in
its own way and which comprises the

transition from birth to death, from
the organic to the inorganic, which
is the individual's necessary material
fate.

Against the awareness of his
material fate, the individual erects
many defenses: art, pleasure, ethics,
God, religion, immortality—ideas,
sensations, and acts whose continuity
in him are preserved by constant cul-
tivation, periodic renewal, unconscious "testimony." These constitute
his moral identity in the social order.
In them resides the essence of his
being, the law of his contentment (such
as it be), and his rational ability to
function from hour to hour. In the
lives of the persons of *Rashomon*, where
this objective order prevailed, utter
chaos was suddenly injected. Each
person was shaken out of himself,
became part of that blind flux which
joins the intuition of the suspense-
before-birth with that of the suspense-
before-death and whose name is terror.
This was largely because of the tragedy'
physical violence, which temporarily
vanquished human reason. If we look
at the terror of war as depicted in
Picasso's "Guernica," we observe a
social cataclysm of which the forest
episode in *Rashomon* is a microcosm.
Curiously enough, "Guernica" happens
to be divided vertically into four
main sections or panels, which Picasso
has subtly unified by overlapping
certain formal elements. Thus, while
the great massacre is of course highly
simplified here in visual terms, it is
moreover synthesized by means of four
stages or views. As wrenched by
violence as are the individual forms,

they congregate, so to speak, to make order out of confusion. Though Picasso was not recomposing from memory, he might have been; in any case, the drive of art is toward formal order and the individuals in *Rashomon*, as proto-artists, have this same drive. As gradually accumulated, the sum-total of *Rashomon* constitutes a *time mural* whose unity lies in the fact that, however different are the imaginations of the four witnesses, whatever harsh vibrations their mutual contradictions set up, the general design (as the film-makers have moulded it) remains and dominates the work's final aspect of great beauty and great truth.

Rashomon as Modern Art is printed in *City Lights* through the courtesy of Mr. Tyler and the cinema 16 society.

---

cinema 16 and the author are
interested in your answers to the
following questions:

1: *Do you agree with the preceding theory as the proper way of evaluating this movie?* (Yes *or* No)

2: *If not, do you have a different approach of some special kind?* (Yes *or* No)

3: *If you have no such approach, do you think the person responsible for the warrior's death in this movie can be identified with ordinary detective methods of reasoning?* (Yes *or* No)

4: *If your answer to Question Two or Three is Yes, will you briefly say who, in your opinion, is the killer, and why?*

please send your replies
to the address below
cinema 16 also exhibits and distributes
unusual films: for information
address

cinema 16
175 lexington ave
new york 16
new york

The Great Tenor Man

LESLIE SMITH

THE RESERVED sign was whipped off the table and the chocolate colored hand deftly brushed the table clean. The black face nodded over the starched dickey as Margaret squeezed onto her chair. George was finding room for his feet among the oxblood gunboats all around him. The Negroes at the surrounding tables watched them without seeming to, and remained sprawled out where they were, not yielding to these *ofays* who blocked their view.

"This table is perfect," Margaret said to the man who seated them, and the dinner jacket disappeared into the smoke beyond the orange spotlight.

The spotlight glittered on the chrome bridge of the electric guitar that the blues-singer was playing, and it yellowed his coal-black shine.

"...*I'm so all alone...lonesome...*" he sang, from across the empty dance floor.

He struck a wild chord on his guitar, a twang that lingered under his voice.

"*...And blue...withoutchew, baybee!*"

"That's Dallas Slim," George shouted at Margaret.

Then came the tag ending and the metallic chords, burning from the amplifier.

Dallas Slim bowed low. The spotlight whirled through four colors and the house lights came up with the applause and cheering.

The M. C. jumped to the microphone. "Well, all *right*! Solid, solid, solid!"

He flipped his head over to glance at the gathering of musicians at the back exit. He held out his dark glasses in a comic gesture of long range vision.

"Short intermission," he mumbled. "Lots of *bee-you-*tiful gals out there eager to take orders for your favorite drinks. Yeah!" He switched off the microphone.

A jukebox came on, from the bar up at the front end of the nightclub.

A waitress popped up out of the floor by their table, all thin arms and legs of creamy black. She planked down a glistening ashtray.

"What would you like to drink?" asked George. "They don't serve beer after nine, when the show goes on."

"Oh, they don't," said Margaret. "Gee, then I can't decide, George. What are you going to have?"

"I think I'll have a bourbon and water."

"Oh, that sounds good. A bourbon and water, too."

The waitress leaned over for the order, her perky figure inadequately clad in starched ruffles.

" Gee, George, it's just too *wonderful* here, " said Margaret, indicating all of it with a refined wave of her hand. " I'm so glad you brought me. "

" Well, I said I would, on your birthday. "

" I *know* you did, George. And I really do appreciate it. This is the best birthday party a girl could have. Honestly it is. "

" This is a good table we got, " said George.

Margaret laid the tips of her fingers on George's hand. " You're not angry with me for insisting on this table, are you, George? "

" Gosh, no! You sure twisted that head-waiter around your little finger. "

" He was nothing, " Margaret said. The smile went out of her eyes for a moment as she watched George.

George cleared his throat. " I usually stay at the bar when I come here, when I'm alone, that is. "

" Oh, then you must come here often, George? "

" I drop in to see the fellows once in a while. "

" The fellows, George? "

" The musicians. *You* know. I like to keep up with what's going on in the music business. For instance, I'm a Bumps Grainger fan. I always come to hear him and so he and I got to be friends. I guess he's about the most progressive musician alive. Do you see what I mean, Margaret? "

" Sure, George. Sure I do. Why I think that's wonderful. I didn't have any idea about this side of your life. My goodness! All these celebrities! "

" I only know Bumps at all well. " George looked up at the ceiling, reverently. " He's a great tenor man. "

" It's all so exciting, George. Will we see him tonight? "

" I don't think so. He isn't working right now. His band broke up. But you never can tell, we might. "

Margaret puffed on a cigaret while George was shelling out the money for the drinks. She looked around her, peering over her shoulders and squinting out across the room. Then she laughed and leaned close to George, in intimacy.

" What is it? " asked George.

" This is such a funny little dance floor. "

" Oh, that, " said George. " Sure, it is. That's all they need. "

They clinked glasses and drank, with George smiling, knowingly. " You see, " he said, " this bop ain't... isn't much good for dancing... "

" What's it good for then? "

" Well, that isn't the idea, exactly. It's progressive, it's irregular, it's like *they* say, 'frantic.' "

" *They* dance to it, don't they? "

" Well, sure they dance to it, Margaret. *They* dance to anything. "

" Those records you brought over the other night sounded as if a person could dance to them. "

" Oh, those...Well, some of those weren't real bop. Take the Charlie Parkers, now... "

Margaret's gaze shifted away while

George explained the Charlie Parkers
and the Dizzies. He talked with the
intense zeal of an enthusiast.

" George?"

"...then they add augmented chords..."
George was going strong.

" George?"

"...like in one of those weird runs
by Dizzy..."

" George, please. I'm sorry to interrupt."

He stopped.

" There's a colored fellow over
there who's been watching us..."

'' Where?"

" Wait a minute." She held George's
sleeve. "He's with those other fellows.
Over your shoulder."

George shot a quick look around,
then another slower one.

"Oh," he said. " My gosh!"

'' What is it, George?"

'' That's Bumps Grainger."

'' Who?"

'' Bumps Grainger, you know..."

"Oh, your friend? That explains
it, then. He was staring so."

" Bumps is all right," said George,
but he kept his eyes on the table.
" He won't bother you."

"Oh, don't worry about me, George.
I was just wondering, that's all."

" You don't need to worry, Margaret.
They won't bother you."

'' Goodness! I can take care of
myself," said Margaret, and to show
that she could, she smiled broadly
over George's shoulder.

" Bumps is all right," insisted
George.

Bumps was all right. Bumps was
fine. When Margaret smiled, he pushed

his long body away from the wall with
his shoulder and threw his arms out in
a gesture of happiness. Exaggerating a
slow motion getaway, he walked a step
or two from the musicians he was talking
with, then looked back for the effect,
his mouth wide open in a laugh, his
teeth like snow.

" He's coming over," said Margaret,
not able to look anywhere else.

George still looked at the table,
The great tenor man stopped when he got
to their table and his smile looked as
though it would break open his face.

" How you doing, man?" he said to
the middle of the table. " How you
all tonight?"

There was a kind of flowing bow for
Margaret, imperceptible in degree but
immense in intention. The man was
moving all over all the time, imper-
ceptibly really, but powerfully like
the tide. He created his own rhythms
where he went.

George practically knocked his
chair over getting up. He put out his
hand and the huge black paw slid through
it like oil.

" How's everything, Bumps," said
George, loud enough to be heard by
the hat check girl.

" Mellow," said Bumps, laughing as
though he'd been tickled. " Mellow,
mellow."

He took worlds of time about everything he did, and he was always doing
something, something definite. He
was either looking at someone or laughing, or talking serious. You could
always say what it was...

He looked at Margaret, not laughing
but just grinning in the friendliest,

politest kind of way, a slice of white across his black face. He wasn't just black, he was coal black and blacker than that. There was a satin sheen to him. His hair was plastered down until it was almost straight and it ended in a row of tight ringlets which hung just above his collar in back. His shirt was lavender and the tabs were six inches long. His tie was short and wide with a big gold saxophone painted right in the middle of it.

"This is Miss Ritter," said George, "Mr. Grainger."

"Knock my eyes a kiss! How you doing, honey? This is a *real* pleasure, a real *gone* pleasure, honest." He nodded quickly a couple of times, his eyes sparkling with black laughter. Then he laughed aloud.

Margaret watched him, entranced, her eyes wide at first and then narrowing, watched him hold out that immense black hand. The black fingers closed around her hand, shutting it off from the rest of her at the wrist.

"Won't you have a drink with us?" asked George, tottering between standing and sitting, his knees still half under the table.

Bumps turned his attention completely away from Margaret. He switched himself off and then a different self on again.

"Why, man, that's real fine." He was extremely polite.

His hand reached out and came back with a chair in it and he was sitting at the table, his elbow on the table.

He turned his eyes to Margaret. When she looked at him he laughed again. He seemed to be keeping time to some music with his shoulders, to the juke box, maybe, or something farther away than that, something farther back.

George was having his old trouble. Feet were mixed up with his chair again.

A waitress popped up from somewhere.

"How you, tonight?" Bumps asked her.

"Real fine, Mr. Grainger." She grinned widely. "What you drinking?"

"Why, whatever these folks are drinking, honey."

"What you all drinking?" asked the girl.

George was just able to sit in the space between his chair and the table. There were feet all around him.

The waitress bent over beside George and when George turned to her, Bumps leaned forward, filling up the space in front of Margaret. His face was changed; he was frowning.

"Say, what's this cat's name?" he asked.

"You mean *George?*" Margaret's voice was filled with surprise.

"Oh, yeah? *George,* huh? Ha! George!"

Bumps shoved himself back in his chair. When George turned away from the waitress, he was laughing.

"Well, what's new, George?" he said. "How's everything going with you?" He laughed briefly, then waited for George, pointedly, breathlessly.

"Oh, everything's going very well," said George, cautiously.

" That's fine, " said Bumps. " Why, that's real fine! 'Everything's going very well.' You said it, George! " His face opened up with laughter again.

The three of them sat there around that little table, Bumps laughing fully, having a wonderful time. Margaret began to grin.

Bumps turned suddenly to George and poked him with a finger that looked like a toy flute.

" You got a pretty girl here, George. "

He swung his eyes to Margaret and back to George.

" Yeah, man! You're really in there! "

George just opened his mouth. Nothing came out. Both Margaret and Bumps watched him. He might have had something stuck in his craw.

Bumps leaned forward with both elbows on the table. " Hey, hey, " he was dead serious, suddenly.

" Sure, " said George, all ears.

Margaret was frowning from the influence of Bumps' serious mood.

" Yeah, well dig this real careful...

" I was driving down the boulevard this afternoon, along about eight o' clock, you know. And this chick was with me. She's a blonde, you see, a friend of mine. "

Margaret's mouth opened, just for a minute, as though she needed air.

" Well, this officer comes along, you know. First on my side, and he looked at me, so I dig him, too. He's riding along like this... " Bumps rode the motorcycle along, like the officer. " ...and I'm sitting there driving, doing about twenty-five,

see? "

He turned to Margaret. " Maybe you don't wanta hear this, honey? "

" Oh, please, yes. I'd love to hear it. "

Bumps held her eyes while he turned back to George.

" All right, so then the officer goes on to the other side, and he rides along over there and he looks in at this chick. So she digs him the same way. The same routine.

" She says, 'Maybe you're speeding', but I show her, see? Twenty-five. Everything's cool. But then he gets behind us and he comes on with the siren. Vunnh... "

Bumps relaxed, suddenly, like a deflated balloon. Margaret and George both jumped, jostling the table. A grin spread across Bumps' face, and the two listeners began to breathe again.

" Well, we stops...

" The officer, he wants to know, have I been drinking. So I say, 'Oh, no officer, I just had breakfast'. And that kills him, see? Breakfast in the afternoon! He couldn't dig that. So he says, 'All right, young man, come on out here, I want to talk to you'. He gave me that young man routine, you know.

" So we walk back to his motor, and he says, 'Who's that woman you're with?' And so I say, 'Why, man, that's Mrs. Wilson', see? I thought I'd have some sport with the officer. So he asks me, have I been drinking, and a lot of questions.

" Then he goes up to the car and talks to the chick, and he asks her

her name and she says, 'Miss Wilson', see?"

Margaret kept watching, watching his every move, watching his mouth form the words.

" So he comes back to me. A real athletic cat, you know? Back and forth. 'I thought you said her name was Mrs. Wilson,' he says to me. 'Oh, no,' I says, 'officer,' I says, 'you know how we colored folks is, how we all drawl out our words...'"

Bumps pushed himself back in his chair and roared with laughter. He laughed until he was limp.

" What happened?" asked George.

Bumps stopped laughing. " He let us go, man! I'm here, ain't I?"

He looked at George incredulously, about as incredulously as anyone could. Then he turned his attention to Margaret. " And how's everything going with you, honey?"

Still serious like a little girl, but with just a trace of latent capacity for fun hanging onto the corners of her mouth, Honey frowned at the black volcano. Then she ventured out into that forbidden pool, where it was over her head, too, and.. she just jumped in. She opened up those frank hazel eyes and leveled off, swimming.

"You laugh all the time," she said.

" Honey, you gotta laugh to be happy, you just gotta."

The little flute started out at Margaret and then folded up and waited.

The auditory part of Bumps' laugh, really just a kind of minor accompaniment to the good humor which seemed to flow, naturally, from him,

was a soft voiced " Hee, hee," like the soft, high tone Billy Holiday gets.

Margaret's smile began to come on like a sunrise.

" I'm beginning to feel strange, " she said.

" You feel good. That's what it is. You're mellow, now. Yeah!" Bumps accented his assertions with vigorous nods.

Margaret brought a red-tipped little white hand out from under the table and laid it tremulously near Bumps' enormous black paw. The long finger jumped out and touched it and then withdrew.

" How you doing, George?"

George's face was all furrowed.

" I'm cramped in here," he said. " I haven't enough room."

" You haven't enough room?" The volcano bellowed at the injustice of of George's plight.

" Give this man some room, " he ordered the world.

The table was picked up and placed a foot, maybe two feet out into the dance floor, all in a gust. Margaret shifted over, laughing, and George followed along, pulling his chair behind him.

They ordered another round of drinks. Bumps suggested a kind of fizzed eggnog, a house specialty, and Margaret went along with him. George stuck to bourbon and water.

The house lights went down and the spotlight came on. Two sax players were standing at the microphone and there was a drummer and bass man in back of them. The piano player jumped up on the bandstand and ran off a chord and the drummer let his brush ride on the traps.

"Hey, all right, now! Well, looky here. I do declare, ladies and gentlemen." The mad M. C. was back at the microphone. "That solid little combo, the Jones Boys. All right, let's give them a hand. All right, all right! Solid, solid. *How High the Moon*."

His little spiel accelerated to a rapid scream, stimulating wild applause from the customers. He just had time to duck out when the alto sax stated the theme, once over, simply, and then they were off.

Look out!

Bumps sprawled out all over his chair and one arm flopped across the table. The alto was blowing right down on him, across maybe ten feet of dance floor.

"My boys," he yelled up at Margaret.

And he grinned idiotically, soaking it into every pore.

George sat still in stiff amazement, in open-mouthed wonder

They whistled and cheered. These boys were mad. And there were dark couples gliding furiously through the spot. Not bouncing, gliding smooth, like oil. First there were a few and then the little dance space was packed.

"Hey, aren't you cats dancing? What's the matter, man?" Bumps sat up at attention, deeply concerned. "You should dance. Yeah!" His frown deepened. He looked from George to Margaret.

"Don't you like to dance?"

Margaret tried to make herself heard. A black ear was put before her.

"George says you can't dance to this music," she yelled into the ear.

Bumps gave his amazement plenty of time to register. He seemed not to be able to put it into words.

"Do you wanta dance, honey?"

Margaret drew in a long breath.

"I'd love to," she said.

"George?"

"George?"

George's mouth contorted into a sickly grin. "Sure, go ahead."

He waved them away, magnanimously.

They whirled right at the table, brushing it, and Margaret, holding off, kept space between them. She danced awkwardly at first, her legs stiff, unyielding in their spike-heeled pumps. But gradually the force of their whirling pulled her close to Bumps. She began to soften.

Bumps found an opening in the dancing crowd. They were gone.

The Jones Boys dragged out *How High the Moon* into twenty minutes of mad improvisation. Even George worked up a sweat, just sitting at the table.

Two or three times Bumps and Margaret appeared out on the periphery of the crowd. They were molded together. Margaret's eyes were closed. Her head nestled in the cup of Bumps' shoulder.

But there was just a hint of something amiss. A suggestion of a kind of ageless racial immobility had come to settle over Bumps' face. His eyes sought release for his spirit in the cean of more familiar experience in the room about him. Margaret had abandoned herself to him but he wasn't with it anymore.

At the end of it, the band dissolved and the M. C. came back to turn off the microphone. The lights came up. Bumps and Margaret ambled across the floor, holding hands. Margaret laughed and held back as Bumps led her to her chair.

"Thanks for the dance," Bumps said, pushing the chair up for her.

Margaret twisted around and smiled up at his face.

But Bumps stepped back, watching her, and he took a quick sober peek at George. He whirled on one foot, then tapdanced his way around the table to George.

"Hey, George, man, I gotta cut out. I got a call to make. You gotta make calls to get results. Huh?"

He put out his hand, and while George unscrambled his arms and legs again, he glanced at Margaret. He gave her a little wink, a kind of goodbye.

When he left, silence, dead silence came along. Margaret's smile went with him. She folded her hands on the table in front of her.

"Well?" said George.

"Well," said Margaret, studying her hands.

"What do you say, Margaret?"

"What do you say, George?"

Something snapped in George. He started out in a great fury. "What do you expect me to say?" Then he sighed. "Nothing," he said. A

"nothing" as flat as a drink spilled on the table.

"I guess we'd better go," Margaret said.

"It doesn't matter to me," said George. "It doesn't matter to me."

"Wait a minute, first."

"Sure," said George.

He nodded as she picked up her purse and walked self-consciously to the rear door, brushing at her skirt.

George drank what was left in all the drinks on the table. And the waitress popped up through the floor again.

"No," said George. "No."

So the waitress cleaned everything off the table except George, and left a RESERVED sign for him to read.

He squirmed in the chair, peering around, then sat rigid. Margaret and Bumps were just inside the rear door, together. Margaret was backing away from Bumps into the room. Bumps was talking to her, fast, and gesturing with his palms down.

Abruptly, she turned from Bumps and made her way toward the front of the place, her head high. As she passed near the table, she motioned to George.

George had to detour around the room. He caught up with her, briefly, at the checkstand where she threw her coat over her shoulders and then went out the door. George dug up the quarter for the girl.

She waited for him outside.

"Take me home," she said.

"What happened, Margaret?"

The Negroes in front quieted down and watched them apprehensively.

"I don't want to talk about it,"

said Margaret.   "Take me home."

"Did Bumps do something?"

"No," said Margaret, turning her head away.   She bit her lower lip and squinted her eyes.

George squared his shoulders.   "He did something, and you're going to tell me, Margaret."

"He didn't do anything, and you don't want to hear about it."   She tried to walk on but George held her.

"I'm going to get to the bottom of this," said George, gallantly.   "Now tell me what he said to you."

"All right, George."   She looked at him, square in the eyes.   "He said he didn't want charity..."

"He didn't want what?...I don't get it."   But his face showed that he was beginning to.   "What did he mean,

Margaret?"

"He said when I grew up to come back and see him again sometime.   He said I was too easy.   He said..."   She turned her face away.   "Now will you take me home?"   she asked.

George drew in a long breath. "Yes.   Yes, I'll take you home." he said, wearily.   "Come on."

They walked up the street together, not touching.

The sharp Negroes relaxed and went on with their interminable conversation. The door to the night club swung out for a moment and the voice of Dallas Slim rose above the sidewalk chatter.

"... 'I get the blues at midnight, Baby.   Baby, when you're away..."

"Twang, twang," went the guitar. The door knifed shut again.

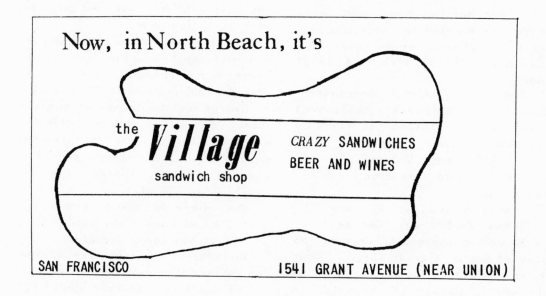

A Note on Reading Poems

When we read a poem we call successful, one of the things we could mean is that here is a poem that has invited, has necessitated our entry into an unalterable universe that is this poem. We must leave our preoccupations if we are to enter this world. It seems more apt to say leave our preoccupations than to say leave our world, because so few of us know who we are or what our world is or whether or not there is a need to know. If this is a helpful way to think about what happens when we read a poem, than we are faced with questions about the relation of one poem to another, of poem to painting and to music, of poem to criticism, of poem to our deeply held beliefs and our daily experience.

If we can agree that each poem, each painting, each work of music can realize within its limits a self-explaining universe, can it then be proposed that art is a means by which we unify, clarify, intensify and expand our reality? It seems unlikely that masterful connoisseurship necessarily increases the order and, therefore, the usefulness of reality. If we depend too exclusively on art works to condition and to sharpen our uses of experience, we would become extremely sensitive persons, but, very likely, fragmented persons.

On the other hand, it could be said that the universe of Shakespeare encompasses enough for the majority of us; he provides a definition of human experience so amazingly complete and so properly complicated that if we can encompass his world, we shall, indeed, return to our own world well equipped to organize it and, by organizing, give it meaningful existence. And, of course, we have his text nearby to re-galvanize us if we falter. Our religious tradition uses the Bible in the same way. Shakespeare and the Bible have been proved an efficient combination. If, in their twelve years of formal education, our children could begin to assimilate these two texts, they would have the basis for ordering experience, of knowing hheir joys and tragedies for what they are, and thereby have available the means of knowing who they are and what they are doing.

What would seem to be required is a text that includes enough of human experience, encompassed with sufficient cogency to excite religious assent; which is, in turn, to say that various and fragmented experience, in order to be manageable, must enter a pre-existing order. It follows, then, that a poem gains when read by a person who has a world to leave from and return to. Can we further say that a fundamental activity of criticism is the discovery of the art work's possible relations to an inclusive, standardized, and widely-known reality?

The emphasis in assigning the activity of the critic is on the discovery of relations and of the terms adequate to the accuracy description of these reactions. To be able to employ these means presumes a critic who not only can effectively avail himself of a standardized, inclusive, and widely-known reality, but also exists in relation to this reality. If the poem has worked, it has suspended his thinking on self, and thus he has transcended self and cannot talk about self's experience of the poem when he returns. So if he is to talk about anything, he must talk as one outside of the poem, and although he can look back, recollect, and point to the complex of words as having a kind of tangibility; and although he can name certain characteristics that suggest relations with other formed experience, he can at best only approximate what it is like to be within the world that is the poem. The poet, as he well knows, stands in a similar relationship to his poem after it is written. Revision of the poem grows out of a re-experiencing of the poem and becomes an increasingly delicate matter as the poem approaches realization of its being. The reader, editor, critic function in a similar way. If one of these sense deficiencies, like the poet he ponders possible revisions; but how many times, upon the poet having tried a suggested revisions, has he felt his poem come tumbling down around his ears Still, the poet and critic are faced with the same rigorous demands that are made upon anyone who is willing to undertake the ordering of his life. The poet's engagements are, even so, more sharply and more frequently met and the tentative results are more quickly known than are the engagements of the majority of us. Further, the artist knows better than the rest of us that there is no easy way to detach from self, to know the qualities of another consciousness, to accept knowingly the collective consciousness working within his own, to catch momentarily the essence of an experience. The majority of us, maybe all of us, know the need, and make the attempt, to extend our accountability, and we also seek the means of arresting moments of insight into our successes and failures in this attempt, so that by contemplating, we can extend these moments. It is the artist, however, who dedicates himself to arresting our knowing and rendering it into permanent, intelligible form. So our thesis is that poems should be approached as things in themselves; that the successful reading of poems requires us to give ourselves every chance to be translated from our own consciousness into the consciousness of the poem. What happens afterward depends upon the success of this act.   H. K.

LLOYD FRANKENBERG

fourth floor ladies · a love poem

Ladies, ladies of the topmost story;
Ladies of graces, ladies of fury:

1

One in a corridor sits and rocks,
hands in her sleeves and her sleeves in knots:
    I'm a harebell.
    A syringa bush.
    I'm a piece of blue silk. I cost twelve-fifty.
    You can't get away from a man.

Blows out her cheeks and leans far over,
Straining against the camisole string.
Curls her heels up under her:
    Do you want me to tell you what I am,
    Mr. Pine Tree?
(Whispering;
a smile like a twisted strawberry)
    I'm a poor little oyster. It took me
    three thousand years to cross the ocean.
    Rock-a-bye baby
    in the tree top.
    Like sweet bells jangled, out of tune.
    Teddy has a gold cock.
    You're a ferocious looking brute.
    You can't get away from a man.

Lady of the green refractory eyes
and Rabelaisian heraldry;
lady rocking, rocking lady
who kicked me when I wasn't looking
and graciously included me
among unseen inaudible friends:
    Do you want to know about God?
    They finished him off with a baseball bat.
    Look out! There's a derrick coming.
    You can't get away from a man.

2

Someone paddles across the porch,
flannel gown and pallid feet
over the bleached and drying boards,
up and over the laundry heaps:
>Give me a dollar. I gave him four dollars.
>You're a good boy. You're a lovely girl.

(a jig and a smile) Ta-*tum*-ti-dee.
>I want to go home. You must let me go.
>They'll never let me. They'll never leave me.
>No.
>No.

3

Comes a lady with fountain hair,
cup of mendicant,
saint's demeanor;
blesses the air with orange juice;
anoints the door
(In Hoc Signe);
washes the floor with her fountain hair.

4

And My Lady Gabble-Gabble
winking through the slotted door:
>Here they call it high.
>*I* prefer to say elated.
>Might I trouble you for water?
>I could spit.
>They brought me here. They took away
>manicure scissors, mirror, comb.
>What have they done with *me*?
>They've left me feeling like a cocoon;
>half in, half out.
>Me, Madame Butterfly!

5

Sewing lady, dripping shreds;
tyrant of the Fourth Floor kitchen;
bulging like your reticule;
went to the Good Will Store for thread;
left a note on the fire-hydrant;
just a little too sensible:
>Do you wait for the people who sold you the holey
>sweater to mend the holes?
>Are we waiting for the people who put holes in us

to patch us up?
Of course I'm crazy or I wouldn't be here.

6

Stock in the center of wavering hands
stands in the untouchable rock of rage,
monumental in nudity:
   Why *shouldn't* I murder anybody?
Her dress, her cards, her kotex shed
between the weave of the iron screen
over the needle-laden boughs
more worthy to adorn than she;
making her runes of Broadway tunes,
behind the Bronte-fronted house
she keeps a perpetual Christmas tree.

Ladies, ladies of the topmost story;
sleeping or waking, endlessly rocking
ladies of graces, ladies of fury;
mouthing bedsprings; fisting glass;
oh what has frightened us out of our wits?

Dance, under the mansard eaves.
Stand like a fixture.
Stare like an owl.
Alternately laugh and bay,
Turn your chameleon-many selves.

Let yourselves go
in your mind, in your clothes.
Come to in a room with softness lined,
window-barred,
eating off tin and gently treated;
allowed to pick flowers once a week
in the little garden
behind the Bronte-fronted house;
ladies of graces, ladies of fury;
ladies, ladies of the topmost story.

LLOYD FRANKENBERG, poet, critic, author of THE RED KITE (poems, Farrar and
Rinehart); PLEASURE DOME: on reading modern poetry (Houghton-Mifflin); and
editor of PLEASURE DOME: an audible anthology of modern poetry read by its
creators (Columbia Records). During the war, as a conscientious objector,
Mr. Frankenberg spent a year as an attendant at a psychiatric hospital in
Maryland.

Hollywood Chronicle : 1942-1948

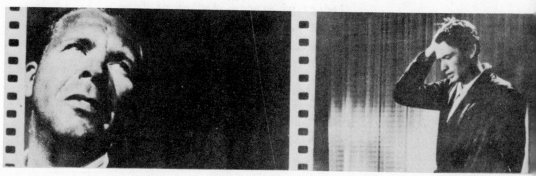

A Long Way From Home

BARBARA DEMING

. Doleful Regions

BANDON all hope, you who enter here!" Dante found this warning inscribed above the entrance to Hell. The same warning is appropriate here, before e reader enters the world through which this book would lead him—the rld which has been shaped upon our movie screens the past several years. That rld upon our screens is the image of ourselves, and the image of these past ars is discouraging. Let the reader be comforted that the image is incomplete. do not speak of that direct likeness of our times which Hollywood films offer. is not as mirrors reflect us but, rather, as our dreams do, that movies most uly reveal the times.* If the dreams we have been dreaming these past years

do not speak us happily, let it be remembered that—like that first book of Dante's three—they show forth only one region of the soul. Through them we may read, with a peculiar accuracy, the fears that beset us, the confusions; we may read, in caricature, that Hell in which we are bound; but we

* I am of course not the first to note it. See most especially Siegfried Kracauer's fine book on the German film, from CALIGARI TO HITLER.

may not read, more than glimmeringly, where hope for these times lies. That would be for another volume. The matter of such a volume could not be Hollywood.

That our films do reveal specifically this hapless side of us, is due not to any innate quality of the film medium but to the role the film makers have chosen. To give the public "what it wants" is how Hollywood describes its function. It is apt to announce, in answer to its critics: "The public dictates". Hollywood exaggerates its own passivity, yet there is in its statement something of the truth. It is true that it must meet the public "where it lives" The public must be able to identify with the heroes and heroines on the screen, able to imagine itself set down in the situations in which they are set down. But films may then so dramatise the motions of these heroes and heroines whom the public finds "sympathetic" as to illumine their situations, and the destiny in life they suffer; or they may relieve their yearnings, extricate them from their plights in comfortable fashion—supply the happy ending. It is in this latter sense, proverbially, that Hollywood chooses to provide for the public's wants—in this, of course, hardly alone among the "popular arts". Its films offer not that release of which Aristotle writes in THE POETICS, comfort akin to that of which the Bible speaks ("The truth shall make you free"), but another sort; they provide for the wants not of waking man but of the prostrate dreamer who, in sleep, would seek respite from the truth. They offer, as dreams often will, indulgence.

As with dreams, it is a veiled indulgence they offer. The fact is less obvious than with dreams, which frequently, if taken literally, make no sense at all (some films, to be sure, make almost as little sense) but the drama here, too, is a secret one. The glamor that movies hold for us is often said to reside in the thrill of identifying with creatures so unlike ourselves—of imagining ourselves, for an exalted hour or two, Humphrey Bogart (or one beloved by him), Ingrid Bergman (or one beloved by her), or similarly of imagining ourselves a millionaire, a musical genius, a jaunty gambler. The more crucial fact is easily ignored: that the conditions of life in which these screen figures are placed are ones which, in essence, the spectator knows too well. The heroes, heroines who are most popular, most glamorous at any particular period are precisely those who, with a certain added style, with a certain air of distinction, express that predicament in which we all find ourselves. But the movie goer need never admit to himself what is the real nature of the identification he experiences, what that condition really is from which he is being relieved, vicariously. Virgil describes the circles of Hell to Dante as that blind world where the good of the intellect has been surrendered. And so here with these other "lost people", whom the darkness of the movie theatre luxuriously encloses.

It is because Hollywood films are designed to gratify the public blindly that they can reveal little of what is hopeful for these times; they can reveal only those false hopes which, themselves, constitute our extremity. The policy of the industry is that each film should please, if possible, each of us; it should appeal to a common denominator of feeling. So one may add that in unsettled times like these, most especially, a common denominator is hard to find in terms of impulses to improve our plight. They are too diverse. It is to be found only in terms of a certain dim sense among us of that plight itself.

If the dreamers know only darkly what it is they dream, the men who weave these dreams know little more than they. They do consciously enough provide indulgence; for it pays. Those who argue that the public would put down its money only for this, perhaps belittle that public, which has been given little chance to prove the contrary; but to figure as the film makers do is to play safe; and, as in any mammoth industry, safety comes first in Hollywood. One can speak also of a political instinct here. Films which open no eyes, stir up no trouble. Like many another, this industry is not without its stakes in maintaining the status quo. (Within Hollywood ranks is to be found a variety of political opinion; yet all, more than they would like to admit, involve themselves in this conspiracy. The Committee on Un-American Activities need not really have excited itself about our movies.) These men consciously enough provide a blind indulgence. But their cunning at providing it is, itself, largely blind. The plight from which these dreams extricate hero or heroine is, I noted, disguised for us. The film makers may well protest having intend- ed this. But here is involved no art.

Rather, it takes art to know always what is the subject with which one is actually dealing. One may be shrewd to spot a subject of general appeal, and at the same time quite ignorant of the true nature of that appeal. The hero's happy extrication from the discomforts of reality is effected often by sleight of hand. The film makers may again protest that they were unaware of executing any such intricacies. Cunning of that sort need not be plotted; it is instinct. The least knowing among us cunningly enough delude ourselves. It takes again precisely art to avoid these motions, which, even when one attempts an honest representation of life, have a way of spontaneously intruding themselves.

If the nature of the medium does not dictate that films must offer this blind fare, and specialise in sleights of hand, it lends itself very especially to this. The audience at a movie plays a more passive role than at any other art, and so is in a more suggestible state. It is seated in darkness. The screen, the only source of light in this darkness, easily usurps attention. This is so of the lit stage at a play. But here is a difference. At a play, the eye of the spectator himself must move to follow the action. At a movie, the camera performs the work for the eye. It turns our heads for us, to follow some look or gesture; it squints for us more closely to note a detail. The camera is alert; we need not stir; our attention is quite literally rapt.

Sleight of hand is peculiarly possible for a further reason. A movie communicates both at the visual level and at the level of the word, and it is all too easy for it to distract us with words spoken, with a name given an event, while the underlying sensuous appeal it makes remains unacknowledged—and may have very little to do with these words. This is again possible in the theatre. And something very comparable is possible on the printed page—where the interpretation given events by an author may be belied by his actual evocation of these events. But in the movies it is so to a new degree, because of the freedom of the camera to range through the sensible world—and quite casually it would seem. (To those who make the films, it would seem casual, too; here is especial leeway for the involuntary.) It is quite possible for one in the audience to ridicule the film he has seen, point out glaring absurdities of plot, instances of complete illogic—and yet, in spite of himself, to have responded to this film very actively, at a less obvious level. A man can wake from a dream, too, and say: I just had the craziest dream; yet he has acquiesced, he has dreamed it.

For all that he laughs at it, the dreamer carries his dream with him through the day—unless he untangles it. This book attempts to untangle those dreams we have been buying, all of us, at the boxoffice, to cut through to the real nature of the identification we have experienced

there—to that image of our condition which haunts us, unrecognised by most of us, unacknowledged, yet hanging over our days.

Because it is a blind indulgence which they offer, our movies are hard to read in this fashion individually. But in unison they yield up their secrets. If one stares long enough at film after film, the distracting individual aspects of each film begin to dim, and certain obsessive patterns which underly them all take on definition. Film after film can be seen to place its hero in what is, by analogy, the identical plight——the dream then moving forward carefully to extricate him. From such a constellation of instances one may deduce a plight more general, sensed by the public (and by the public-minded film makers)— a condition which transcends the literal instance featured in any single film, though it need not deny any such instance its own validity.

The heart of this study has been the juxtaposition of many texts. And the number of films I have viewed in this way is a substantial one.* But the number of films I will actually cite is small. This is so for a reason. One who writes of the movies may never assume that the text he is discussing is a text common to him and to the reader. With the exception of certain favorites which do tend to be revived fitfully from year to year, films make their sudden multiple

---

* For 1942, 1943 and 1944, in the capacity of film analyst for the Library of Congress, I viewed a quarter of all features released. For 1945, 1946, 1947 and 1948, I viewed something less than this, but, in the basis of published synopses, carefully selecting what films I would see, with a view to missing no new trends.

With the exception of four films mentioned in passing, I talk in this book of no films I have not actually seen——and for those four I read either the script or a detailed synopsis. And I do not rely upon memory. At each film I took lengthy notes in shorthand——a very literal moment by moment transcription of the motions of the actors and of the camera, of dialogue, of sound effects. Quotations I make may not be verbatim but are very nearly so.

appearance upon the nation's thousand screens, and as suddenly fade from those screens. No comprehensive film library exists. The reader may not turn to a certain text at will. Even if the films were available, to consult a particular film is a more complex process than to pull a book from a shelf; but they are not even available. The Museum of Modern Art, in New York, has pioneered in this field, but its selection from any given year remains, appropriately enough, a limited one; and this collection stands as yet virtually alone. The Library of Congress in 1942 undertook to establish a national film library, but subsequently, Congress demurring, abandoned this project. Not even film scenarios are readily available. Even the Gassner-Nichols publication of " best film plays" for the year has been discontinued, after only three editions. There has been insufficient impulse among either the makers of the films or the public ' to review the substance of all these enchanted hours. It is the special task of the writer on films to provide the reader with some sort of substitute for that text to which he cannot turn, in some degree to evoke it for him, that he may judge for himself whether or not the pattern the writer discerns resides there in fact. And this one may do for a limited number of films only, if one would not tangle the reader in plot upon plot. Nor is it easy to examine certain films in detail but to refer to many more in passing, for as the real substance of a film lies never on the surface, it cannot be " noted briefly" If by the end of this book those analyses I do make

have seemed to the reader legitimate, and if those figures I trace in representative films of a variety of genres seem to compose a world that is consistent with itself—the one " Hell", really—it may perhaps be ventured that any other film chosen from the same years would contribute to that image.

My attempt in the chapters that follow is to give that world—that hapless image of ourselves—the boldest definition that I can, and to this end I shall omit certain references which might be included but which would make it more difficult to keep the image in focus. It would be interesting, for example, to refer along the way to other popular media, and especially where a film is derived from that source. But the image I would evoke is elusive, easily veils over. My concern is to hold steadily before the reader's eye this one complexity.

I offer no overt interpretation of this image. My conviction is that it stands alone; that if it is beheld not in fragments but in proper intricacy, then, like any poetic image, it wakes in the heart of the reader echoes more resonant than could any special interpretation one might offer. Such interpretations have their own justification, but that original totality remains always something more than the sum of all its readings.

The world that I evoke will not be startlingly new to the reader. Here is imagery that has been on the tongues of poets for some years past. But this is the special significance of the exploration of a mass medium: the poets are sensitive in advance of

others to the nature of the world in book covers, the populace as a whole
which they live, but here is evidence sensed in its bones.
of what at last. in the years this

April 1950

Layout of title page by Blair Stapp.

Picture credits (reading from top of the page and from left to right): Paramount Pictures (HAIL THE CONQUERING HERO), RKO Pictures (NONE BUT THE LONELY HEART), Warner Brothers (RHAPSODY IN BLUE), Warner Brothers (PRIDE OF THE MARINES), Metro-Goldwyn Picture Corp. (THE CLOCK), Warner Brothers (CASABLANCA), RKO Pictures (CORNERED), Selznick, Releasing Org. United Artists (SPELLBOUND), 20th Century Fox (DARK CORNER).

Remaining chapters of A LONG WAY FROM HOME *will be printed in subsequent issues of* CITY LIGHTS

ANNE LOUISE HAYES

decision

If choice might be in fact
The movement of the will
Once to the single act,

We might consent and stand;
Though we were human still,
We might be as we planned.

But this is not the case
What we have meant to do
Shifts, though we pray for grace,

Shifts, for the choosing soul
Is changed by each consent.
So we have shaped the whole

As, bit by bit, we choose,
Wondering what we meant,
Wondering what we lose.

JACQUES PRÉVERT

translations from *Paroles*

LAWRENCE FERLING

the dunce

He says no with his head
but he says yes with his heart
he says yes to what he loves
he says no to the teacher
he stands
he is questioned
and all the problems are posed
sudden giggles grip him
and he erases all
the figures and the words
the dates and the names
the phrases and the traps
and despite the threats of the master
to the howls of the infant prodigies
with chalk of every color
on the blackboard of misfortune
he draws the face of happiness.

school of fine arts

From a plaited basket
The father picked a little paper ball
And he threw it
In the bowl
Before his fascinated kids
Then sprang up
Multicolored
The great Japanese flower
Instantaneous water-lily
And the children were hushed
Wonderstruck
Never later in their memory
Could this flower fade
This sudden flower
Made for them
Instantly
Before them.

autumn

A horse collapses in the middle of an alley
Leaves fall on him
Our love trembles
And the sun too.

breakfast

He put the coffee
In the cup
He put the milk
In the cup of coffee
He put the sugar
In the café au lait
With the coffee spoon
He stirred
He drank the café au lait
And he set down the cup
Without a word to me
He lit
A cigarette
He made smoke-rings
With the smoke
He put the ashes
In the ash-tray
Without a word to me
Without a look at me
He got up
He put
His hat upon his head
He put his raincoat on
Because it was raining
And he left
In the rain
Without a word
Without a look at me
And I I took
My head in my hand
And I cried.

sunday

Between the rows of trees on the Avenue Gobelins
A marble statue leads me by the hand
Today is Sunday the cinemas are full
Birds on branches watch the humans
And the statue kisses me but nobody sees
Except a blind child who points at us.

one shouldn't

One shouldn't let intellectuals play
with matches
Because Gentlemen when left to itself
The mental world Gennntlemen
Isn't at all brilliant
And as soon as it's alone
Works arbitrarily
Erecting for itself
Out of so-called generosity in honor of
building-workers
an auto-monument
Let's repeat it Gennnntlemen
When left to itself
The mental world
Lies
Monumentally.

JOSEPH KOSTOLEFSKY

cupid at the burleycue

In yellow-slicker shoes with pointed toes,
A store-bought suit, bright-checkered, ample padding
Swathing the limbs Corinna found so fair,
In celluloid collar, rose-oil on my hair,
Dressed to the nines, the third man at a wedding,
I wait for the ritual taking-off of clothes.

Nor feel any shame that it should come to this:
Cupid, well-fleshed, with paunch as round as a plum,
The doted-on darling of gentle spinsters' dotage,
Primed for a tamed felicity in a cottage.
What wonder if the sounding brass goes dumb,
Or cracked lips prowl the track of Juno's kiss?

Why frown if Campaspe's nectar is Crackerjack,
Love's stately dance ground down to a hussy's grind?
Love had its chance, but tripped too quick a pace,
Demanded too much, beggared its store of grace.
Now all I feel is its nudging in my mind,
Its hobbled chargers panting at my back.

In swimming pool, in hospital, in jail, in debt, indemnified,
Marked with the scuffed insignia of loss,
Beauty is dead. On the runway her shadow stalks,
Her passing marked by bumps and dirty jokes,
Laid to rest with old shoestrings and dental floss,
And an old man's cough to praise her when she died.

Outside it drizzles. Footprints track the snow,
Trailing chilled beauty. Desire steams my collar.
I pant, an old man, chafing, dreaming of sun.
Down to essentials, the last veil comes undone.
Clasping that groin to my opera glass, I holler,
"Take it off, baby, off now. Go, girl, go!"

Two Views of *Limelight*

1. A Probing of Identity...

THROUGHOUT theatrical history it has been generally accepted that the true clown must be simply, totally funny regardless of how unhappy he might be and irrespective of what urge he might harbor to express an occasional serious comment on life.

As far back as *The Kid*, Chaplin has challenged this basic concept of the clown's role. He " 'as not known 'is plyce." as a good servant should. His is a strong ego which has preferred mastering a medium to " serving" a public.

Implied in most of his work is the question, "Must I always be funny?" With *Limelight* he brings this question out in the open and answers it with a resounding " No! "

He chooses for his central character Calvero, an aging music hall comic (he refers to him as a " comedian" , not a " clown", incidentally) who has lost his touch with audiences. Calvero can no longer be funny; his basic attitude towards life has become too serious. Unlike his creator, he lacks the inclination—and probably the. self-confidence—to attempt serious character roles and is one comedian apparently without the urge to play Hamlet. In terms of the need to eat and the need to create, this is an unfortunate situation for an actor. We suspect that Chaplin feels this way, too, and that his comment on

Calvero may be, " There but for the grace of God... "

For the purpose of showing us Calvero, Chaplin has reworked a situation familiar to us from previous films (such as *City Lights* and *Modern Times*): the hapless heroine befriended by the pathetic, funny little man. Previously the waif was a saccharine, one-dimensional character, misty and unresolved because she was forced to fulfill opposing functions: she was both a foil for Chaplin's clowning and the tool of his rebellion against a narrow definition of the clown's role. His rebellion is still there, but now he gives us Terry—a live, rounded character who invites our admiration and compassion without being in the least cloying. The waif is no longer a shadow standing between us and Chaplin's glorious comedy, but a necessary part of a serious drama.

The pathetic, funny little man— formerly at once smaller and larger than life-size—has also become a real and immensely likeable human being. Though it is Calvero who concerns us most, only in the light of his relationship to Terry can we understand the film's philosophical meaning. Terry's suffering and her love for Calvero point up his acute sense of life made tragic by an awareness of failure, decay, imminent death. Hers is a youthful suffering, the young's perpetual search for life's meaning. His is a knowledge born of experience and a stale, almost comfortable misery. "Life is not a meaning, but a desire," he tells her.

Though he knows this in a general way, his is the tragedy of a man never sufficiently acquainted in a deep, highly personal sense with his own specific needs and desires. He is disintegrating because he has not solved the riddle of his own identity. "Who am I? What am I, clown or philosopher?" These questions, implied throughout the film, confuse him. He drinks to solve the conflict—to weight himself temporarily on the side of comedy, for without liquor he cannot trust himself to be funny. ("I'm alwaysh funny when I'm drunk.") Neither can he be wholly serious for more than a few moments at a time without self-mockery and self-slighting getting the better of him. In contrast to Terry, he will not permit himself to sound the depths of his suffering. He can neither give up the compulsive necessity to be funny nor accept himself as a basically serious man. Unlike certain real-life clowns (Bert Lahr, for example), he cannot even settle for being serious off-stage and comic on-stage. His professional and personal lives have become intermingled in such a way that both suffer. He lives suspended between laughter and tears. His self-mockery appears, then, as a brutal weapon used against himself rather than as any magnificent defense against the world.

Chaplin's technique for showing us Calvero's self-mockery is an old one of his, that of breaking a serious mood with a sudden thrust of comedy. In his earlier films a pathetic moment is followed by a longer, often boisterous comic bit—such as the slapstick brawl in *The Kid* which breaks the mood of " the little tramp's" woeful anxiety over the threatened loss of his " adopted" son.

Despite the many serious scenes in Chaplin's films, the funny scenes have been more numerous and of longer duration. But in *Limelight* the old technique undergoes a shift of emphasis. The serious moments are longer and more frequent, and the amusing ones have more the effect of a pinprick than a jab.

This basic technique has two variations in the film; one forces us to wonder how seriously Calvero is meant to be taken, the other, how seriously he takes himself. When we first see him, he is drunk—and drunks are always good for a laugh. But more than that, he is obviously amused, not distressed, by his condition. In this opening scene, the variations of the comic technique are merged: we laugh at him; he laughs at himself. In subsequent scenes, the variations are usually used separately, and the one designed to reveal him laughing at himself predominates.

He frequently manifests a flip attitude towards himself: he is too casual about having had five wives; he comes perilously close to travesty when he conjures up the facile dream of how Terry will be reunited with her " true love" ; he has a way of ending a serious comment with a quip; he himself (not just the audience) is aware of the comic juxtaposition of breakfast kippers and morning philosophizing.

In a few scenes Calvero is a figure of fun only for the audience—such as

the scene in which his earnest prayer for Terry's success is interrupted by a stagehand's removal of the scenery behind which he is kneeling. Yet— although Calvero is not mocking himself at this moment, he is shown as being unable to pray openly and unabashedly; he is a little ashamed of his strong feelings.

This inability to follow through on his own deep emotions; the constant need to cover them when they have reached an uncomfortable intensity; the compulsion towards the comic— these may explain why Calvero did not make an effort to become a serious character actor after he lost his ability to make audiences laugh. It is a final irony that he recovers his touch only with the aid of liquor and with death staring from his eyes. When he suffers the fortuitous heart attack, he is freed from the inner obligation to repeat his last, unrepeatable success. And by dying he has gained the only legitimate entry into the tower which lies beyond both comedy and tragedy.

The question, " Must I always be funny?" was destructive for Calvero in a way that it has not been for Chaplin. Calvero's comic genius suffered from a compulsive quality which defeated him both on-stage and off and prevented him from finding answers to the larger questions, " Who am I and to what committed?"

" Must I always be funny?" has haunted Chaplin for years—a persistent inner voice. Even in his early works he found his comic materials among the tragic litter of life: poverty, illness, alcoholism, loneliness. At first, despite their basic seriousness, he used his materials in the interest of being " simply, totally funny".

As the inner voice grew in volume, he incorporated undisguised pathos into his films, and with *Modern Times*, *The Great Dictator*, and *M. Verdoux* he added increasingly articulate social comment. (In the case of the latter, he met with strenuous opposition from the public, who felt that the comment was, if anything, antisocial. Certainly the vindictive final scene in the courtroom was jarringly out of tone with the rest of the picture.) *Limelight* is an attempt to resolve, in artistic terms, the conflict engendered by Chaplin's persistent preoccupation with " Must I always be funny?" In contrast to his Calvero, he does not leave the question hanging by a retreat into a neither/ nor state of being—but meets it head-on. The picture itself is a stirring negative answer to the question, " Must I always be funny?" — which is the specific for the general question implied in it, " Who am I and to what committed?" Out of the artist's own conflict and concern with these questions has come the stuff of renewed creative effort. The theatre is for him " an escape into life".

Chaplin is most surely committed in the deepest sense to the theatre, in a way Calvero could not be. (Perhaps Calvero is an embodiment of a shadowy, residual fear of noncommitment.) In *Limelight* Chaplin makes often self-conscious, always artistic use of several theatrical arts for the purpose of exploring a personal (but also universal) problem of identity. His capacity for prodigious effort, his enormous skill, and his intensity of feeling testify to a basically whole-hearted and serious (as opposed to a frivolous) approach to the art of the film, and beyond that, to life itself.

2. Some Notes on Chaplin's *Limelight*

PAULINE KAEL

A REMARK overheard: " I don't care if he is a genius. I don't like that man. "

If the audiences which attend *Limelight* in San Francisco are an adequate sampling of Chaplin's American public, he now attracts a somewhat segmented art-film audience. This is not the same audience he used to play to—but the reasons are considerably more complex than the " complicated" ones Calvero indicates to explain why the headless monster turned against him.

The majority audience (if some cleavage is necessary, let us say roughly the people who voted for Eisenhower) resents him partly for political reasons, partly for moral ones, and, more basically, because he appears in the guise of genius. When the mass audience became convinced that the clown who had made them laugh was really an artist, they felt betrayed. This is the same audience which turned Garbo into an object of ridicule when her beauty and distinction raised her to an eminence they could not tolerate. Then she, too, became the adored beauty of the minority.

The minority audience was always fascinated by the stills which revealed the beauty of Chaplin—the depth and expressiveness beneath the tramp make-up; the majority was perfectly satisfied with the mask of comedy. In a chance glimpse we thought we perceived a tragic countenance under the mask. Now Chaplin has given us too long a look—the face has been held in camera range for prolonged admiration—and the egotism of his self-revelation has infected the tragic beauty. The illusion, the mystery are gone—and with them possibly a good section of the minority audience as well. It is difficult not to be interested in what Chaplin will do next, but the bated breath has acquired a faint wheeze.

* * *

Oddly enough, for all the mind and sophistication attributed to Chaplin, the hero of *Limelight* is surprisingly like the conceptions of the artist held by the vast American film audience (although this audience suspects, and quite rightly, that there are other elements...). *Limelight* is just as sentimental and high-minded about life and theatre as show people might wish. Possibly theatre people will see it as true and beautiful, just as so many Jews saw *The Great*

Dictator as an awesome achievement. (Just as an analyst friend thought *Mourning Becomes Electra* the greatest film ever made.)

It is dubious, however, that Chaplin can regain the mass audience with this film: the suspicion that he is not a regular fellow is fairly widespread, and the simplicity of the film is pompous enough to mislead neighborhood audiences into thinking it is that abhorrence—art.

* * *

Chaplin's range as an actor is quite probably as wide as he thinks it is, but his range as a creative intelligence is certainly considerably less. He is almost the only man who is in a position to use the film medium for a personal statement. (It is questionable if other creative film-makers would wish to do so: his aim may be as unique as his opportunity). His ideas and personality have pervaded his last three films. *Verdoux* remains fascinating, impudent enough to make one toss overboard some minor reservations. Mercifully in *Verdoux* the ideas are not nearly so explicit as in *The Great Dictator* and *Limelight* where the failures of taste and creative insight are alternately embarrassing and infuriating.

As Robert Duncan remarked, "It would have taken W.C. Fields spitting into Calvero's passed hat to restore the comic genius."

The Chaplin of *Limelight* is no irreverent little clown; his reverence for his own ideas would be astonishing even if the ideas were worth consideration. They are not—and the context of the film exposes them at every turn. The exhortations in the directions of life, courage, consciousness, and "truth" are set in a story line of the most self-pitying and self-glorifying daydream variety. Calvero's gala benefit in which he shows the unbelievers who think him finished that he is still the greatest performer of them all, his death in the wings as the applause fades——this is surely the richest hunk of gratification since Huck and Tom attended their own funeral. It was humor in Twain's day; Chaplin serves it at face value a hundred years later.

Calvero is not a little tramp who happily wins his waif or pitiably loses her. Calvero *renounces* his waif and renunciation carries a certain amount of prestige. Of course it was all "Platonic" anyway. Terry does however carry conviction when she says he loves him——we suspect she wouldn't love him if it weren't Platonic. For this Terry is the embodiment, the incarnation almost, of the recurrent Chaplin heroine—even to the name, Claire Bloom. Surely she has produced herself out of the same wonder and daydream from which Chaplin has drawn his images of the lovely waif. She is a very serious young actress and she moves with authority—she knows she is the real thing.

In early Chaplin films two babes-in-the-wood met. Calvero, though just as pure and innocent in heart, represents the wisdom and experience of age—and hence renounces Terry. Somehow, whether intentionally or not, we are not made to feel that any great sacrifice is involved. It's as though genius has removed the necessity for human relations. Chaplin has composed a curious idyll of the sexes, replete with a second pure-in-heart young lover for Terry in the person of his son. The Svengali-Trilby theme is presented not for horror, not for satire, not even for laughs, but just *straight;* Calvero is enobled by imparting strength to Trilby and still has it both ways, emerging himself triumphant as an artist.

* * *

Chaplin was a great comedian, but the demonstrations of Calvero's stage routines are, despite amusing and hilarious moments, rather mediocre. This is difficult to account for. Robert Hatch, in an otherwise excellent review in *The Reporter*, suggests that the acts " are deliberately not very good because comedians like Calvero were not very talented and their material was shabby even in 1914." This is ingenious but it doesn't fit the idea content of the film, nor can it account for the worse than mediocre ballet, performed presumably during the great days of Diaghilev period. The mediocrity is scarcely intentional; on the contrary, it seems the not uncommon result of aiming at greatness.

Calvero is meant to be great allright. When he awaits Terry in the darkened theatre after her dance and says, "My dear, you are a true artist, a true artist," this is intended as " the shock of recognition." The camera emphasis on Chaplin's eyes, the emotion in his voice are intended to give depth to his words. This

ghastly mistake in judgment and taste—
this false humility which proclaims
his own artistry in the act of asserting another's—this is not a simple
mistake. It is integral to the creative mind which produces a *Limelight*.

* * *

Chaplin apparently is not content
with the ideas which can be realized
in comedy performance; nor is he
content with the subtle riddles posed
in *Verdoux*. He wants a wider range:
he wants to *state* his ideas about
life. The Sunday thinker is likely
to think he knows some " truths"
that people should be told and more
than likely he'll make an ass of
himself in the telling. It is several
thousand years since Socrates investigated the minds of artists and
concluded that " upon the strength of
their poetry they believed themselves
to be the wisest of men in other
things in which they were not wise. "

* * *

The Sunday composer who is in the
position to have his music written
down for him, orchestrated, and even
performed, is a rare bird indeed.
The layman's desire to appear as a

great composer is no less grandiose
than Chaplin's score. Significantly,
his derivations are not from the
moderns, but from the popular masters
of the 19th century, the patron
geniuses of Hollywood music. If we
compare his music to a typical Hollywood score, it sounds indistinguish-
able from others. But this is not the
comparison he invites——and if we
take him on his own terms and compare
his score to an interesting film
score, to Auric, Honneger, Prokofiev,
or Walton, for example, Chaplin dis-
appears from discussion.

One wonders what Chaplin makes of
the developments in his own medium in
the last half-century. Though a contemporary of Griffith, he is also a
contemporary of Dreyer, of Cocteau of
Carne and Renoir, of Bunuel and De
Sica, of Carol Reed, Huston, Mankiewicz.
The full measure of the dismal failure
of *Limelight* comes when we place it
against its contemporaries. We have
been told that Chaplin is a man of
wide culture, but *Limelight* might be
the work of the fabled young man who
was afraid to read a book for fear it
would spoil his originality.

WALDEMAR OLAGUER

Three Poems

the alien

Straight out of China walked this wanderer
Into a nest of relative fools. He was thin,
Suffering from miasma, brittle as a river reed:
And they denied him his tall ambition.
Age was the matter with him. They inquired into
Origins,—the century's curse, asked bright
Questions about his head, his heart, and other facts
That covered an entire biography.

Born of the everlasting East, they really did not see
What to declare of him; yet, if judging by the
Four distinct humours of the Medeival Mind, you know
He's warmly mingled of sanguine with melancholic.

Chart the fever of his ascent to freedom,
Deduce the inner picture to its closest premise,
Send him out with complacent best wishes, until
Broken within, he chokes with tears and numbers,
And recalls dead Camelot and ruthless Carthage;
But having closed the gates, you only prove human laws
A mockery. Now witness a heart's dying.

On reaching the dank and dismal room, he takes
The old machine, and renewal in his ageless eyes,
Indites a warm entreaty to the Pentagon.

pledger's monologue

" Why are people so divided on me? Some reverence me;
Others don't, they revile this satyr behind
The bachelor facade. Say, what's the idea anyway, of
Making me a controversial guy, when I have been—"
The telephone. He goes to answer it. (Connoisseurs' conversation.)
It is an honest man's apartment. Cozy chairs. Antiques.
A clock which ticks efficiently. There is a signed
Sepia picture of Gehrig on the harpsichord.
And all the novels of James T. Farrell.
" Why, I have been quite forward with my life,
That is, made no pretenses, taken everyone
At market value." He looks unbelievable in the
Twilight: he has matured morally in fifteen months of this.
" Pledger is sound. He's sane, a mixture maybe of
Something slightly devilish, bits of the rake;
Considered aesthetics, but he's not a romanticist.
I remember the time contralto Caveney sang here,
Tremendous ovation; with everybody gone
We had a nice personal duet, in the bedroom. What was that
Evidence of? My passions or my pastimes?
Take Guy Manso and that thoughtless evening:
We drove to Carmel, took a swim. The motor accident;
His arm fractured, and at home, while
Guy was in Dante's hell, I calmly played at solitaire.
We're still friends. The boy must recognize my heavy streaks.
I had a dull childhood; puberty was worse, but they had
Their mellow moments; for I took my glaring poverty,
And outbalanced that with developing my gifts;
And though no da Vinci, I am old Pledger,
Many-faceted, serene, obvious to the touch,
Unknown to science, Maecenas to the arts.
The accretions of a life well-spent surround me:
Baseball, beer and babes. Sometimes, admittedly,
I'd exchange Blake for some Pabst, young hours with
A tavern floozie..." A cat howls from afar,
The clock reads eight—the number's
Meaningful. Old Pledger yawns decisively,
Turns a page of poetry, and blinks.

" Time to let in Hannibal. He's probably cold out there,
And he'll want a saucer of milk, if he hasn't
Caught mice. Ah, such is existence,
The present that combines eternity with time,
When one is quite the kaleidoscopic vertebrate
I am. Here Hannibal, here Hannibal..."

minerva remarks on pledger

Orpheus in Hades couldn't be more tragic
Than this rejected, grieving swain,
Lost over a dubious woman named Maisie;
He takes to intellectual games, like calculus, for
Ease from pain, winds up star-gazing
Through the winter night. What's he, and
Where is his direction? Minerva answers...
" A sensitive instrument,—a cello which, twanged
Carefully gives absolute music one always listens to.
I'd use him for my oracle, if he knew Latin,
Had an elegiac property of voice; but Pledger,
Brought up on hardness, deadened to basic dignities,
Despises ritual. He'd make an excellent artisan
Carving marbles with sure character; or else
A conscientious athlete. I've seen him, at one
Stretch, win forty-three card games
Without moral wavering; and at the end express
Boredom at the symmetry of constant winning.
There is both the ape and the dove in his blood;
Pursuing their separate identities."

" But of his footsteps, I do not know;
All wisdom from Olympus fails me.
These are some of the best pieces that are
Pledger; scattered in their brilliance, sitting
In strange niches—food for himself in solitude,
All contrary one to the other, and

Unreconciled; of which the clashing center is the universe,
And the chaotic ending is the sea. "

Witness Again:

A Critical Donnybrook
Concerning Marjorie Farber's "Witness: to What?"

1. The Squeeze Play

LESTER HAWKINS

IF WE could neatly single out acts for praise or blame, then we should be grateful to Whittaker Chambers for revealing the espionage activities of Communist agents in America. But actions form a dynamic sequence, and when we consider the use Chambers has made of his evidence for Republican propaganda and against the free use of the intelligence, we must conclude that he has only helped deliver us from one enemy to hand us over to a not very different one. I was surprised to discover that precisely these aspects of Chambers' book most pleased Marjorie Farber.* I had never suspected that she thought this was

much of a time for adopting an embarrassingly outspoken sentimentality in the place of analysis and a " standard as simple as stepping into the dark" in the place of statistics. To me, all of the literary and moral aspects of Chambers' book are undeniable corn. But, as usual in these cases, we are not so much sickened by the sentiment as by what goes with it. The chorus of sweet moral voices is growing... What is it they are trying to say?

We must face it. This is no longer the innocent talk of an Oxford Movement—to that it is only akin in its flabbiness; this is dead serious. Like Stalin, these people are playing

---

*Marjorie Farber: " Witness to What?" *City Lights*, Oct., 1952.   Mrs. Farber does not mention that Chambers' " profoundly religious" document comes to earth now and then to praise the F.B.I., the munitions makers, Luce, Nixon, etc., and to damn the C.I.O., the N.L.R.B., the Welfare State, the State Department, etc.

for keeps. The challenge of our time, says Whittaker Chambers, a great admirer of Toynbee as we know from his notorious articles in *Time*, is to make this a century of great religious wars instead of social upheavals.

Mrs. Farber, like Chambers, thinks that the present situation is rigidly bound to two alternatives—*either* a religion of personal morality *or* communism. This statement is then made to equal: *either* an anti-communist crusade *or* communism. The first pair of alternatives—religion or communism—would leave many of us in a void. Most thinking people I know find the idea of God flatly contradictory, and, if He does not exist, it seems pointless to "imagine ourselves creating" Him. However, the second way of stating the choices—an anti-communist crusade or communism—we can recognize as the basic analysis accepted by the Republican party. In other words, although we may not know what people mean by ",God", we can often find out what they intend to do in His name.

The Anti-Intellectual

SHALL THE intellectual knowingly embrace McCarthyism? Could he, in fact, do so? Mrs. Farber seems to think he can, and her reasons for thinking so are to be found, at least in part, in her type of analysis of our relations to the world. I believe that her method tends to dictate its own peculiar conclusions, and since it is a method that has become increasingly fashionable in this country in recent years, it must be taken seriously.

The method consists of a continual referral to some fancied internal dynamism of the human being. Statements about the world become psychic forces that live a curiously expanding life of their own, and, so transformed, they work inevitably and relentlessly both in history and the individual. A progress of values and emotions is described without reference to the situations that called them forth, and we are urged to look within to find Good, Evil, Guilt, and other master keys to our predicament. Thus, historical materialism is an Evil that inevitably issues in the horrors of the totalitarian state because it poisons our values; to refuse the church is still to find oneself unconsciously playing out a religious rite; to concern oneself with civil liberties at this time is symptomatic of an internal force that will surely land us in the Communist party. Our analyses of our situations, our reasons for our acts, and our stated ends have nothing to do with the case; either we embrace the Good or we find ourselves solidly "in" with the Evil.

How do we know this? By examining our hearts. Unfortunately, however, the examination does not remain within the heart, for it gives us not only judgments about hearts but about situations as well. By throwing the issues into this internal mill, what is gained? The life is squeezed out of them and we are left with dogmatic pap.

Mr. John Strachey has pointed out that the anti-communist Crusaders strangely resemble the communists. Both are, he says, Absolutists, and he might have added, dogmatists. Both define the world anti-historically by reference to Good and Evil. To the hysterical anti-communist the free intellectual is "tainted" with communism, just as to the communist he is "tainted" with "Trotzkyism" or "Bourgeois reversion". Every thinking person today is experiencing something of the great squeeze play of the Absolutists. You are told that you are "really" a communist if you are a liberal thinker, yet who have the communists killed off in their purges and betrayals if not the relatively free intellectuals? To the communist, the intellectual is a traitor to be eliminated; "Ike" has promised that he too will boot out the "intellectual elite". Even the artist is experiencing the squeeze; the communists want an art of social realism, and Archibald MacLeish wants an "art that will help us survive". The absolutists of both sides agree that they have found the bedrock final answers to our predicament and that this is the time for action, not for thought.

There are many other similarities between the communists and the crusaders, but one stands out as important above all others and perhaps fateful for our civilization. These are people who see only menaces; they are the Paranoids. Reasoning as they do by symptoms and willingly creating an atmosphere of trials, confessions, and betrayals, what else can we call them? They want all

their enemies, both real and imaginary, to confess their "errors". An enlightened society does not expect its criminals to confess, but attempts to prove them guilty. Why did the Inquisition force its witches to confess? Because there was no other way of proving that they had been riding on broomsticks. No one expected Al Capone to confess and no one went around the Italian slums looking for potential Al Capones to put in jail. As for the intellectual, the only "error" he can confess is that he has not always been liberal and intellectual enough. We must not recreate the Moscow trials in America.

We misunderstand the paranoid if we assume that his fears are all unreal. Rather, what is peculiar about him is his fascination with a menace— perhaps very real—to the exclusion of all else and his consequent failure to erect a constructive position of his own. The German phenomenologist, Scheler, has spoken of the "sheerly negative" man, the man of resentment who defines himself by a continual "no". The man who is only "against" is a man who lives in fear and is too neurotic to think, although he may spend time trying to. Unable or unwilling to analyze situations, afraid of all change, he lives a perpetually regressive life, bound to a vanishing past. In place of analysis and well-defined ends, he offers us a mass of uninformed, changeable and often exceedingly dangerous recommendations. Use the atom bomb, invade China, quick! get the hydrogen bomb, route them, stall them off, arm the Germans, on the other hand get out of Western Europe because they'll take it anyhow. We are beginning to see first hand why some of the greatest crises in history have been fumbled by idiots and children.

What we must ask the fanatic and paranoid is, does he have any consistent plans for our own welfare and our foreign policy? Does he know economics and does he have any plans, other than anti-plans, for our internal economy? In general, what kind of ends does he have in mind for the American nation and the human race? But he cannot answer these questions, not reasonably at least. In all probability he is too busy saying, Roosevelt got us into this mess; we should have known that Japan and Germany were not our true enemies; we have been listening to a bunch of Reds and Pinks.

What I have been describing is a mentality that is perhaps understandable in a professional bigot or a remarkably ignorant general. But why should it be recommended by intellectuals—or, rather, ex-intellectuals? What part of their situation has made them victims of fear and negativity? The only answer to these questions I know is that the situation of our time is tough and not a little confusing. Many people prefer to retire within themselves; they are Seekers after Salvation. Now this *is* something we have no time for, this search for the impossible.

The anti-intellectualism of our time is familiar enough; practically all human thought has been accom-

plished in conditions very much like it, if seldom quite so severe. It's not very amusing to have to go back to fundamentals again instead of getting on with things, but I suppose it will be necessary so long as there are people around who don't seem to know why we think, or why we think freely, at all.

The Intellectual

OUR FIRST job is to define the intellectual, i.e. a person who thinks at least part of the time. The fact is that most of our ideas about him have lost their force, not because they are so often repeated— they are usually taken for granted, but because they no longer apply. In addition, academic empiricism, with its bias toward a dead and desert world of neutral "verifiable" bodies, has portioned out this world, the only one it knows, to the various special sciences. From the empirical standpoint, there is no place for the thinker who attempts to name our situation and sketch its ends, because from this position the idea that we are in the first instance involved in a living and situated relation to things is unintelligible. In this view, our involvement in our situation and our efforts to bring its ends to light become "value judgments", i.e. statements which are useless to guide behaviour since they are non-verifiable and non-descriptive and are themselves only behaviour. These "values" cling to human beings like properties to things. In other words, for the empirical scientist human behaviour becomes an object for thought only when viewed by another and when its living implications are past and therefore dead. If we take this position, the intellectual becomes a mere amateur scientist. But the difficulty then would not only be to restitute to the thinker his functions, but to reconstitute the most ordinary functions of living.

We are, however, always functioning and always in a situation. This means, as the German philosopher, Heidegger, has said, that things are first present to us as things of use, grouped into situations by a mass of instrumental connections. The tool nature of things is not grafted onto "sense-data". It confronts us as an immediate concern, and the very being both of our emotions and the matters of which they are composed is intrinsically purposeful and projectful. The "thing-tools" that compose our situation have a forward throw; to understand this future potential of the things of our world is to discover and fix their meaning. In short, we find ourselves continually in immediate situations which are felt about and cared for, and which always present us with new possibilities. To proceed in this manner is to go beyond the specialized sciences. Our "field" is already prepared for us in each instance of thought, and we are made aware of it by the anxieties and felt evasions present in the predicament given us by history.

For example, if our situation is that of a great depression, as it was in the '30's, then we may be forced to examine economics, and we may borrow heavily from the technical thought of economists and sociologists. The economist may have recommendations, but when it comes to dealing with that area of practice which consists of ends-means questions and which is, by empirical standards, partly economic, partly political, partly sociological, partly psychological and partly moral, then we find ourselves in the special field of the intellectual, or of the economist or sociologist now acting as intellectual. Here, in other words, we are not only concerned with "scientific" material, but also with ends and the perennial human attempt to comprehend that total synthesis of our situation in which, knowingly or unknowingly, we are involved in all our emotions and acts. This is an effort with which the artist, in his special way, is also concerned. It is an effort that goes beyond science, as Marjorie Farber suggests, but it is not therefore mystical.

The situation which is given to the intellectual is contingent; he didn't make it, but found himself in it. This is not true, however, of his ends, which are ways of assuming a situation based on a free analysis of it. The ends are, in other words, the supreme moment in the function of our intelligence; they are not value judgments which simply form parts of our nature as various value theories would have us believe. To subscribe to certain ends is to make a stand in a situation, and to make a stand is to be prepared to defend ourselves with analyses and repeated references to those ingredients of our situation that most people refer to when they talk about "hard facts".

Thus, for example, the intellectual may have a sentiment of equality based on the repeated observation that only when human beings are content to treat each other as equals can the spectacle of their relations be free of the more nauseating types of bad faith. Of course, statements about ends can be misleading and can indicate inadequate analyses. But all statements are addressed to others and it is in the process of discourse that we must hope that the true ends-sketching, situation naming activity will emerge.

Thus, acting, knowing, and the setting of ends are related processes. We must continually re-define our situation and in the process continually remake ourselves. To acquiesce in the already established and already defined is not to eliminate the necessity of forging new definitions and finding new ends, but to evade our changing predicament and to invite regression, confusion, and sterility.

One could perhaps imagine a society in which there was no specialized function for the intellectual, not because of an absolute hegemony of specialized science—the empirical sciences could never take this role, but because everyone could become what we now think the intellectual to be. Such a society would consist of thinking individuals, all of whom had a minimal knowledge for carrying on a continuous and free discourse; it would need no heroes to make its

decisions. This is admittedly utopian, but it is an ideal for training and the remodeling of our institutions; no society can be totalitarian if its individual members demand the right to know and to suggest.

As things stand, however, the bigot is anti-intellectual and the uninformed citizen is non-intellectual. The intellectual, when he is an intellectual, i.e. when he thinks clearly and is not just a failing victim, is always involved in searching for new solutions and is, by definition, a liberal, in the only clear meaning I can see for the term. His eyes are not looking within or in the dark; his ends come from a situation and refer back to it. The bigot relies on what Marx has called an ideology, i.e. a set of ideas which are no longer applicable but are used in lieu of analysis and in bad faith. Self-interest is scarcely the word for the bigot. In a sense, the intellectual is also self-interested; it is always his own anxiety he is trying to name. If he "generalizes", he is not making a special ethical effort so much as searching for true causes and adequate descriptions. This attempt to understand our conditions would never be questioned if it were not for the difficulties created by the bigot. We do not think in order to become martyrs to truth, but simply to know.

"We"

I WAS TOTALLY bewildered by Marjorie Farver's portrait of the liberal intellectual and her various uses of the rhetorical "we". Among other things, a liberal intellectual is never a "communist dupe." As part of knowing his situation, he makes it his business to know the communist party line; he knows where it stands and he knows where he stands. He knows its motives and ends and he knows his own. If he takes a position like that of the communists, as in the popular front of 1935 or on a Jim Crow issue today, he knows exactly what he is doing. If he changes his stand, it is because the situation has changed, not because Moscow has given him an order.

An intellectual did not "wake up" in 1938 as Mrs. Farber did and find that half the world was communist. On the contrary, he was following and worrying about the events in China and Czechoslovakia. He knew, in 1946 for example, that Chiang Kai Shek was an incompetent ally and an unpopular oligarch. Mrs. Farber should realize that if we are to understand the events of the past, we must analyze them in terms of what made them situations when they occurred. Otherwise our analysis is playing checkers with time and we can then say that Roosevelt ought to have... or "we" ought to have...in a way that has no meaning. Statements like, "We ought to have stopped the Reds in China" are not legitimate opinions since they do not imply a full analytic appraisal of a situation.

Likewise, a liberal intellectual has never possibly been "wrong" while the editors of *Time* have been "right". I can see no way in which

Luce could have arrived at the "right" position with his methods. Reasoning like Marjorie Farber we could say that, earlier than Luce, Goebbels was "right" about the "communist menace". However, can we possibly think that either Goebbels or Luce have given us that kind of total response to a total situation that we can accept? For the total situation of man, what counts is not the kind of prediction any fool can make, but a total analysis. We are forced to judge Luce's anti-communism against the taste and intelligence generally displayed in *Time*; only in this way can we find out what communism means to him and how his anti-communism differs from our own.

Most particularly, I found Mrs. Farber's estimate of 1948 as the peak year of American liberalism extra-ordinarily strange. I don't remember anyone then calling for the nationalization of steel or the P.G.&E., but I do remember that this was when some of us began to worry about the methods of the F.B.I.

Finally, I don't think "we" were ever so complacent nor ever ever so completely political as Marjorie Farber suggests. Most of my thinking friends have often had their attention forced onto the problems of their own artistic and other non-political projects and the narrow concerns of a disastrous marriage or a difficult job. They have thought, if anything, almost too much about the issues of personal morality and the unaccountable ways of love. Above all, they have had an enforced sense of humor;

most of them have laughed themselves
half crazy over all these things.

The Situation in 1953

WHAT IS the present political situation of the American intellectual?
One part of the answer, at least, is
clear. Since he cannot possibly join
either the Communist or Republican
parties, he must concentrate exclusively on a third alternative. Since
there is danger of war for reasons
that do not depend on him, he must
support drives against treason, but
he must also make a stand for freedom.
Unlike the bigots, he will not confuse
these issues. He must try, in other
words, to prevent backward senators,
grandiose-minded military leaders, the
Peoria Women's Club, and all other
boobs from using the drive against
espionage as an excuse for stamping
out freedom in this country. Very
few people in Washington can define
a communist and many of those who can
are, unfortunately, willing to mistake
liberal thought for a " symptom" of
the evil. The difficulty is made
greater by the fact that the intellectual has a duty to this country
to be subversive by Republican standards. After all, the prime reason he
is not a communist or a Republican is
that he prefers and needs freedom, and
if he is going to have it, he must use
it for what it is for—for a change.

Every liberal intellectual favors
some revision of our economy from a
strangling oligopoly toward some kind
of more democratic control, whether in
the direction of socialism, syndical-
ism, or a more limited corporate
enterprise. This is his platform

because he wants greater freedom and
a more responsible morality. He has,
however, the glaring example before
him of the failure of an ostensible
socialism in Russia, just as, I might
add, he had an instance of failure of
corporate enterprise in Germany and
Italy.

I think that any theory of the
causes of the Soviet failure and any
assessment of the Marxist movement
ought to start from the fact that
Marx, living in democratic England, so
trusted the liberal institutions of
his day that he neglected to write a
political theory. That had been done
by the enlightenment. He concentrated
his attention almost exclusively on
the economic forces that threatened to
undermine the principles of these
institutions and sap their meaning.
Today, we can see that a political
theory is even more important than an
economic one; but that was not part of
Marx's situation. His eyes saw only
an economy that drove toward imperial
expansion, the wholesale exploitation
of labor and depressions every ten
years. Economic laws were to Marx
what repressed instincts were to
Freud; they were forces working in the
dark to the ruin of the individual and
society, and they had to be brought to
light. Marx saw rightly that those
who claimed that the facts of economics were those of nature, not to be
changed, were inconsistent. We do
often study nature to change it. If
we study a flood, for example, it is
to construct dikes against it; if we
study the currents of the economy, it
is because they are flowing against us
and we must divert them.

Unfortunately, Marx was fascinated by the wealth of material he un-earthed. He came to think that the cure of capitalist contradictions was the entire cure of society and that a scientific study of them would dictate our historical course. This view was mistaken and led the later Marx to an irate dogmatism. Still, I cannot think that he defaulted his situation in anything like the degree of those who, faced with putting his recom-mendations into practice, failed to devise adequate and humane means for doing so. Having accepted Marx as dogma, without a political theory and without liberal inventiveness, Russian communists went from expediency to expediency and finally ended in para-noid fear and bigotry. This danger, however, is open to us all. We are always under the obligation to sup-plant new patterns and analyses for old ones before the old ones kill us off. As Kant remarked, civilization is a race against time.

The problems of democracy remain, despite the Russian question and the threat of war. If a marked amount of decadence, a substantial percentage of our crimes (including "white collar" crimes,) and much of our anxiety is attributable to the conditions created by capitalism, they remain so at-tributable regardless of the kinds of evil the Russians have created. If the N.A.M. tells lies, they are still lies. After the Russian revolution came Stalin and after the French revolution came Napoleon. Neither of these facts justifies the treatment of labor as a commodity and the re-pression of freedom for fear of a

worse evil.

There have always been many of us who have been highly impatient of the "lesser evils" of liberal reform measures like the F. E. P. C., the minimum wage, and the various acts of the British Labor Government. Our present circumstance being what it is, however, I see no alternative but to work in these directions, although I also think it highly important to continue to plan more radical changes, for which the need is desperate.

The immediate problem is consider-ably more grave if we consider the backward nations overseas. If we do not use our privileged position in the world today to stand for equality, for reform of the *latifundia* and for help toward industrialization, then we shall continue to lose friends to communism.

In sum, I think the main factors in our present political predicament are the threat of war, the failure of Russian Marxism, the threat to our freedom, our need for allies and the inequality and regimentation of our own society. What do these mean, taken together, i.e. as a situation? That totally dislocating change is out of the question, but that standing still is disastrous. I think that the intellectual today is, in this sense, a reformist. Tomorrow will be a different matter, a different situation.

Thought and Feeling

TO MARJORIE Farber, the world sharply divides into fact and feeling, the objective and the subjective. On the one hand is science, the arid art of politics and the rational; on the other is the very real world of values within. This dichotomy is, in one form or another, well known in the history of Western thought. On the one side are the rigid metaphysicians—Descartes, Leibnitz, Hume, Kant, Hegel; on the other are the " subjectivists"—Pascal, Rousseau Hamann, Kierkegaard, Nietszche. In our own times, this division of the two realms has often been made by the naturalist philosophers Mrs. Farber opposes. They at once give us rigid rules for verification of the " objective" and a nonverifiable realm of high-sounding values that would have pleased the heart of the wildest neo-Platonic metaphysician, except that it means nothing.

However, if we take a fresh view of what we are doing in the world, we can see that this position is absurd. Our emotions and our ends as well as everything else are neither within nor without us. An emotion is in the world like everything else, but it is in a present, humanly situated world, not one that has been reduced or codified for theoretical or technical purposes. In other words, the exhaustive description of a situation is the exhaustive description of the emotion that comprehends it, as we know from adequate novelistic or dramatic treatment. If we have fear, it is because the world presents fearful things or fearful aspects; the fear is a synthetic quality of the world. If we have ends, it is because our situated world comprehended by our emotions has a future potential—something to do. In the first instance the world is organized as a concern.[1]

Instead of dividing the world into an Either/Or of facts and feelings or values, we should rather start with the fully constituted world and ask why and how various reductions come to be made and how, by analysis, we can improve them for purposes of discourse. We do not then fall into the danger of erecting a realm of psychic forces inside and a strictly indifferent situation to fit them into; taken in all seriousness this dichotomy would alienate the most hardy individual. If we start from things as situated we can more profitably answer such questions as: How do we have psychic

---

1. I think that the view of values as within, as properties of a person which somehow infect the otherwise neutral objects of perception, is based on a confusion caused by certain peculiarities of the interpersonal. For example, if a soldier goes into battle alone and has fear, he will be entirely concerned with the horrors of the war he is witnessing and in which he is participating. His world will exist in a state of emergency and certain privileged things will be useful to him for safety or flight. The situation will not be questioned. If, however, another soldier, who has no fear and from habit no longer finds the war so horrible, or at least so strange, should appear and call attention to the first soldier's cowardice, we can get a glimpse of how we begin to think of the emotions as inside. The first soldier now suffers a kind of rupture in his situation. He continues to see the war as horrible and strange, but he has just been told that he sees it this way because of what *he* is, not what it is he is seeing and doing. It is the soldier himself who is now contingent. He will need to re-establish an actable world, i.e. find ways of assuming his situation. If there were space for more complicated examples and analysis the point could be made somewhat clearer.

facts at all? What are the full implications of the existence of others?
and what are the differences among
theoretical, artistic and moral com-
munications? To have recourse to an
inner, final realm of values or to
God is to cut the analysis short and
to deny ourselves the ability to make
statements that analysis offers.

In other words, part of the situation of the American intellectual
in mid-century is the inheritance from
the immediate past of a markedly insufficient philosophy which has taken
the successful physical sciences for
its model as the Greeks, to their
detriment, used geometry. The answer
to this predicament does not consist
of a retreat to any position of the
past. The solution rather is to be
found in the analysis of what is
peculiar and unsatisfactory about a
philosophy of descriptive (scientific
or verifiable) and non-descriptive
(prejudicial or value) statements. We
can readily discover one reason why
this procedure is unsatisfying—the
"non-descriptive" side of the ledger
includes all our ends!

Our total situation includes the
political, the moral, the artistic and
the theoretical. We are only con-
strained for purposes of clarity to
carry on these types of discourse at
different times and, perhaps, to
specialize in one or the other of
them. If we choose among them it is
to fulfill a role in the total discourse of men; it is not to throw the
other activities out of our lives.
Thus, for example, justice (the
political) and love (the moral) are
not opposites; they are concepts that

prove remarkably difficult on analysis
(and in living) and they are indications of connections between two
different sets of things, both of
which occur in the situations of us
all.

The division of the world into
facts and values is like the division
into communists and crusaders in that
both procedures constitute recipes
for alienation and despair; both give
grim choices that force us finally
into sheerly negative positions.
Thankfully, both dichotomies are false.

Reconsider

THE AMERICAN intellectual and artist
has always faced the task of trying
to win his way out of a regional
thought, literature, painting, and
music toward a more fully self-
conscious and universal position. I
think a certain progress has been made
in this direction, but it could be
shattered by cutting ourselves off
from Western Europe and joining forces
with the provincial bigots and little
minds of the Republican party. Now,
as never before, we need to maintain
our contacts with England and France,
with the people of *Esprit, Temps
Moderne,* and the *New Statesman,* whom
we should hopelessly alienate by
pitting ourselves against inventive
freedom. I am certain the crusaders
will exert every pressure to force us
to capitulate. But most of us will
refuse this suicide and I strongly
urge Mrs. Farber to reconsider before
accepting it.

I think many of us have been led
into a kind of pessimism by our attempts at honesty about ourselves. It

is true that Whittaker Chambers' portraits of Senator Nixon and Henry Luce are far prettier than the self-portraits intellectuals tend to make of themselves. But I hope I don't need to plead for this kind of truth against that kind of calender art. The anti-intellectuals are preening because they think they now see their great historical chance. It is in-credible to think that these are the people who find the liberal intellect-ual unpatriotic. Against them, I can cite those of my friends who have been willing to lie for their country when abroad, as Milton did for his when he reassured the aging Galileo that England was the place of freedom he thought it to be.

2. A Reply From Marjorie Farber

I GATHER from the general correspondence that Whittaker Chambers is a black-hearted revolutionary, second only to Mc-Carthy, MacCormack, T.S. Eliot, or the Luces. Anyone who defends Chambers against the pack of doctrinaire "liberals" who had fallen on him like wolves becomes an even blacker reactionary. Even Claire Luce has not recommended that we " embrace McCarthyism," as Mr. Hawkins tells me I do. It is dis-couraging to report that a large group of readers seem to know what I think, not because of anything I said, but because they already know what "re-actionaries" think. Since I have been confused with so many people, from M. Camus to Senator Taft, and have had at least five philosophic positions ascribed to me with which I am in rad-ical disagreement, I wonder if we ought to call this process " reading" at all. It looks more like that "stim-ulus—and—response" reaction to certain words which modern psychology is pleased to call " communication."

Under this system of " communi-cation" there are only two sides to any question: Either the Red/Or the Black. Certain words flash " red" to some and " black" to others; otherwise the process is the same. Now we know how many moderates, conservatives, and liberals have been lumped together by the other side as " Red." Does the "liberal" ever stop to think how many millions of people—how many centuries of human life—he lumps together as " reactionary"? The word ranges from the scoundrelism of McCarthy to the vicious stupidity of MacCormack or the " paranoia" of Pegler; it includes stubborn nostalgia, naive opportunism, liberal-minded conservatism, religion and traditionalism. It includes not only Bilbo and MacArthur but those Southern poets who once proudly called themselves " reactionaries." They called themselves this not because they approved of lynching negroes but

because they were disgusted with the
illiberal opinions and the opinionated
temper of the self-styled "liberal."

I am sorry to see that Mr. Hawkins,
despite his philosophical sophistication, has included himself in this
illiberal group. His communication,
repeating Sartre's argument with Camus, is interesting enough in itself.
However, since it is always well to
know who we are, I had better say that
I am not M. Camus. In fact all these
un-subjective, neo-Hegelian systems
of *Existenz,* fashionable in Paris,
strike me as somewhat of a parody on
the existentialism of any good novel-
ist or poet—to say nothing of the
Jewish and Christian metaphysicians.
Even Heidegger and Jaspers (at least
from what I have seen translated)
fail to make the distinction clear, as
Buber and Kierkegaard have done, between our subjective being and all
philosophic knowledge of *Being.*

The quarrel between Mr. Hawkins
and me is over subjectivity and definitions of *Morality.* But since his
communication is so remote from any
statements or beliefs of mine, I will
try merely to answer the one unspoken
question which accounts I think, for
most of the sound and fury over Chambers. How can someone labelled "rea-
tionary" appear in any way liberal—
more liberal, even, than most of his
"liberal" accusers—except to another
reactionary? That is the question.

Let's find something to agree on—
say Joe McCarthy—and decide what makes
him black. Insofar as he can be said
to hold beliefs, McCarthy believes in
certain stupid or vicious doctrines of
the 19th century which we do not call
reactionary, but let that pass. Can
we agree that what makes Joe a true
reactionary is not only his beliefs,
but the fact that his methods are so
illiberal? He appears, like Bertie
MacCormack, to lack that curiosity or
openness of mind, that humility or generosity of spirit which enables the
liberal to find out what a man thinks
before attacking his ideas. Mc-
Carthy is not curious about what a man
thinks, because he already knows;
all the words flash "red" to McCarthy and MacCormack. So if MacCormack
reads a book, he finds nothing there
but what he knows already. If McCarthy labels Governor Stevenson a Red,
this is not because he has heard anything Governor Stevenson has said,
but because Stevenson has associated
himself with "Reds" like the anti-
Communist Wechsler and the anti-Communist Schlesinger.

Now we, being liberals, do not call
people "reactionary" merely because
they are associated with someone called
"revolutionary". We (I hope to
use the pronoun in such a compliment-
ary way as to cause no disagreement)
never display that illiberal spirit
which closes itself to new ideas ar
says, "I already know what you think."
We read even our opponents with care.
What is admirable in them we admire,
what is wrong we deplore—having first
examined our own beliefs to see if
we, by any chance, have been harboring

such wrong ideas ourselves. We do not look our opponent straight in the eye and say " I have never been wrong in my life. " We let him know exactly how and why we disagree with him. And since we treat even our enemies with magnanimity and honor, naturally we treat our opponents with courtesy. I do not mean social manners. I mean that patience or curiosity which bespeaks a lack of arrogance and may be nothing but the minimal sanity of regarding oneself as human—i.e. neither omniscient nor infallible.

And though none of us lives up to this ideal entirely, this is at least what *liberalism* means. As an historical absolute, as an absolute value developed historically, this is what we try to live up to if we are liberal-minded people, and not merely doctrinaire " liberals" . Liberalism was born in the liberal 18th century, which insisted that the State was to be a servant of man and not the other way around, as the 19th century was soon to claim. Marxism was born in the 19th century. By that time we had lost that minimal sanity which regards oneself as a limited, imperfect and not even quite perfectible, being. We lost this because it was associated with some unacceptable religious metaphors: " miserable sinners all" , or " equal in the sight of God" etcetera. " What rubbish! " people said—echoed by Mr. Hawkins, above— " No God exists. Men are equal in the sight of Man. " Forgetting M. Voltaire, who believed that men had always invented God because God was such a necessary invention, men in-

vented a new kind of " freedom" instead.

What happened? Nature was invented, to whom man was enslaved as a natural animal: a cog in the biological machine. An organic State was invented, to whom man was soon to be enslaved as a social organism: a cog in the social machine. A new science of medicine and a medical psychology were invented, in which man was scarcely an animal at all, but the " human machine" itself. Men were no longer thought to read, write, or think. They " reacted" , *produced*, " solved problems" —like rats in a maze, like a chimpanzee with a stick; they " communicated" their reactions to each other, like machines having their buttons pushed. A new Romantic " freedom" was invented in which all social forms and manners were a sham, and only the natural, only the animal, only the nobly savage were real. And so began a new enslavement to our animal, our primitive, our childish natures— ending in the totalitarian enslavement of man to man. It was not freedom that was re-invented, but slavery.

It happened to be religion which provided our restraint upon the natural barbarism in man: that barbarism of the child who believes himself to be absolutely right and thus absolutely capable of judging his opponents to be absolutely wrong. (Though we cannot do without absolutes, we must discriminate one absolutism from another.) The remedy is not a return to orthodox religions which (as I hope to show later) are based on the *same* absolutism, derived from the *same* theory of knowledge, as modern Science. Yet if we do not find a substitute for loving one another in the impersonal, old-fashioned way, as God's creatures merely—or as men—I fear, with Mr. Auden, we shall die. If not physically as animals, at least we die as men.

Now the " liberal intellectual"— as defined by Mr. Hawkins above—is a man who, if not absolutely right, at least has never been wrong. Anyone who disagrees with him must be a reactionary. In this kind of " either-or" thinking, whether of the Right or Left, no half-shades exist: no half-right liberals, no half-right con-servatives, no fallible human beings at all. Whittaker Chambers is not a man, wrong in his opinions but liberal in his temper; confused in his think-ing but clear in his heart—mag-nanimous even in defeat. Whittaker Chambers is a *reactionary*. Anyone who defends him is a *reactionary*. Any magazine which prints such a defense is *reactionary*. Shall we allow such a magazine in San Fran-cisco? If the government is too reactionary to suppress it, we can at least resign, withdraw support, tell everyone it is *reactionary*. That is enough to know, just as it is enough for the other side to know that we are *Red*.

The " liberal intellectual" is a man who, to the best of Mr. Hawkins' recollection, has never been wrong. It seems that he cannot, almost by definition, make a mistake. He " is never a 'communist dupe'...In the popular front of 1936 or on a Jim

Crow issue today, he knows exactly what he is doing." If this awe-inspiring definition described a human being, I would congratulate the " liberal intellectual" on being one. But I am afraid it describes only his third-person recollection of himself. Are there any other aging liberals like me, who *remember* the year 1936?—This is where the pronouns " I" and " we" come in handy, for simple historical accuracy.

So to address you correctly, Mr. Hawkins, I have read your communica-tion with much interest and agreement, and can only conclude that you were under some strong enchantment when you read mine. I do not claim that you were ever a Communist nor even a Marxist, but only that you have a strange recollection of the year 1936. I do not consider you any of the things you call me: paranoid, senti-mental, absolutist, philosophical Idealist, nor an embracer of McCar-thyism (though when you speak of " the sweet moral voices" being raised, I think I will take that as an unintended compliment). I am saying only that your definition of the " liberal intellectual" contains a certain amount of " double-think" which would, in an ex-Marxist, in-dicate some hang-over from the Marxist past.

You may remember that I said " no reviewer can fail to be moved by such a record of suffering, unless he is totally blinded by the Marxist faith." It is a little shocking to hear this suffering judged in nothing but pseudo-aesthetic terms as " corn" or " kitsch" . None of the reviewers went this far, except the man who called Chambers " a monster with mysticism ". But there are many non-Marxist intellectuals today who display the same peculiar blindness toward the moral, the personal, the " human". It is almost a hatred of morality.

To conclude now with my voting record—which I am afraid we cannot assume to be irrelevant. I believe I was one of the few reactionaries in the country who was out pushing doorbells for Stevenson, and though my readers will have no trouble in figuring out motives for this, I'll be glad to tell you why. I think I was also one of the few liberals in the country willing to believe that Stevenson meant everything he said. Since I swallowed his platform whole, including all his references to Communism or religion, I found no campaign oratory or expediencies to forgive him for—as the " liberal" *Nation* found it surprisingly easy to do. It seemed to me that only a

liberal would say " After 2000 years of Christianity we are still debating civil rights?" and only a conservative would insist that the State remain a servant of man. So I found this liberal-conservative position of Stevenson's something new in the 20th century and began to hope that, under his leadership, liberals might begin some belated process of self-criticism. Even now it seems just as true to say that, without some healthy self-criticism, no party can develop or survive.

Just as a radical New Deal may have saved capitalism from political reactionaries, so I believe only a radical re-examination *from within* can save liberalism from its Marxist and totalitarian flaws. Few readers seem to share my hope. So far most liberals are willing to criticize only *other people:* those labelled " Communists", or ex-Communists or " Marxists". No one has yet explained how we, as liberals, can possibly criticize liberalism unless we consent to criticize ourselves.

3. Wilder Bentley

Dear Peter Martin:

On my return from Stockton today I found two copies of the second issue of *City Lights* awaiting me. As one of the supposedly " confused liberals" your Marjorie Farber writes about, I was ruffled rather than confused on first reading the opening paragraphs of her defense of Chambers, in your

leading article. On the whole, however, I must thank her as author, and *City Lights* as publisher, for her outspoken attack on logical positivism and naturalistic determinism, and for her apology *for* if not defense *of* theistic realism or practical mysticism. In short, I now feel confident that your publication has taken the

kind of stand that I hoped it might
have taken in its first issue. It has
decided to live up to its lights—in
this case, to its inner lights, the
several consciences of its Editors.
After this, whenever I catch you and
your peers slumming over on Third
Street, I'll know you for unorthodox
lay Franciscans rather than for morbid
documentary seekers!

There are only two aspects—or
perhaps I should say implications—of
Mrs. Farber's apology for mysticism and
against the "modern distemper" with
which I disagree: first, her over-
concern with guilt and death; and
second, her grasping at straws, religious straws, if you will, but still
straws.

Granted that all of us share the
collective guilt, and some of us more
than others, I fail to see how this
obligates us liberals to ally ourselves with the counter-revolutionaries as a kind of penance for past
sins. Supposing, for example, that
we happen to be neither revolution-
aries nor counter-revolutionaries but
evolutionaries or gradualists? As a
matter of fact, I can not believe that
Mrs. Farber herself has faced up to
the implications of her stand with
the counter-revolutionaries, if,
indeed, it does represent her true
stand. For certainly she can not
mean that we who stand for freedom
of conscience are forced to choose
between " anti-communism" and " anti-
anti-communism"? What kind of choice
is this? In the same vein, she seems
to imply that even Rankin and other
members of the Un-American Activities

Committee are mere instruments (rather
than instigators) of a great grass-
roots movement of sane rank-and-
filers not only to purge America of
communist " traitors" and " saboteurs"
but also to put the misled dupes
amongst our liberal intelligentsia
(and I have the disagreeable feeling
that she lumps us all, intelligent or
not!) in our proper place. Not a very
elevated place in the popular imagination according to her, if I read
aright!

In the name of true humility let
us assume that we liberals deserve
more punishment than we get these
days; does that mean that as true
penitents the remission of our sins
must depend upon our climbing upon
the motorized tabernacle of Gerald
L.K.Smith, in the same seats with
McCartny, Rankin, Tenney, Nixon,
Levering, and McCarran, in order to see
this crusade against communism carried
through to its logical conclusion—an
America purged and *communized* in order
to compete on a wholesale-retail basis
with communism abroad?

Again, though it may sound too
complacent of me in view of the mass
blood purges of the past two decades,
may I suggest that we liberals need
not nourish our sense of guilt until we
are driven to the isolation and despair
of Kierkegaard or to the doomsday neo-
orthodoxy of Niebuhr? If Whittaker
Chambers really believes what he professes (and his own confessions, even,
I grant, his perjuries, lead me to
believe that he may), then as a "First-
Century" Christian he should by now
be living as the "new Man"—in the

"rebirth"—as the "fool in Christ", *only the negative aspect of which religious experience Mrs. Farber keeps referring to as his death in the flesh!* It is this emphasis on his " death" rather than on his " rebirth" which leads me to wonder whether his defender would have us revere him as a secular crucified hero-god scapegoat or consider him rather of the unorthodox order of Melchizedek, along with William Blake, George Fox, John Woolman, Mohandas Ghandi, and other practical mystics? If Chambers belongs to this latter group, then it is my humble opinion that he has already been elevated above our praise or blame; though in making such value judgments as these two alternatives suggest, one lays oneself open to the charge of naive naturalism or of naive spiritualism as the case may be. Yet, may I suggest that those honest, introspective ex-Marxists who., like Mrs. Farber, no longer find tenable a political credo based on scientific determinism alone, might do well to read widely and deeply the accounts of the kinds of religious experience that have led and still do lead *to a revolution in the hearts as well as in the minds of men;* for this split in man's nature, which Mrs. Farber decries in philosophical language, actually stems from a tendency in the West to view the intellectual revolution of the Renaissance as something distinct from if not at sword's point with the spiritual revolution of the Reformation. I submit that we still need both these private, individual revolutions in the minds and hearts of men

on virtually a universal scale before we are in any position to institute political changes in society at large. To realize the truth of this one needs only consider how sporadic and short-lived the political revolutions of the past three centuries have been as a result of the precocity of their leaders and the immaturity of the masses that followed them.

I must further take issue with Marjorie Farber's tendency to idealize that which she does not understand, a common failing of many of us. In Mrs. Farber's case I should term it religious straw-clutching—a phase through which many of us pass during moments of extremity. In her case, as well as I can construe her public confessional, her former *Thesis* (economic determinism, or more particularly, dialectical materialism) has played her and some of her confreres false; *ergo* her present *Antithesis* (anti-dialectical materialism, or is it Russophobia?) must be the only alternative (plus some mystical religious component for which she cannot account but which she holds responsible for Whittaker Chambers' triumph over the flesh). Though in other of her statements she affirms herself unready to embrace some "neo-orthodox" form of Christianity or Judaism, I should say that she certainly is ripe!

While not condoning either fascism or communism for their systemized use of torture, terror, and death, I doubt whether even an honest parson, priest, or rabbi would give Mrs. Farber her naive premise that Christianity or Judaism has succeeded in eliminating

papan scapegoatism and blood-sacrifice
by the mere rite of substituting the
chalice and the wine-cup for the
Mythraic marble slab; or, to put the
case in more contemporary language,
organized religion has failed to find,
let alone apply, what William James
termed "the moral equivalents for
war". (Apparently the science of
psychology has also failed if we are
to believe the Einstein-Freud correspondence during the '30's!) In fact
the very revival of the term "witch
hunt" from its theocratic context,
both Catholic and Protestant, for
present-day political purposes suggests its true origin. Then, too,
certainly Mrs. Farber must have heard
of the systematic massacre of the
Albigensian "heretics" in southern France and of the Spanish *auto-
de-fe*, both conducted under Catholic
authorization, and of the bloody
Lutheran purges (Martin's very own!)
during the suppression of the German
Peasants' "Revolt", to name only
three instances from Christianity's
two gory millennia! In short, this
trend of recent years toward secular-
ism and away from religionism may
have stepped up the tempo and scope
of torture and destruction considerably but it has invented few if any
new means or greater intensities!

Thus religion *qua* religion is no
open sesame to the kind of integrity
and disinterestedness that Mrs. Farber
admires in men like Whittaker Chambers;
nor, for that matter, is patriotism
qua patriotism (which, by the by, she
finds hard to differentiate from religion), despite the fact that an age

which has tried to make a religion out
of politics must now become as morbidly
absorbed in the anatomy of treason as
our ancestors were for diametrically
opposed reasons morbidly absorbed in
the anatomy of heresy! —*Apropos*, one
wonders why some shrewd and enterprising department of political science, say at Columbia, Yale, or Prince-
ton, has not set up an agency for the
sale of political indulgences.

In summing up, I think we must
admit that the genuine religious experience, by which I mean the kind that
revolutionizes and unites mind and
heart, is of an immediately apprehended
or mystical sort and hence is the privilege of only a rare few individuals
in each century whatever the so-called
Zeitgeist or "culture-climate" of the
century in question may be; and that
special pleading for communal or mass
conversions to this or to that religious or political *parti pris* based on
dogma must always resort in the end to
coercive "conversions" through violence
or its threat, in which event *genuine
conversion,* a highly subjective, freely
assumed, individual concern, becomes
debased into mere mass exorcism.

And now for the good or the bad
news of this letter, depending on the
attitude of its Editors who have stated
in good conscience in their second
issue and on the first page of Mrs.
Farber's article: "Marjorie Farber's
analysis of Chambers' motives and the
liberals' response is so individual and
so challenging that we are devoting
most of this second issue of *City
Lights* to it." As a liberal who has
attacked neither Hiss nor Chambers but

who has rather taken the stand of deploring the whole nasty business of the trial for its sensationalism and clouding of justice, and as a "Contributing Editor" to *City Lights* with no power over its editorial policies I shall have to tender my resignation from your staff unless you permit me to *contribute* the above statement in the certain assurance that it will be published in the columns of your next (third) issue. For I submit that I can not subscribe to a magazine that devotes one-half (25 pages) of an issue to an attack on liberalism itself by blanketing all liberals as carping turncoats (some are!) or as dupes of the Party—dupes or deliberate fellow travellers, indeed! If this be true, then Milton who, as I understand it, shares the honor with Charlie Chaplin of being a patron spirit of *City Lights*—is a Catholic "renegade," a Cromwellian "stooge," a "subversive" Leveller, and an "atheist" Mortalist by turns!—Smear him, O *Time!* Purge him with "Hisses," O *Life!*

Wilder Bentley

4. Horace Schwartz (editor of GOAD)

Dear Peter Martin:

I hope you will not be offended at the things I am saying in this letter. I have admiration for you and for CITY LIGHTS, and hope that you will continue to publish the magazine, and will encourage every evidence of honest talent.

I read the long piece by Marjorie Farber in the last issue. I read with disbelief and dismay. I could not understand how an obviously intelligent and sensitive person could come to the embrace of Whittaker Chambers, for any reason or on any grounds. My feelings were motivated not necessarily by a sympathy for Alger Hiss or any of those who mixed with Stalinism and came out badly, but by inability to conceive of a professed liberal praising a poisonous madman. I could call a roll of those who have gone mad under the strain of the present political situation. Do you read Dwight Macdonald or James Burnham etc...? I knew a young Anarchist lady who told me the saviors of America were Senator McCarthy and the Hearst press, because they were exposing the Stalinist Dean Acheson. But I imagine you know them.

Because the long tradition of humanism has gone awry under the punishment of Stalin Communism, we need not turn to either Catholicism or some kind of mystical (I am afraid I must use the word) Fascism. If one wants to maintain a position as an intellectual, it is not necessary to make a fanatical religion of anti-Stalinism. The laws of economics are still working, though a bit obscured. It is still true that America is a land of giantist capitalism, and that it will kill itself by its own contradictions. (Because the Stalinists say this it does not make it less true.) The world will still be better Socialist, and with all the inconvenience of it, it will still be better than what we now have. Even in America, there will soon be a time when poets and painters and musicians will be treated as honored citizens, as the real legislators, not hounded to death as now.

Because the time is slow in arriving, there are those who make intellectual or financial capital out of denouncing humanism and exposing "traitors." It is obvious that this is what Chambers and the like are doing. It becomes a sad and outrageous spectacle when such a decent and generous person as you print such as the Farber article. (I must say I thought the article was caused by some social snub the author had received in Fairfax or wherever she lives. I cannot possibly account otherwise for her lumping of Republicans and Communists.) This kind of thing becomes the gospel of American fascism. If the Macdonalds and Burnhams and Farbers think they are going to be the Rosenbergs and Goebbels of McCarthy's cabinet, they should think hard about it.

Possibly Chambers will be enshrined (after he is gassed or shot) but the scribblers now twisting reason until it screams, to make an apologia for the coming Apocalypse, will get the same treatment as the lowliest Jew.

If their defection from Stalinism has driven all these ex-Stalinists mad, let them get treatment, or remain silent. They are only hastening the inevitable butchery.

Horace Schwartz

5. Other Comment

...I think I have thought about the case–though perhaps not very intelligently–as much as any thoughtful person not directly involved has thought about it. I take it back. I certainly have not thought about it as hard as Marjorie Farber–at least not in such unintelligible (to me) terms. At times, I thought I was catching on to what she was saying, but I could stay with her for no more than one or two paragraphs before I was rudely bumped off the track by a conglomeration of pseudo-something-or-other phrases. Reminded me of some articles I used to wade through in *Horizon*–I think they're known as esoteric–capable of being understood only by the initiated–but on the whole I enjoyed *Horizon* and nothing in it completely threw me.
...This I understood: " ...the general public, often deceived by a writer's ideas or his aesthetic merit, is almost never deceived by his tone." I certainly had the feeling that Mrs. Farber was utterly sincere, and I also felt sympathetic to her view when I was able to catch a bit of her meaning.

I guess I'll have to read *Witness* and then take another shot at her article.

--R.D.S.

...It is a remarkable sequence of monographs, which, by the way, I read at a single time and with many-angled interest. That is saying much on the credit side; now on the debit–I feel that Marjorie Farber has overestimated, overcomplicated, and overdramatized her subject; and the intellectuality covers the pieces rather like semantic coloration. I mention this feeling the intellect of an author is more effective when less concerned with itself. Though, to me, these extravagances damage the series badly, I repeat I read the whole six pieces without stopping; they were that fascinating. And, of course, nothing is perfect.

--L.S.D.

...Marjorie Farber's article on the Hiss and Chambers controversy...I find almost impossible to criticize. I disagree with practically everything she says, and of course, that's quite an obstacle to an appraisal. I could nearly say I disagree with everything *except* (1) the religious character of communism; (2) that the Communist party and the Catholic Church are mutual counterparts; (3) that economic justice does not solve all problems. Marjorie is apparently one of those sensitive souls who swing from ecstasy to revulsion, and from revulsion to ecstasy. Having discovered, belatedly, the religious aspects of communism, she now believes that " *Time* was more nearly correct about the important things than the vast majority of liberal opinion," and that the Un-American committee is a beneficent institution, which has saved our democracy. It is the same old story which you find in the *40th* chapter of Gibbon's *Decline and Fall*–describing the early ecstasy and later disillusionment of the Greek

philosophers under Justinian with regard to the Persian empire.
...Moreover, the article pays no attention to the fact that Chambers'

" martyrdom" is one in which he is
free, whole, the author of a best-
seller, and in possession of a personal
fortune, probably around six figures.

6. A Last Word

MARJORIE FARBER

I feel grateful to any readers willing
to give Chambers or me the benefit of the
doubt; I think this shows a liberal mind.
Undoubtedly my defense of Chambers would
have been less positive and extreme had the
" liberal" attacks on him not seemed wildly
overdrawn, improbable, even lunatic. I can
understand why so many adjectives have been
applied to me—from ex-Communist or Fascist
to " hysterical", " exaggerated", " provoca
ative" and others meaning " interesting if
untrue" —while the educated opinions familiar to us all seem so self-evidently sane
and sound. A few years ago it seemed that
way to me: I thought all rebel reactionaries, poets, hotheads, or religionists on
the "other side" needed to be psychoan-
alyzed.

Now I'm not so sure. Having spent six
years trying to reconcile two nearly ir-
reconcilable positions—the subjectivity of
a Pascal or Kierkegaard with the Hegelian
"objectivity" of a Freud or Malinowski—I
believe both the scientific and the religious positions to be wrong in many ways:
in many of the same ways. Yet an acceptable humanism needs something from both
sides: it can't be All or Neither. These
arguments are long and tedious but I hope
some of them, if or where they appear, will
answer Mr. Bentley's objections. Here I
can mention only the one chief misunderstanding which is partly my fault. Certain
omissions or a general over-emphasis in
the Chambers piece, published in the heat
of an election campaign, have been identified with familiar reactionary or religious positions. Nevertheless, this confusion itself reveals the same old "liberal" prejudices.

The same three assumptions have been
made by nearly all correspondents: (1)
that only an orthodox Christian or near-
Christian could discover the anti-Christian
bias in our current thought; (2) that only
a Marxist or ex-Communist would "confess"
to the inhuman qualities or consequences
of Marxist liberalism and (3) that only a
reactionary or Republican would criticize
the liberals. Why? One needn't dislike
art in order to criticize a painting. It

is possible for a liberal humanist to criticize what passes for liberal humanism today without being a reactionary, a Christian, or even an ex-Marxist.

Not many years ago liberalism was Marxism: predominantly so. What short memories the liberals have! What I was "confessing" was only that I have been a self-
righteous educated citizen, complaisant
toward Communism and contemptuous of
religion; somewhat lazy or dishonest in my
thinking; illiberal toward all I failed to
understand. That seems to me quite bad
enough. Had I been a thoroughgoing Marxist,
I should feel worse; a Communist—worse
yet. Had I been a Communist spy, I should
feel, with Chambers, that only death or
penitence would serve. Now if any liberal
seemed in danger of beating his breast or
falling into a frenzy of repentance, I
should consider this excessive. As it is,
the liberals have turned the full fury of
their complacency against the man who confessed—insisting that he is absolutely,
qualitatively different from themselves.
Yet, as I tried at some length to demonstrate, it is they who consider Communism
"farther Left" and reveal, in every other
way, that the difference between Communist
and Liberal beliefs has been one of degree
only.

The point of the Chambers piece was
this: Only the Catholic Church so far,
and a few Anglican or Southern poets, have
discovered the radical flaw in the 19th-
century tenets of our contemporary thought.
And they arrive at certain conclusions unacceptable to the rest of us. I thought
it was time for the humanists and liberals
to take a hand in this.

Finally, I hope intellectuals in
San Francisco will carefully consider
this question: do you really want a
magazine designed for a liberal exchange of ideas-including unfamiliar
and unpopular ideas? Or do you want
various sectarian organs of opinion,
designed for the ritualistic purpose
of keeping everybody's prejudices
flattered and his mind unchanged? The
latter is what we have always had
before.

TURK MURPHY'S JAZZ BAND

"turk murphy is unquestionably the most driving force in . . .
'dixieland' music today." [nesuhi ertegun: SOMBRA, rio de janeiro,
december, 1950.]

featuring

BOB helm

" . . . probably the strongest jazz band clarinetist
since jimmy noone and johnny dodds . . . " writes
mr. ertegun, currently teaching the history of
jazz at u. c. l. a.

wally ROSE

from joplin to scarlatti . . . equally at home in the
concert field, rose has been called "the finest living
exponent of authentic ragtime."

"the temptation is very strong
to say that this is the best white jazz of all time..."
– GEORGE avakian of columbia records, record changer, may, 1951

dancing   thursday through sunday nights 9 to 2

the italian village
columbus at lombard – san francisco

A NEW MAGAZINE

IN SAN FRANCISCO

Behold now this vast City;
a City of refuge, the man-
sion house of liberty...
should ye suppress all this
flowery crop of knowledge
and new light sprung up and
yet springing daily in
this City?

Milton

Number **4**   Fall 1953   35 c

CITY LIGHTS is published at 261 Columbus Avenue, San Francisco 11, California. Telephone DOuglas 2-8193. Copyright, 1953, by CITY LIGHTS for its contributors. Manuscripts are invited, but no payment can be made at this time. Rates: thirty-five cents a copy; two dollars for six issues. Advertising rates upon request.

Editor, Peter Martin. Associate editors, Junius Adams, Herbert Kauffman, Joseph Kostolefsky, Eileen Martin, S. Tenenbaum. Business Manager, Raymond Davidson. Production, Natalie Gumas, Hubert E. Ricci, Jean Taylor. Presswork and format, Richard Pool. Process photography, David Leong. Lithographed in U.S.A. by Pool and Associates, Inc., 115 New Montgomery St., San Francisco.

Albums

Jules Laforgue

A translation by C. F. MacIntyre.

I've heard of the Far West, the Prairies, life in the raw,
and my blood groaned: "Oh, if that were my fatherland!"
Cast off by the old world, without faith or law,
out there I'd be king, a *desperado*--grand!
Out there I'd scalp myself of my brain from Europe!
To prance, turned to a virgin antelope,
no literature, living by chance, as a roughneck,
wheezing the California dialect!
A genuine rancher, stockman, architect,
hunter, fisherman, gambler, beyond the pandects!
Between the sea and the Mormon State! With venison
and whiskey! clothed in skins, having for bedding
the grass of the Prairies, under the primitive sky,
rich as the baskets of flowers at a wedding! . . .
Then what? Campfire to campfire, Lynch law, the tough
life; today with diamonds in the rough
on my fingers, faro or poker. Then to shrug it
off and dash back to the hills and go nuts after nuggets!
Grown old: a farm that faces the morning sun,
a milch cow and some children, and for fun
a sign on the gate: "Tattooer for everyone."
Just look at mine. Then, if my heart were lured
by Paris that was singing: "Not yet cured?
And your children too still gadabouts out yonder!"
And if your flights, O Rocky Mountain Condor,
showed me the Infinite, enemy of content,
oh well, I'd found a religious cult, or invent
a social code, empirical and mystic,
for all Pastoral Peoples, a hash of modern and Vedic.

.　　.　　.　　.

Oh, what fine bonfires of straw! These crazy joys,
these picture-albums, my grand unbreakable toys!

Jules Laforgue   *Des Fleurs de bonne volonte*
1860-1887

The Study of the City

An Informal Overture

DAVID RIESMAN

EVEN WITHIN the last one hundred years, the attitude of both town and country people towards the city has undergone extraordinary oscillations. Mindless worship of cities and of industry, Spencerian optimism about progress, are hard to find today in a thinker of distinction. Indeed, it could be argued that virulently pro-urban, pro-industrial outlooks go together with the worst abuses and miseries of early and rapid urbanization and industrialization--as if to cover by rhetoric the human waste involved.

The fact is that praise of cities represented a minority note in a chorus of late 19th-Century protest against city life. The camping movement, as a recent thesis by Lee Bramson and Marianne Rigsbey explicates, was inaugurated in this period as a high-minded repair movement for the alleged deleterious consequences of city life upon the young; it goes without saying that the woodsy people who started it and gave it its philosophy were city people. (A personal consequence for me was that, as a college student working in a settlement house in the North End of Boston, I was required to teach campcraft and Indian lore to Polish and Italian kids whose entire experience was urban - it was this experience, I suspect, which first led me to wonder about the possible development of an urban pastoral, more meaningful than an Indian or scouting pastoral in their situation. Even the games they were supposed to learn were largely of country derivation, roller skating being, as Mark Benny has pointed out, one of the few inventions other than team sports such as basketball, adapted to urban terrain and space.)

To be sure, there were some who were discovering the city in the late 19th Century with more curiosity than concern. This was mainly the province, it appears to me, of the great novelists, from Balzac to Henry James, for whom the streets and even the slums of Paris and London exercised a many-layered fascination. Lesser novelists, like Bellamy and Dreiser, were more apt to preach against the city; Bellamy, in his novel *EQUALITY*, urged that cities should be limited to a maximum of 250,000 inhabitants; his attitude, which would rob the city of its vices, secrecies, and mysteries, survives today in Lewis Mumford and in many city planners who favor surgical remedies for the chronic ills of cities. And many sociologists, practising our trade of

* This article is developed from a paper presented at a conference on " The Urban Person: A Program for Research" at the Fourth Annual Symposium of the Committee on Human Development, University of Chicago, January 31, 1953. The Committee is a teaching and research group which includes its faculty anthropologists, psychologists and psychiatrists, sociologists, and physiologists. It is sponsoring several studies of the metropolis, in Chicago and in Kansas City; I have been engaged in the latter enterprise and draw on its initial stages for the paper.

studying the vulnerable rather than the impregnable centers of society, have looked at cities as problems, leaving a residue even to our own day of courses and texts on urban disorganization, the pathology of race and cultural contacts, an overadmiration for " roots," a dispraise of marginality, and other ingredients of an anti-urban attitude based on a rural model of the good life.

It should, moreover, be clear that this rural model has virtually nothing in common with the romantic pastoral attitudes of 18th-Century Parisians or classic Romans and Athenians. The latter were highly sophisticated city-bred people, with the fondness city-bred people have for dreams of the country, city people toying with an imaginary world of innocently lecherous shepherds and ivory-scrubbed sheep - a pleasant setting for poetry and painting. To be sure, there might be tinctures of moralism involved, of a belief that some child-like human state had been lost in the shift to urbanity as a way of life. But on the whole, what could be more urbane than this version of pastoral?

Very different has been the moralism of those sociologists and poets who have viewed the city through the eyes of a folkish ideology of consensus, hard workmanship, and a simplistic view of the integrated, well-adjusted homey individual. What these observers have admired about rural or small-town life has been less its pleasures than its pieties - pieties often only possible because of the " export" of adventure to the cities, pieties often exaggerated by the nostalgias in the mind of an observer unfamiliar with the forms rural deviance takes.

These pieties are apt to be too crude and fundamentalist to be attractive to us today. When, located in an American setting, we need merely recall William Jennings Bryan attacking city people as sinful blood-suckers and pleasure seekers. But we can still appreciate an exotic version of this religiously-inspired pastoral in CRY THE BELOVED COUNTRY, which eloquently upholds the healing qualities of the country-side as against the slums and sluts of Johannesburg. The film - a far cry from John Fiske's dream of an urbanized Africa - struck me as less a brief against detribalization than a rural-based protest against the city and the shanty-town. (I saw the movie in a Negro neighborhood theatre, and to judge by the audience comments and restlessness, it made these well-dressed American Negroes very uncomfortable, perhaps, as Everett Hughes suggested, because their fur coats and Buicks contrasted so sharply with the abysmal poverty of their African racial brothers - and perhaps also because their sophistication was made uncomfortable by the devotedly religious whites and blacks of the film.)

A very different picture of an urban shantytown is MIRACLE IN MILAN, a good example of the genre which looks in cities for the pleasures and innocences the earlier poets and dramatists found or pretended to find in the country. MIRACLE IN MILAN was made by, about, and for people habituated to cities, and to city poverty and slums, for quite some hundreds of years - people truly civilized. I think we can find some American analogies. Even a film like THE ASPHALT JUNGLE, which pictures the entrepreneurial niceties and risks of a jewel robbery, treats the city with sympathy, with Whitmanesque lyricism - with evident affection for its more morbid types. Reuel Denney has suggested that the charm of these cityscapes can be appreciated particularly by city people who have moved to the suburbs and who are the more fascinated by the inner circle of urban blight and over or de-population because they no longer live there. Alfred Kazin's reminiscent book, A WALKER IN THE CITY, springs in part from a similar impulse to rediscover what has become an unfamiliar terrain. These works, and the attitudes they express and call forth, illustrate what I mean here by the terms "urban pastoral." An illustration of a different sort can be found in the cartoon film, GERALD McBOING BOING, with its light-handed treatment of the urban media and urban family life - a far cry from BUGS BUNNY. What makes GERALD urbane is not only its NEW YORKER magazine kind of humor but its abstract forms, in art and music as well as theme - as against the literal exaggerations which often mark the Disney style.

Reference to the NEW YORKER reminds us that some cities are more urbane - hence more given to urban pastoral - than others. Yet there is nothing inherent in these valuations; instead, they too, oscillate widely. In the first several decades of this century, the literary and socio-logical exploration of Chicago's Gold Coast and Slum, of its waves of ethnic succession, its architectural monstrosities and innovations, excited widespread fascin-ation. Even the gangsters, as the urban reply to the cowboy, helped give this city a legendary quality. In fact, the myth of Chicago was one of the inducements to my wife and me to come and settle here. Now we are sad and surprised to find how little this city's glamorous past and present potentialities are appreciated by the natives. The 'reaction to the Liebling stories in the NEW YORKER is a case in point; the humorless defensiveness of Chicagoans seems testimony to their guilt for their own disparagement of the city - though to disparage seems to me one of the inalienable rights and privileges of the city dweller. Mark Benny and I, discussing last year what sort of interview one could use to get at people's attitudes towards Chicago, concluded that simply to ask them direct questions would in most cases pro-duce a stereotyped bill of complaint; they would mention the dirt, the traffic, the water, the alleged corruption, the lack of this and the poverty of that. We felt that

we would have to use a "non-non-directive interview" to explore what might be some of the unexpressed and taken-for-granted values which these residents find in city life. For instance, we would want to know whether they are aware of the advantages of being as near as most dwellings are to a shopping street with stores, taverns, sodas, other pharmaceutical services, movies, and a whole gamut of consumer amenities. Do they make use of these amenities or simply complain about some of the consequences, in traffic and arrange-ment, of having them available? Perhaps an interview of this sort, we felt, could help the interviewee discover some of the qual-ities in city living which he actually enjoys, and so to enjoy them more.

I recall in this connection a column which Sidney Harris wrote several years ago in the CHICAGO DAILY NEWS complaining that there was no true community in Chicago, that he never saw his friends in Evanston unless he met them in New York or Pasadena, and that we really all ought to live in the country where we could see our friends every day. I observed to Harris that it was because he had the base of Chicago that he could be cosmopolitan, that he could see his friends in such pleasant settings elsewhere, and that if he lived in the country as a country-man he would be most unlikely to have friends; he would have neighbors, from whose gossips and from whose limitations he would long to flee to the city. I know perfectly well that for myself my long summer residence and occas-ional winter residence on a Vermont farm is only made possible by city earnings, and hospitable by city friends and values. Such values have increasingly spread throughout America. In fact, one can find in the West and elsewhere farmers and ranchers as cosmopolitan as you like, and the pages of the FARM JOURNAL and other city-edited rural media carry many of the same advertisements and articles which

teach the arts of consumption to sophisticated urbanites and suburbanites.

The urbanization of America, then, is
largely accomplished in fact, if not wholly
in feeling. We are fortunate to be living
in a period when the worst nightmares of
the transition to city life and to industry
are nearly at an end for the great majority
of the American people; the complaints we
now register against our cities, for
instance against Chicago, seem relatively
superficial and trivial in comparison with
the depths of animus engendered by the
previous epoch's break with a long rural
and small-town past.

But by the same token it seems to me
that it is time to moderate the fantast-
ically wide oscillations of sentiment
towards the city which I have hinted at
more than described in my remarks so far.
It is no longer a question of embracing the
city or rejecting it like many contemporary intellectuals, but rather of a more
differentiated stance which builds on the
attitudes of our predecessors and takes a
fresh look. Since we learn what to think
of our cities in large part from novels,
from the press (particularly, as Helen
Hughes documented,* from its "human
interest" stories), and from social science,
this fresh look can have revitalizing
effects on observer and observed alike.
To some of you it may sound strange that in
a program devoted to research I have spent
so much time on this question of stance, of
attitude. My own repeated experience with
students is that a stance is the beginning
of a research program. So it has been with
the interest a number of us have in popular
culture, represented in the soap opera
studies of Warner and Henry** and in the
study of the patronage of the symphony
orchestra which is being undertaken in
Kansas City. Popular culture is of course

all around us, but students need "permission" to consider it a field. More than
that, they need to enjoy it to work at it
with more than half a heart. Sometimes a
student will come to me and say: "I understand you are interested in the comics; I
want to do a thesis on the comics." And I
will say, "Do you enjoy reading them?" The
student may be startled: enjoyment is not
part of his Ph.D. program; I will add:
"There are lots of things to study. I
won't object to your studying something you
hate; one finds out things that way, too.
But life is short, art long; why read
comics, or anything else, unless there is
some intrinsic pleasure in it? Do not be
so unselfish a devotee of scholarship."

Something of the same thing is true of
the city, and the classes within the city.
There are many students who grit their
teeth and go into lower-lower homes. To
establish rapport with the underprivileged
is for them less a form of cross-class or
cross-cultural adventure than a pious
penance for their own privileges. In the
same way, we do research in small towns,
even if we don't like small-town people.
I hope we will never get to the point where
we do metropolitan research because that is
the thing to do, or because "cities are
America," or the future, or any such effort
to justify our curiosity by pretentiousness.
"Field training" for our social scientists
is (among other things) an effort to get
students to enlarge the range of their
skills while they are still free to fool
around, to experiment, before too much is
at stake. But no student ought to feel
continuously pressed by the conviction that
the people whom he finds it hardest to
reach, or most boring to interview, or most
unpleasant, are therefore more "real";
even research, much as we love it, can be
bought at too high a price.

---

* Helen MacGill Hughes, NEWS AND THE HUMAN INTEREST STORY (Chicago: Univ. of Chicago Press)

** W. Lloyd Warner and William E. Henry, "The Radio Day Time Serial: A Symbolic Analysis," GENETIC
PSYCHOLOGY MONOGRAPHS, 1948, Vol. 37, pp. 3-71.

And conversely this leads me to say that that some of us in the Committee on Human Development are studying Kansas City for strategic and publicly defensible reasons to be sure, but also because, when we went there last spring, we were captivated. Community Studies, Inc., our hosts there, impressed us as a remarkable experiment in continuing self-observation by a city - in p'anning through research rather than through official manipulation. We were struck by the layout of the city, its Quality Hill where (except for some new apartment buildings) the non-quality live, its Country Club District, to which most anyone can be elected who has the price of a house and will put up with a realtor's archaic taste; its network of railroads, which symbolize the city for those of us who grew up before the air age; its half-pleasant, half-unpleasant Southern exposure, represented in the slouch of some of its Negroes and in a certain serenity. As I read the interviews done by our field staff there, I sense a growing eagerness on their part to take a sector of the city as their own domain, quickly aware of who lives where, and of the variety of life-styles to be found even within a city block. And the best interviews are those where the interviewer has not been afraid of his respondent, but curious about him, not too remote in human or class terms, concerned with the quality of the respondent's life but not threatened by it or by over-identification.

In these interviews our field staff has been experimenting with ways to get at the whole life-cycle of an older person, to carry him back in his memories and forward in his hopes and fears - to tap his recollection for points of crucial decision, whether marked by ecological shifts, by crises of death or illness, marriage or birth, by occupational change and leisure innovation. We have wanted to tie these private memories wherever possible to public events, to war and depression, to legisla-

tion and shifts in public attitude, to changes in the polity and layout of Kansas City and the smaller communities which feed population to it. We have wanted to see what uses our respondents have made of the city, and the city of them. It may be that we will find people of so "folkish" a temper that they are incapable of the abstractions involved in responding to so searching an interview. They may be living, for all practical purposes, in a village - but not a village such as many are today, with urban values and connections, but a village of the type common fifty years ago: quite conceivably, the city contains not only some of the most advanced but also some of the most encapsulated sets of people in America. The inescapable contacts of such people may not make them urban but simply shrunken, for not everyone is influenced positively by the culture of those who are his ecological neighbors. And yet I would be surprised if we found many people, at whatever social level, who did not in some fashion think of themselves as citizens of Kansas City (whether in Missouri or in Kansas as the case may be), and not only citizens of this or that bloc or block or ward or "natural area."

Furthermore, while some of our exploratory interviews are turning up elderly people who, after the frequent fashion, bewail the good old days of gentility before those other people - those other values - came, other interviews - and, much more, our informal discussions - show that pride and hope in Kansas City are still very real. While I myself, with my notorious fondness for non-intellectual and unfanatical politicians, might regret the passing of Pendergast and Binaggio, the interviews reveal the very real elation of many people in the liberation from the corrupt tyranny of the machine: they are still too close to Pendergast to make a new version of urban pastoral out of his doings. But they are far enough away from the plutocratic pirates of the pre-Depression era to admire and memorialize the men who made Kansas City the metropolis that St. Joe (with possibly an even better location on the Missouri) might otherwise have become.

As I became very aware in studying ports and railroads twenty years ago, most American cities are where and what they are because dynamic men moved earth and defied heaven to bring boats and railroads, warehouses and power stations to one place rather than another. Richard Wohl[*] and I, after some discussions of the entrepreneurial history of Kansas City, believe that we may well find that at each turning point in its development, it had men on hand who saw to it that these essentials were provided for so that this particular city of the plain would remain well-watered and green-backed. The coming of light industry to the city in the post-War period is only the latest of such moves of cautious expansion and intelligent enterprise. Indeed, it is not too far-fetched to regard our study itself as a light industry of a sort, which was attracted to Kansas City by some of the same entrepreneurial talents which once brought stock there from Texas, soldiers from Ft. Leavenworth, and more recently a sizeable adult education project from Pasadena.

To be sure, this is only a very cursory guess. It would take an enormous amount of detailed digging to find out what led to the location of certain plants in Kansas City during and after World War II. Perhaps Kansas City had less to do with it than we suppose; perhaps it was done to Kansas City by the Pentagon, by managers in Wall Street, State Street, and Wright Field, for whom Kansas City was not much more than a place-name on a set of maps of railroads, labor supplies, power grids; perhaps when a city reaches a certain size, it gets beyond the power of its local enterprise   either

greatly to restrain or greatly to expand its pulling power. At this point, it may be that Kansas City just keeps rolling along, with energy needed only to divert or contain.

These last remarks are indicative of another reason why our attitude to the metropolis is important in the design of our research. For I have briefly touched upon some of the ways in which the history of the city will, although we and our interviewees may not always know it (in fact are likely not to know it) influence what our interviewees will tell us about their own personal history. In fact, I would make the flat statement that if we only study contemporary attitudes we will not properly gauge what is ephemeral and what perennial in those attitudes--the mere intensity with which an attitude is expressed does not, of course, mean the attitude will endure. The anthropologist who goes to Dobu cannot tell us how seriously to take what he hears from informants precisely because they are his only source, in the absence of trader reports or archaeological evidence. But the student of the metropolis is far less helpless in understanding the past that lies outside the purview of contemporary response -- though, indeed, the memory of those who talk with him will in turn be influenced by the sorts of historical sense that their literacy allows and encourages. On the contrary, our helplessness is the result, not of our paucity but the immensity of data: we are overwhelmed by the stored social memories of the city, so much so that we hardly know where to begin. And so we are constantly tempted by the instrument we know best how to use -- the interview with a randomized respondent -- and we are appalled by the labors involved in tracing the social history, not of Jonesville,[**] but of a city

---

[*] Richard Wohl, an economic historian, is coordinator of the Research Center in Economic Development and Cultural Change at the University of Chicago. He is now preparing a brief social history of Kansas City.

[**] Cf. W. Lloyd Warner and associates, *DEMOCRACY IN JONESVILLE* (New York: Harper and Brothers, 1949).

of 800,000.

Nevertheless, we are in the city rather than in another Jonesville because we are tempted and challenged by difficulty and complexity. (I need hardly point out that my colleagues who have worked in various Jonesvilles are well aware that these communities do not want for difficulty and complexity, only it is easier to miss it.) And because we are in a sizeable city, we have the opportunity of recruiting allies who have been drawn to the city by not dissimilar needs, and who have made the study of the city a profession or an avocation. Kansas City has, in the University of Kansas City, a young and vigorous center (including Ernest Manheim, a distinguished sociologist); it has several colleges, among them Rockhurst and nearby Park College; it has an enterprising public library, a determined city manager, and, in Community Studies, a unique city-wide observatory. It is Simmel's theme that it is the nature of city men to make systematic observations and abstractions,* and Robert Redfield has recently declared that only in a civilization (as against a folk society) do men make protests, comparisons, and serried discoveries.** Only with a certain degree of population density are men directly and continuously confronted by conflict and stratification, by alien ways which have somehow to be embraced, rejected, managed, understood, rather than regarded as part of the order of givens in an unchanging universe. Existence itself for humans involves some of this, but the search for and partial control of differ-

entiated existence seems to spring from city life. And I value differentiation, in thought as in emotion, and am prepared to pay the price.***

These matters, too, are debatable. We require concepts for our Kansas City projects that will help us rediscover the city and its historical significances, as an effort to create a scientific working version of urban pastoral. In doing so, I hope that we will maintain a very strenuous dialectic between the abstract and the concrete, especially the concrete person who confronts us in our interviews, as well as between the historical and the contemporary.

But, no matter what abstractions we develop, they will contain something of how we feel about Kansas City, about cities, and perhaps inescapably about America. We are the emotional heirs of the 19th-Century ambivalence about the city, just as we are the heirs of its earlier students, such as Rowntree and Park, James and Zola. As heirs, our enthusiasm is a chastened enthusiasm, our disgust a chastened disgust. Meanwhile the city itself is not what it was when you began this article. All we can do in our research in Kansas City, and in other metropolitan areas, is to begin anew the endless process of rediscovering our own values in the course of discovering the world, bringing each to bear upon the other, trusting to our curiosity, and unafraid of the anxiety and confusion stirred up in us when we embark on a topic of so enormous a scope and so long a history and prospect.

* See *THE SOCIOLOGY OF GEORG SIMMEL*, edited by Kurt Wolff (Glencoe, Illinois: The Free Press, 1950).
**In *THE PRIMITIVE WORLD AND ITS TRANSFORMATIONS* (Chicago: Univ. of Chicago Press, 1953).
*** Cf. my article, "Values in Context," *AMERICAN SCHOLAR*, 1952, vol. 22, pp. 29-39.

Brothers In The Light
A Story

BORIS SOBELMAN

Benjy Schein sold disability insurance for a company which used direct mail advertising to find its prospects. Every week the company sent fifty thousand letters out to the householders of Los Angeles reminding them that sickness strikes, that accidents happen and that no man can say when and to whom. Against these hazards the letters offered protection; not the gift of perpetual well-being, for no one could offer that, but the only realistic thing which would help, a steady income during periods of disability. There was a postcard for reply in every envelope with a printed request upon it which read, " PLEASE SEND ME YOUR FREE BOOKLET EXPLAINING HOW I CAN GET ONE HUNDRED DOLLARS A MONTH WHEN SICK OR HURT, " and these cards, when they came back to the office, were turned over to the salesmen, among them Benjy, who called on the senders.

As a salesman, Benjy was neither the worst nor the best but he was certain he could be better. There were examples all around him, men like Morrie Gross and Petey Burke who made three times as much money and with hardly half the effort. Morrie Gross had once had a furniture store of his own but had given it up because he found selling much easier. " No headaches, " he used to say, " that's what I like. No financing, no overhead. Where else could I knock out three bills a week without a dime invested! "

Petey Burke was almost as good as Morrie. He believed there was no such thing as a man without money, and this belief, he always claimed, was what made him successful. " I send 'em borrowin' to the neighbors and relatives, " he would say, " I got a special pitch to make the relatives get it up. I ask 'em how much they think

they'll be stuck for if the guy breaks his back and is laid up ten, fifteen years. You should see them start thinkin' after that. I once even drove a mooch down to the hock shop to get a loan on his wife's wedding ring. I says to him how long is the ring going to feed you when the quivering eephus strikes?''

The office manager was a former oil lease salesman named Marty Jay. Selling oil leases had brought him into contact with people of great wealth, and possibly as a result of this, he found himself unable to admit any superiors into his world. People were either his equals or his inferiors. The President of the United States himself was either only as good as Marty or a jerk. He excepted only geniuses, men like Einstein or Thomas Edison.

The number of calls any salesman could get depended entirely on Marty. If a man was a good salesman, what Marty called a " producer, " he not only got all the calls he wanted but could work any part of the city he chose. Morrie Gross did even better than that. Morrie picked the calls himself out of a box Marty kept on his desk and even this privilege didn't seem to impress him. " Stinkeroos, " he would say, putting a batch into his pocket, " is that the best you could do?''

" Well, " Marty would answer, grinning, " I got to save the good ones for the coxeys. "

Coxeys were the polar opposites of producers. They were poor salesmen or they were men Marty decided couldn't sell. There were seven coxeys in the office and they spent hours waiting for Marty to give them cards. They always looked apologetic and unhappy, and showed animation only when they listened to the stories Petey

CITY LIGHTS

Burke or Morrie Gross told about their sales. Whenever they were privileged to hear about some particularly shrewd or bold or cunning bit of selling they became infused with confidence and hurriedly wrote the details down to be conned over later. If they became sufficiently uplifted they would say to Marty, "Why can't we have talks like this more often.? It's money in the bank just listening to Morrie. If we could have a talk like this twice a week we'd close twice as many sales."

Benjy Schein fell somewhere between the producer and the coxey. He had ups and downs and was hard to classify. Marty Jay couldn't quite regard him as a jerk but on the other hand wouldn't admit him to the company of his equals. His attitude to Benjy was one of continuous bafflement, like an innocent confronting an hermaphrodite. Just when I'm beginning to think you're a coxey," Marty would say, " you come in with a load of business." When Benjy had a bad week Marty became certain he was a coxey and angry with himself for having wasted so many good calls on a jerk, and Benjy would have to explain just why the leads had yielded no business before he could get any more.

After Benjy had been working in the office several months he discovered a method of breaking the news of a bad week to Marty without endangering himself. He would put the two or three policies he had written, rather than the expected seven or eight, on Marty's desk, and begin an involved story about the marvellous ingenuity and sheer selling audacity that had gone into closing them. When he was finished he would say, "Morrie Gross himself couldn't of done any better." Marty used to bite on the end of his cigar and grin with pleasure and glee as the drama of the trapping of the customer was unfolded and when it was over he would say, "That's the way to sell. My confidence in you is up a hundred percent."

Benjy would then say, " But the rest of the leads were real stinkers."

"Well," Marty would answer, "they can't all be good."

There were always a great many leads in the office none of the salesmen would take. These were cards across which the sender had written, "No agents, please," or " By mail only," or, from a more communicative soul, "This sounds like a gyp but am interested. Send literature. Will contact you if want representative." Some were from people over seventy whose age made them ineligible for insurance, and others had a return address which looked plausible enough but were signed with such names as Mahatma Gandhi, John D. Rockefeller and Rex, the Wild Horse.

These leads were reserved for the coxeys. "Now fellas," Marty would say, gathering them around, " everybody has the wrong ideas about cards like this. They think they're no good or phonies and won't go near 'em like they was a jinx.

" The truth is they're just as good as the rest.

" Now here's a guy," he would go on, holding up a card, " says he wants literature. What do you say to him? Knock on his door and tell him you are the general manager and ask was one of our salesmen out here before and insulted him? Why do you ask, he says, and you say, showin' him the card, it says here send mail only and we figured one of our men had been out here and insulted you. If you will be good enough to give us the guy's name we will have him fired. Well no, the guy'll say, all I wanted was something to read. So you say, what do you want to read for? I'm the general manager and can give you all the right information. Just give me five minutes of your time.

" After that," Marty would conclude, " if you can't get a deal you should turn in your kit and go get a job in a factory."

These instructions given, Marty would dole out the cards, the coxeys standing around, glum and sullen with no faith in

what he said. When later, the cards had
fulfilled the meagerness of their promise
Marty would look sourly at the men and
appear too emotionally frustrated to speak.
The coxeys would become even more apologetic and go out to another room asking
each other what was wrong and how would
Morrie Gross have handled their leads, or
even look at Benjy Schein as if he were a
being of different order from themselves.

Benjy felt sorry for the coxeys but
there was nothing he could do to help.
Besides he had to be careful. If Maxie
ever saw him becoming friendly with them he
might suddenly decide that Benjy was after
all a coxey too, and Benjy would find himself calling on people named Benito Mussolini and Oscar the Octopus.

As a matter of fact he was never really
out of danger. Any card which by name or
address seemed to have been mailed by a
Negro was automatically his. Nobody liked
to call on Negroes. They never had any
money. Marty had worked out a special
pitch for them but Benjy found it impossible to use. It revolved around the idea
that Negroes were not normally eligible for
insurance but because the company had made
them an offer through the mail, it would be
a violation of the postal laws to refuse
them this time. Powerful as this argument
was, no one had much success with Negroes;
and the fact that these cards, though far
beyond the reach of a coxey, were never
given to men like Petey Burke or Morrie
Gross was Benjy's true measure in Marty's
mind. Benjy was never unaware of this
and never allowed himself to forget it.

The only way to improve this situation,
he knew, was to become a better salesman.
For one thing he would earn more money, but
more important he would be released from
the onerous task of inventing strategems
for Marty. There were times when he wanted
to quit the business entirely but whenever
he thought about it he remembered he had a
wife and was unskilled for any kind of job.

He had even become a salesman accidentally, and in fact through Morrie Gross.
His mother in the East had written him
asking that he drop over and convey her
regards to a woman she had not seen in
years, a girlhood friend. The night Benjy
called a dollar limit poker game was going
on and Morrie Gross was the big winner.
When Benjy introduced himself the woman
went into ecstasy and insisted on bringing
out a special bottle of whiskey and having
him shake hands with everybody. The woman,
whose name was Mrs. Reynolds, began remin-
iscing about the days she and Benjy's
mother were girls, then broke into tears
and kissing Benjy began repeating over and
over, "That God should let me live to see
this day."

When this passed she insisted that Benjy
tell all about himself. This he did as
well as he could, selecting those elements
of his life he considered she would find
interesting. He said he was married, was
working and was happy. This made Mrs.
Reynolds weep all over again and she began
to reminisce once more, but this time she
was cut short by Morrie Gross. "Who wants
to hear about an old bag like you," he said
jovially. "Let the guest of honor talk."

Benjy didn't know what else to say and
while he was trying to think of something
Morrie Gross said, "What do you do for a
livin', kid?"

"Well, right now I'm working in a ware-
house," Benjy said a little uneasily,
remembering the dollar limit poker game.

Mrs. Reynolds began squealing, and
clutched Morrie's arms. "Put him in your
business, Morrie. Put him in your business. You must do this for me. You owe
me a favor for a long time."

Morrie bit off the end of a cigar, lit
it and pontificated with himself. Then he
said, "Ever hear of the A&H racket, Benjy?"

"The A&H racket? What's that?"

"Insurance. Accident and Health."

"He makes three hundred dollars a
week," Mrs. Reynolds broke in, unable to

control herself.

"And without a dime invested," Morrie added. He puffed on the cigar again. "Benjy, my advice to you is get in it. Meet me in the office in the mornin' and I'll see you're broken in and introduced all around. I can tell by lookin' at you you'll be terrific." He took Mrs. Reynolds' hand and shook it and said, "Thanks for sendin' us a great salesman, Mrs. Reynolds. That's another favor I owe you."

Mrs. Reynolds' husband at this point caught Benjy's eye and nodded significantly. "If Morrie Gross says to do a thing, do it," he said.

Since that time Benjy had learned a lot about selling. He had found that salesmanship was not wholly the natural talent it appeared to be in men like producers but could be learned like anything else, although the process was slow and difficult. The trouble was the companies were not interested in teaching the men. A newcomer had to be immediately capable. If he was not, he became a coxey after a week or two, which meant that he earned barely enough to keep himself alive, and in secret nourished himself with visions of lucky breaks like selling ten policies in one house or stumbling on the president of a union who not only bought the coverage but ordered every one of the seven thousand members of his union to do the same.

Some of the coxeys were young men who had worked in banks and brokerage houses and looked upon the insurance business as a profession, much like medicine or law. There was always a great turnover among them, as the older ones, wounded and bewildered, drifted away and new ones came in. Some were men who had taken correspondence courses in selling; others had been brought in by Marty's ad in the papers which always began, " IF YOU CAN'T MAKE TEN THOUSAND DOLLARS A YEAR WE DON'T WANT YOU! " They were the untouchables of selling and accepted the treatment they receive as something pre-ordained, immutable. Collect-

ively their eyes all beheld the same vision: they saw themselves as producers, swaggering around the office like Morrie Gross or Petey Burke.

One day Benjy got a card on which the name TITUS A. BEASLEY was printed in strong large letters. There was an address, and on the line marked for Occupation, " Man of Jesus and Jehovah. "

The Reverend Beasley lived in a house which had once been a notions and dry goods store and which still bore on its peeling frontage the foot high lettering of the word MERCHANDISE. It served now as both a dwelling and a tabernacle. A dragging, hand-painted sign hung from one end to the other informing the world that this was the Church of the Scientific Revelation, and that all souls go upward being lighter than air.

The Reverend himself was a robust, whitehaired, very black man in his sixties, with shining teeth and a bassdrum voice, and Benjy knew after only a few minutes of talk that he would buy a policy. This put him at his ease and made him become friendly and even intimate; he began calling the Reverend by his first name.

They were seated at a table in a corner of the living room, which by the looks of it served also as the congregation's meeting place. One end was piled high with five stacks of folding chairs. There were several pictures of the Reverend on the walls, a few framed mottoes like " HOME IN THE ARMS OF THE LORD" and " BLESSED ARE THE SAVED, " a large lithograph of an elephant, a photograph of Haile Selassie, a map of the world, a calendar with a blue and white banner with the crocheted words, " CHURCH OF THE SCIENTIFIC REVELATION. " The Reverend's wife made a brief appearance from the kitchen where she had been washing dishes, laughed when she was informed an insurance salesman had come calling, and then went back.

Benjy looked the room over interestedly, hoping approval would show in his face, and noticed the banner with the crocheted words.

"That's a beautiful piece of work, Titus," he said. "It must be a pleasure having something like that around."

"It sure is, boy," the Reverend Beasley answered with conviction, "that's an uncommon inspiration to all of us an without bein' bragadocious about it was knit by Smiley, one of our sisters, who I saved one night when she was fixin' to poison herself."

"Poison herself," said Benjy, surprised. He was also a little sorry he had mentioned the banner. There was a story to be told here and he would have to listen.

"True as I live," said the Reverend Beasley, "Sister Smiley was right there in her house mixin' up some ant paste when the neighbor woman come runnin' over and told me. Said Sister Smiley been tellin' the whole street she was suffering with the hemmridge and was sure to pass on any day. Went runnin' over there hitchin' my pants all the way and start prayin' as soon as I come in. Prayed all night, prayed the next mornin' and the day after and the day after that and was finally so tired I fell asleep right there on her floor. When I woke up what do I see but Sister Smiley shinin' in a new white dress, raisin' her eyes to the sky and sayin', "Praised be Thy Name."

"And she didn't die?"

"That's right boy," answered the Reverend. "Not only didn't die but was born again. And been born again ever since."

"That's wonderful," Benjy said, a little uncomfortable. "You really saved her."

"Not me," said the preacher, with robust modesty. "Believin' did it. Savin' is a matter of believin'." He went on, pleased with Benjy's reaction, "A plain scientific fact. No man can be saved lessen he wants to be saved, and when he wants to be saved he just asks for it and someone will be around to save him."

He got up from the table and began to pace back and forth. Benjy felt that he had become excited talking about Sister Smiley and the best thing was to wait before bringing up the matter of the insurance again. He lit a cigarette and remained silent waiting for the Reverend to sit down but instead the preacher suddenly placed a hand on Benjy's shoulder and said in his deepest tones, "Would you like to be saved, too, boy?"

Benjy didn't quite know how to answer this question, even assuming its intention were merely rhetorical, which he more than suspected was not the case, and he felt deeply chagrined for having ever mentioned Sister Smiley's banner. He had no idea what the Reverend Beasley did when he went about the business of saving someone, whether it could be done on the spot, or required another place and time. One thing, however, he sensed from the preacher's deeply portentous tones : if he gave any other answer than a "yes" the sale he had been so confident of getting would never be made.

"Well," he said, hoping to temporize, "if a man is given a chance to be saved he wouldn't be much of a man if he turned it down."

This answer resulted in exactly those actions he had hoped to avoid when he made it.

The Reverend Beasley shouted "Hallelujah" and then called to his wife in the kitchen, "Nancy Jo, they's a brother here is ready for the light," and Mrs. Beasley sang back from the kitchen, "Praise the Lord," and a moment later appeared carrying three Bibles. She handed one to Benjy and gave another to her husband. Benjy tried to make some kind of protest but upon handing him the Bible Mrs. Beasley began praying in a loud sing-song, and while he was still making up his mind how best to stop this, the Reverend's voice had already come in with "Amens" and "Hallelujahs." There was no way out.

Mrs. Beasley continued for a few minutes, then her husband took over, and after several minutes of this they got down on their knees, motioning Benjy to do the same. The Reverend announced that all should open their Bibles to a certain page and read aloud together. The reading was short, a few pages only, then the Reverend put an arm around Benjy, hugging him strongly, and said, "You are now a brother in Christ, Hallelujah."

"You are now a brother in Christ," Mrs. Beasley sing-songed. She was a thin woman with a weary, flattened face, but now it actually shone as she and the Reverend embraced Benjy.

A deep sense of shame overcame Benjy and he found he couldn't say a word. Mrs. Beasley went into the kitchen and came out bearing a tray with cups and saucers and a pot of coffee which seemed to have been waiting for just such a moment. The Reverend Beasley poured with pride and told Benjy to be sure to come to the prayer meetings Wednesdays and Fridays, and of course, Sunday mornings. Benjy sipped his coffee and gave up the idea of disillusioning the Beasleys or hinting they might have made a mistake. Their confidence in his salvation was too profound. But he did tell them he couldn't see how he could come to the weekday meetings because he had to work every night. This perturbed the Reverend Beasley somewhat but he finally accepted the fact with a biblical quotation and a certainty he had somehow gained that Benjy would be there Sundays.

"You got to hear me Sundays, boy," he said, "I'm all fired up Sundays."

Benjy had been hoping that his talk about working would remind the Reverend that he was there to sell insurance. He wondered how he could mention it without being, under the circumstances, too indelicate. Thinking about this made him forget to some degree what he had just been through. The thought occurred to him that if he lost the sale after such an experience he would never call on another Negro again, Marty Jay or not. The Reverend Beasley, at this point, saved him any

further introspection.

"Now about that insurance," he said suddenly, "we ain't forget. Write me one up, and Sister Beasley too, and if you could only come to prayer meetings Wednesdays and Fridays you could prob'ly write a few more."

Benjy took their applications and all he could think of while he was doing so was that Marty Jay would be pleased with him in the morning. It was, after all, a double sale, nothing too common, and as he worked he began to feel more and more like a salesman and less and less like an involuntary convert. When he left he had progressed so far back to this older role that he parted thanking the Beasleys for their business and was able to omit any reference to the religious.

The next morning the incident had already become transformed. It became another story about selling, and judging by the reception, a good one. The coxeys looked at him with admiration and Marty Jay became so full of glee that he forgot completely he had ever suspected Benjy was a jerk.

Benjy himself began to believe that only a first rate salesman could have had himself saved by the Reverend Beasley. The feeling that he was a good man stole upon him, and the possibility that he could become a producer followed. He might even have tried to do something about these beliefs except that Petey Burke made him change his mind. Petey had heard the story too, but Petey was not a coxey. He was a producer and his mind had its own ways of working.

He showed up at the Reverend Beasley's a few nights later and asked to be saved. This request being granted he told the Reverend that though this was all right as a first step, what he wanted was to pray and to pray as often as he could. He joined the congregation at their Wednesday and Friday meetings and attended the sermons on Sundays. At the end of a month he had sold more than fifty policies, and when he felt

every possibility had been realized he
abruptly terminated his churchgoing.

The Reverend Beasley called the office
to find out why Brother Burke no longer
came to prayer meetings and Marty told him
Brother Burke was sick. When The Reverend
asked what the nature of the sickness was,
Marty said a severe case of the quivering
eephus. The Reverend called every day to
say that each Sunday the congregation
prayed for Brother Burke, and to ask if he
was getting well, and every time Marty said
he was getting worse. Finally one morning,
he informed the Reverend that Brother
Burke's ailment had become complicated with
Oriental gongo and symptoms of crud and
that he had died during the night. The
Reverend asked where the burial would be so
that he and some of the congregation could
come down and say a few prayers. Marty
replied it was too bad but because of the
contagious nature of Oriental gongo the
Government was flying the body out to ·the
South Pacific and having the burial there.

During all this Benjy Schein experienced
a heavy guilt and was oppressed with the
thought that he had committed some monstrous crime against the Reverend. And all
his ideas about becoming a producer faded.
They were obviously unreal in the face of
what Petey Burke had done in the same
situation. The best he could hope for,
Benjy told himself, was to become a little
better, just good enough to be secure.
Petey Burke was miles ahead of him and
Petey wasn't even as good as Morrie Gross.

James Cleghorn

Existenz (to Abe Kleinberg)

this is no public legend but my own
that throve on dying and will soon be gone -
a hopeless gesture followed by a yawn.

cause and effect may casually postpone
their usual issue in this desperate case
let them forego these atoms if they will
whose little shadow watches at its sill
the comic downfall of the human race.

who, nourished at the knife in mother's breast,
remembering bitter blood until he dies,
by tireless memory and thought possessed,
although not even saddened or made wise,
has not felt sometime as if earth and sky
came to a close within his closing eye?

Deferment

A Story

BART ABBOTT

SALINAS was warm that summer and fall. This was '42---about eight months after Pearl Harbor. I had been working on a Henry J. Kaiser defense project which had recently been turned into a war job. There were twelve or fifteen of us on this job-- riggers, riveters, some carpenters and electricians, a crane operator and a boss. We were working on a storage tank for magnesium. This was a small side project of the main job, which was the construction of two large magnesium reduction plants.

The clothes under my leathers were sodden with sweat before nine in the morning. I worked along steadily, burning the welding rods down to half an inch. The stubs fell lazily to the ground fifty feet below as I squeezed the handle of my "stinger" and inserted a fresh rod. In another hour I would be on the shady side as the sun rose high and later slowly slid toward the edge of Monterey Bay fifteen miles away.

The deafening thunder of the rivet gun a few feet above was no longer bothering me. I had worked my way into the welcome cool of the tank's shadow. The metallic staccato of the riveter always merged into the background after a couple of hours on the job and no longer interrupted my thoughts. As I paused for a smoke I watched the careless ease of the rivet heater on the ground as he tossed the white-hot rivets from his tongs to the passer above me. Each rivet described a precise arc on

its flight upward, paused before falling back toward the ground, and then the passer's cornucopia of tin slid under it. There was a tiny clink as the rivet hit the tin. In three seconds the rivet gun would begin its clatter, wind up to a crescendo and suddenly fall silent for a few seconds, and then the "clink" again.

When I began to think of the cold beer and tacos I'd had the night before in a little Mexican joint across town, I knew it was time to go back to work. I flipped the butt away and snapped the hood down across my face, and began to make fire. Soon my thoughts took me away from the job again.

Welding is lonely work. Other workers can't work too near your job without getting their eyes "flashed" from the arc's powerful rays. A flash can knock a man off work for a week. Even when you work next to another welder, the hoods covering both your faces make conversation just about out of the question.

I was thinking of the war and the draft, and the dough the government was pouring into this job and others like it. I wondered if I'd be drafted soon, and if there would be any jobs after the war. The old-timers said it would be like after the last war, unemployment and bad times for working stiffs. I worried about Ell and the kid, and the new one coming in the spring. I wondered if I'd ever get to know Ell the way I'd got to know people before the war. It seemed like I could learn people warmly and intimately then, (people who were not nearly as close to me as Ell was.) Was she somehow different from others I had known, or was this an effect of the war that climbed right down into people's personal lives, undermining and weakening their relationships with others?

The arc splattered along in front of me with its nasal whine shutting me off from the outside world. I ran out of rod and took off the cumbersome hood as I smoked again.

It was getting close to noon. Waiting for a lull in the rivet gun's almost continuous roar, I yelled down for the time to a carpenter who was working fifteen or twenty feet below me.

"Won't be long now," he grinned up to me, "twenty till."

I decided to wait till lunch before going down for more rod, so I got out of sight behind some staging rope. As I puffed on the cigarette I watched the heavy Lorraine crane snatch up the pre-cut I beams and plates as the guys on the ground slung them up and hooked them on. As soon as the load was clear of the ground crew, the operator would start the crane's turn. Up, up and around, clearing the high tension wires strung along the road, the plates and beams would come to a motionless stop a few inches from their final place of rest above me on the tank's framework. Two riggers up there would drop a couple of temporary bolts into the rivet holes, whip the nuts on, connecting the new iron to the skeleton, cut the piece loose from the crane and move to the next spot, leaving the rest to the rivet gang and me.

I watched this operation for several minutes, admiring the crane operator's skill. As the steel left the ground it moved in a smooth, graceful arc, never slackening its speed until it stopped with scarcely an inch of swinging motion beside the riggers. That operator was smooth, plenty smooth, and fast, too.

But in watching how he did it, I began to wonder why he didn't bring the steel across the railroad siding instead of across the wires. It was obviously a safer route. The tension wires ran down one side of the job and the rails down the other. The crane and the tank were in the middle between them. It seemed to me that the distance for the crane was the same either way and to swing the stuff across the rails would be safer. But hell, nothing would happen, nothing ever did, and this driver knew what he was doing.

Then Mike, the foreman, blew his whistle for lunch and I scrambled down the ladder and made for my pail.

After we finished our sandwiches, we usually sat around together, because there weren't enough of us on this job to make it sociable to split up. The guys were batting politics, women, and the draft all over the lot. A young carpenter, the same guy I'd asked the time of, was riding high over his deferment. He had it coming, any way you looked at it: three kids and another on the way, a damn cute wife, and an option on the eighty-four hours a week we were working in the hot Salinas sun on this job.

We sat on the ground against two tool sheds, a dozen construction Joes in two rows facing one another and panting in the shade. The older guys started kidding Curley, the carpenter, about his deferment and the wife he was crazy about in spite of three and a half kids, five years of marriage, and seven twelve-hour days a week on the job.

"That deferment's going to grow wings and fly off in six months," grinned Eddie, the rivet passer.

"Yeah," threw in one of the riggers, "and then your troubles begin. First you'll worry that no one'll look after Jean, and then you'll worry that someone will. You're gonna be in a sweat over that for sure!"

We all laughed, even Curley, because he knew that Jean was the one thing he didn't have to worry about. She was as nuts about him as he was about her. They were still,

after five years, constant targets for new-
lywed jokes.

"Okay, have your fun," laughed Curley.
"The trouble with you guys is you're so
wore out you can't get a woman who can
stand you, or if you can, she ain't worth
having."

We all laughed but he wasn't far off in
his point. After roasting twelve hours on
that job it was pretty hard to be any good
in bed. And as I said before, it took
quite a woman to put up with a construction
Joe's life: a month here, six months there,
and in between jobs no paydays.

The talk drifted back to the war and to
the money it was making for " the old man. "

Freddie, the rivet heater, a short guy
with the longest arms for his size you've
ever seen, was musing over Kaiser's expansion. "He starts out with a couple of
rock crushers and a gravel pit, and look at
him now! Top man in the construction
racket, top man in ships, magnesium, and
pretty soon airplanes, even...all that from
one goddam gravel pit..."

Curley stopped him. "What are you
beefing about? If he's smart enough to get
it, more power to him. Your trouble,
Freddie, is you're sour when anyone else is
getting it. Besides we're not doing so bad
since the old man came along."

Steve, a long-nosed rigger with an even
longer scar down the side of his cheek from
some forgotten accident on an equally forgotten job, broke in, "That's okay for
clowning, Curley, but you don't stop and
think things through. A lot of these Kaiser
dollars are gonna be bloody. All this
speed, these twelve-hour shifts. This
hurry-up from the pusher, the super screaming for more speed. That's gonna mean
bloody dollars. Just wait, you'll see,
Curley."

The rest of the "old heads" didn't
dispute the gloomy forecast, but neither
did they approve of such talk. Their
thoughts were summed up by one who remarked, "Talk about those things and you
bring them on. "

The whole gang, depressed by recollections of construction accidents, attempted
to bring the bull session atmosphere back.
The attempt was short-lived and a failure
besides. Jokes on Curley weren't funny any
more, talk of women had become dull and
meaningless, submerged by the preoccupation
of all construction Joes: When will my turn
come? How will it happen? And then the
rationalization: Not me. I'm careful. I
watch the game.

Mike's whistle was almost welcome and
we all returned to our jobs with unaccus-
tomed willingness.

I opened a fresh can of welding rod and
picked up a rectangular cover-glass to replace the spattered one in my hood. Shoving
eight or ten pounds of rod in the " quiver"
on my belt, I went over to the welder, spun
the crank and started her up. After
twisting the dial slightly to insure a
hotter arc, I began the climb to the
staging where my stinger lay.

I began the first pass along a butted
joint and in ten minutes realized that it
was better to face the ray burns and
splattering of the arc than to keep the
leathers on any longer. The rays wouldn't
bother until tonight, and every welder gets
used to " hot ones" that find their way
under the leather coat. Jiggle your arms,
your legs or your belly at the moment of
contact and you can shed a hot bit of metal
or slag even more effectively without the
cumbersome leathers.

An hour later when I stopped for a
smoke, I still hadn't shaken the thoughts
of the lunch hour. The crane was still
making its graceful ellipse up from the
ground to the tank frame. Below me, Curley
and another carpenter were building a
scaffold along the wall of an outbuilding
which was to house machinery. The crane's
boom passed within two feet of Curley and
his scaffold on its course across the
tension wires. It was safe so long as
there was no change in the boom's pitch.

The riggers, bolting on, were working up the tank, not around it; it was unnecessary for the crane to move on its tracks or boom up or down. And besides that operator was smooth.

I noticed the superintendent's pickup truck jouncing up the road to the job and decided it was a good time to start burning some more rod.

I had been working half an hour or so when my rod failed to spark. Throwing back my hood, I saw Curley had shut off my weldor and was waving me down. As I started down I noticed that the rest of the gang, except for myself and the riveter, were gathered around the super. When I got over to the pickup, the old man had just started to talk to them.

"Fellows, you've done a damn good job here. You haven't wasted too much time and you seem to know how to order your materials and use them without ten tons of scrap laying around at the end of the job. You ought to be finished here day after tomorrow and I know you're all trying to figure out what part of the country to head for next."

There were expressions of agreement from the whole gang on this last statement. Half the secret of success for construction workers lies in their ability to dovetail the beginning of a new job into the ending of an old one. Letters are sent to friends around the country for leads on new jobs. News reports on congressional approval of funds for dams, post offices and bridges are discussed among friends with a sharp eye for pertinent angles, pros and cons, all of which makes a congressional committee consideration of these questions look like blind man's bluff.

The superintendent continued, "You guys made me a bonus from the Company and I want you all to have a few drinks with me over at the Cantina after the job tonight."

"You don't know what you're getting into, Charlie," one of the guys ribbed.

"Now boys, you put me in so good with the 'brains' that they've given me the rock crusher job over at Le Grand and I want you guys to stay with me. This Le Grand job will mean four hours' pay a day for riding time and five bucks a day subsistence on top of a ten-hour shift. It's gonna be a good money job."

All of us with families had figured the money before he finished his words. I slapped Curley on the back and both of us danced around sparring at each other like kids. Our wives had put up with rotten cramped living quarters on this and many other jobs. We had stayed in cheesy auto courts where the kids had nowhere to play, and the girls went nuts trying to cook on two-burner kerosene stoves. Having enough money to rent a cottage with a real gas stove would be heaven on earth to both our wives.

Curley and I felt pretty good the rest of the afternoon and worked at a faster clip thinking of the promised drinks and the news we would bring home to our wives afterward.

At quarter after five I stopped for a smoke before starting down the ladder to shut off the machine and put my tools away. Curley was up on his scaffold with an electric drill making holes for the bolts that would secure the rafters. I tossed a rod stub at him and it stung him on the neck. He slapped at the spot, and turning his face up in the direction it had come from he cussed me out goodnaturedly and then went back to his holes.

I lowered my stinger and cable to the ground and started down the ladder. Halfway down, I stopped to watch the crane hoisting the last section of steel for the day. It swung high in its graceful arc to clear the high-tension wires. Curley let up on the drill trigger and waited for the boom to pass his scaffold. He winked up at me and stretched out his arm to give the slow-moving boom an affectionate pat as it passed.

The grin on his face remained, frozen,

masklike. Long blue sparks danced around his head and arms, concentrating their fantastic blaze on his two hands, one holding the drill, the other stuck to the boom as though to flypaper.

At the moment he had touched the boom, the steel hanging from its sling like a teeter-totter had gently dipped its heavy end just enough to brush the topmost of the wires under its path.

The crane operator froze on his controls at the horror on the scaffold above him. The drill in Curley's hand was grounding 11,000 volts, the current passing down the crane and through Curley on its grounding course. I gripped the ladder rungs with nerveless fingers and watched, hypnotized, as the drill cord burned in two under the tremendous load. Curley's stiffened body relaxed and toppled in slow motion from the scaffold.

I slid down a rope that hung beside the ladder without noticing the skin I left on it on the way. I reached his body first, feeling sure that he was dead from the juice before he had touched ground. Unbelievably, he was breathing and softly moaning. He had landed chest first, the impact had expelled his dead breath and reflexes had started the heart and lung action again.

Someone else came up and we carried him over to level ground. Curley's eyes were open but he couldn't seem to see. His lips were moving, and I bent close trying to catch his words. They were becoming clearer. He was muttering a couple of words over and over. At last I began to catch them. ''Oh shit. Oh shit.'' His voice strengthened until we all could hear. '' Oh shit. Oh shit. ''

They weren't uttered meaninglessly, or in anger, but only with the greatest and deepest regret I've ever heard in a human voice. He was regretting the end of life, life he loved, life with his woman, his children, life that was for him only starting, that promised so much for the future, life that had been squandered without thought of its ever ending.

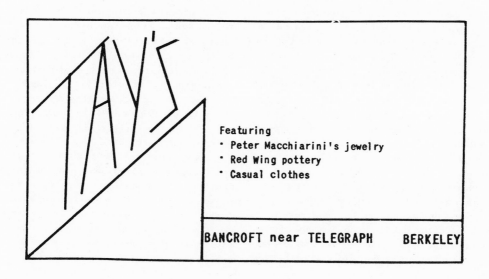

The Live Dog

-or a Dead Unicorn

MARJORIE FARBER

WHEN A critic writes about painting, he has a whole theory and tradition of the craft behind him. When he approaches movies or television, he lacks even a definition. What is a movie -- Art? Entertainment? Or something psychological, like a daydream? Something sociological, like a mass opiate or mass hypnosis? Or is it something anthropological, like myth or ritual?

If he decides that some movies are art, then the rest must be something else: an entertainment for the masses. He will praise only the *pastiche* or imitation-art, and admire the popular artist only when he is dead, or no longer popular. There is something about this Fine Arts approach to movies which brings out the worst in our aesthetic theories: all that 19th century romanticism and deification of the artist, with its sublime indifference toward the artist's craft. Chaplin has been praised in terms that would make a craftsman blush: they sound like Hawthorne praising Michelangelo. But this is not, of course, criticism of the popular arts. It is rather a sign of exemption from them: an elevation to the rank of Fine Arts.

If a critic decides that movies have nothing to do with art, then craftsmanship becomes even less important. He will take no interest at all in the formidable techniques of acting and direction; of cutting and editing and camera-work. A movie will appear to be all psychological motive or response: a collective daydream created by the audience in their seats: or the psychological know-how of movie makers, cleverly shaping the mythic content of a plot to fit the daydreaming demands of the audience. It will not occur to this critic that an audience may be held enthralled by nothing more hypnotic than strong interest and pleasure. Or that plots, with or without their daydreams, may be just something the audience ignores: a writer's daydream, maybe, overlooked in favor of something else -- all that action, all that make-believe projection of the real, or simply the actor's real-life projection of himself. Who knows what makes the movies fascinating?

To judge by television, it is the projection of real life which audiences want. A small flickering screen may be as "hypnotic" as a big one, although we are kept more outside it, less uncritically swallowed up. For whatever reason, television tends toward "reality" in some sense. Whether it's the backstage drama of a benefit, a folksey M.C. and the amateurs on quiz shows, or just the amateurish mishaps at the local studio: whether it's the grim realism of the best dramatic shows put out by Goodyear, Philco, Ammident and Lever Bros., or just the make-believe "realism" of the serial crime shows; whether it's the deadpan "Marlon Brando" style of delivery as developed by Rod Steiger or Wally Cox (a sort of penetrating Brooklyn mumble carried, with the aid of sound-engineers, to electrifying lengths) -- television can powerfully project the illusion of real people, moving without artifice in real-life situations. Even the sketchy sets of the dramatic shows may force us, like the Elizabethan stage, to create our own illusions. And as for the dramatic shows themselves -- the best of these, freed from box-office theories of "art" and "entertainment," have been experimenting in some fresh and instructive ways with such unromantic topics as alcoholism, mating habits, war, death and bereavement in the contemporary world. One of them deserves at least a footnote here.

> An hour-long drama, called ONE LEFT OVER, shows how a man gets through his first night and day of bereavement, after learning that his wife and two children have been killed in an auto wreck. Nothing happens, except the unrelenting details of hospital, police, insurance, funeral business, inept well-meaning neighbors, social workers, laundry men. The dramatic question is whether he can preserve his human dignity long enough to get some sleep, shave, drink his coffee and break the news to his surviving child. His efforts to " keep going" build up a nearly unbearable tension, relieved only by a neighbor who finally manages to say some very ordinary right things. So much dignity surrounds this tension, however, that the neighbor's parting line -- " Sleep tight, chum. Take it easy"--wakes echoes of goodnights, " sweet sleep" and tender partings of high drama.

Now I think if I were able to describe this play properly, in terms of its own craft, the question would not arise " Is it art? And if so, is it an imitation of the Fine Arts or a new and living art? And if it is an imitation, does that raise it above the status of 'popular entertainment' or cast it below the status of 'living arts'?" A similar question arose in the 70's. How could the awful daubs of Cezanne or Matisse be called " art" ? They could not, because critics had forgotten -- and had to learn again -- what the craft of painting is. In doing so, a whole aesthetic was re-created. In poetry and music, too, critics went back to Aristotle to find what a craft is. Poets and "New Critics" in particular have found the classical concepts of poetcraft rewarding.

Unfortunately this aesthetic, tailor-made for ancient crafts, will not fit new and unfamiliar crafts like television or the movies. It is only by analogy with Fine Arts criticism that a new aesthetic can be made -- much as "New Critics" worked out theirs by analogy with Aristotle. But while a few beginnings have been made, in movies as in jazz and bop, the general tendency of intellectuals is to call these crafts "mass entertainment," reserving the word " art" for the entertainments of the few.

It is surprising how much of the present dismay -- the "alienation" of the intellectual from his culture and so on -- can be traced to this one habit alone. For, while craft is not the whole of art, it is nearly the whole study of aesthetics. Art depends on craft to about the same extent a man depends on his body: that is, art is something "more" and better than its body, yet nothing at all without it.

Other parallels are evident. You can always define the whole of art -- both soul and body, so to speak -- in the same terms as you define a man. The early 19th century tended to define them both as vague spirit, soul or " feeling." Or both can be defined as they often are today: nothing but physical body, nothing but aesthetic craft. *

A better metaphysic might define the body as the objective means whereby you achieve your subjective ends; craft as the aesthetic means by which the artist achieves his non-aesthetic ends. Then it would be no substance, " mind" or " spirit" making up the non-physical ends of man, but meanings, values, activities of specific kinds. And these same meanings and values make up the non-aesthetic ends of art. It is dangerous to call these values of art-moral, intellectual, or metaphysical -- all by the same name: " aesthetic." For that is to define a man in terms of art, as the 19th century has done.

This ends in a vicious circle, with

* This whole terminology is misleading because it is only objectively that the " mind" or " soul" appears to be within the body. Subjectively, your body appears to be within yourself -- your self as thinker, mind or soul. Subjectively too, the art work exists within the imagination of the artist, and not within the physical artifact. If it is true to say the soul is in the body, we must add that the body is equally in the soul. Craft has a similar relation to art, as the " part" which mysteriously determines the whole.

poetry or movies defined in whatever psychological terms are currently defining men. The remedy might be to call aesthetics "The science of art's craft" -- much as medicine is the science of man's body. The "psychological" critic who ignores the craft of movies would then be as unscientific as the doctor who ignores a broken leg. For if craftsmanship is not the whole of art, it has subtle powers to affect the whole.

For example, we are often annoyed with the critic who tells us that a novel or a movie is technically deficient -- when we have found it moving, entertaining, or instructive. Yet some time later we discover that its moral, social, or philosophical values were as stale and derivative as its craftsmanship. The critic who is concentrating on craft is probably protected somewhat from the passions and pressures of his time. Certainly it is chastening now to observe old war movies on television. When the hero points his finger at the gangster, we know how many paces he will take, how slowly he will raise his hand, what the tone and rhythm of his speech will be, and exactly what he will say: "The time has come for you and Your Kind. Little People everywhere are rising.." etcetera.

When it comes to old familiar arts, we are all good critics. When it comes to new ones, the critic needs more than familiarity: he needs a theory. Let us see what the advantages are of approaching any art or entertainment in terms of craft: i.e. the means and methods whereby an artist achieves his end. It is the advantage, as well as the limitation, of a craft to define its larger ends within its own craft-terms as means. Thus the end of baseball is simply *baseball*. But this carries an aesthetic judgment: it means good, well-played baseball. To win games-- to win success or fame: these are not the ends of craftsmanship. The end of cabinet-making is a well-made, functional table. Such a table will be both salable and

"beautiful" to one age, and useless to another. Another age will consider a well-made carriage, automobile or helicopter "beautiful." But a craft which is untimely -- like a folk-song which brings us the news of 1653 -- may still have relevance to our musical requirements. And a craft which is merely timely -- like a Stalinist "folk-song" of the 30's --- may have no relevance at all.

In craft-terms, the end of movie-making is to make a movie: that is, neither a novel nor a play, but a piece of cinematic craft which as yet has scarcely been defined. The more familiar craft of poetry, too, has no further end than to make a poem. To call a poem "beautiful" -- like a "beautiful operation" or a "beautiful shoe" -- may be only a redundant way of saying that it really is a poem.

Who decides whether a poem is a true authentic poem, or a pseudo-poem? At present it is the poet's fellow-craftsmen-- poet-critics -- who decide this: their judgments handed down from highbrow to middlebrow or mass journals of opinion. But we cannot deny that poetry is an unpopular craft today. Only the outstanding poet achieves this downward reputation, while many good poets do not.

If we turn to the "popular" arts, we find that some of these are less popular, really, than the Fine Arts. Such lowbrow crafts as bop or science fiction will each have its coterie, however, dedicated -- like the highbrow coterie -- to its particular craft. I can think of only two crafts today which so reach across the gulf of "high" and "low" as to be truly popular. These are comedy and sports. And of the two, only sport has achieved a critical frame of reference: a widely agreed-on theory of its craft.

With a few exceptions, the writer who comes closest to being a true critic of the "popular" or lowbrow arts -- the man who displays the same intimate knowledge and involvement with his subject as a "textual analyst" devotes to poetry -- is the sportswriter. He is the true aesthete of sport, untroubled by metaphysical problems of definition. He doesn't care whether baseball is "art" or "entertainment" so long as it is *baseball* -- with a long theory and tradition of its craft behind it.

So another advantage of the craft-approach is that it cuts through nomenclature (or shows us, perhaps, how important nomenclature is) in relation to our enjoyments. At present our enjoyment of a movie depends too much on our ability to call it "art." Hellenic bards and Gaelic minstrels probably never asked themselves if they sang "art" or "entertainment," so long as it was song or *poetcraft*. A painter doesn't care much what you call it, so long as it is a painting; neither does a good movie critic care much whether a movie is called art or entertainment (though he may draw the line at daydreams) so long as it's a *movie*.

We can see how well this operates in poetry. The "New Critic," working safely in the concrete text, not only helps the poet achieve his ends; he may even help him define his ends. At least he does not merely hinder or confuse the poet by telling him that his end is some highbrow opiate, escape or daydream. Carefully distinguishing the aesthetic ends of craftsmanship from the moral and metaphysical ends of art, the critic of craft knows that these moral-metaphysical ends are no mere symptoms of psychology. He knows how much knowledge, observation and deduction -- "scientific method" -- is required for poetry, and how little use mere "feeling" or mere inspiration is. He knows that a feeling may, in fact, be nothing but a half-formed or undeveloped thought -- or two undeveloped thoughts at once. The less

developed these are, the more complicated and confused will be the "feeling." *

If our enjoyment of a movie depends on our ability to call it "art," this works in a circle. The more we reject it as non-art, and treat it as a problem in sociology, the less knowledge or enjoyment we shall have.

A sociologist has to ignore the aesthetic means of art if he is concentrated on its theoretical end -- especially if this end is not to produce art, but to produce something psychological like a daydream. Here the end is defined as a beginning: as a motive. In this he resembles the romantic artist, who also considers the end of art to be a psychological motive -- disguised, however, as vague pseudo-religious aspirations, divinely inspired and confusingly called "aesthetic." The romantic artist wants little more than "feeling," inspiration, intuition, or unconscious dream to work with. Craft, technique, hard work, knowledge -- these are not sufficiently "artistic." To call him a good technician is like calling him a good mechanic.

Thus even if the romantic or the psychological critic does describe the craft of movies, this is less the craft of art than of psychology: some device or drug for producing dreams and other symptoms. (The same devices for inducing sleep may also induce "automatic writing," free association and hypnosis. But it takes a good craftsman to produce a good poem in his sleep.) So whether the dream is some Freudian "truth" of the Unconscious, or an unconscious Revelation from on high, the romantic criticism remains psychology. It is not criticism of the movies.

The Fine Arts or museum approach to movies, on the other hand, has a different

---

* Poets and critics have not only these advantages; they have also a much older tradition of the *human*. Defined in non-romantic and pre-scientific terms, to be "human" meant to be different from Nature, distinguished from animals, and neither divine, perfect nor omniscient. Insofar as we are ruled by common sense, or even sense of humor, we define ourselves in these ancient ways. But insofar as we are ruled by our prevailing education or philosophy -- i.e., by the last three centuries -- our human norms may be just the opposite of these.

fault. Instead of describing them in terms of no craft, it describes them in terms of the wrong craft. So even when we exempt certain movies as "art," we are breaking the first rule of aesthetics which is to describe an art in terms of its own craft (as I fear I broke this rule in my own too-arty description of the television play).

What I have been suggesting here is that any valid approach to the popular arts must be neither "aesthetic" nor "scientific" in romantic terms, and must be aesthetic in more classical terms of craft. For such an approach, three things are needed. First, movies and television must either be dignified as "arts," or "entertainment" must be dignified as one of art's functions. Secondly, a movie-aesthetic must be defined as a movie-craft. Finally, a new aesthetic can be worked out by analogy with the craft-aesthetic practised in painting, music or poetry. We could then decide what relation good craftsmanship may bear, even in a comic strip, to some other kind of excellence.

This is exactly what a few movie critics like James Agee or Manny Farber have been doing. Only by not being "aesthetes" in the usual sense have they succeeded in becoming movie critics. And only by their attention to craft have they given us the beginnings of a theory or a point of view by which to approach all the popular arts. I believe similar beginnings have been made in jazz and bop -- with the "hot" and "cool" musician each performing some valuable, if unverbal, service as a critic of his culture. The "moldy" jazzman may in fact, like the traditionalist in poetry, be criticizing present culture by preserving a past good, while the cool musician like the romantic rebel may escape from past and present ills toward some better future.

The danger here is that defenders of jazz, more "defensive" than critical, will take up jazz as an end in itself. We see

already that the intellectual's response to popular arts has gone to one of two extremes. Either he exalts certain of them to the rank of Art, and thereby denies this status to the rest; either he "understands" them as sociological phenomena and enjoys them as surreptitiously or as dutifully as a parent enjoying a scout trip -- or he goes to the opposite extreme: he takes up an aggressively lowbrow position, from which to write as jazzily as possible about the live arts as though we had no others -- as though museums were not full of dead arts of far higher quality than these.

And here of course is the crux of the matter. It is very hard to pretend that jazz or bop is better than a Baroque gigue or folk-tune, or that Bartok is even half as good as Bach. On the other hand, it is equally hard to maintain that a live dog is not better than a dead unicorn. It is the present we dislike, really, more than its arts. And yet our present arts, since they are living and not dead, are performing a unique function. Whatever we may think of them, even comic strips help to define our culture; and whatever we may think of that, it is the only culture we have. This demarcation of culture into high and low -- with its implication that what the masses have is no culture at all -- really doesn't help us much to change that culture. But our dissatisfaction with our present arts does become clearer if we speak of them as "present," not as "popular."

To help us here we need more than devotion to a craft: the bop musicians and science fiction fans couldn't be more immersed in theirs. To find a remedy for the values we deplore, we should have to know what caused them. Not the present arts or "mass media" of entertainment; the disease is surely older than any of its recent symptoms. In fact, our tendency to blame our troubles on such late peripheral symptoms is part of the disease. It derives in general from the habit of placing other values first, above the human, and in particular from placing aesthetic values first. This causes us to see art as the source, rather than the reflection, of cultural values.

So Hollywood is blamed for a general debasement of values which began three hundred years ago in Europe, when Beverly Hills was a primeval swamp. This is especially handy for Europeans who can blame the history of Western Europe on "America" -- that is, upon a present age composed of coke bottles, frigidaires and television sets for which the synonym is now "America." At the same time, poets are urged wistfully to create some new god or myth for us to live by. Art is not, of course, that powerful. Even the occasional prophet like Dostoyevsky or Lawrence has little power to affect our myths -- and then only if the century happens to be going in his direction. An artist derives his values, like the rest of us, either from an older metaphysic or from the definitions of his day. For the past three hundred years, prevailing definitions of Man have taken the same direction -- away from "the child of God" and toward "the child of Nature." But never, I believe, have men looked to the artist to tell them what "God" or "Nature" was. The artist is expected rather to illustrate, to uphold and celebrate a prior *mythos* and cosmology.

Magic & Entertainment

If we go beyond craft or aesthetics as the "body" of art, we are at once in the realm of metaphysics: of that which defines the human. Within this cloudy realm, however, we can perhaps distinguish *myth* and *knowledge* as the two broad values of art which help to define the human. That which celebrates and that which instructs: these two together seem to make up the whole extra-aesthetic purpose of art.

Every myth must have its ritual celebrations, of course -- for which the traditional word is *magic*. Magic is the ritual in service to the myth. And if we define myth as the ruling values of a culture -- from its cosmology to its social and political institutions -- then the magical arts would be those, even today, which most clearly celebrate or uphold our ruling values. The arts of knowledge, on the other hand -- the more "civilized" arts of drama, history or the novel which do not celebrate so much as they observe, record, examine human history and behavior-- these bring us, through the medium of *entertainment*, our most explicit knowledge of people. As *magic* serves to uphold the myth and to celebrate our values, so *entertainment* serves to increase our knowledge and to instruct us in the ways of the human.

Traditionally, too, this later or more civilized kind of art has served as entertainment for the few, while the earlier or more primitive kind has served as magic for the many. Although every art may include both magic and entertainment, the purpose of magic can be distinguished as the opposite of entertainment. Magic aims to arouse emotions useful to the common good, emotions which are meant to be discharged outside the aesthetic experience: carried over into life. Entertainment aims at the sort of "catharsis" which Aristotle believed to be the purpose of every kind of art: the emotions aroused are meant to be discharged then and there, within the aesthetic experience, and not carried over into life. Thus it is the entertainment-purpose of art, excluding the magical, which has traditionally formed the basis of aesthetics.

For this reason, prevailing aesthetic theories -- from Aristotle's "unities" to Eliot's "objective correlatives" -- properly define the entertainment purposes of Euripides or Chaucer, but are misleading when applied to the magical-religious purposes of an Aeschylus or Dante. The

arts of religion, like those of folk-magic
or of social propaganda, may be "aesthetic" in their craftsmanship, but they are
clearly magical in their purpose. In
secular times such artists as Dostoyevsky,
Whitman, Lawrence, Eliot, who have celebrated some kind of religious values, have
not been content with the "pure aesthetic"
of the entertainment arts. Even the great
non-religious art of the Renaissance and
Romantic periods -- Beethoven's quartets or
Shakespeare's tragedies -- seem chiefly to
be celebrating something: perhaps the human
condition   itself.

Although we can make no hard-and-fast
distinctions (Dickens, for example, combined entertainment with moral-social
propaganda in about equal parts), we find
that many dramatic artists have aimed far
less at magic than at the entertainment
purposes traditionally called "aesthetic."
Euripides and Chaucer, Shakespeare in his
comedies, Racine, Moliere, Sterne, Defoe
and most of the 19th century novelists --
these are the artists who entertain as they
instruct, and bring us our best knowledge
of human behavior.

The popular arts, although magical by
tradition, now include much of *entertainment* in the classical sense. The
comedy of Harold Lloyd or "Mr. Peepers,"
as well as the more serious B movies and
television plays, instruct as they amuse.
If they move us, it is not to any social or
political action, but rather to the "aesthetic" and of entertainment: we are moved
to enjoy an aesthetic experience. And if
this seems a lesser experience than we gain
from Moliere or Racine, it is not the
aesthetic values which are at fault, but
something moral-philosophic, metaphysical
or religious: all those normative values
which define the human. Despite our gains
in moral freedom, we have only a broader

definition of the human; the older artists
had a higher one.

In the 16th and 17th centuries, for
example, an educated upper-class enjoyed
the kind of music, painting or drama which
we call "Art" but which served them as
entertainment. This was entertainment of
such high craftsmanship, however, and such
high moral and philosophic value, as to
make the rustic celebrations of the country-
side seem a rough child's play: superstitious peasant games. "Art" came to
mean the high entertainments of the few --
with everything magical or religious either
excluded, or explained in "aesthetic"
terms of the entertainment-arts. *

The folk-magic of the countryside,
despised by the 17th century, was nearly
wiped out by the enlightened 18th century--
along with all the other "myth and superstition" of the Middle Ages . By the time
a few remnants of these had been recovered
by poets and scholars of the Romantic Age,
everything was being called "Art." So
these ancient dances, songs and mythic
tales which had conserved old social and
religious values reaching back to primitive -- perhaps even prehistoric -- myth,
were inaccurately called folk "arts." As
such they came to be highbrow entertainments, enjoyed "aesthetically" by a cultured few. And since the romantic "Art"
includes so much of idol-worship too, the
"folk-arts" were treated as reverently in
some quarters as a Raphael Madonna or
Romanesque cathedral.

Something of the kind is happening
again. An "Art" which now includes all
dead magic or religion, as well as all
aristocratic entertainments of the past,
may include even the Sennett comedies of
yesterday -- adored reverently as "folk-
arts." What this "Art" rules out, as
always, is only the live contemporary magic

* This definition of "Art" in terms of entertainment derives in part from Aristotle. He lived in
a similarly late period, when the magical-religious meaning of the Aeschylean drama and the Oly-
mpian sculpture had been forgotten, and the arts had come to be a civilized entertainment for the
few.

of the many. Whatever vital magic there may be in movies, television, pocket books and comic strips is despised as mass commercialism, childish dreams and "entertainment," or as bourgeois myth and superstition. If the educated reformers had their way, all this magic would be wiped out once again. And each time in recent Western history that a folk-magic has been wiped out, it has come back thinner, more impoverished and debased. We cannot deny that our enlightened education has been leading us, in some ways, straight downhill.

Yet oddly enough, it was this kind of museum-thinking -- the 19th century worship of " Art" at the expense of myth or magic-- which became in itself a curious form of highbrow magic. Even today the ritual of calling other people's magic "entertainment," and one's own entertainments "art," serves as a morale-building activity, designed to keep the highbrow loyal and hard-working and contented within his special class or group. Indeed it is by his powers as an aesthete or art critic (rather than as moralist, historian or philosopher) that the intellectual most often distinguishes himself from the "masses." And yet these highbrow entertainments include not only past art but every entertainment which is currently passing for art -- whether it is imitation pseudo-art or highbrow propaganda and instruction.

The give-away, as R.G. Collingwood points out, is that much highbrow " art" is said to "date" like women's fashions, whereas if it were really art -- well, " Le temps ne fait rien à l'affaire."

> The simpler and more vulgar (say) *I know what I like* The more refined and artistic reject this idea with horror. It makes no difference whether you like it or not, they retort; the question is whether it is good. (This) protest is in principle perfectly right; but in practice it is humbug. It implies that whereas the so-called art of the vulgar is only amusement... the art of more refined persons is not

amusement but art proper. This is simple snobbery...The cliques of artists and writers consist for the most part of a racket selling amusement to people who at all costs must be prevented from thinking themselves vulgar, and a conspiracy to call it not amusement but art. *

So the educated reformer, following the highbrow practice, decrees that all our entertainments must be either " art" or " education." Education is anything suitable for teen-agers to their sophomore year, while art means every dead art, pseudo-art, *pastiche* or imitation copied from past ages. That dreary form of instruction known as " adult entertainment" falls somewhere in between.

The result of this particular snobbery, or highbrow magic, is a vast factory extending from Broadway to *THE NEW STATESMAN AND NATION* for the wider distribution of a standard education and for the mass-production of imitation art. Continual pressure is exerted on the artist to " communicate" understandably to the educated middle group; while such lowbrow media as television or the movies are exhorted to " raise" themselves toward the standard of *THE NEW YORKER* or the *SATURDAY REVIEW* . Not only the comic arts of vaudeville, but such low folk-tales as may be found in comic books or Western movies, are as unacceptable to this middle group as the " arty" entertainments of the highbrow.

Nor can this situation be blamed all on the " middlebrow" or " mass man" of an industrial culture. Some of it must be laid at the door of the too-aesthetic highbrow himself, with his persistent identification of art with culture. Museums, operas, English courses--all " cultural" pursuits. Yet this Fine Arts " culture" is the exact opposite of " a culture" in its living or historical sense, by which we mean the central myths, ideas and institutions under which men live.

Much of the present " alienation" can be traced to this 19th century identification

---

* *PRINCIPLES OF ART*: Oxford, 1938.

of art with culture and of entertainment with non-culture. Whenever we think enviously, for example, of some past or primitive culture, it is generally an aesthetic quality or condition we are admiring. It is the cathedrals, the counterpoint, the pottery or canoe -- the harmony of living socially under a religion pleasing to the inner eye and ear -- this is the picture of a dead Europe which most often makes us say that art is dead, culture is dead. This is an aesthetic picture -- or rather a nostalgic **Fine Arts** picture, like a picture in a museum -- kin to that aesthetic pleasure which many intellectuals are finding in old religious rites. It is also a sentimental picture, which leaves out too much history.

This article will be concluded in the next issue of CITY LIGHTS.

Philip Lamantia

The Game

Man is in pain.
 Ten bright balls bat the air
 falling through the window on which his Double
 leans gelatinously: a net the air formed
 to catch the ten bright balls.
Man is a room
 where the Malefic Hand turns the knob
 on the unseen-unknown Double's door.
Man is in pain
 with his navel hook caught in a stone quarry
 where ten bright balls choose to land.
 and where the Malefic Hand carves on the gelatinous air
 --a window to slam shut on his shadow's tail.
 Ten bright balls bounce
 into the unseen-unknown Double's net.
Man is a false window
 through which his Double walks to the Truth
 that falls as ten bright balls
 the Malefic Hand tossed into the air.
Man is in pain
 --ten bright spikes nailed to the door.

Salvages An Evening Piece

Robert Duncan

A plate in light upon a table is not a plate of hunger.
Coins on the table have their own innocent glimmer.
Everything about coins we obliterate is use and urgency.
How lovely the silver dull disk glimmer is. Shells without remorse.
The rubbd antique nickle dated 1939 Liberty portrait relief of
Jefferson and, beyond, darkend with use, a grimy patina beautiful 1929
buffalo Indian head nickle.

Bottles. An aluminum tea pot with wicker handle. A remnant length of
Italian shawl worn by my grandmother in the 80's, this too increasing
as beauty in dimness; the reds, ochres, blacks and once perhaps almost
white natural cotton yellowd. The wearing, the long use, the discoloring.
It would be becoming to beauty in words worn out. As a poetry, to be
discolord.

It is not the age it is the wearing, it is the reversion to the thing
from its values. One nickle; then two dimes, a brighter, a newness,
fresh-minted (yet when I look--in god we trust--it is 1944, the god is
Mercury with wingd helmet; the other a bust of Deus Roosevelt Roman style
with sagging chin and stuck-up defiant non-descript head--this is 1947--
in god we trust). Then two nickles--the grimy ones. One shiny fifty
cent piece above (beyond) a fourth nickle showing Montecello E Pluribus
Unum.

This mere ninety cents is more, is all piece by piece, in art, as they
are here, pieces of glimmer as rare as the mysterious chalice with faces
and figures or the cast from the greek horse and rider.

Notes on use and values.

    Then the litter. The gleams of silver and nickle seen as coins of
light in the litter. A key--another gleam--an ancient evocation; a
coinsilver spoon, a chippd cheap cup-shaped cup with grey glaze without
the imperfections of beauty beautiful because it is a cup. A large brown
glass bottle of vitamins that look like beans. Papers. A letter from
a friend, a program in my own script black and definite (defiant) arranged
over the hite paper. Matches. An envelope.

In the ate hour left after the history of the day, taken with a will
before bed-time, how transformed the wor is. The silence almost reaches
us in which an original--all that has been left behind, tossd about--of
s--remains.

    Beautiful litter with thy gleams and glimmers, thy wastes and remains.
The tide of our purpose has gone back into itself, into its own counsels.
And it is the beauty of where we have been living that is the poetry of
the hour

OUR HERO...
MOON MULLINS!
A GREAT GUY ACCORDING TO HIS AUTOBIOGRAPHY.

MOON

DANIEL J. LANGTON

EILEEN MARTIN

THE FACE of Moon Mullins is as indelibly stamped in the minds of most Americans as the flourish letters of Coca Cola, the copper head of Abraham Lincoln, the knotty little body of Popeye (the sailor man), or the heavy, handsome face of Clark Gable. For many of us his face recalls, not a single incident or a series of incidents from the comic strip life of this man, but his *manner* of living and the general atmosphere of his world. The observation of his life has become a casual habit with us, a thing we might or might not choose to do over morning coffee.

The casual but persistent popularity of *MOON MULLINS* might be attributed to the purely comic world in which he lives, a world that uses the situations and language of our time, but never in any *specific* contemporary sense, so the situations do not lose their liveliness with the passing of time. (Even the city in which Moon lives could be the city of twenty years ago or now: buildings rise large but formless in the background of his life, and the people wear clothes that represent the

extreme jazzy and lowbrow tastes of a number of years--from 1915 to 1953.) Or the popularity might be because Moon himself is the great American slob--a believable one, as contrasted to the outlandish slobs that come and go in the Lil Abner world of Al Capp.

Moon is not an admirable man; in many senses he is a complete failure in society. He is a banjo-eyed, pool hall sport. He wears his straight hair combed down flat with pomade, and there is usually a derby clamped on his head. He wears bargain basement sport shirts of the loud variety, and saggy pants. Once in awhile he dresses up, puts on a coat and a novelty tie, and goes out to see a chick or have a few beers and some poker or dice. He has a contemptuous, easy posture, and there is usually an unlit cigar in his mouth. Moon doesn't smoke the cigar much--it is there to complete his attitude. His coat is never buttoned.

Moon spends his days hanging around the house or bumming around town, and his evenings are spent doing mostly the same thing, with a little more drinking. He lives in Lord and Lady Plushbottom's rooming house with his kid brother, Kayo.

Kayo is a runt of a kid, tough and wise. He was raised in an atmosphere of cigar smoke and sweaty undershirts. He wears baggy trousers and suspenders, and he hardly ever removes his big black derby hat, which is even bigger than Moon's. He

MULLINS

and This Place He Lives In

FRANK WILLARD: *Colonel Patterson had an idea for a low-brow roughneck strip and called me in because he thought I could handle it.*

GILBERT SELDES: *Art in the comic strip is the primary faculty of being able to create a compact universe that adheres strictly to a logic of its own.*

likes to carry a slingshot. Moon and Kayo usually stick together, and Kayo, though just a kid who comes only to Moon's knee, has learned a lot from his big brother about the ways of the world.

Lady Emmy Plushbottom, the landlady, is a gaunt, stringy woman who is constantly worried about her appearance. She often goes around in curlers, but usually she has elaborate, beauty-parlor ringlets and puffs on top of her hawk-like head, and she likes to buy silly Easter Basket hats and frilly blouses, in which she postures, skinny elbow mid-air, her hand clapped over her boney hip. She leers out at you in an attempt at sexuality, her beady eyes shining through steel-rimmed glasses. Her pre-occupation is being attractive again to Lord Plushbottom or to any man, and sometimes she even buys reducing devices and sits in her petticoat while being massaged by rubber belts and rolling contraptions-- a ghastly sight of cold, bony nudity.

Lord Plushbottom has money, and he is a gentleman--though one never sees his money and there is a suspicion that it doesn't exist, at least not in great quantity. He acts more like a dignified pensioner playing rich. He wears a curious combin-ation of elegant clothing--a morning coat, striped pants, wing collars, and starched white dickeys with a spotted or floral-design tie. It is never clear just exactly what he has on--because, for one thing, he is often in a state of undress. (He is

really too fat to wear clothes comfortably.) He is forever sitting around in haughty posture, half-dressed, smoking his pipe and playing cards. He likes to chase the chicks that Moon likes, pitting his wealth and manners against Moon's able-bodied brassi-ness--and he likes to stay out late at night, boozing, gambling with the boys. But he never loses his dignity, he never welshes on a bet, and he wears his polished moustache high.

Uncle Willie and Aunt Mamie (Moon's

AND MOON'S KID BROTHER... KAYO!

relations) are servants in the boarding house, but they have become members of the household. They too sit around, heavy and indolent, in a state of undress. Willie is almost bald on top, but he has a great growth of black stubble around his mouth, and he chews a stubby black cigar. When he is not in his undershirt, or one of Plushy's (Lord Plushbottom) cast-off wing collars, he wears glaring checkerboard suits. He, like the others, likes to spend his time in pool halls and roll his eyes at girls. He fights almost continuously with his wife, Mamie, for Mamie is always exasperated by his indolence. Mamie wins every fight because she is an enormous, muscular woman who wears a lady-wrestler look on her face and tattoos on her arms. Mamie seems to be the only one who ever works around the house, and though she spends a lot of time sitting around and complaining, she seems forever involved with a scrub pot or a stack of dirty dishes--her hair knotted on top of her sweaty head, her house dress sagging, and her mouth wide open with reproach.

From day to day these six sit around at home, the men playing cards or watching from the window the pretty doll with the mink coat and blonde hair who is always moving in next door, the women complaining; the men losing money in saloons or pool halls, the women beating them up--and now and then they ride into the country with their black cigars and baffle a farmer by their city ways. Their doings are always of a low nature, for the minute one of them tries to exalt himself, a member of the boarding house is there to check him--they have spent too many days together in sweaty undershirts; each knows how crummy the other one is.

There are, as of now, about 10,000 Mullins strips, dating back to July 1, 1923, when Moon made his debut in San Francisco. Frank Willard was twenty-nine when he started the strip; he will be sixty this September. Thus, barring something called

KITTY HIGGINS, which was never more than a dashed-off filler, this strip has been truly a life's work.

Frank Willard was born in Anna, Illinois. He fled from this town after being asked by the school board to leave, and went to the Union Academy of Fine Arts in Chicago. He fled the Academy, too, in three months, and took a job in an insane asylum. In 1915 he submitted a cartoon to the *CHICAGO TRIBUNE* which was accepted, and he threw up his job at the asylum to work for Col. McCormick. He was a sports cartoonist for the *TRIBUNE* until he was drafted in 1917, and when the war was over he spent four years as an anonymous cartoonist for one of the giant syndicates. About this time, Col. Patterson, who was owner of the *NEW YORK DAILY NEWS*, started assembling a stable of comic-strip artists who were to become famous. Col. Patterson dreamed up the situations, and even the names of the main characters. (One of his strokes was to add " and the Pirates" to a strip called

MRS. WM. P. MAMIE MULLINS! SHE CAN TEAR A NEW YORK TELEPHONE BOOK IN HALF—MAKE HER MAD AND SHE'S LIABLE TO DO THE SAME TO YOU.

TERRY that later crossed his desk.) Then he went out and found his artists. Thus, at the same time, GASOLINE ALLEY, LITTLE ORPHAN ANNIE, DICK TRACY, SMITTY, THE GUMPS, HAROLD TEEN, and MOON MULLINS made their appearances--and Willard began to work for Col. Patterson.

Moonshine was quite a common name in 1923, and Mullins was a name associated with the laboring class. (Willard borrowed it from a plumber.) The strip started as Moonshine Mullins, but was soon changed to Moon. The first MOON strips reveal an uncertain and frightened Willard borrowing right and left for both ideas and style. The situations and drawings were awkward; the dialogue strained.

In his first years, Moon was alone. He had to struggle to make a living, and his beginning was as a trainer to Mushmouth Jackson, a colored fighter who was considered by Moon to be a challenger to Jack Dempsey. The ineptness of those first

UNCLE WILLIE...
HE'S PERFECTLY SATISFIED WITH HIMSELF EVEN IF HIS WIFE ISN'T.

strips is hard to believe. Though it was a continuous narrative, it is doubtful if Willard read the old strips before starting the new. Twice a week he used the same situation exactly, only changing the drawings and dialogue: Mushmouth went to jail, but the next day Moon was in jail and Mushmouth was outside attempting to help him escape. When Dempsey fought Firpo, Moon bet on Firpo, and although Firpo lost, Moon won the bet. And so the muddled strip stumbled on, while a patient audience watched.

Through the Twenties and Thirties we can see how Willard was gradually finding his way, introducing his characters. First Little Egypt, a dancer, was added for sexual attraction, with the extra piquancy of being married to a professional strong man. She was to remain Moon's libido for over twenty years. Suddenly, On March 23, 1924, Kayo, the perennial kid brudder, was introduced without an explanation and became a prop for Moon's observations on life. In December of that year, Moon became a member of a lodge and was made treasurer---a poor elective choice, for he left soon after for Gary, Indiana (with the lodge's funds), and took a room in the boarding house of well-to-do Emmy Schmaltz, at 1402 Goatsnest Street. Except for brief sojourns, he has been there ever since.

Little Egypt then came to town to work at a theatre owned by Lord Plushbottom, who had left England under a cloud. (His identical twin was a thief.) She had divorced her professional strong man and was being ardently wooed by Lord Plushbottom. Plushy, thus introduced, came to stay. Uncle Willie (Moon's relation) showed up then as a bachelor, disappeared, and turned up a year later with a wife, Mamie, with whom he had eloped in 1928. Willie and Mamie also came to stay.

During these years, Moon, who was chronically broke, accepted a proposal of marriagefrom Emmy (she offered him sixty-eight thousand dollars.) But he reconsidered on learning of five previous husbands, and

LADY EMMY PLUSHBOTTOM!
THE EFFICIENT LANDLADY... IN SPITE OF NATURE'S BEING A BIT STINGY WITH HER IN THE DEPARTMENT OF LOOKS AND BRAINS.

went to Florida, where he became an out-fielder on John McGraw's Giants.

Later, when he was traded to Chicago for a catcher's mitt and some second-hand jock straps, he quit the game in a huff. He went back to Emmy, who forgave him, and upon her upping the ante, they were re-engaged.

But again he reconsidered, and took a job as valet to Sir Mortimer Bathwater. While he was gone, Emmy married Lord Plushbottom (as part of the ballyhoo for the Chicago Fair of 1933).

Since 1933, the strip has been set: Moon and Kayo, Plushy and Emmy, Willie and Mamie; and these people have gone on with their poker parties, chaste love affairs, bicker-ing and nonsense without a change of an eyelash in method. Had Willard worked the dreary chronology of *GASOLINE ALLEY*. Lady Plushbottom would now be seventy-five, while Kayo would probably be in Korea. Instead, he has evolved " a universe that adheres strictly to a logic of its own."

Now to Moon, and to the special qualities that make him, in his way, worthwhile. Moon is a bum. In the past he has been a prof-essional athlete, a carnival worker, a fight trainer, and something of a part-time lout,

but he has not done a day's work in over twenty years. During the war, Moon was the only comic strip character not employed by the government in War Bond posters. While Joe Palooka, Mickey Finn, and Skeezix Wallet marched off to war, and Daddy Warbucks made war bucks, Moon shot pool and read nothing but the sports page. He is seldom attracted to a woman unless she is rich or married. His neglect of both his attire and his kid brudder's education are shameful. He drinks like a fish, would rather fight than argue, and has never read a book in his life. He is a low-brow and a rough neck, and no better picture of one has been drawn in our literature. His faults gape at you. He believes in, and prac-tises, a sort of democratic anarchy Thoreau was so sure would die in the cities, and he treats everyone with the casual disinterest that only a truly classless sub-society could produce. But he has a certain dignity. He would never stand being lectured to, he is incapable of hyp-ocrisy, and in his scattered, off-hand

LORD PLUSHBOTTOM...
ONE OF NATURE'S NOBLEMEN— WHO'S WIFE HAS SUPREME CONFIDENCE IN HIM...WHEN SHE IS WITH HIM.

attention to his brudder Kayo, he has produced a boy who will be able to spot and puncture pomposity and self-love in others as long as the strip lives

Willard, like Moon, never seemed to care much about the events that have been tearing through man, these past thirty years, and he has carried his independence to an extreme: no one whose only reading matter was *MOON MULLINS* would have known there was a Second World War. But Willard, like Moon, has dignity. (His treatment of the Negro, often crude and jarring, is a model of un-self-consciousness and basic respect for the Negro which some of our Southern writers would do well to study.) It is said that Willard picked the name Mullins from among the plumbers in the phone book. It may well be that this was the last book he ever opened, and for this he may be deplored but not dismissed.

An art has grown unattended and scorned among us. Many believe it is a blight that steals from us the time that could more profitably be spent reading great books. But some are coming to the conclusion that we should ignore it no longer, if only for an analysis of its casual popularity. But Willard, by drawing his people as they are and only as they are, will be rejected for his lack of cleverness and literary all-usions. His failure to educate the masses will be deplored, and his total absence of " aesthetics" will make him difficult to those educated people who are now finding Art in some comic strips.

But if, instead of looking at Moon Mullins from any existing definitions of Art, we look at it as something created according to its own standards and judge it for what it intends to give its audience, then we may discover an art in this frivolity. Surely there is an art in Willard's firm, decisive line, with which he generously rounds out plump bodies, saucer eyes, swollen cigars, and the heavy, soporific, overstuffed furniture in which Moon, Mamie, Willie, Emmy and Plushy loll eternally, apathetic to any other world. There is an art, too, in the flawless language of the people who live in this place--a language where everything is explicit, nothing, in the end, is left unsaid; even the silences reveal the deliberate intentions of a man carefully feeling his own way. There is an art, perhaps, in Moon, one arm wrapped around his blonde, the other grasping the steering-wheel of his roadster, muttering through the cigar in his mouth,

" Let us take a trip to this place, honey, and see my aunt who lives there."

Drawings by Frank Willard, courtesy of CHICAGO TRIBUNE--New York News Syndicate, Inc. Copyright 1953.

Red Blanchard and His *Zonch* Cats

NORMALLY the studios of radio station KCBS, here in San Francisco, are quiet, even somnolent. San Francisco radio is characteristically unhyperthyroid; there are no zany quiz shows, no autograph hound audiences, no movie stars - in short, none of the hustle, bustle and frenzy of radio that obtains in larger cities like New York, Hollywood, and Chicago . Network shows are piped through to the transmitter, announcers read the news, disc jockeys spin their platters, and occasionally there is a small, genteel, live-audience program. To a visitor sitting in the KCBS lobby the place seems to have, except for a low-volume speaker that continually retails the program of the minute, an almost institutional quiet, like the outer office of a plush law firm or the waiting-room of an expensive private sanitarium.

But of late this calm has been rudely shattered. Six nights a week the *Zorchest* juvenile audience in the world files in to attend its own special radio show. It's quite an audience. Many of them have their hair and eyebrows dyed green, their faces painted in weird designs with lipstick or eyebrow pencil. They wear tattered old clothes festooned with outlandish gadgets and hand-lettered slogans (DROP DEAD RED). Their hats are immense floppy creations studded with bottle caps, ostrich feathers,

flashing lights, and anything else that appealed to the creator's fancy.

Their faces tend to be solemn. Adults in the same masquerade get-up would have that giddy exuberance that comes with the knowledge one is doing something silly. But to these children, most of them in the nine-to twelve age group, the Red Blanchard show, "What is it?", is more of a formal social ritual and they wear their costumes much in the way an adult wears morning clothes. Only the older teen-agers become rowdy and treat what they are doing as a joke.

But when the kids after much jostling are finally seated in the studio auditorium, " All hell," as one of the KCBS staff prosaically put it, " breaks loose." To the casual listener, tuning in for the first time in the middle of a program, " What IS It?" probably would sound like a combination football rally and election night shindig. The audience screams, laughs, boos, shouts commercials in unison, and cheers itself hoarse. Here and there in the midst of this bedlam Red Blanchard reads a skit in one of his many voices (Lowell Bogardus, Louella Bogardus, The Flat Man, and dozens of others), plays silly records, conducts interviews, and allows some of his listeners to shout a cheer into the 'bully' machine (an electronic gadget that produces multiple echoes: the child says " bully"

Is it,

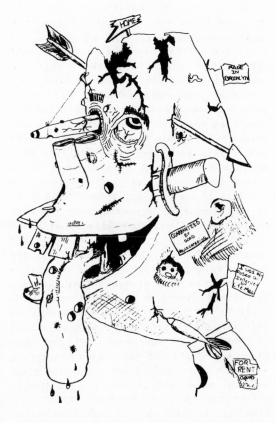

WILLIAM EISENLORD AND JUNIUS ADAMS

and it comes out BULLY bully *bully bully*..)
The total effect, if you fall in with the
mood of the show, is of an electric excitement comparable in intensity to that of a
good revival meeting.

The Red Blanchard show has been attracting a lot of interest in radio circles. Not
only has Blanchard captured a huge juvenile
audience, but he has achieved with them
that rare relationship where they almost
literally do " rush out and buy" any product he happens to be sponsoring.

There seem to be two main reasons for
his success. One is that Blanchard has a
real knack for starting fads. Radio ad-
vertisers are always trying to start fads,
but usually in a superficial, patronizing
and graspingly commercial manner. (" Send
in 15¢ and a Zippies box-top for your new
Captain Magoo Space Goggles! All the kids
are getting them! Be one of the gang! ")
Blanchard, having a better understanding of
his audience, knows that they will respond
best to an idea which is useless, ridiculous, and at least mildly messy or destructive. One of his earliest campaigns
was: " Send us some dirt to fill in San
Francisco Bay! " The dirt poured in by the
ton, cluttering up the mails with bulging
packages and envelopes of all kinds, many
of which undoubtedly broke open in transit.

Other campaigns for empty orange juice cans
and used bottle caps produced a mountain of
scrap. His latest campaign is one to " stamp
out TV, " an idea less productive of chaos
but still negativistic. In the same way,
Blanchard's approach to commercials gives
the impression, at least by implication,
that buying his products is also a useless,
ridiculous, beautifully pointless activity.
One of the particular joys of buying a Zorch
Hat at Roos Bros. or chartreuse colored
shoes at Price's Shoes is that one's elders
will almost undoubtedly *not* approve.
Even turning back a Zorch Cow at a soda
fountain because it is not made with Belfast
Root Beer is a kind of gleeful negativism.
(Red does not really try hard to tell the
kids Belfast is *better*, he sells them on
the idea of *insisting* on Belfast.) The
Hale's commercial (the kids all shout: " Go
to HALE'S!! ") is another example.

The other ingredient of Blanchard's

success is that he realizes the extent to which children are fascinated by certain adult preoccupations. Many of Blanchard's skits are written by his fans, and almost all of them turn on some theme which is usually dealt with by and for adults. They are usually take-offs on adult radio programs such as *DRAGNET* or *THE WHISTLER*, or else they deal with "monsters from outer space." The humor is usually adult radio humor: like Jack Benny with his 1916 Maxwell, Red Blanchard is again and again provided by his juvenile scriptwriters with a "1917 Jaguar pick-up" or an "1863 Zorch Special Twelve." Of course there are more childlike touches; the skits usually end with a horrible, gory monster, slimy and many-tentacled, enveloping the hero in its death-dealing embrace. Faced with this "thing," the hero always "does what any red-blooded American boy would do..." He "blacks out" and "as you black out the last thought that flies through your mind is 'What is it?' Braaaagh!!!" And when Blanchard blacks out he makes a staggering spectacle of it, collapsing across the stage amid the encouraging cheers of his audience. (Of course, here is another reason for Blanchard's following, the fact that he can get and use material which is so powerfully thematic to children, and which prissier and more school-teacherish entertainers would never know how to handle.) But in the main, the scripts Blanchard uses (some of them are reprinted here), are not-so-childish parodies on 'adult' topics; they are replete with 'gorgeous blonde canaries', tough private eyes, and characters such as 'Humphry Bogardus' and 'Katherine Heartburn.' Probably many of these touches were originated by Blanchard, but they are taken up, amplified, and perpetuated in the hundreds of letters that pour in through the mail every week, along with letters, poems, drawings, insults, and packages containing booby traps and practical jokes of all kinds.

Another aspect of this preoccupation with adult and semi-adult activities is the slanguage Red and his Zorch audience use. It is a kind of converted bop talk which takes the lingo of the cat and the hipster and brings it out of the marijuana den and into the soda foundain. Phrases like "I dig that," "Crazy man," "It's the end," etc. are liberally used. In addition, there are some new terms which give things a kind of Freudian overtone, words like "nervous," "mixed-up," and "threatened."

Blanchard also has, of course, a sizeable adult audience. Many of his skits are performed in an inspired manner which is equal to the best of Henry Morgan and other good radio comics. And the show is fascinating to listen to for the sheer excitement of it. Many professional people of a psychiatric or psychoanalytical tinge are known to listen (with a certain priggishness, one would suspect) because they feel that here the American child is exposing his psychological innards. And a number of parlor sociologists watch closely too, fascinated by Red's ability to transform, through the simple gimmick of satire, the socially disruptive attitudes of the hipster into the good-humored affirmations of *Zorch*! But most of us probably listen to Red for the various sound reasons summed up by the Night Special Delivery Mailman at KCBS:

"I stop in and watch Red because it **helps me keep a perspective on everything.**"

Dear Red – Some Zorch Documents from Red's Listeners

DEAR RED,

I am sending you my drawing of the " I Listen to Red in Bed" card. I hope you like it. I just drew a picture of a mug of Root Beer in the right hand corner of my drawing because I live in Glendale and have never seen a bottle of Belfast Root Beer. Your artist can re-draw it though.
I think I deserve an " I dread Red" card for all the work I put in on this drawing. Please send me one.
I saw the article about you in Time magazine, and I thought It was excellent. The picture It showed of you in that " Zorch Hat" made you look like a kid in his teens. I sculptured a large head of " Captain Space the Planet Man" to send to you but I dropped It and It broke. I will try to make you another one if I ever get around to it.
I am mailing this in June 30, so I just get under the line for the contest. I could sure use that $50.

DEAR RED,

Thanks loads for using the two minute drama I recently sent in, and thanks too, for the certificate, in fact the following dramatic gem was written on the back of the certificate. Hope you can use this, and if so, will notify me when so I may hear it, as I don't catch your program every nite.
(VOICE) I'd like now, to tell the story of a man who overcame many hardships to become one of the greatest private dicks in the business. This is the story of Dick Dixon Private Dick, who solved all his cases lying in bed, (he was sometimes known as an UNDERCOVER MAN.) Our story is entitled " Murder on the Golf Course, or he shot her 72 times, as that was par for the course." To best know the story, we first have to delve a bit in the personal life of Dick Dixon Private Dick, a fellow who while in college lost both arms, both legs, had his

eyes put out, and lost his hearing (in a fraternity initiation prank), but despite all this, with courage, and the heart of a lion, he went on to become---a burden to his parents. Dick's father owned a Chinese restaurant, and many times he would sit in the window of the restaurant disguised as a bowl of chop suey, the disguise so he would be unobserved in his fight against crime.
One day a little boy came to Dick in the the restaurant window and told him there was a dead woman lying in the street, Dick muttered in two words," Im-possible," but he decided he'd better investigate first he put in a call to Homicide--Homicide was on vacation, so Dick Dixon Private Dick would solve this case alone. Arriving at the scene of the crime a single look at the body told him, this shrewd observer that she was dead. He went through her handbag to check for identification. It contained the usual things a woman carries in a handbag, keys, a lipstick, a Yo Yo, a hard boiled egg, and a package of beef jerky, no clue yet to her identity. He heard a noise, stealthily glancing around, but noticing nothing, he continued his search for clues to this woman's identity. He opened her coin purse, and there he saw a box of cornflakes. At least one part of the mystery was solved..the noise. You see these were the crispy crunchy kind. Somebody had called the police in the interim (the phone booth was filled) and while Dick was pondering over the many puzzling clues in the case, the coroner came over to the body and said in his most professional manner, " Man check that real crazy stiff." Dick paid no attention. He was too busy with his thoughts, he was determined to solve this real puzzler. Another look at the body, a careful scrutinization of the facial features, and Dick suddenly had the feeling that this woman's face was familiar, who

is she Dick spoke out loud, who, who, who an owl flew down on Dick's shoulder and said "Father."

That's it, Dick exclaimed, I'll check with father. Brushing the owl off his shoulder, he put in a hurried call for his father. (The phone booth was still busy, so he too, had to use the interim.) Presently his father arrived on the scene, and met Dick just as the coroner was preparing to send that real crazy body down to the morgue. Together they made their way to where the police were, they were eating the corn-flakes, Dick asked his friend Lt. Byrd of homicide if he could get another look at the body, but the Lt. was feeding the owl the beef jerky, and couldn't be bothered-- undaunted by this apparent lack of cooper-ation Dick showed his father the body, father agreed, she did look familiar, but who he said who, the owl left his meal of

beef jerky and came back. Suddenly out of the blue a bolt struck Dick I have it he said, shouting with jubilation, I'm not positively sure, but it looks like my wife Mary Jane, I'll look again said his father, " By Jove you're right," his father ex-claimed, Dick you've done it agair " Father and son arm and arm, walked away from the scene, jubilant with the knowledge that once again Dick Dixon Private Dick had solved a crime that baffled the police. Today friends when you pass a certain Chin-ese restaurant and see two eyes peering out from under the noodles in a bowl of chop suey, that's Dick Dixon Private Dick, help-ing in his own little way to help combat crime.

(*The preceeding was a true story only the names, places, facts, dates and incidents were changed to protect the indecent.*)

YOUR name is " 4 eyes" Bogardus. Yes, you are one of the blind umpires of the Perump baseball team. You are better known yet as " The Ump From Perump." After a hard day's work at the ball park, you hurry home in your souped-up 1863 " Szorch Special Twelve." This has become quite a habit, hasn't it, " 4 eyes?" After all, you've never wanted to be late for the Red Blan-chard show, your favorite educational and cultural radio program, did you? No, of course not.....but tonight, you somehow feel very, very brave. So you decide not to listen to the Red Blanchard Show but rather you go into the living room and turn on your TV set and watch Red Buttons. Yes, now you have broken your bond of loyalty to Red Blanchard just because you wanted to watch another comedian perform, and on a TV set, IMAGINE THAT! Now you are in for it, " 4 eyes!" Now you've really done it. But wait.....will you dig that crazy trade mark on the TV? Why...yes, it's one of those real, cool CBS Columbia sets. Now you KNOW that Blanchard's feelings won't be hurt and that everything is just fine, isn't it? So you sit back and relax in

comfort and say to yourself, " Nobody will ever know." Just then you hear a noise from behind you. You quickly turn around and come face to face with Szorch purple colored monstrosity with its long and slimey tent-acles reaching out towards you. One of its arms smashes your 3½ inch thick reading glasses, the other 20 wrap around your body so that they crush you in a terrorizing way and all you can think of is " WHAT IS IT?" " BRAaaaaagh!"

TURK MURPHY'S JAZZ BAND

"turk murphy is unquestionably the most driving force in . . . 'dixieland' music today." [nesuhi ertegun: SOMBRA, rio de janeiro, december, 1950.]

featuring

BOB helm
" . . . probably the strongest jazz band clarinetist since jimmy noone and johnny dodds . . . " writes mr. ertegun, currently teaching the history of jazz at u. c. l. a.

wally rose
from joplin to scarlatti . . . equally at home in the concert field, rose has been called "the finest living exponent of authentic ragtime."

"the temptation is very strong
to say that this is the best white jazz of all time..."
– GEORGE AVAKIAN of COLUMBIA RECORDS, RECORD CHANGER, may, 1951

dancing   thursday through sunday nights 9 to 2

the italian village
columbus at lombard – san francisco

Ace on the Road

A Recent Hollywood Tradition
and the Man Who Took Over

JORDAN BROTMAN

AMONG all the developments that changed the face of the Hollywood movie after the war, two must be singled out for the strong and contrary influences they have sought to exert over our lives. One is the rise of a new kind of film, based on part of the common experience of postwar life. This is the "highway movie": it gave us most of the best pictures of the late 40's. The other is the rise of an undistinguished young actor named Kirk Douglas, now an established name in Hollywood. Kirk Douglas carved out his career in the highway movie and decided its fate. His climb had been a challenge to Hollywood ever since CHAMPION (1948); his last highway movie, ACE IN THE HOLE (1951), showed how much had been at stake--and was lost. In this article I want to examine the highway movie and Kirk Douglas together, and point out their double role in the last few ill-defined years of Hollywood's entertainment life.

If we were to try to pin down the distinctively American quality of so many good postwar movies - KISS OF DEATH, CHAMPION, THE PROWLER, RED RIVER, and others - we should soon come across the fact that all of them were dominated by an image: an image of the American road. The road, the great theme of both our geography and our inner lives, has been faithfully, and as it were involuntarily and painfully reflected in our pictures. Think of RED RIVER, the story of a cattle exodus from Mexico to the Abilene railroad. With its primitive subject, RED RIVER only gave us our broadest land-bearings; yet these could never have been transformed, as they were, by such sensitive devotion to every inch of the way, by such a hunger to consume distances, if we were not in the habit of seeing the roadstead and the highway as part of our most personal, unhistorical selves.

This link, between the road and ourselves, is the emotional clue to many successful movies of the late 40's, like SUNSET BOULEVARD. Strip SUNSET BOULEVARD to its essential situation, and you have William Holden racing through Los Angeles a breath ahead of the finance company - a down-and-out film writer in a city of highways, terrified at the thought of having his car taken away from him. There is something momentous about this escape, not only because we all know Los Angeles, but because there is a Los Angeles of the mind, and William Holden flitting like a moth from road to road down to the oldest road in civilization - Gloria Swanson's stately, decayed boulevard - becomes Theseus in an American labyrinth.

In such pictures as this, the discovery of the highway gave the movies a new dramatic grasp of the *careers* of men, their rise and destiny. The "career" is preserved in its literal sense, as a rushing over a road - even in big-city movies like *KISS OF DEATH*. A hero is forced out of the common life and travels his road alone, either to come to terms with life or repudiate it and get run down. In either case he cannot escape his nature; the road, always beckoning as an escape into chance and the elements, comes to signify the course of his real character - he travels on his humanity alone.

The sources of the highway movie - with its moral intensity, its manneristically severe photography can be traced back to any number of traditions: the suspense film, the tough detective film, the American-at-war film, and furthest to the Depression film and the documentary. But these are not all. Hollywood's central tradition derives from its audience. The movies reach out into the population for new stars who then eventually reproduce their *own* inner lives on the screen, and their connection with the older heroes may be simply that they themselves have grown up going to the movies. This connection was explicit in the highway movie. The men who starred in it were speaking for an emergent new proletarian type - the unfinished, partly educated (and incidentally movie-minded) young veteran, the American who went to the last war and had his first moral awakening there, and came back painfully procuring an identity out of all he could find: uncertain of his aims, desiring freedom and security at once, divided between ambition and moody despair. And just as the war precipitated a vast awakening (the G.I. Bill was its momentous result), so the highway, crowded with the wanderings of army-camp days and the unsettled numbers of unmarried adults in the first years after the war, again witnessed

the national and historical hardship. These were bitter personal experiences, but they were a mass experience. It was the highway movie that found this out, that caught the personal image of the time and tapped its energy.

Hollywood's actual receptiveness to the new period was measured by its *casting*, a highly developed skill that exercises a subtle leadership over the story line, and has continuingly and increasingly substituted for skilled acting. The highway movie brought forward a number of specialized new stars and cut across established lines. Van Heflin, for example, an actor who had been stymied for years playing emasculated roles for the women's market, turned up not too long ago in a fine highway movie: *THE PROWLER*. Whether or not anyone responsible saw the hidden connection between Heflin's earlier roles and this story of voyeurism and deceit, of a man cut down on the highway because he cannot get into life, *THE PROWLER* remains Heflin's central role. A similar change took place with Victor Mature, who after years of erotic opportunism suddenly came to with *KISS OF DEATH*, a serious movie which discovered his childlike, urban pathos.

The point about these men - and new ones like Richard Conte (*THIEVES HIGHWAY*), Sterling Hayden (*THE ASPHALT JUNGLE*), Montgomery Clift (*RED RIVER*, *A PLACE IN THE SUN*), Burt Lancaster (*THE KILLERS*) and others - is that they came into their own because some casting director caught in them some of the common look of moral ambition and moral collapse. They were proletarians (even the film writer in *SUNSET BOULEVARD* is glamorless) - not of "circumstance" but of social and psychological conditioning. They were presented as failures more often than not, for, as Kirk Douglas's sudden rise will show, Hollywood is drawn to failure. They were not insignificant men; but the precision of the casting office cut them all to size. Thus they left the highway movie in a state of suspense, of potentiality, that sooner or later must be recognized and broken in upon by someone with more encompassing ends in view - for better or for worse. And Kirk Douglas had them in force.

I first saw Kirk Douglas in *LETTER TO THREE WIVES*, a successful comedy in which he played a gentle high-school English teacher married to an ambitious, scattered woman who writes radio scripts, and who almost wrecks his home by throwing it open to her raucous agency sponsors. Kirk Douglas has never returned to this role,

a unique exception among his pictures, but it throws light on the movie personality he later developed in the highway movie.

The point to be noted is that Mankiewicz, who directed the picture, failed to see what he was really doing with his English teacher. When Kirk comes back to his miserable, repentant wife, shyly lectures her on the humanities, and wins her promise to write radio only on weekends, we are informed that the small truth is sweeter than the big lie: culture, armed with nothing but light, has slain the hydra of radio. But what has actually happened is much less agreeable.

Distracted as she is, the wife is really the stronger, more productive, more self-reliant and realistic of the two. The teacher is a coddler. He sucks sweets of memorized poetry; he is "hurt" by radio; he nurses his injuries for future reproach. The real point is that the humanities are nice because they are so *weak*, and Kirk Douglas knows it. At the end, the wife, who does not have the means of valuing her energies and is more at the mercy of her husband than she knows, has to take him in again; even so, her promise about weekends sounds just like a pampering concession for a little more sex.

It is the more striking that Mankiewicz could have been taken in by this story, since another story in the same picture, about an illiterate department-store tycoon and an aggressive salesgirl (Paul Douglas, Linda Darnell). shows how two strong people come together because they are strong, and to their own surprise discover love; here sweetness belongs to power, as it does in all real comedy. But equally remarkable is how fittingly Kirk Douglas is cast. With his charmingly passive gravity, the way his eye casts about for the caress of **approval**, Kirk Douglas shows that he grasps instinctively and only too well what is expected of his English teacher. Some sympathetic streak directs the actor to a part that is essentially pose, since the teacher's values are counterfeit. What comes through is Kirk Douglas's obvious confidence of deserving everything a teacher (or a musician. a journalist, a statesman - why not?) *should* deserve, as if, rather than acting a part, he were declaring his existence alone enough to suffice for any achievement.

This seductive kind of prowess opens up into a rougher, more violent prowess in Kirk Douglas's later pictures, but the connection with *LETTER TO THREE WIVES* is more basic than this. *LETTER TO THREE WIVES* brought an enlightened, liberal species of Hollywood opinion carefully before the public. It is precisely such opinion - if we think of it as that cluster of vague, ingratiatingly liberal attitudes upheld in the character of the English teacher - that has fallen time and again, in modern life, to the seduction of sheer power. And sheer power, having found the right opportunity,did take over in the later Kirk Douglas movies behind the persistent liberal haze - a power putting itself forward as more spectacular than anything it cares to attempt or than any world it cares to live in. Above all, the writers, the directors, the "progressive" producers from Stanley Kramer on down were not simply helpless before the spectacle of the Kirk Douglas personality, but acted with it in a fascinated collusion.

This situation emerged in the most demo-cratic of all Hollywood's picture forms: the highway movie. How acute it became can be seen from a look at three Kirk Douglas highway movies: *CHAMPION* (1948): *YOUNG MAN WITH A HORN* (1949); and *ACE IN THE HOLE* (1951).

CHAMPION, as Ring Lardner originally wrote the story, was about a hoodlum who makes good in the prize ring by crushing one life after another. The opening sen-tences are typical: "Midge Kelly scored his first knockout when he was seventeen. The knockee was his brother Connie, three years his junior and a cripple." Hollywood transformed the piece in two ways. First, it made a flowing highway narrative out of a small hotel-room story; second, it made - or almost made - a tragedy.

The movie has a momentous sweep that was quite beyond Lardner's idea. It begins with the two brothers going west on the bum and ending up on the Pacific beach, highway's end; there are a roadstand owner's daughter, a few fights, a growing crowd of hangers-on; finally the long trek back to New York and the Garden, from training camp to training camp along the road. The highway is the scene of the career; and, standing for the double obsession of pursuit and escape that possesses Midge, it *is* the career.

The obsessive motif marks the picture's second break with the story, the step into tragedy. Ring Lardner made Midge a skulking moron and scored his main point against a system that showered Midge with honor. In the movie Midge is a fighter of heroic dimensions, greater than the system, greater than all the dependents of the system: the system crucifies whom it honors. About the basis of Midge's greatness, however, Kirk Douglas and the movie disclose a fundamental disagreement. And because Kirk Douglas is allowed to carry the last-moment decision, a spell is broken.

What *CHAMPION* meant to say is that Midge's greatness lies in his striving, vulnerable innocence. A brilliant alter-ation of Lardner's story will point this out. Both Midges have to throw a certain fight. In the story this is a sordid affair in which Midge haggles over his cut of the take and then lies down in the second round. In the movie, it is Midge's fatherly and worldly-wise manager who stands for throwing the fight in the interests of making the big time the right way. And as willing as he is, Midge cannot bring him-self to throw the fight. He is driven to betray his prospects and his loyalties for a vision beyond his control.

This is the tragedy of a simple, powerful man caught between two forces, the one created by his dependents and the world they know how to get along in, the other by his obsessive reason for being. Midge attracts parasites helplessly, and it is they from whom he seems to be struggling to free himself in the ring. The lame brother (Midge does not beat him in the movie) is a moral cripple too; the manager is a sensitive weakling; the women throw themselves compulsively at Midge, without asking what it is they are helping to destroy. These people prey on Midge's conscience, goading him into coarseness and brutality and making him pay with his eventual death in the ring. They are the price of his single, impossible drive to fulfillment in the dream.

But even so, the movie ends by endorsing the pious denunciations on every face as the hero's body is dragged away, and then we see that it has really intended - on Kirk Douglas's initiative - to endorse them throughout. Hollywood is not always able to follow through with its moral commitments, and Kirk Douglas has forcible commitments of his own, backed by the urgency of a physical personality. If the world of Midge's followers remains morally bankrupt for all to see, it is really because that world and its pieties represent the whole, incapacitated moral world for Kirk Douglas - the world in which he means to distinguish himself. As Midge, Kirk Douglas plainly wants greatness *with* guilt: he wants to *compel* Midge's followers (along with the great movie audience beyond them) to participate in his guilt and to forgive him, forgive the naked athlete for sins that lose their identity in the strong, sweet solvent of personality. At the end of *CHAMPION*, the hero's appeal goes over the heads of his pious detractors and directly to the public: Midge is to be forgiven.

The audience is enticed among the weaklings, and the splendor of *CHAMPION* passes

away with a bad taste. The producers have deserted their theme and surrendered to a virtuosity that seeks out a degraded world to be guilty in - in order to assert its freedom from *any* moral structure that could assign guilt. In compromise, the camera fixes on the surfaces of Kirk Douglas's body; it is in love with that body, its softness and its rages, like any other compulsive among Midge's followers.

How Ring Lardner's doctrinal little story could have evolved a true highway tragedy and its fatal deterioration at the same time, only shows how inventive Hollywood is - and after that how easily intimidated, despite all the intrepidity of the camera. That such intimidation could lead to further and finally total surrender remains for our two later Kirk Douglas movies to show.

YOUNG MAN WITH A HORN is after Dorothy Baker's romantic account of Bix Beiderbecke. It was not a clear account, perhaps because one thing about Bix was only too clear: Bix was a great musician. This fact is turned into the pivotal lie of a movie that glitters with all the surfaces of emancipated Hollywood.

Kirk takes on Bix's career (a highway career too) as a rejected child, a waif picked up by a Negro band. The leader teaches him to play and becomes his dependent. Negroes are to this picture what the women and cripples are to *CHAMPION*: they succour and forgive, only, being negroes, they are content with token returns. The movie plays up the sexual situation, varying it to fit Kirk's fantasy; in the end, like abandoned lovers, the negroes become very aged, spiritual, and full of massa. The camera suggests excitement with highways rushing toward fulfillment and doom. Doom does come: Kirk has a breakdown and recovers in the clutches of a loyal white woman. The price of those dark flirtations has thus been, in Kirk's terms, fatal.

A complete surprise comes in the middle of the picture: an episode that forces the issue. Kirk, as Bix, has made the Cafe Society circuit and meets Lauren Bacall, well bred, expensive, a sociology student at Columbia and the daughter of a doctor. They have a touchy romance and decide to marry, and Kirk moves into Lauren's penthouse. But Lauren soon displays clinical symptoms: she grows sexually colder, more abrupt and critical; she won't come home; finally she drops Kirk and the penthouse too, and is last seen making a grim effort to reinstate herself at school. Kirk falls into an alcoholic coma.

At last, we think, Kirk has pushed his way into something too big, the movies have taken his measure. Certainly Lauren's plight is more interesting than his; she is father-dominated, striken with "uncreativeness" and vagrom impulses, but she has brains, courage, and culture. She wants Kirk because Kirk is "reality," and when she quickly undeceives herself she turns away to impose an even sterner punishment on her pride. The facts are there; but the movie stands with Kirk's wounded sensibility against hers. If something bigger than Kirk exists, its bigness is demonstrably bad, selfish, frigid, and lame. Lauren Bacall stands for the civilized world that always lurks in the background of Kirk's resentment, and now comes forth a a suicide.

ACE IN THE HOLE, biggest and most challenging of the three highway movies, brings us a Kirk Douglas who is no longer pulling his punches; and Hollywood has brought out its heavy equipment to back them up. A movie so ominously mounted against the southwestern mesa and sky, so massive with contrasts of highway and winding catacomb - here human beings must be stripped down and the stakes must be high. They are: Chuck Tatum, the movie's hero, is doomed; and so humanity is doomed.

Kirk Douglas, as Chuck Tatum, plays a washed-out New York reporter who lands a job on an Albuquerque paper and waits for the big break that will send him back to his thousand-a-week dream. On a routine assignment he stops for gas at a soft-drink stand in the desert; behind it is an Indian burial mountain, and inside one of the shafts a man is trapped. Sensing his big lead, Chuck braves the shaft ("I like the odds") and stays to oversee the rescue. The victim can be carried out in a day; Chuck schemes to keep him buried for a week - time to awaken the nation and bring New York to its knees.

The rest of the story traces the coming of the great carnival crowd to the scene, Chuck's guileful brutality, the sensuality of the victim's wife - and finally that inexplicable moment of paralysis and regret, when Chuck discovers that it is too late to save his man. There is a struggle with the wife, a flash of scissors. Mortally wounded, Chuck climbs to the loudspeaker on top of the hill. "Leo Minosa is dead," he snarls at the crowd. "Go on, get in your cars and go home. Go home." Then he speeds back to town and slumps in front of the editor's door with the failing cry: "You looking for a thousand-a-week man? You can have him - for nothing!"

So ends lunacy - or does it? The movie observes the code of punishment after crime, but Chuck Tatum's long death agony points to something else. It is his supreme cry of rage and contempt against humanity - the sadism of the crowd, the malignity of women, the cowardice of officialdom, the greed of New York. Behind these, more quietly yet more insistently attacked, are the stupidity of simple folk and the sickliness of the innocent. In a world so debased, Chuck Tatum's agony becomes the voice of a greatness that can find no redeeming response in life, and his crime a cry against a human justice that is boneless, impotent to acquit itself. Who is to judge Chuck Tatum, when Chuck has judged with his life?

ACE IN THE HOLE prepares for Chuck's verdict with calm integrity. In the background stands the great herdlike crowd, mounted by the camera in bare closeups and high panoramas (taken from a helicopter). The secondary characters emerge in detail: big, babylike Leo Minosa in the cave; the Indian mother snuffling into her rosary; the Spanish father, stooped and cringing; the sheriff with his pet rattlesnake; the somnambulistic Lorraine. And towering above all is Kirk Douglas's overdeveloped physique with its machinelike completeness, asserting superiority over men and suppleness under danger. The camera fixes on all these elements with a lingering, skilled fascination that is like intelligence itself, caught in the ultimate reality.

That a picture as bankrupt as this one can, in fact, make its point with so much enlightenment, shows clearly where Kirk Douglas draws his biggest assets. All the approaches of ACE IN THE HOLE are made from the right side. The picture's ethical discriminations are, as it were, democratic - the public vs. the mob, the social vs. the antisocial - and it attacks the evidence in a sociological way. Its impulse is to present its subject as a critical test case, and, without shrinking from the evidence, to return a liberal verdict on human society. And if it does turn out that society is subhuman, that the strong man who can give it its real name remains our only sanctuary - why then, the documentary style is its own unanswerable justification.

Kirk Douglas was quick to exploit the high mood of the picture. Here were courage, realism; and Kirk met the challenge with a daring bid for "unpopularity." "I think," he wrote in an accompanying press release, "American audiences are adult enough to appreciate the impact of this frank, hard-hitting picture." He refers to the "heated controversial discussions" that greeted the first screenings of the film. "Many people said it's stark and pitiless. Even more said that ACE IN THE HOLE is vivid...exciting...realistic. That it portrays true-to-life *people* as they really react to a desperate situation."

Life *must* be seen as it is, and Kirk tears the veil: "You know there *are* women as greedy, as heartless, as unfaithful as Lorraine, played by Jan Sterling. And there *are* men like Chuck Tatum, the ruthless man that I play who lets neither men, women, nor morals stand in his way. You may hate me as Chuck Tatum...or cheer me...but as long as it stirs you, excites you...as an actor I'll be satisfied."

To turn from these artless remarks to the picture itself is to turn to Kirk Douglas's private hell. Like all hells, it is insensitive and redundant, and if it looks like reality it is because a sensitive camera has conformed with a highly selective realism. The nerveless landscape, the stunted Indian figures only secure Chuck's insensitivity to landscape and to the spirit abiding in the Indian dead, or abiding anywhere. And the vacant faces of the crowd only secure Chuck's insensitivity to the human. A great crime has been committed in this picture, yet the only event of equal magnitude here is Chuck's coldness before the crime itself. Rage and regret perhaps, but never moral realization, which cannot happen in a Kirk Douglas movie because nothing on Kirk can be final and binding.

The Chuck Tatums cannot face the demands of life, but they can bear even less to be alone in their hell. They want power; they want life as it "really" is and invariably find it among the shabby and deformed. What is Lorraine Minosa, for example, but the indispensable guarantee that sex is a sham? And Lorraine is just deadly enough to put the fact that Chuck is inadequate with women almost beyond recognition. There is one relationship in the movie: there is an adolescent boy who worships Chuck, and upon this child who has had no prior life of his own Chuck confers something like admission into his own orbit of self-love. Here, of course, we have the essential relationship of all Kirk Douglas movies: Midge Kelly and his crippled brother, Bix

and the negroes. In *ACE IN THE HOLE*, where
life is impoverished of all resources and
where Kirk Douglas, paragon of muscularity,
consequently takes on spiritual qualities,
the relationship with the young boy becomes
the most aspiring of such relationships and
yet rests on the most desperate device: the
corruption of a child.

IN THESE three movies we have traced the
defeat of a moral community: the moral
community that defined the sombre but con-
sequential world of the highway movie. In
CHAMPION Kirk Douglas was already well
enough in control to undermine that movie's
tragic, affirmative character with a seductive anarchy of his own. In *YOUNG MAN
WITH A HORN* he enlisted the audience to
denounce moral and cultural complexities
only too vulnerably exposed in Lauren Bacall
In ACE IN THE HOLE he unmasked the mob in
society, and offered moral sanctuary behind
his iron-fisted reproach. And no one was
to guess that the audience, menaced, privileged, and excited at once, was to be
turned into a mob itself.

This transformation of moral community
into mob - in the highway movie and out-
wards, by insinuation, to the world of the
audience - has been the achievement of one
man, undistinguished other than by his
capacity for punchy fatalism. The question
is: how has Kirk managed to swing it? What
has brought big Hollywood so meekly behind
him? Not the box office entirely. Compared
to truly mass products like the musicals
and the "women's" films, the Kirk Douglas
movies can count on no more than a modest
take. Their aims are expansive, but they
are essentially designed for the scattered,
curiously distinct public of the highway
movie, and they take their stand on the
relatively free, initiating level of that
form. The point is that it is just here -
at its own level of free initiative - that
Hollywood has fallen to Kirk Douglas.

The answer must lie, then, in Hollywood's
attitudes toward itself. Negating the

consequences of all action with the glamor
of brutal, sheer performance, Kirk Douglas
seems to have brought *decision* to a Hollywood that has not really wanted to face the
more difficult decisions involved in its
widening contact with American life. Evidence of this widening contact was the
highway movie, which, as if accidentally,
tapped the enormous contemporary significance of the image of the road. If the Kirk
Douglas movies were able, at the right
moment, to take over the new impulse with
a grotesque individualism that looked like
its fulfillment, it was only because they
had the backing of Hollywood's permanent
sense of inadequacy.

Unrest and self-contempt are still the
lot of the liberal, intellectual writer in
Hollywood. It is to the writer that we
finally turn, because the writer's position
in the industry is vital - and because Kirk
Douglas has entered into a flirtation precisely and curiously with him, with his
mind; the Kirk Douglas movies savor of this
flirtation. At the root of things, perhaps,
is the writer's own guilty sense of compromise. This is exercised in him daily by
his imagined subordination to a system that
supposedly puts an incredible money value
on "talent" only to follow through with an
incredible lack of interest. The fact is,
however, that this view of his position
only affords the writer a comforting escape
from the recognition of what he most intimately fears and hates: his possession of
real power. In this the Hollywood writer
faithfully reflects the predicament of
liberal culture at large, its refusal to
take up the lonely and besmirching responsibilities of power, to take frank
hold of the main, vulgar opportunities
for power available in the time. This
state of things has interacted with liberal thought itself, which, clinging to
its accustomed innocence about the role of
power in human affairs, has acquired the
characteristic softness and passivity that
we noted in the role of the English teacher

in *LETTER TO THREE WIVES*. Liberal culture has always disparaged Hollywood, dramatizing the corruptions of power with its clamor about "the big sellout." The peculiar virginal shame thus preserved in the Hollywood writer has made him susceptible to the attentions of dissident forces whose secret it is to be quite at home with power. Hence, for example, the virulence of Stalinism in Hollywood: at the core of its ethical persuasiveness, Stalinism stood for the preservation of personal dignity and purity - and for the formulation of power decisions by others. Hence, too, the minor but significant appeal of Kirk Douglas.

Kirk Douglas represents an old romance in the life of the writer: the romance of the intellectual and the pugilist. Oddly enough, in this case it is the pugilist that has the intellectual initiative. Kirk wants the writer above all, wants to get possession of that elusive, envied, private mind; and to that end he is gifted with an intuitive sense of where weakness and virginity truly lie. The writer, flattered by an appeal that would redress the injuries of childhood, cooperates, identifying with a promiscuity and moral destructiveness that seem to take bold vengeance upon the human lot. The result, in the script itself, is the production of a spurious toughness, a spurious display of power, seeming to answer the continual demand by society at large for an intellectual leadership that can deliver, but in fact only betraying what Kirk Douglas has sensed and manipulated in the Hollywood writer all along: the soft spot of virginal withdrawal, of incipient disloyalty.

The Kirk Douglas movies, taken alone, give us hopeless feelings about liberalism in Hollywood, at the same time that they raise a very real, involuntary hope that keeps us in an unpleasant suspense. The road movie, in its original form, came to an end with the entry of the ace on the road. But no idea, no form, is ever permitted to stand still: sooner or later, an ace was going to get on the road, a new moral threat would challenge the idea to grow greater by encompassing it. The idea, we see, surrendered some movies ago. And the threat keeps coming at us again and again, in the tireless repetition of Kirk Douglas's face, always closer to us, more obvious, more grimacing. Yet just here it is almost as if the movies - "movies" by themselves - had some inherent way of taking care of their too prominent faces, distorting them and finally dissolving them; as if the movies on their own might just give the ace his come-uppance. This, at least, is the irritable hope that keeps us waiting for word of the new Kirk Douglas movies - and even, for all we know, going to them.

1953 POSTSCRIPT: Since this article was written (1951), three new Kirk Douglas movies have appeared. Two of them are milestones of a sort. *THE JUGGLER* (1953) is a highway movie set not in America but in Israel, where it transplants, by a kind of cultural imperialism, the social bleakness of *ACE IN THE HOLE*. *DETECTIVE STORY* (1952) celebrates the marriage of Kirk Douglas and the Broadway theatre. This was inevitable. Broadway, in its senescence, must have rejoiced in the show of strength provided for the stage by Kirk; we can only guess at Kirk's feelings on gaining this high preserve of cultural respectability.

a winter hanging

William Millett

I

January is a wind
sprayed on every snow flake
and the clouds are heavy as
        prisoners in a jail.

The sun falls into an edge
of blazing ground
and the sky melts
like a castle of sand.

Birds scream overhead
        like flapping sheets
and the flat-faced moon
is a sterile bandage
on the lacerated sky.

II

I see a black land,
the green hides like lead
in a cavern of death
and the willows stand nude
in the snow.

I hide in the woods, dark woods,
and hear the drums of animals
and their secret dances
shattered by those fog-echoed, valley voices.

My eyes roll
        suspended from a thin wire
as the Klan search for my
        paralyzed scent.

III

They come rope-drunk
faces wrinkled
gloves wet with fear
looking like cellophane on fire.

Strong as Knight's armour
sheathed in honor and sword
I feel their fingers deep in my throat
and my blood begins to drop in palm hands.

A large ball of silence
chokes me with a hooded weight
dark as a paper bag
and something makes round, cold lines
above my shoulders.

Out of brilliant lights
I see the great basic face of
death lifting before me
saying Christ is a colored man
you will be with him tonight.

SHANE as Serious Drama

F. W. HOWTON

GEORGE Stevens, who made *A PLACE IN THE SUN*, directed *SHANE*. We are not surprised to find that *SHANE* is a marvel of subtlety in the use of the camera, the composition of scenes, and in the effective exploitation of symbolic values. Many pages of careful analysis could be and should be devoted to critical appreciation of these strictly cinematic aspects. However, since most people who take movies seriously are already convinced that Stevens is an outstanding film artist, this reviewer feels that a more pressing task is to show that the excellence of *SHANE* includes plot and dramatic development as well as directorial technique narrowly construed.

It is my contention that *SHANE* is serious and important drama, not just "poetry in film" or "musically ordered images," to mention two of the more beguiling cliches currently heard. That the basic story is traditional and that the characters -- superficially viewed -- are stock is not necessarily a liability for *SHANE* any more than it is one for a Verdi opera, or, to take a more pertinent example, *THE BLUE ANGEL*.

American movie audiences, harrassed by the second-feature system (unless one is warned in advance, how hard it is to walk out on a Universal epic that just might turn out to be another *D.O.A.*!) have developed a psychosis about "formula stuff." Too often "familiar" means "formula" and "formula" means "stinker." The unfor-

tunate result is a thoroughly perverse preference for plotless porridges. This animus against clear, simple, and familiar plotting is at the root of the charge currently heard that the plot of *SHANE* is unimportant and to be dismissed.

SHANE is a familiar story with familiar characters in a familiar setting presented with extraordinary skill and sophistication. Moreover, it is conventional realistic drama with a tragic motif. The central character, Shane, wistful sojourner among "real" people, copes throughout with a moral dilemma of universal scope and appeal.

Shane, the aimlessly roving gunfighter, always tied to his great burden of guilt -- guilt for being stronger and abler and at the same time more capable of violence and destructiveness -- is inevitably an outcast. His great talent for violence obsesses him and constitutes a tragic flaw. His is the fate of all exotic specialists: to be known by one uncanny skill, to exist in a single aspect. All of his relations with men are dominated by the legend of prowess that pursues and envelopes him like a poisonous cloak. Bad men seek him out to measure their might against his; good men shun him because his strident example of vengefulness threatens their virtue and their self-esteem.

Ascetic individualism is the object of an old and continuing preoccupation in literature and moral philosophy. The poignant image of man as set off from and tragicomically coping with Society -- Society seen as a congeries of raw, brutish forces analagous to the forces of nature in their utter unconcernedness with individual human needs and goals -- has been a never-failing subject of dramatic inspiration. The theme of *SHANE* might be described as the paranoid variety of this larger theme. The character Shane cannot relate to others as a "whole" person because he fears that his association will be contaminating and destructive. He believes that, willy-nilly, he must bring tragedy to those he would love.

The character Heyst in Conrad's novel *VICTORY* is beguiled by the diametrically opposite obsession: he fears that association with others will be hurtful and destructive to *him*. Both Heyst and Shane are ascetic individualists; both have sadly and reluctantly renounced intimate personal relationships through fear of the destructive results they are sure must follow. The difference is in the anticipated object of the evil consequences. Heyst fears for his lily-pure soul; he believes that any close contact and involvement with the depraved world of men must result in his moral destruction. Shane, on the other hand, fears not for himself, but for those he touches.

The movie treatment may be considered in three sections or phases. In Phase I Shane, from out of nowhere, "happens by" a sodbuster's homestead. The essence of his dilemma appears immediately in the contrast between him, the aloof and subtly dangerous horseman, and the warm, solid family group of the Starks. Each fascinates and yet repells the other as only opposite human types can--and must. Each is strong in the area in which the other is weakest. They regard each other as potential selves, and in the poignancy of that disturbing vision they sense a basis for union, a kinship of oppositeness. Stark, Marian—his wife, and their young boy exemplify for Shane what he wants most and can never have: peace and love. Shane, for the Starks, stands for freedom and invincible power.

On impulse born of his ambivalence, Shane lends moral support to Stark, who is being intimidated by the local cattle baron. Riker, the cattleman, wants to clear the homesteaders off of "his" range. Stark is grateful and more--he urges Shane to stay on as a helper. Shane, somewhat to his own surprise, it would seem, accepts.

Shane feels that to embroil himself in the Riker-sodbusters dispute is to bring bad trouble to them and himself as well. This motive is the basis for his refusal to fight one of Riker's bullies in town, an act which stamps him as a coward in the eyes of both parties.

Clearly, from what I have posited of Shane's character, that action is strongly heroic rather than cowardly; the effort it cost him to suppress his hyperdeveloped propensity to fight back must have been very great. Only the knowledge that his fighting back would promptly involve him as an active party with ultimate destructive consequences upon his irresponsible little idyll with the Starks has held back his hand.

(The barroom scene is one of the early highpoints of the film. Shane, in awkward loose-fitting brand-new denims and work shirt, invades the accepted sanctuary of the cattlemen to buy--soda pop! Calloway, big, tough Texas cowboy dressed in well-cut saddleworn clothes, heckles Shane, implying that he "smells of pigs." The physical contrast between the two men-- clothes, manner, speech--symbolizes the real social gulf between the cattlemen and the sodbusters. The meek, family-bound homesteaders fear and envy the strength and glamorous audacity of the cattlemen; they, in turn, look wistfully at the settled, constructive family life of the others. Calloway's shy admiration of Torrey's daughter (the girl fascinated by the hats in Grafton's store) is certainly a factor in his defection from Riker, after Torrey's murder.)

Phase II begins with Shane's fight at Grafton's store with the same Riker hire-

ling, Calloway, who had heckled him before.
Although he attacks the cowboy on his own
initiative and clearly has no intention of
involving the sodbusters in a brawl, he is
soon overwhelmed by numbers. Stark, wielding
a pick-handle, comes to his rescue. Back to
back, the two friends fight the four cattlemen to a draw. The significance of this
action lies in Shane's apparent commitment
as an active party in the Riker-sodbusters
dispute. Henceforth he can no longer be the
idle stranger with known sympathies but with
no responsibilities as a combatant.

(Portentous of his growing involvement
and apprehension is the gun-handling lesson,
in which Shane demonstrates to the boy
proper technique in drawing and firing. The
"lesson" is, of course, no more than a
pretext. Ritualistically, Shane wants to
reassure himself that the familiar power
and skill are still there. The boy is the
ideal auditor and foil for the gunfighter's
anxieties. On the boy's urging, he explains
how the gun is used--and then demonstrates
it with terrifying effect. In a split
instant the heavy gun is out of the holster
and in his hand, firing three shots in one
long sustained roar. The quick flick of the
camera from the boy's face to Shane's and
back serves to reveal our own mixed feelings.
The boy's face is a study in single-minded
awe: Shane's, through the billowing smoke
and dust, the mask of a man transformed by
fear and unshakable will into a tensely
efficient killer.)

However, his status is still not defined,
except negatively, since he carefully avoids
implicating himself further either by advice
or act. Except for the incident described
above, his gun is kept wrapped in his bed-
roll and his temper kept even enough that
he can tolerate such provocations as fence-
cutting and the smirks of an imported gun-

man, known to him, who clearly recognizes
Shane as his prime adversary.

The gunman, Wilson, brutally provokes
one of the more hot-headed of the sodbusters, Torrey, to draw on him and, with
sadistic slowness, kills him. At the funeral Stark is able to persuade the other
farmers to stay on only by virtually promising that he will "do something" about
Riker. Shane, pointedly asked his opinion
during the deliberations, is careful not to
commit himself. This is the most convincing
evidence of his continuing determination to
avoid embroiling himself; he knows that,
given his special nemesis, to fully identify
himself with the sodbusters in their dispute
is to commit himself to violence and death
and to the end of his friendly relations
with the Starks. *

Phase III sees precisely this development. Calloway, sickened by Riker's tactics
and Wilson's murder of the little Southerner,
Torrey, deserts Riker and warns Shane that
the proposed meeting between Riker and
Stark is a trap. Stark is to be killed.

At last the issue is perfectly clear:
Stark must be kept from attending the meeting and Riker and Wilson must be killed.
Shane knows, now. No doubts trouble him,
only his familiar sadness and remorse.
For he must (1) prevent Stark from fulfilling his manly obligation to fight his
own battles, and (2) he must break off with
the family and move on.

Stark is a courageous and determined man
and Shane has to knock him unconscious to
prevent him from going to his death. (Director Stevens, fully realizing that the
fight is the dramatic climax and resolution,
stages it magnificently with heavy and
effective use of symbols. The bleak moonlit
farm yard is the backdrop. The nervous
skittering of the horses and the lunging,

It also offers a convincing refutation of the view urged in most of the reviews that Shane is
nothing but the familiar "lone ranger" or "Robin Hood of the Old West" character, the very embodiment of disinterestedness and altruism who goes around righting wrongs. Wilson's murder of Torrey
was a particularly outrageous wrong; yet Shane was unwilling to stir himself even to the extent of
lending moral support to his friend Stark when Stark is seeking to persuade the others to stay and
fight for what is theirs.

crashing and bellowing of the cattle conveys nature's shock and outrage at the unnatural spectacle. Stark's wife and boy, torn in their loyalties, chorus our own mixed feelings. Stark, the more human of the two, we know is under terrific tension. On the other hand, Shane is clearly the tragic figure, forced by circumstances to take up his gun and revert to type--the type which he has learned to abhor, but too late. The fight with Stark is so desperate precisely because he would like nothing better than to lose. At one point Shane is apparently down for the count. How easy it would be just to stay down! If Stark should be killed, Shane would take over his place and family and escape at last from his exile. And all this with Stark's blessing! No wonder he couldn't find the strength to beat Stark "fairly," but instead had to clout him on the head with his gun.) Then, provoking a showdown gun battle, Shane kills Riker and three of his henchmen and

sets out for "where I ain't been before," secure in the knowledge of his fate.

Unlike *VICTORY*, *SHANE* contains no lesson for living, and there is a very basic structural reason for this. We must infer in *VICTORY*, that Heyst *could* have chosen to be different; indeed the novel carries the message that he *should* have so chosen, and that we, informed by his example, should teach our hearts to love before it is too late. Shane, on the other hand, acts like a man irretrievably doomed from the very beginning. *Being* the kind of man he was, he made himself expert in the technique of fighting back. Only gradually (we may surmise) did he come to realize that in thus single-mindedly fulfilling himself he had struck the mold of his own unhappy destiny.

SHANE, in its dramatic aspect, is concerned to reveal the character of a good man doomed by a tragic flaw---a flaw of excellence.

A Long Way From Home

Some Film Nightmares from the 40's

BARBARA DEMING

II. *I Stick My Neck Out for Nobody* (War Hero)

W HAT is this pumpkin pie Americans
are fighting for?" cries a youth
just arrived in this country (in *They
Live in Fear*, 1944.) "Gosh," he is very
soon writing to his mother, "People are
quite willing to die for it, and I too!"

At a casual glance, our films about
the past war would seem well summarized
in this child's cry of delight. Listen
to the voices which join themselves with
his: "In other wars, men haven't always
known why they were fighting, in this war
we are all fighting for the same thing!"
(*CRY HAVOC*); "We all see eye to eye!"
(*THE YANKS ARE COMING*); "This has been a
happy home" (*CROSS OF LORRAINE*); "We are
fighting for our lives" (*CRY HAVOC*);
"When it's all over...just think...being
able to settle down...raise your children...and never be in doubt about anything!" (*THIRTY SECONDS OVER TOKYO*). One
could go on quoting from film after film.

My warning in the past chapter would
seem a curious one. Where are the doleful
regions of which I spoke—the sighs, the
plaints, the terrible outcries? Men die
in these films, for this is war, but they
fall on a battlefield bright with visions
of that life they "almost happily" die to
secure; each with his family photograph,
his letter from sweetheart, wife or mom,
with news of the home town he is proud of ,
warm in his pocket; or the page torn from
the magazine—"Your Ideal Home." "We
shall utterly defeat the enemy," the government film *A Prelude To War* quotes General
Marshall. And to his words, a bright

bright globe eclipses a dark.

A few of the war-time songs chirped in
the musicals of those years insert that
they look forward to "a world that is new."
But wait: what the song means is that,
through this war, the rest of the world
will come to know some of the happiness
that we know now. After the war, "the
people of the whole world will meet together at one big table" (*Three Russian
Girls*), and there the whole world will come
to know the taste of—"What did you call
it?" the Russian girl asks the American
aviator. "Pumpkin pie!" he tells her
again. When an American in one of these
films would explain to a stranger what it
is for which we fight, pumpkin pie comes
most readily to the mind: we set it out
for all who would gather round, we dole it
out in equal share, because "one big family—that is America," someone sums up
(*They Live in Fear*).

On the field of battle, clear evidence
of this happy family meets the eye where-
ever it turns. *Guadalcanal Diary* (1943):
Here is Catholic side by side with Jew;
here is Brooklyn cabbie next Philosophy
teacher; here is (briefly) Negro next to
white. *The Purple Heart* (1944): Here are
artist, laborer, lawyer, football player,
arm in arm; one of Italian extraction, one
Irish; one, again, Catholic, one a Jew.
Eve of St. Mark (1944): Here on the one
team are a boy from a small New England
farm; a poor city boy, Irish Catholic, who
is a Dodgers fan; a rich Southerner from

an aristocratic family, who likes to quote
poetry. Again one could continue for pages.
Tiny little tensions are sometimes drama-
tised, but they are always quickly resolved. In *A Wing And A Prayer* (1944),
there is a little bit of tension between
officers and men; but before long the men
come to understand why the officer had to
behave as he did. In *Cry Havoc* (1943),
there is a little bit of tension between
rich girl and poor: but their differences
dissolve. In *Destination Tokyo* (1943),
there is a little tension between the doctor, who claims to be a materialist, and
one of the men who is deeply religious:
but events soon prove just how serious
this difference is. After the usual operation at sea such films feature, the
doctor, to the boy's muttered prayer, mutters a fervent "Amen!" Fundamentally

"we all see eye to eye."

Where is that darker landscape of which
I spoke? "This," the voices chorus,
"is America." But one may ask oneself:
are the voices overbright, the tableaux too
carefully composed, one-of-each-of-us
placed too punctually in the happy group?
Then one may remark another invariable.
In film after film there erupts some really
harrowing moment of violence. This is war.
One could put this down to realism and
pass on. But is it here the mere documentation of reality? Watch: the jugular
vein, pierced, spurts its blood directly
at us, spurts, it almost seems, straight
from the screen (*Cross of Lorraine*). As
the Jap screams, the armored tank charges
right over us, as if we were its victim
(*Guadalcanal Diary*). The hand to hand
fight between the Yank and the Jap end-

lessly protracts itself. We suffer in closeup each killing blow (*Behind the Rising Sun*). The emergency operation will never end. The camera cannot have its fill of that face, where teeth bite lips, eyes suddenly swoon away (for this, name at random almost any film). Here is no controlled rendering of the facts of war. The camera voluptuously involves us in the destructive moment, moves in too close, and dwells overlong, inviting us to suffer the ecstacy of dissolution, the thrill of giving it all up.

One may ask: does not this compulsion, betraying itself in film after film, bely the bright tableaux arranged, the bright cries carefully mouthed, and hint at some very different sense of the actuality of things, repressed but secretly insistent? A long look confirms just this. The figure of the clear-browed soldier with the dream in his eyes grows dim, turns insubstantial, .and another figure looms up, member of no happy clan, a figure of bitter aspect, withdrawn upon himself, who cries, "Don't you ever wonder if it's worth all this—I mean what you're fighting for?", who cries, "I stick my neck out for nobody...I'm not fighting for anything anymore, except myself!...All hail the happy days when faith was something all in one piece!"

THESE particular words are taken verbatim from one of the most popular films of 1942—*Casablanca*. They might seem shrill enough to discern without straining. One might, in fact, ask why some official ear did not catch them and have the film withdrawn. But the truth is that the film is one of the last a censor would take notice of. It is one of the last that would shake up in an audience self-questioning and doubt. The reverse is its very design: to relieve and still any such commotions. At the film's beginning, the hint is dropped that the hero may be speaking words ne does not mean. He is presented as a cipher, a man behind a

mask, and the film poses the question: if it should come to a trial, might he not perhaps be shown to possess a fighting faith more real than all the rest? Just such a trial is gradually framed, and the film delivers its answer in the affirmative. The very nature of the drama here—the very nature of that question which makes the wheels of the film turn—might still seem to give away much. And cold on paper, I believe it does; but not for one sitting out front. Here is the film's real magic: not only does it bring to the question the right answer; it brings the right answer without letting the audience become fully aware of what the question is; it drowns out the bitter cries without letting the audience become fully aware of what the cries have been all about. (I repeat that all this is likely to have been unconscious on the part of the producers.) But here is the film itself, in synopsis:

It is set abroad, and just before Pearl Harbor, the fight in question not yet our fight. This, to begin with, makes the tale seem more innocent; though if one looks twice, it makes it simply a dream about our entrance into the war. The hero, Rick (Humphrey Bogart), runs a cafe in Casablanca. Next his cafe lies the airfield from which planes take off to Lisbon—and from there to America; so Casablanca is crowded with people trying to flee occupied Europe. Visas are pitifully hard to obtain, legally or illegally, and while they seek, and wait, "everybody goes to Rick's." Rick's is a limbo, peopled by the sad and frantic. But among all these displaced ones, Rick himself is marked out for us, a homeless one among the homeless, exile in some special degree. In his case alone the nature of the exile is not an apparent one. Our curiosity about Rick is provoked long before we are allowed to see him. The manner in which we are finally introduced to him carefully prolongs the suspense: a waiter has just informed an eager newcomer that Rick never drinks with customers; we see a check handed across a table; a hand puts an okay to it; the camera draws very slowly off to take Rick in—and we are left more curious than when we had started, our introduction is to the very figuration of that question on which the film turns: Rick's glooming deadpan. He sits alone, staring at a drink, " no expression in his eyes. "

As the drama unfolds, various facts about Rick's background are provided for us, by the characters who press upon him, each, for his own purpose, seeking to guess him right. But always the sense is imparted that the key to the puzzle, that which would make all the other pieces fly into place, remains to be found. Almost everyone wants something of Rick, starting with poor little Yvonne, " fool to fall in love with a man like" him; but there are two characters who most particularly strain themselves to decipher him. They are Renault (Claude Rains), French prefect of police, and the Nazi Major Strasser, who is in Casablanca to prevent the escape to America of underground leader Victor Lazslo. Two German couriers have been murdered, and letters of transit have been taken from them. Strasser is concerned to see that these letters do not get into Lazslo's hands. He and Renault both come to suspect that Rick knows where they are hidden. We know that he knows. We have seen the little rat, Ugarte, leave them in his keeping (" Just because you despise me, you're the only one I trust ") And Rick may do with them what he will, for Ugarte, who had his own plans—he helps, at a price, those who are desperate –is promptly arrested for murder. We first see Renault trying to figure out how Rick will behave in relation to this arrest, for he plans to take Ugarte at Rick's place. " I stick my neck out for nobody, " says Rick. And when the time comes, and Ugarte goes scrambling to him, he *doesn't* move to help. This tells us nothing, for why should Rick risk any

thing for one like Ugarte? The episode—with several others in the film—is a teaser, keeps the guessing going. But Renault has also tried to sound out Rick about Victor Lazslo. In the process ,he has provided us with our first tangible facts about Rick's background. A flicker of interest has crossed his face at Lazslo's name , and he has bet Renault ten thousand francs that Lazslo will manage a get-away; but what makes Renault think that he, Rick, might do anything to help? " I know your record, " Renault brings out, watching him; " In 1935 you ran guns to Ethiopia, in 1936 you fought in Spain on the Loyalist side. " " And got well paid for it on both occasions, " Rick returns, deadpan.

Another note out of his past is sounded for us, but this more vague. Rick has run into the interview with Renault by wandering onto the terrace of the cafe. From here the airfield is visible. The sound of a plane warming up pulls Rick's eyes in that direction, and he watches mesmerized as , caught in the glare of the floodlights, the plane speeds down the runway and turns to a speck. " You would like to be on it?" Renault probes. " I have often speculated on why you do not return to America. Did you abscond with the church funds? Did you run off with the President's wife? I should like to think you killed a man. " " It was a combination of all three, " Rick grunts, eyes still captive of the speck of plane.

Renault introduces Rick to Strasser, and Strasser in his turn tries to get some rise out of Rick, with Lazslo's name. Rick lightly comments that his interest in Lazslo is a sporting one (he refers to his bet) –" Your business is politics, mine is running a saloon. " But " You weren't always so carefully neutral, " says Strasser. He has a dossier on him. " Cannot return to his country, " he reads, watching him; " the reason is a little vague. " His words fail to disturb the expressionless mask.

And then, suddenly, the film takes a

turn. Suddenly we sit up, expectant. Enter
Ingrid Bergman. (Enter Mrs. Victor Lazslo.)
She walks into the cafe with her husband,
and from their table she spots Sam, the
Negro pianist -- Rick's only intimate. Sam
spots Ingrid, too, and his glance is nervous.
When Lazslo leaves the room for a moment,
he crosses to her quickly. "Leave him
alone!" he begs, "Leave him alone, Miss
Ilse!" And we hold our breath.

We are at the point at last, we feel, of
finding him out. When they come face to
face, this feeling is confirmed. She has
insisted on the music that brought him.
"Play it once for old times' sake. Play
it, Sam. Play *As Time Goes By*." Sam,
resisting, mumbling resistance, has played
it, and Rick has come storming in: "I
thought I told you never—," his face at
last registering an emotion. In the few
tense sentences they now exchange, it is
obvious that Rick's past confronts us right
here, in Ilse's person. We cut to a later
hour, and Rick alone over a drink, the
lights out, the customers all gone, everyone
gone but Sam, who pleads, "Don't just sit
and look a hole in that drink, boss." But
"Tonight I've got a date with the heebyjeebies," Rick announces. "You know what
I want to hear. If she can stand it, I
can! Play it!" So Sam, at the piano, fingers
out the song. The veil is about to be torn.
The music, as we know, will softly rend it,
"The fundamental things apply, as time
goes by..." Sam murmurs out the words
"Woman needs man, and man must have his
mate that nobody can deny..." We move
up on Rick, on the drink before him, and
dissolve—into a day in 1940.

An idyll: Rick and Ilse in Paris, in
love. They have met but recently, we
gather, know nothing about each other's
pasts. "Who are you really?" he asks,
gazing, love-struck. But she: "We said
no questions." Love-struck, he acquiesces.
In the background, Sam plays their theme
song; they drink the last champagne. For
the Germans are advancing on Paris; they

will have to flee; but they will flee together. They name the train at which they
will meet. There is one thing first to
which Ilse must attend. But then we cut
to Rick there waiting at the station, in
the rain; and Ilse does not come. He
waits; she does not come; the train is
about to pull out—the last train out of
Paris. Suddenly Sam arrives, with a note:
she cannot see him ever again, she writes—
but believe that she loves him. The rain-
drops pour down upon the letter, smudging
the writing; the train utters its baleful
departing whistle, boo hoo, and we dissolve
back to Rick over his drink. He looks up
and there is Ilse standing in the door,
come after all these months to explain.
Rick doesn't give her a chance. Bitterly
he mimics for her now her words back there
in Paris: " 'Rick dear, I'll go with you
any place. We'll get on a train together
and we'll never stop. All my life, for-
evermore!' ...How long was it we had honey?
All hail the happy days," he lashes out,
"when there were no questions asked, and
faith was something all in one piece!"
She gives up and leaves. Rick, giving it
all up, too, sags over the table; his
drink tips, spilling over the cloth; the
scene fades out.

So we know him now. He is unmasked.
He has had his "insides kicked out by a
pair of French heels." This is his secret.
And this, note, is the context in which he
utters that cry: "All hail the happy days
when faith was something all in one piece!"
As uttered here, this is not the cry at
all I seemed originally to report. The
veil has been torn aside on the portrait
of—a man betrayed in love. A wounded
lover's cry, this cry; nothing more.

Actually a veil has been subtly drawn,
not parted—silkenly slid before our eyes,
to music. Look again and see the sleight
of hand. Review the puzzle pieces which
supposedly assemble for us into the portrait of a man betrayed in love: He never
drinks with the customers, is cold to poor

little Yvonne—this will fit. He who
fought in Spain and Ethiopia, now will
stick his neck out for nobody. A man embittered in love, of course, will extend
that bitterness to life in general. Then
note further: for reasons unknown he cannot
return to his own country. Here is a
piece which refuses to be fitted into the
place assigned.

It refuses, that is, here on paper; but
not upon the screen. Rick's " date with
the heebyjeebies" is worth going over
again, this time in full detail. In this
scene, all the variant notes I have just
mentioned are struck again—but in the
instant are gathered up, and blur into the
one note. As one watches, it is persuasive.

When we see Rick sitting there at his
bitter drink, he is lit dramatically through
the cafe window by a circling finger of
light from the airfield—which visibly
enough recalls that trip to America he can
never make, that exile over and above the
exile Ilse has brought him to. And listen,
now, to a more complete text of what passes
between him and Sam. " Don't just stare
a hole in that drink," Sam pleads, but
Rick answers that this night he has a date
with the heebyjeebies. Then he breaks
out—" strangely," comments the script*—
" They grab Ugarte, then she walks in.
That's the way it goes. One in and one
out. Sam, if it's December 1941 in Casablanca, what time is it in New York?...I
bet they're asleep in New York. I bet
they're asleep all over America. Of all
the gin joints in all the towns in all the
world, she walks into mine!" Then: "Play
it!" Look at what is here casually woven
in, in sight of all. "One in and one out"
of Ugarte and Ilse. Look at this pairing..
Ugarte personifies the perversion of a
good cause through opportunism: he takes
his risks for a price. Rick's feeling
about this sort of a betrayal of a faith
here blurs in one split second with his

cynicism about love's promises. Note,
next, the date " December 1941"—making
this just pre-Pearl Harbor. " I bet they're
asleep," in the light of this date, takes
on a meaning more than literal. Thus
cynicism about political opportunism, cynicism about political naivete, are gathered
up in turn and in an instant blurred with
the very special cynicism of the jilted
lover. Finally, when at the fading of the
flashback, Ilse appears at the door, it is
the circling finger of light from the airfield which picks her out, virtually materialises her; so here even *that* variant
note, with which we began, is gathered
in, and *visually* confounded with the other,
the lover's bitter loss.

As Ilse stands there now, all bitterness can be said to have been focused on
her person. From here on, Rick may come
out with whatever he will; it will be
harmless. And note: if the film can now
somehow dispel that very particularised
disillusion of his -- in this girl -- by
subtle act of substitution, all other
harsh notes that have been introduced, and
blurred into this note, will be dispelled.

As the film proceeds, Rick does come
forth with ever more cynical outcries.
The way to listen to them, as I set them
forth, is to forget his characterisation
as the jilted lover, to abstract the cries
from this context, and listen to them in
themselves. The film proceeds:

After Ugarte's arrest, Lazslo is advised
that Rick may have the letters of transit.
But when he goes to Rick, Rick turns him
aside coldly—" The problems of the world
are not in my department. I'm a saloon
keeper." When Lazslo retorts that once,
he's been told, he was a man who fought
for the underdog, Rick comments, " Yes, I
found that a very expensive hobby." The
characterisation of sulking lover is quickly reanimated for us; we are quickly reminded that it is love Rick found to be

---

* *CASABLANCA* is included among the Gassner-Nichols *BEST FILM PLAYS*.

expensive. He goes on to say that he may
not ever use the visas himself, but he
won't give them to Lazslo: and when Lazslo
mutters, " There must be some reason... "
replies, " There is. I suggest that you
ask your wife. "

Then Ilse herself goes to see Rick for
her husband. " Richard! " " So I'm Richard
again? " he mocks her, " We're back in
Paris. I've recovered my lost identity. "
But in this interview too one can, if one
will, listen to his words in terms of a
lost identity not simply that of the happy
lover. " Do I have to hear again what a
great man your husband is and what an important Cause he's fighting for? " " It
was your Cause, too... " " Well I'm not
fighting for anything anymore, except myself. I'm the only Cause I'm interested
in now. " In desperation Ilse pulls a gun.
" You'll have to kill me to get them, " he
tells her. " If Lazslo—if the Cause means
so much to you, go ahead! "—with this
equation, again safely reducing all to a
wounded lover's terms.

She, of course, cannot shoot; she breaks,
she drops the pistol—and flings herself
into his arms. " I tried to stay away...
If you knew...how much I loved you...still
love you! " And the film fades in on them
a little later as she explains at last
what happened that fateful day. She had
been married to Lazslo already, when she
met Rick, but she had heard that he had
been murdered in a concentration camp .
Then that day she had learned that he was
alive, had escaped, was waiting for her.
She had had to go. But now, she cries,
she'll never have the strength to leave
Rick again. " I can't fight it anymore.
I don't know what's right any longer.
You'll have to think for both of us, for
all of us. "

" I've already made up our minds, " Rick
answers her. But he does not reveal his
decision. The question of how he will act
is stretched out to the very end. Rick

continues inscrutable. The script notes
with the same regularity " His expression
reveals nothing of his feelings " And
he continues in cynical utterances. We,
of course, more and more tend to suspect
that such utterances mask his real intentions. We even with some anguish now suspect this

Lazslo ducks into Rick's to elude the
police, who have broken up an underground
meeting, and Rick, sending off Ilse by a
back way, gives Lazslo a drink to settle
his nerves. Here it is that Rick demands,
" Don't you ever wonder if it's worth all
this? I mean what you're fighting for? "
Lazslo retorts that he sounds like a man
" trying to convince himself of something
that in his heart he doesn't believe. "
And we in the audience at this point would
gladly be convinced, ourselves, if we could.
There is only one level of meaning at which
we would think of taking his words; and the
price asked does seem a dreadful one.

As Lazslo and Rick stand there, Renault's
men burst in and declare Lazslo under
arrest, on suspicion of having been at that
meeting. Rick grimaces at Lazslo a dark
smile: " It seems destiny has taken a hand. "
And now he takes his most seeming cynical
step. He calls on Renault and suggests a
deal. If he'll release Lazslo, Rick will
give him a real charge against him. He
does have those visas. He'll pretend to
give them to Lazslo, and this will give
Renault the chance to walk in and arrest
Lazslo for complicity in the murder of the
couriers. Under cover of the excitement—
if Renault will help—he, Rick, will make
use of the visas himself, to depart for
America with Ilse. Which should put
Renault's mind to rest about his desire to
help Lazslo escape. He's the last man
he'd want to meet in America. " I'll miss
you, " Renault tells him; " apparently
you're the only one in Casablanca who has
even less scruples than I. " So Rick goes
to Lazslo and offers him the visas for a

hundred thousand francs. He tells him to come down to the cafe, with Ilse, a few minutes before the Lisbon plane is to leave. When Lazslo tries to thank him, he cuts him short: "Skip it. This is strictly a matter of business." One cynical gesture is here wrapped within another.

This particular gesture is soon enough annulled, in a little stint all to itself. When Lazslo does try to hand Rick the money he refuses it gruffly: "Keep it, you'll need it." In this small instance, at any rate, his cynicism has been proven insubstantial. But we wait to see how he will act in the main matter. Ilse thinks that what he intends to do is send off Lazslo on the plane, alone. But nobody at this point really knows how anybody else is going to act. Rick is not at all sure about Renault. The film has been building him up as a minor puzzle. "Rick, have you got those letters of transit?" Renault has asked. "Louis, are you pro Vichy or Free French?" Rick has retorted. "I have no convictions...I take what comes," Renault has declared; but on his face, too, the camera has dwelt teasingly, the smile there ambiguous.

Suddenly everything begins to happen fast——though in a fashion, still, that keeps us guessing. Renault walks in and—— Lazslo and Ilse stare——declares Lazslo under arrest again. "You are surprised about my friend Rick?" At which Rick pulls a gun and informs Renault that there will be no arrests -- "yet." And he orders him to check with the airport that there will be no trouble. Renault pulls a fast one, and pretending to call the airport, really calls Strasser, who races for the field.

At the field, at last, all our questions are answered. While Lazslo is off somewhere checking arrangements, Rick tells Renault to fill out the names on the visas. They are: Mr. and Mrs. Victor Lazslo. Ilse, dazed, protests, but Rick tells her

gently: she knows and he knows that the Cause needs Lazslo, and Lazslo needs her—— she is part of his work, "the thing that keeps him going." "What about us?" she cries, but he answers her, "We'll always have Paris. We didn't have. We'd lost it...We got it back last night." And "I've got a job to do," he tells her: "Where I'm going, you can't follow." Lazslo returns——"Everything is in order." "All except one thing," Rick adds, and he tells him of Ilse's visit. She did it to try and get the visas, he tells him. To get them, she tried to convince him that she was still in love with him. And he let her pretend. "But that was long ago." "Welcome back to the fight," Lazslo salutes Rick; "Now I know our side will win!" And he and Ilse walk off toward the plane.

Strasser bursts in. Further decisions are called for. Renault cries out that Lazslo is on the plane. Rick has Strasser at gun point, but Strasser calls his bluff: he jumps to the phone and asks for the Radio Tower. Rick shoots Strasser. The French police burst in; and the next move is Renault's. There is an extensive pause as he and Rick exchange stares—faces, to the last, expressionless. Then: "Round up the usual suspects!" Renault barks, and the police dash off. The roar of the ascending plane is heard. The two men turn their eyes. The beacon light sweeps them. The plane roars up over their heads. It might be a good idea to leave Casablanca for a while, says Renault. There is a Free French garrison at Brazzaville. The ten thousand francs he owes Rick—"that should pay our expenses." "Our expenses? Louis," says Rick, "I think this is the beginning of a beautiful friendship." Arms linked, they walk off into the twinkling dark.

Look where the film has brought us out: the embittered one who would stick his neck out for nobody, steps spryly into battle. Look what has been accomplished: the final note here is the very one documented at

this chapter's beginning. Arm in arm with
comrade, he steps forth, to music, the
dream in his heart intact. "Everything
is" indeed "in order" magically. The film
has permitted a most disturbing figure to
take shape, and there before our eyes has
struck him harmless. More than that, it
has comfortably recruited him. Lazslo may
well cry out, "Now I know our side will
win!"

What is more, the dream has recruited
this unlikely warrior without even leaving
us with the sense that we have witnessed a
remarkable translation. The love story
has borne the brunt of the work: it is the
guise of the jilted lover that has allowed
the figure to take shape at all, and utter
his bitter cries; and it is the scene in
which he finds again his lost faith in
the beloved that enables us to cancel
out those cries, and believe in his entry
into the fight. But note a further magic:
the impression we are left with at the end
of the film is that even had Ilse never
returned to explain her leaving him, if it
had come right down to it, Rick, for all
his gloominess, would of course have rallied
to the Cause. This the dream accomplishes
by having him continue his bitter gesturing
to the end. When we are given proof how
insubstantial is the cynicism about "the
problems of the world" that he professes
after Ilse has returned to him, automatically we extend even to his original
bitter aspect the same judgement; retro-
actively we dismiss it, too. Thus as the
film ends, that glum mask, shaped there
before our eyes, has been interpreted as no
disturbing sign but sign, rather, of a faith
deeper than other faiths. "Just because
you despise me, you're the only one I
trust," Ugarte has blurted to Rick. The
dream, in effect, manages the tour de force
of defining Rick's relation to the Cause
analogously. It leaves us with this half
conscious feeling: Just because he wears
the aspect of utter cynicism can one be
sure that he is the real man of faith.

Precisely by this contradictory sign can
one spot the man who really cares, the man
to be relied upon. And so in the dark,
the shadow of our dim disquiet is dispelled.

Some readers will perhaps at this point
protest: why cannot the film be taken at
face value? The film is a love story, and
it is complicated by the fact that the
bitterness the hero feels toward his beloved he transfers to life as a whole;
but that, they may protest, covers the
matter; to read any more into it is artificial. Even at a strictly literal level,
however, the label of jilted lover cannot
be made to adequately cover Rick's case.
At the end of the film one thing remains
altogether unexplained: why it was that he
could never turn to his country. For
the purposes of the dream, this stray end is
gathered up neatly enough, with Ilse's
final departure. As Rick's eyes turn this
last time to follow the plane's flight, the
one exile is fused forever with the other;
an audience is very unlikely to remember
that they are actually separate matters.
For our purposes, though, the distinction
stands and—even to be altogether literal—
does raise the whole question of a wider
reference for the drama enacted than any
love alone provides. In that last cry of
Lazslo's—"Now I know our side will win!"
the producers of the film, themselves, unconsciously acknowledge the more crucial
identity of the hero, the more general
nature of the crisis of faith he suffers.

But it is in unison that films most
clearly yield up their secrets. It is the
joint evidence of other war films that
above all exposes the drama of Rick as
something more than a drama of love in a
war setting. One can name film after film
about the war which raises dramatically the
question of the hero's faith, then moves
forward to confirm that faith, and step
him briskly into battle. Among these
films, the hero is by no means always a
disillusioned lover—though this note, too,

is repeated. He may be any one of a variety of figures. Of any of these figures, **viewing him individually**, one could say, as of Rick: this is a very special case, or a case, at any rate, without any general application for the American public. The hero very often is not even a citizen of this country. But line them all up and the question that looms is: why do the American film makers so persistently seek out remote cases of just this sort with which to satisfy their public—unless the identification made is actually one that is not remote at all? Here now are a succession of these "special" figures. Stare at them all together, as I line them up, and watch the special markings fall away, the figures curiously blur...

The conclusion of this chapter and remaining chapters of A LONG WAY FROM HOME *will be printed in subsequent issues of* CITY LIGHTS.

Still photograph on title page from *CASABLANCA*, 1942, Warner Bros.

Joseph Kostolefsky

The Doppelganger Brothers

Along with the swaying **Pole on** his swaying pole,
The juggling Serbs,
And the man who played *TREES* on his teeth,
Enter, in tights, the Doppleganger Brothers
Hugo and Udo, desire and duty, linked
Arm in arm, slack hand on solid skull.
(Whatever they lack, the act is seldom dull.)
Hugo, it seems has had one nip too much,
And keeps one eye intently on a blonde,
Just off the second aisle.
Of course, he slips,
Sooner or later he stumbles, tumbles down.
Their option won't be picked up for a second week.
On stage or off, the balance is seldom right,
Someone will stumble,
Somewhere the grip will break,
Udo will go to confession, or Hugo to jail,
But the torn halves will be joined,
The Brothers made whole, the Brother rise again.
They'll get another engagement soon,
The two-headed, whole-hearted man with the Prussian spine
And the eye that winks like a beacon,
But it's no good.
The balance is off, forever,
The parts awry,
Mingling and separating until they die.
We all want our money back. We've all agreed
The Brothers are a sorry act indeed.

A Letter from LOS ANGELES

BORIS SOBELMAN

SEVERAL years ago, the gentleman-novelist, Mr. Evelyn Waugh, finding himself unaccountably in Hollywood, used the occasion to cast a cold eye on the city of Los Angeles. Considering the height from which this orb must have been focused, and considering the further fact that a roil of smog undoubtedly obscured the view, we must score it as a triumph of sorts that the Forest Lawn cemetery, if nothing else, was seen. But seen it was-- for not long afterward, Mr. Waugh, his eminent self untarnished by his travels, used it as the subject for a novel in which he hee-hawed mightily at the burial customs of the local barbaroi.

It would be idle to attempt a rebuttal, particularly when no counter argument lies available. Forest Lawn with its art-works and everlasting music is still here, and will remain, conceivably, for a good long time, attracting to itself all those who consider such things beautiful. In the meantime, the suppressed spiritual side of us longs for something that will reach beyond the Middle West and bring out among us the higher beings of *VOGUE* and *HARPER'S BAZAAR* with their parfums, their Rouaults, and their middle-aged decolletage.

The fastidious Evelyn, I'm afraid, has beveled us to the edges, but before the admission reaches him, let us throw in one last counter: a sight never before seen on this green earth; a thing as quintessential of Los Angeles as ambergris of the whale, and something, in its mystical denotation,

so profound that the great sage of Zurich himself, did he know of it, would immediately order the world-wide Jungian network to drop everything and pay attention to more important matters; this, a funeral cortege racing down a freeway, delivering a stiff to its final rest with a speed and unction unknown to mankind since live burials first became crimes.

Something here activates the hackles. Oswald Spengler, were he enabled to be an observer, would not be slow to recognize the terrorizing Destiny so apparent; Faustian man, dead as a doornail, still conquering Time!

But this is worth dwelling on more. As an old reader of little magazines, I can tell a symbol from a handsaw even when the wind is bad, and though it is not my intention to give the secret away entirely, one small clue is in order. The speeding cortage has this implication--by its means the dead are made quick.

Let the finical Evelyn match that. This is a city where the symbols dig deep. And in this matter of fast funerals, supremacy is ours; hands down. We have the cars, we have the freeways, and by Harry, we've got the cemeterie too.

There were two events of some cultural importance here in the last several months which between them roughly symbolize the period we now find ourselves in. The first was the conversion of the Esquire Theatre, for many years the showhouse of foreign and art films, into a delicatessen restaurant, and the second was the appearance of Gypsy Rose Lee and Paulette Goddard in a movie, which unfortunately, due to the press of much more trivial business, I failed to see.

The demise of the Esquire came without warning and it seems impossible to discover the reason. Television, that smiler with the knife, can hardly be culpable in this case. The people who patronized the Esquire are hardly the kind who would voluntarily give up the pleasures of Art for the commercializedcoma now available in the living room, but on the other hand something must have been keeping them away. Much as one would like to know why, no answer presents itself. There is a growing tendency in this city to blame business failures on the absence of parking facilities and the Esquire had no facilities of this kind at all. Yet in the past this was no drawback. People would park as much as a mile away, and then saunter through the streets to this pleasure dome glowing under the stars. Whether the fare was better then or not is hard to say. My own feeling is it doesn't matter. Considering the disillusion which might follow THE BICYCLE THIEF after its enormous ballyhoo, or one of the more symbolic omelettes cooked up by Cocteau, it is easy to think that a rebellion of taste occurred, and lasted just long enough to throw the Esquire into the clutches of a cabal of sinister sandwich-passers. As the devout might say, would to Heaven it were so. But it is too hard to believe.

Thinking back over the past several years, evidence comes to mind quite readily to prove the Esquire audience a dumb and long-suffering beast, one not too likely to find Italian films the last straw. In fact the suspicion that it enjoyed them hugely is quite ineradicable. Charisma abides in things as well as men, and anything haloed, however faintly, with Art, can be the source of a pleasure independent of the means. Here indeed we confront again the dilemma noted by so many great and voluble minds: good ends and bad means. My impression of the Esquire audience forces me to say that for it, at least, the end was all; the means nothing. In what other way can one explain the profound, even acute pleasure, derived over so many years from so many dull, boring, and even bad films? How else explain the eminence of, say, Sir Laurence Olivier, undoubtedly the greatest practitioner of amateur theatricals the world has ever known.

Can we conclude then that the end of the Esquire signifies the passing of the charisma? And as a corollary state that Art is not as long as too many opinions have led us to believe? Personally I have no answer, but as a bit of *noblesse oblige*, I went to what was once the Esquire and had a hot pastrami sandiwch. All in all, looking at every angle, and conning such imponderables as might occur to me, I must say it was more enjoyable than Rosselini, and just to make everything fair, I even threw in three novels by Moravia.

The other event, the showing of a movie starring Gypsy Rose Lee and Paulette Goddard, may not be as cultural, perhaps, as some would like, but for myself anyway, the fact that I missed it is still a matter for self-reproach. I have no illusions about what kind of beer this pair might brew, but a charisma of another kind is in attendance here; the *ruach* of the good old days. Can you think of Paulette and Gypsy Rose without thinking of other times? And can you think of other times without some nostalgia? It is good indeed to know that these two rough old dames are still around, and with enough push and hustle left to make a movie.

Paulette (and I hope she will pardon this familiarity) was always one of my favorite movie actors. She is one of the few people in Hollywood, and possibly the only female, who ever possessed modesty. It was a living pleasure to watch her. Every mannerism, every gesture, everything she appeared to do was informed by a sense underlying which seemed to say, " Look! Here I am, starring. At the top! And what did I start out with? Nothing! No talent, no ability, not even real interest. All I had was a little energy and lots of ambition and look at me. Right up here with all these sensitive people." Well, bless you girl, you were always a real innocent. You had twice as much sensitivity as anyone around you, and not half the ambition , I'm sure.

So here it is now, this film,and let me vow that the next time it comes around I'll be there no matter what the sacrifice. The fact that it is undoubtedly television bait of a rather supreme kind, is no deterrent either. I will step up to the boxoffice as we used to do in bygone days, lay the money on the line again, and in the dark abysm (which soon enough will be closed to the public) range back to the time when machine guns and billy clubs couldn't force me to see a Paulette Goddard film. Good old days those must have been, and if a whiff of them is available only through a total turnaround, then the turn will be made.

Anne, O'Neill

To Which the Heart

The known doom and the silver sun slipping
Down alleyed streets on a winter day,
Snail-tracks over the cobblestones, and the grass
Beginning to spring between the stones, and summer
No different, nor autumn. Where lies the snow
And where the frightening beginning of the year?
No April shatters here.

The known doom to which the heart returns.
The turn of no seas, the knock on no door.
Forsaking the chilly roofs and the copper-green griffins
Wearing snow-caps - moths swarming in the golden light
From street to sky and the snow covering the blue steps
Three flights down under the curving lamp post.

What fantasy of escape, where the brown hills
Are no less sullen, nor the water more silver.
Mistbinds, choking in the throat
Weaving blind across the eyes. Sonorities
Blast from the searchlight rocks
Where the livid small waves gleam like pennies
And sink copper heavy into the black.
                              No alien sound.
The hills are bones and the body's dust. And no escape
But the known doom, to which the heart returns.

PREVIEWS

at the

Pocket Bookshop

Recognizing the growing importance of the paper-bound book for American readers and publishers, *CITY LIGHTS* magazine has opened the CITY LIGHTS POCKET BOOKSHOP, which will specialize in good paper-bound books and magazines. Write, call, or visit our new shop and office at 261 Columbus Avenue in San Francisco, phone DOuglas 2-8193. We have a complete stock of Anchor Books, Penguin Books, Bantams, and Signets and Mentors, as well as a wide selection of paper-bound titles from Modern Library, Open Court, and Hafner Publishing Companies. In addition, we stock a wide selection of magazines, from *LIFE* and *THE NEW YORKER* through *PARTISAN REVIEW* to *CITY LIGHTS*.

New Paper-Bound Titles

THE LONELY CROWD
David Riesman and others. *Doubleday* (Anchor A-16), $.95 10/8 A provocative sociological study of the changing American character from the 19th to the 20th century. Abridged and revised by the authors for this edition, with new material.

NEW WORLD WRITING: *Fourth Mentor Selection*
New American (Mentor Ms96), $.50 10/28 The latest volume in a series that pioneered in the field of original paper-bound literary anthologies. Contents includes: short stories by Gore Vidal, Shelby Foote; part of a novel by William Sansom; the work of 10 Irish poets; articles; a play; drawings. Intensive promotion.

AVON BOOK OF MODERN WRITING
Ed. by William Phillips and Philip Rahv. *Avon,* $.35 Original fiction, essays, poetry, autobiography, most of it previously unpublished in any form, collected by the editors of the *Partisan Review*. Contributors include: Colette, Diana Trilling, Eleanor Clark, Patrick O'Brian.

DISCOVERY: NO. 2
Ed. by Vance Bourjaily and John W. Aldridge. *Pocket* (C-115), $.25 10/1 Pocket Books' second notable entry in this field. Short stories, poems, essays by Muriel Rukeyser, Pietro di Donato, Babette Deutsch and others, all published here for the first time.

in the Magazine

AMBASSADORS TO THE MACHINE
David Riesman
The author of *THE LONELY CROWD* and *FACES IN THE CROWD* discusses "Living in Industrial Civilization."

FILM AUDIENCES AND WHAT THEY SEE
Pauline Kael
Who goes to the movies today? Miss Kael asks. Children, of course -- and a smaller audience of "educated" people. And what do they go to the movies to see? *People.*

GUS AND THE SATURDAY MATINEE
Herbert Kauffman
A story.

I'M A BIG RED-HAIRED MAN
Jay Caldwell
A story.

THE FARM AS A FRAGMENT OF THE SOUTHERN CALIFORNIA CULTURE
Curtis Zahn
A poem.

GUM SANG TI FO
Lilah Kan
Big City *(Gum Sang)* is the Chinese name for San Francisco, California. Miss Kan writes a personal account of her experience in this great Chinese community, where she has lived since she was thirteen, when she came here from a totally different environment in Chicago.

SUBSCRIPTIONS

ARE INVITED. RATES ARE TWO DOLLARS FOR SIX ISSUES. WRITE, ENCLOSING CHECK OR ORDER TO BE BILLED, TO

CITY LIGHTS
261 COLUMBUS AVENUE
SAN FRANCISCO 11, CALIF.

FINE COLOR PRINTS

from 10 cents up

ONE MAN SHOWS

by local artists

and

Books of The Peregrine Press

at

THE PORPOISE

628 Montgomery Street, Room 239

Hours: 12 to 4

Closed Sundays and Mondays

Number 5   Spring 1955   35c

CITY LIGHTS 5

Television Issue

CITY LIGHTS is published at 261 Columbus
Avenue, San Francisco 11, California.
Telephone DOuglas 2-8193. Copyright,
1955, by CITY LIGHTS for its contributors.
Manuscripts are invited, but no payment
can be made at this time. Rates: thirty-
five cents a copy; two dollars for six
issues. Advertising rates upon request.
Editor, Peter Martin. Managing Editor,
Richard Miller. Associates, Eileen
Martin and Mary Adams. Lithographed
by Red Arrow Press, 216 Market Street,
San Francisco.

The Television Illusion

Leslie Farber

I T HAS been an error to assume that television at its best would be a sum of radio, stage, and movies at their best. It may be that radio and theatre people still predominate in the television industry, to the despair of those concerned with cinematic techniques, but it will not be long before Hollywood experts will have wholly replaced the engineers and Broadwayites who began the industry. Yet the mere transposition of movie methods will not help, unless television is understood for its differences from all other media, as well as for its similarities.

To begin with, the quality of illusion in television cannot approach that of the movies. There are several reasons for this. A dark silenced movie house, with all seats facing a screen several times life-size, compels a passive absorption which simply is not present in a living room or bar. Any room in a house will impose our daily life upon us through its decor, its intrusion of familiar lights and sounds - in brief, through its lack of resemblance to a theatre. The introduction of a television screen may diminish but will never obliterate its primary identity as a room in a home. But when the movies end for the evening, the theatre waits darkly for the projector to be turned on again: it has no other purpose in life. For this reason television lacks the whole powerful, prior illusion enforced on us by simply entering a movie house.

Barring fire in the theatre and assuming he finds a seat, the movie patron is almost certainly assured of seeing a movie without interruption. But interruption is the prime quality of television: one never sees anything straight through. Even if the interruptions, ranging from unexpected guests to electrical disturbances, were controllable, there would still be advertising breaks. The very fact of private enterprise requires that illusion be shattered every fifteen minutes. And though most of us would find the alternative - government control or the benevolent dictatorship of an educated minority - as mixed a blessing as free enterprise, the fact remains that these fifteen-minute illusion periods are a harsh experience for the novice viewer.

Much of the persuasive force of the movies comes from the mere bigness of the silver-screen figure, several times life size. Put crudely, one tends to believe in people who are bigger than circus giants yet fashioned with the symmetry of midgets. Conversely, the television screen which reduces its actors, as though reversing the telescope, invites the calculating attitude of microscopy. Although T V screens have advanced from ten to twenty inches, any further increase in size will further decrease the clarity of the image. Add to this the fact that T V sets come with a set of controls which permit each set owner to be his own projectionist, having the uneasy responsibility of judging the brightness or precision of each image. No studies are available, but it is doubtful if movie projectionists make the most trustful movie fans.

Television repair men have a way of approving set reception by announcing, " Man, that's really like a movie! " But as T V manufacturers well know, an advertisement which showed *actual* set reception would not sell many sets; it's better to paste a clear photograph of Milton Berle over the screen. The fact is that American television made a compromise, originally, between clarity of picture and number of channels: to broadcast a sufficient number of dots per square inch would have reduced the number of channels to one or two. And while we may find our present number far too large, we can study the disadvantages of a one-channel monopoly in the British system - where, I am told, the viewer gets clarity and education at the expense of any variety of entertainment or dramatic interest (aesthetic interest too, if Shakespeare or Mozart occur only on Sundays). For the sake of variety, the American viewer is obviously willing to put up with a large amount of optical 'frustration and discomfort.

But there is no real reason why the T V picture should be as clear and detailed as a movie picture; it might be best for everyone if the two media were more dissociated in the public mind. At its very best, by T V standards, the T V picture is imprecise, with outlines both blurred and distorted - the result being a strikingly flat picture. There must be unique advantages in a flat picture, to judge from painting, but these advantages will scarcely be realized by directors who insist that television achieve a three-dimensional image. One film critic, discussing the giant movie close-up, thought there was a point of magnification where the actor's face becomes a kind of abstract representation. In television abstract or non-objective presentation is a continual possibility, not through enlargement but through the mechanical distortion and blurring apparently inherent in the medium.

Everyone who watches television for any

length of time must eventually form his own private picture of the T V camera, and whether his picture matches the reality of studios is somewhat beside the point. He probably imagines an immense steel object, fashioned like a crane, with seats for six operators suspended high above the floor. Each operator wears earphones allowing him to receive messages from the Chief Cameraman, who stands with his head pressed to the viewer. If an actor moves three paces to the right, the Chief Cameraman presses a lever on his intercom, connecting him with the Horizontal Operator, and orders " eight-point-two turns right." Upon receipt of this message (which must be repeated because cameramen do not have the same training in enunciation given to actors), the Horizontal Movement Operator turns a large wheel which has the same general construction as a carnival Wheel of Fortune, but is equipped with a delicate gauge so that eight-point-two may be achieved with precision. Similarly for vertical and diagonal, forward and backward movements. Should an undisciplined acrobat have the stage, doing somersaults and cartwheels, the spectacle of the Chief barking out orders and operators spinning the six wheels must resemble a B-36 instrument-flight through a blinding snowstorm.

An expensive coast-to-coast production like the Show of Shows may have three or four such cameras, each requiring a crew of six skilled operators and one Chief Cameraman. But the smaller-budget programs use only one or two cameras and restrict the crew to Chief and Horizontal Motion Operator. This means that all the action must take place in a rectangle five feet long and two feet wide, chalked out in a manner invisible to the viewer. While this rectangle will accomodate a trio comfortably, a quartet should incline their heads together; and even so the outer shoulders of the first and fourth members will not be visible to us at home.

The evidence for this fanciful conception comes from two sources. * The first is the T.V. comedian who up to now has fought a losing (though often funny) battle with the camera - or so he informs his audience. It may be that his complaints are for purposes of humor, bearing the same relation to fact as his complaints about his gag writers. Yet, even if this is true, the comedians have saddled their audiences with an underlying uneasiness about the manipulability of the television camera - extending even to those programs where no one complains.

The second and more important source is the television show itself, live or kinescoped, as it appears on the owner's screen. The variety shows are the most hazardous, where the top man in a balancing act is more often than not amputated from view. For some reason the camera cannot move back, the way a man with a Brownie can, in order to enlarge the view. Ballroom dancers often disappear from the screen altogether, while the camera tries slowly and jerkily to find them. Presumably the Cameraman signals them that they are lost, and they also try to find the camera.

Variety shows look as though the actors were advised by chalk marks never to move out of range of the fixed head-on view which allows both long shot and close-up. Within this prescribed area they may move as they please, but the restriction is hard on viewers brought up on movies, in which there is at least an illusion that the camera just happened to be where the actors are. Perhaps one reason for the studios' fondness for panel shows is that these provide an easy itinerary - from Interlocutor to expert and back - for the stiff-necked camera to travel.

During the early days of movies, when directors were almost too impressed by the camera's ability to follow the actors wherever they went - and not enough impressed by the ability of audiences to follow a meaning or grasp a point - we

spent innumerable minutes watching actors push a doorbell, turn a knob, walk through the door, come through the door on the other side, close the door - as though Doors were the great enemy, to be overcome by heroes everywhere.

In television so far, the opposite is true. Once an actor leaves the rectangle enclosing him, he never goes but is suddenly arrived inside the new rectangle of his destination. If a contestant on a panel show is asked to write his name on the blackboard, the camera switches from Contestant at Table to Contestant chalking his name. No one can say where the blackboard is in this alleged room, nor whether, for that matter, the event is taking place now or happened at some earlier time.

The Groucho Marx show, evidently a kinescoped version of his radio show, includes only such action as would be visible to an audience at the radio studio. The remarkable thing is how many television shows follow this same pattern, worked out for radio. In such a studio theatre, the televiewer at home gets the worst possible seat. He is centrally placed, on the stage and just in front of the footlights. For the small advantage he gets in the way of close inspection, he has lost his view of the whole stage and simultaneously much of the illusion.

But except for the studio audience, it is obvious that T V is not and never can be a theatre stage. The best live shows try to make up for this by making a cinematic use of the television camera's talent for focus, for the shift from middle distance to the close-up of a stationary object. - So that if we are sitting just over the footlights on a stage, we are also placed somewhat in the director's seat during the filming of a movie scene. If we think vaguely of the difference between a movie seen on television and a live show, we think of many tiny figures hurrying away from us in one case, and in the other of large blurred faces and upper torsos - the

---

*After visiting a local studio, I find that the role of Chief Cameraman is performed by the Director, pushing buttons in his control booth; otherwise the picture is substantially correct.

latter giving us a very distinct sense of dramatic meanings but a very indistinct sense of place. We never know where the characters are, in a live show, though we may know who they are quite as well or better than we do at movies.

The television camera is, in brief, a near-sighted, slow-moving younger brother of the movie camera - a bookish fellow, clumsy at games, whose owlish talent for close study compensates for his inability to catch the broad, quick movement in depth which we expect of movies. The strength of the T V camera lies at present in a nearly static, sculptural tableau shot - like an opera, or an Eisenstein movie. Unlike the old-fashioned tableaux of vaudeville, in which "nude" figures imitated statuary, the T V figures show constricted movements - minuscule motions in a dimension largely invisible to a stage aurience. The closest approximation to this style might be a movie of a Broadway play, filmed directly from its stage.

It is probably for this reason that such sluggish enterprises as the marionette show and panel program have found a new life on television. "Small octaves for small hands," as the accordion-teachers put it. For the small television screen, actors must squeeze themselves together, lap edging lap, while the camera pores over an intricate repertoire of tiny tic-like gestures, most of them fleeting and involuntary. During the early days of "Broadway Open House" Jerry Lester, a pioneer in this development, would push his face into the lens to exhibit a small quivering of his cheek. More recently the television singers have developed a dramatic style which depends on bizarre vermiform acrobatics about the mouth. Though at present this style of acting would seem to have its origins in the Neurological Clinic, it may yet be a portent of the type of dramatic gesture television will encourage.

Nevertheless the tableau shot offers more dramatic possibility than the puppet shows lead us to suspect. In his last movie, *Ivan the Terrible*, Eisenstein at-

tempted a comparable form which many critics found too wooden for their taste. Yet a sophisticated audience, willing to take for granted the movie camera's ability to move, might find novel tensions invoked by its ability to stand still. Twenty years ago the Chase was a fresh and challenging exercise for the camera, providing the audience with an authentic crisis. By now, however, the Chase is a predictable venture, not to be resuscitated by the addition of new gimmicks. Sewer, subway, railroad station, amusement park - these were effective for a few pictures, then returned to their more usual function in the life of a city. But if the Chase is now too threadbare for illusion, this is probably because we were brought up on it: the Chase has so penetrated our imaginations that we no longer need it spelled out.

A similar phenomenon has recently occurred in the theatre. After years of realistic staging, actors in business suits can now seat themselves around a table on the stage and read their parts, trusting the audience to invest their words with the necessary illusion of costume, setting and movement. The device works, of course, because of our history as audience. The same thing has happened to the game once called "Charades" but now significantly called merely "Indications." Where our grandfathers decked themselves out in weird costumes to portray book titles and proverbs, our version of the game specifically forbids the use of props or costumes. We prefer to to take these for granted, relying instead on a dramatic shorthand which would have been obscure indeed to another generation. So while the tableau shot of television may exist by reason of necessity, its effectiveness when skilfully used will depend on the whole history of drama: particularly on our changing notions of what constitutes reality and illusion. We can assume that much of what seems "realistic" to us will become the sheerest fiction or melodrama for our descendants.

Not only the good dramatic programs but sports too, can take advantage of the tableau shot - notably in boxing, where the television camera spans comfortably the small octave that is the prize ring. Instead of chalk marks on the floor, the ropes of the ring keep both fighters and referee enclosed for middle-distance and close-up shots. In fact, the prize fight might have been invented for television. Already it seems hard to believe that patrons once paid for arena seats from which they could barely see the ring. And there is at least one bit of evidence that television may eventually change the form of boxing. This is the new life T V has given to the " in-fighter": a boxer whose principle attack of short slicing blows, delivered with chin on opponent's shoulder, is hardly visible beyond the tenth row. Conversely the classical, standup fighter loses some of his appeal when subjected to the close-up.

Other sports, particularly those requiring large fields and many players, have been difficult for the T V camera, although part of the trouble at this stage is the fact that most cameramen are unfamiliar with the sport they are televising. When cameras become less cumbersome it might eventually be possible for the announcer, who is presumably the sports expert, to operate the camera himself. As it is, football on television emerges as quite a different sport from football played on the field. Treated as a series of tableaux, T V football consists of endless shots of the quarterback taking the ball, drifting back, passing, or being tackled. Meanwhile ends and backs, like the man signing in on the quiz program, are miraculously transported downfield to catch or miss the pass. And since line play is almost non-existent on T V , football fans are forced to rely on their imagined recollections of the game. If, as many promoters fear, succeeding generations should stop attending sports events altogether and their recollection of the game should fade away, then football might adapt itself entirely to the T V camera. This may be even more true of baseball, which offers the most constricted

representation of all. The usual triangular shot of pitcher, batter and catcher not only distorts the flight of the ball but gives us only a small portion of the diamond play. Moreover the action of baseball, with its sudden eruptions, is often too fast for the T V camera to follow. As a final speculation, it is not impossible that sports fans of the future will turn to more private or scholarly occupations, like fencing, which require an area comparable to that of the prize ring.

Because the T.V. illusion is so different from that of stage or movies, it takes the novice televiewer some time to adjust himself to the new medium. I think he does it by never permitting himself to become too absorbed in it. To spare himself the shock of dipping in and out of the illusion, he will try for a more casual aloofness and may thereby achieve a more critical distance as well. If illusion is all-important to the arts, the breaking-down or seeing-through of illusion is the first step toward criticism of the arts.

It is hardly surprising that televiewers read, play cards, knit, make love or do their homework with the set turned on; if they cannot have illusion, let them at least be masters of the situation. It may be this very splitting of attention, rather than any badness of the programs, which accounts for that feeling expressed by all viewers and often decried by educators and psychologists: the feeling of waste. If the illusion were complete, there would be no sense of time or of time wasted. Dramatic illusion demands, in fact, that one's personal time sense be suspended, in order to live through the various days and moments of the action. Actually we experience no sense of weeks or months passing, but live suspended in the present - so that a good movie always ends too soon, and seems to have passed in a moment.

Since imagination is a process much like memory, the same thing happens when we review our own lives: suspended in the present, we are free to roam at will among the re-created and hence imagined events of our past. Having created these like a drama for ourselves, we find such meditations - when we wake - to have lasted but an instant. Out of this illusion too, we may be interrupted or we may wake up when the play is over. Or something internal may cause us to wake ourselves up. When this happens, we usually come to with a guilty feeling: it seems we have strayed from a true creation of the past and begun some false invention, some self-indulgent daydream.

It would appear that illusion breaks down from two causes: either from external interruptions or from some inner sense of falsity and untruth. A bad movie, unless we can believe in it, drives us back into our own time-world; we feel bored, or watch the clock. But a good movie, were it interrupted every fifteen minutes for popcorn and commercials, would be as distracting as a television show. And distraction is a very active state - the opposite of sleep, hypnosis or illusion, and the enemy of all contented meditation. Such restlessness may induce a critical mood.

Certainly there is nothing passive, as educators claim, about a medium which requires such continual control as television: so much changing of stations, fiddling with the knobs, turning the room lights on and off, picking up and laying down of books and knitting. The continual hope is offered, that we may improve the quality either of the picture or of the dramatic entertainment. The continual choice is offered, whether to accept the given or to reject it altogether. Thus we are not in the passive condition of accepting what is given, which our forefathers may have enjoyed, but rather in the over-active modern state: distracted by too much freedom - always with the hope of absolute, infinite possibility looming just ahead. Strangely enough, modern man offered himself nearly infinite freedom of choice at the same time as he stopped believing in the term " Free Will."

It is soothing to enter a movie theatre, to be deprived of all choice, and to have one's evening disposed of. But with a choice of employments forced on us by the periodic interruptions of a television program, the choice of mere " passive" entertainment is bound to seem more frivolous than knitting, housework, conversation or a book. Even those periodic trips to the bathroom or kitchen - which, according to the water companies' records, occur at fifteen-minute intervals every evening in America - even those are apt to seem more real than merely burying oneself in one crime, suspense, variety, quiz, adventure story after another. But here again it is the multiplicity of entertainment which oppresses us. Although an evening at the movies may be one of the most solitary experiences possible to modern man, it nevertheless comes under the heading somehow of social life; there is nothing sordid about it. But to see the equivalent of eight or ten movies in a single night - and every night - that's when we begin to hear the brush of bats' wings and feel the cobwebs settling on us. It is also much harder, if we are at loose ends, to make the decision not to look at television than not go to a movie or not to get someone in for bridge.

All the same, I believe the average television fan is indulging in activities of a far more intellectual and critical nature than he may be aware of. Even the children, who are quick to spot the phony and the fake of old Western movies, are thus functioning as critics rather than contented patrons of the arts. Even though a child may object to any art, once he spots it - preferring his illusion to be " real" - this early training in distinguishing the " fakey" from the " real" may provide as much instruction as all the college courses which will later tell him what is real and good, and require no critical discrimination on his part. As a matter of fact, I have heard college graduates arguing about the social problems of *High Noon* or *Crime and Punishment* as though these were no books or movies, but a history witnessed on the street - forgetting, like the children, that the arts are invented by some very human minds.

I think television forces a certain critical distance on everyone, beginning with the children, and that once a critical distance is achieved some critical discrimination is almost bound to follow. The fact that we do not value or much notice our own critical activities, unless they are expended on something important like a science-lecture, a book of non-fiction, or a political argument, may come from the fact that we do not ordinarily remember how much instruction we have gained from our earliest experiences in fiction: from movies, comic books or fairy tales. Or we may think "criticism" is only what is explicit, as well as positive or "constructive" - forgetting how many complicated value judgments are required merely to dislike a bad movie. The result is that a man may ignore the fine independent taste he exhibits toward the movies, and think of himself as a critic only when he is offering somebody else's stale opinions as his contribution to a political discussion.

This brings me to a second point about television. If it lacks the grand illusion of an art-form, might it not be useful for the opposite purpose: for seeing the truth about politics and public events? When the Kefauver Committee hearings were first televised, critics were so exalted by their new ability to recognize a rascal by his face that they foresaw an early purification of public life. This notion of the camera as a latter-day truth serum reinforced a long-cherished conviction of the average man: namely, that words are tricky and misleading, but anyone can judge a man by his face. And with television's passion for the close-up, it seemed that at long last we had a mass means for measuring Quality in men. A quick shortcut to knowledge, wisdom and experience, the television camera would be to everyman what the Rorschach test is to psychologists.

Of course there is a sense in which a man's character, his probity and intelli-

gence can be discovered in his face. But our vocabulary for describing this - the noble brow, the beady eye, the chin strong or weak, the lips sensual or compressed - comes down to us mainly from literature. Since we can see, to some extent, whatever we have the words to see with, a great deal depends on which novelists we have read, and how well they have communicated their wisdom and experience in physiognomy. There are also the visual sources for our skill in face-reading. Portraits of the famous - Christ, Socrates, Webster, Lincoln - each furbished with those particular features which the artist believed characteristic of goodness and wisdom. And the portraits of the villains of history - Judas, Napoleon, Burr, Rasputin, Kaiser Wilhelm - even the photographs of Hitler and Mussolini. To these lists we must add the Hollywood figures who embody the virtues and vices of our time. Was Lewis Stone *really* wise patient, forgiving, or - given another director with another theory - could he just as well have played an aging fop? Was George Sanders really wicked, or might he have been cast as merely one of the husbands of the famous Gabor sisters? Unlike our literary notions, our visual standards obviously shift with fashion, too often after the fact. Would Costello's face have seemed quite so evil, if we hadn't already known? And Hiss - the greatest setback to physiognomic science since Lombroso: one day a clean-cut studious Harvard type, the next day a cunning spy. With the facts contradicting all evidence of our senses, we had either to deny the facts or to convince ourselves that he had a cold and steely (or a shifty) eye.

As we actually judge character among our fellows, faces are not the only or the most important thing, of course. There are all those gestures, mannerisms, fleeting expressions, tone of voice, choice of words - posture, stance, behavior - in a dozen different situations; above all, speech: what is said, when. But for all this multiplicity of everyday meaning, we have an even less agreed-upon vocabulary than we have for physiognomy. Our critical judgments of men may be sound enough, if we could only express them - or does the lack of vocabulary affect our judgments? With the presidential campaign, every self-made diagnostician took his turn at analyzing the personality of the candidates. Some tremendous gap in quality was apparent to everyone - but what was it? Stevenson, obviously more intelligent, looked better and talked better than his opponent - but was that good or bad? To some that meant he was an egg-head and a slick politician; to others it was Eisenhower and Nixon who looked slick. To this latter group Nixon's televised self-defense appeared the glibbest kind of soap opera; to the former he was really just a barefoot boy, it was Stevenson who was glib. Unfortunately the results of the election cannot tell us whether the American people, recognizing quality when they saw it, proceeded to vote against it, or whether the large vote for Stevenson proves just the opposite.

We do know that a surprising number of experts, recognizing Stevenson's high intelligence, integrity, humility and so on, did vote against him on the ground that an intellectual will not make a politician. The very concept " intellectual" carries such a stigma of neurosis that some social scientists interpreted Stevenson's real doubts about himself as " instability," apparently preferring some more familiar or less modest kind of doubts and hesitations. Eisenhower's weak fumbling with his speeches convinced many that here was a real American, of heart and feeling, no egg-head but a true man of the people born in a log cabin.

In short, Stevenson's advantages were interpreted as everything from a virtue to a vice, and the interpretations were couched in language borrowed from whatever theory seemed congenial - whether religious, psychological, phrenological or economic. As an example, we might recall Time magazine's heroic job of interpretation here: they had the task of converting a candidate they liked into a candidate they liked but

wouldn't vote for. For the first couple of weeks, as you may remember, their admiration for Stevenson lay unconcealed. Indeed here was a man who embodied all those virtues which Time had sought unflaggingly, between campaigns, to instil into its readers. Stevenson's humor, his determination to commit himself on every issue, his ability to make language serve rather than to conceal thought, his theoretical grasp of the anti-religious nature of Communism, his distrust of growing centralization and the Big State - even his genuine apprehension before the task he had chosen - all these qualities represented the enlightened Christian conservatism which Time considered its own philosophy. It may be interesting to recall how each of these qualities was rendered invidious (and not only for Time readers):

Stevenson's humor became his frivolity and lack of serious purpose; his forthrightness became his gift for language; his language became phrase-making. Although a candidate at least for Bartlett's Quotation's, his phrases " wore spats." And not only the Princetonian spats of Wilson, or the Groton-Harvard spats of Acheson and Hiss, they also wore the galluses of old-time demagogues and rabble-rousers: Stevenson became " the greatest stump speaker since Wm. Jennings Bryan." This left Eisenhower as both under-dog and Honest Man: young Mr. Lincoln played by Gary Cooper.

As seen on television, Eisenhower's incompetence easily became his artless virtue. How right that a man of the people should be hopelessly unskilled at public speaking: a doer, not a talker! So each week Time, like an elder Webster, counselled young Mr. Lincoln on his statesmanship, chiding him for laziness and inattention. Their criticism achieved the soft validity of a doting parent, who sees no relation between her son's manners and the man he will become. And each week Time briskly paraphrased those speeches which looked even worse in print - meanwhile frankly applauding the General's opponent as the most polished after-dinner speaker (or glibbest rabble-rouser) since Wm. Jennings Bryan.

Since the American electorate was able, for the first time in its history, to study its candidates in close detail, what equal opportunities for the discovery of truth might have been provided - if only we had some shared theory and vocabulary for expressing it. There really is no wordless, mindless, method for discerning truth or quality. Some verbal art was required for Republican opinion-makers to convert their educated readers to a frontiersman's theory-namely, that distrust of words and intelect, accompanied by a faith in Romantic theories of " instinct," heart or feeling. But how much easier it was for the television camera simply to exhibit the Bold Soldier and Frontiersman (never mind how feeble), pitted against the City Slicker (no matter how sincere).

By now the early hope of revealing some predigested Truth about public life through the television camera begins to seem naive. Telecasts of congressional hearings, U.N. meetings, conventions or parades offer moving, even meaningful moments; yet for information we depend largely on the critical remarks of commentators, as in radio. This early hope came primarily, it seems to me, from the ingenuous faith of the Nineteenth Century (whether it is called Romantic, or scientific, or the philosophy of Naturalism): namely, that Truth is not created but is something lying there, waiting to be discovered - especially by new improved scientific gadgets. The stake we have at present in the hidden camera or tape machine seems largely a hangover from the Romantic eras - calling to mind all those mindless words like " spontaneity," " intuition," " instinct," " empathy," " feeling," " sincerity," and so on. Like marijuana and benzedrine, which offer at least the illusion that one can transcend his limitatiins, so too the portable television crews will, for a while, stimulate the same expectations in their audience. It is said that three years after T V arrives in a city, the high fidelity shops

move in, peddling their brand of infinite exactitude. When Hi-Fi proves no shortcut to music, it will probably give way again to some new illusions of visual " reality," such as three-dimensional color television.

It looks at present as though we couldn't tolerate the notion of " illusion" ; everything must be " real." That is, it must depend on perfect instruments, and not on fallible " human" judgment or imagination. What is overlooked in this, of course, is that the judgments of mathematician or engineer are at present determining our notions of reality. Even when some obviously mistaken view of reality turns up, like the stereopticon perspective of 3-D, we do not lose our faith that the instruments of truth will eventually perfect themselves.

But if television can not bring us the ready-made Truth of our romantic hopes, it will be obvious to anyone that the reality it does bring us is none the less real and true. So far as the real illusion of television is concerned, it is not necessary to think only of the high-powered programs which provide political and other information to the public. There is a tremendous fascination in all the real-life presentations of the T V screen. For all its limitations as an art-form (or because of them) there is tremendous interest in merely watching amateurs move around, or in observing the performance of almost any actor and directors. If I can't have art I prefer, like most people, not to have artiness; and yet there is something about television - its lack of any Grand Illusion- which makes even artiness interesting. The camera-work is interesting on the otherwise dull Garroway show; so is the weirdly inept German expressionism used in the half-hour film show *Counterpoint*. Because of this absence of the more familiar or more successful illusions of art, the viewer cannot help being aware of the writers, actors and producers behind the arty scene - all trying for something and getting B for effort.

At its best, of course, television has

produced a surprising number of creditable dramatic pieces, but at its worst it often has the lovableness of hometown theatricals. Oddly enough, I think the critical distance imposed by the television screen brings us round in the end to a state of sentiment, of friendliness or sympathy, which is at least the first requisite for an aesthetic experience. And perhaps this is just what we miss and feel most cheated of, after being overpowered by the huge illusions of the movie screen. In the movie theatre, we must love or hate pretty much on cue, as though our reflexes were being manipulated as we sit there. But at home we can choose to dislike or grow fond of the shadowy people moving in our living rooms according to much more personal and mysterious standards.

On Watching A TV Boxing Match In October

Jack Spicer

The boxers show an equilibrium
Unmatched this autumn. In the air outside
Winds swirl around the big October moon
While men and boxers seek a place to hide.
Within the focus of a crowded room
The boxers face each other. They pretend
That man can counterpunch real enemies.
They hit each other til the very end.
One wins and they embrace there, while the wind
Grows louder and the screen begins to fade.
Then all the men and boxers bind their wounds
And leave the empty screen, and are afraid.

The Live Show

Reality on TV

David Sherbon & Victoria Mendel

ADMIRERS of various live shows - Mr. Peepers, the Goodyear-Philco Playhouse, Colgate Comedy Hour and so on - may have wondered just how these are produced and how they acquire their particular lively, spontaneous quality. Most viewers probably imagine that a T V show must be a combination of movie and stage techniques - with the director first setting up a stage action, and then shooting it much as a movie director would do. What actually happens, however, is apt to be a very different, a more difficult and impressive thing to watch.

In the first place, since there is no chance for cuts and re-takes and one performance is all there is, the action resembles a first-night in the theatre more than a movie production. But a theatre company may spend many months rehearsing, where a T V cast has hours or days - at most, a few weeks. It is only the rarest, most expensive, most thoroughly planned production which could hope to roll off exactly on cue. What the live performance depends on, therefore, is last-minute teamwork, improvisation, and continuous coaching from the floor-crew and director.

But while the director is supervising every minute of the final performance, even to follow his instructions under this kind of speed and pressure would demand a much greater concentration, flexibility and teamwork from the group than either stage or movie work. They are required to think fast, to make their own decisions and yet to move as a unit: something like the small commando teams of the last war, as compared to a regular platoon. Or a small jazz combo, compared to a big name band. In such groups the leader may have the final responsibility but can never have absolute control; he may be called on to follow the others' lead as often as to issue orders.

So with the T V director in his control booth. His coaching must be done at split-second speed while the show is going on - done moreover from within his soundproof walls, by means of earphones. It's as though a movie director had to do his own cutting and editing in the film room, while relaying his instructions to the actors and the floor crew. The director is not, in fact, watching the live performance at all. He is observing its effect translated into a medium utterly different from both stage and movies, namely, the small T V screen. He knows, too, that the two or three camera views being shown him on his monitor - and among which he must, at every moment, choose - will be further translated or distorted by our blurred and fuzzy home sets, jumping with brilliantly distracting impulses of light. So, while choosing the best and clearest picture, he is also relaying a steady stream of suggestions to the cameramen, and to the " stage director" or prompter (also wearing earphones) who will silently convey these to the actors. The crew on the lights and the sound-booms too will require more or less supervision, depending on the show.

In the midst of these split-second decisions, the director must keep his mind
divided between dramatic values, on the one
hand, and pictorial values on the other.
But pictorial values in this medium do not
go much beyond clarity and visibility.
"Composition" (of a still, or single frame)
is reduced to the elementary terms of a
snapshot or news photo, in which extra
pains must be taken to have the subject
well-lighted, well-centered and visible
enough in terms of line and color contrast:
placed, that is, against an uncluttered,
contrasting background. Nor would it be
particularly desirable if the director did
have time for more artistic composition of
the single picture.

Dramatic values - or rather "meaning":
the point of an action - must come first,
at the expense of pictorial interest. As
an extreme example, we might imagine a
televised football game in which the camera
devoted itself to well-composed close-ups
of the players' faces - missing half the
action. As a matter of fact, the two
political conventions showed us many candid
camera views of the spectators' faces, some
of which had the glowing, sharpened intensity of a Flemish portrait - yet how many
of us would prefer these to the breathless,
backstage excitements of the political
action itself? However well-composed
these " stills," there is always an arty,
static quality when a *moving* picture slows
itself down; the T V cameras were, in fact,
marking time - waiting for the drama to
begin. Outside of clarity and visibility,
pictorial values on T V mean chiefly the
cinematic values of pace, rhythm, timing,
sequence, movement, continuity - in other
words, dramatic values. As one T V director expressed this: he couldn't afford
to stop, he said, and admire a single picture once it was " done," but must be
searching in that frame for the *anlage* of
the next.

On the other hand there is a nearly
absolute difference in quality between the
two media, T V and movies, which we ought
to take a moment to describe. Compared to
movies, T V starts out with two strikes
against it: the size of its screen and the
difficulties inherent in its production
methods. And while these, when properly
accounted for and turned to best advantage,
may become T V 's greatest single asset (as
we shall see), we may assume that the T V
screen will never be as big as a movie
screen - unless, of course, we all start
living in abandoned movie theatres. This
means that we will always be outside the
screen, looking at a two-dimensional picture
moving in a small frame; we can never get
inside the screen, as we do at the movies,
and move around with the actors inside
their universe of action.

The disadvantage here is that T V will
never be able to represent an object, or a
living action, in all the singular reality
and detail of a movie or a Renaissance
painting - whose virtue is to reveal the
quality, the essence, of a living object:
show us a single rose in all its large
mysterious detail. But still less is T V
a Broadway stage whose tradition, at least
in musicals, is to show off a single rose
by massing the stage with a hundred long-
stemmed beauties. What T V can do, however, is to communicate meaning - an idea,
a visual gag, the point and purport of an
action - quite as well as movies can. In
fact, because of the more flexible and
improvised nature of its production, it can
often do this better.

As an example, let us take a very simple
visual gag. An Actor A, hiding from Actor
B, peers around a bush onstage, is surprised
by B; the script calls for a close-up of
" surprise." While Camera One is taking
the bush, exposing Actor A behind it, Camera
Two is moving in, focussing on the spot
where A's head will appear above the bush.
While Two is getting that shot, Camera One is
backing up to catch the whole scene: the
end of " peering" and the beginning of
" surprise." And Two is now moving a little
closer, preparing for the final close-up
of " surprise."

There is the action, as called for in
the script and so rehearsed. But now in

performance , as these four men - plus the director, plus the cue-man or prompter, plus the crew on lights and microphones, to say nothing of various sound engineers and producers in or out of the control booth; as each of these six, eight or possibly ten men begins to concentrate on his own aspect of " peering" and " surprise," some changes may occur.

The director may himself decide that Camera One should back off farther and hold the shot of the bush until Two has had time to get his close-up of A's surprise. This slight variation may then suggest further changes to Cameraman Two, who may decide on a still closer view of A's face. Just as he is trimming this up, the director may ask him to hold it: the close-up has given the actor a new idea: he will lean closer into Camera Two and keep his surprise bottled up until Two starts taking.

Through such fast, well-disciplined moves as these, a visual gag may be put across with much more lucidity than would have been possible from a rigid adherence to the script. The changes above, all tending to exaggerate, to intensify, the single idea " surprise" also tended to simplify and to clarify it by trimming out extraneous elements. The unity displayed by the group would show up on the screen as a heightened unity of effect, and hence would have more impact. I believe the average show on television must necessarily have some of the unrehearsed quality of the small jazz band.

Everything depends on the skill of the group, however, whether we get the " spontaneity" of amateur theatricals (as in the Robert Montgomery dramas, the Campbell *Sound Stage* or the undirected chaos of the Godfrey show), or whether we get the true illusion of spontaneity, carefully planned and executed, of the *Goodyear Philco Playhouse* or the first year of *Mr. Peepers.* Obviously good improvisation means group discipline. For a jazz band to anticipate collectively what each player is about to do would not be possible, of course, without a single " idea" or pattern to

be followed in the musical sequence. And like the T V group following a single pictorial sequence, the jazz band may thereby achieve a greater clarification, a heightened unity, of the musical idea.

So far as the viewer can tell, live shows vary widely in the amount of rehearsal and the degree of one-man direction they get. Some shows look under-directed like the old Berle show; others look over-directed like the new Berle show. The big Kraft and Ford shows simply look badly directed. But the best Goodyear plays achieve an " undirected" look - as though the director had given the actors *carte blanche* to express themselves. And while we can assume this is good direction, it is striking how much the performers depend on the whole production, rather than a single part. Goodyear and Philco can bring out astonishing performances from such movie veterans as James Dunn, Wendell Corey and Eddie Albert (although Albert, left to himself as an M.C. for a variety show, can be a total failure. Conversely, an incompetent production like Robert Montgomery's can make even Cedric Hardwicke look like an amateur. A good theatre man like Hardwicke can improvise his lines, and even help other actors get through theirs, but there is nothing he can do if the camera freezes on him while he is merely trying to get himself offstage. Even a veteran T.V. actor couldn't do much without the fast cooperation of director and stage crew. Usually it's the most expensive stars who get (or give) the least rehearsal time; we've all seen harried comedians rushing in and out of production numbers, fluffing their lines and ruining their timing - especially on the *All Star Review.* On the other hand, the big dance groups often look tired and harried as though they had been over-rehearsed; or rather, as if they had forced a month's precision training into a week or less. But some of the big variety shows go off more smoothly than a movie, like the very good Martin-Lewis show for Colgate recently, which was running concurrently with one of their poorest movies.

Unlike movies, where good direction may be accompanied by some bad writing or a few badly-acted bits (like a movie with Alan Ladd), live shows display a marked homogeneity on all three levels. A good crime show, like Ammident's *Danger* or Auto-lite's *Suspense*, will have good writing, good acting and good direction. In the Montgomery and Campbell shows the writing is apt to be as amateurish as the production. Ford and Kraft are equally competent and equally slick: they buy the same slick-magazine plays and use the same undistinguished acting styles. And *Dragnet* of course carries this uniformity to such absurd lengths that all the characters talk alike. Since the T V director can never be the absolute czar that it is possible, theoretically at least, for stage and movie directors to be, we can assume that much of this homogeneity comes from the teamwork among T V actors and director; also from the executive producer who chooses his talent and buys his own plays. Good or bad, the whole production seems to stand or fall together.

While this is a great advantage in such performances as the *Goodyear-Philco Playhouse*, which compares favorably with anything coming at present from Hollywood or Broadway, there is a less fortunate kind of uniformity to be discerned in some of the over-praised or so-called "highbrow" shows: *Omnibus, Studio One,* Sid Caesar's *Show of Shows* and the present *Mr. Peepers.* Despite the variety and unevenness of these programs, there is a certain drift toward one dead-level taste, as though the original talent had been overruled by a board of directors. And whether this taste is the callow Broadway sophistication of *Show of Shows* or the more pedantic sophistication of *Omnibus* and *Peepers,* or the genteel artiness of *Studio One* , it aims always to be *different* - different from Milton Berle, different from Molly Goldberg and Lucille Ball. In elevating the popular taste, the idea is not to give the public what it presumably wants. The results are often painful, as when *Omnibus* inflicted an hour-long bit of stale whimsy on Jack Benny - one of those supernatural numbers with angels in funny costumes - which was exactly the sort of thing we see every other week on the popular *Kraft Theatre.* Or was *Omnibus* descending to the crowd? In either case, Jack Benny was made to seem extremely dull, which was no favor to anybody. It is usually safer when *Omnibus* and *Studio One* stick to the classics, which they do very well, and do not try for anything original - especially in comedy.

Mr. Peepers is the saddest example of all. Originally the show with the funniest visual gags, the best comic writing, acting and directing to be seen anywhere - at least since Harold Lloyd - *Mr. Peepers* has turned so consistently away from comedy that it is now some kind of "highbrow" soap opera. With the introduction of love interest, Wally Cox no longer plays an absurd and *therefore* lovable character, as in all good comedy. Peepers is played straight as the lovable young science teacher whom we are nevertheless asked to find absurd - why? Not because any of the other characters find him so; he is actually the *raisonneur* of the piece. If he is absurd, it is only the sophistication of writer and viewer which tells us so - as though humor might depend on the dubious assertion that all science teachers are ridiculous. With a similar abandonment of visual gags - perhaps on the theory that farce is inferior to "situation-comedy" - there is only one truly absurd, funny or lovable figure left in the show. This is *Mrs. Gurney,* as played by the remarkable English comedienne Marion Lorne. And Mrs. Gurney is soon to be married off. Of course this failure may be a simple exhaustion of ideas and talent - farce is much more difficult than situation-comedy; and yet it would have been so easy to give *Peepers* a foil, a straight-man. When Cox appeared on a variety show with two such formidable straight-men as Tallulah Bankhead and Milton Berle, he was as absurd and lovable as ever.

These are all interesting examples of what may happen when a producer tries to avoid what is popular, instead of avoiding what is bad. But of course no one knows what makes Milton Berle or *Dragnet* or *I Love Lucy* popular. To know that, we should first have to distinguish the good from the bad in those programs, and then decide which it is the public prefers. As it is, one set of producers makes the blanket assumption that everything popular is bad, while another set of producers assumes that everything popular - or at least high-priced - is good. And strangely enough, one assumption gets about the same results as the other. Many routine filmed shows have been brightened or retrieved by simply hiring some expensive camera work and direction. This is the reason Loretta Young's weekly soap opera seems mysteriously better than it should be. And if you add good writing and good acting, you'll get a good show from the most unpromising format - like *My Favorite Husband* which started out as an upper-class *I Love Lucy*, aimed at the carriage trade, and is now one of the best-made comedies on the air. Far from depending on its social snob-appeal (as Peepers depends on intellectual snob-appeal), it often achieves the kind of social satire which Peepers tries for and doesn't always get. The most bitter and touching satire of the middle classes to be seen on the air today is probably the carefully written *Ethel and Albert* comedy.

In view of the many depressing examples of uniformity cited above, it has been all the more encouraging to watch so many actors and writers blossom forth under the uniformly good productions of Goodyear and Philco. This Playhouse has turned up a surprising amount of good writing, well suited to its particular style: a kind of Chekhovian naturalism, infused with Stanislavsky, and a delivery which gives the effect not of an actor reading his lines, but of a character groping his way through some urgent feelings of his own. While this style would be ruinous to Moliere,

Congreve or even Shaw, it is very well adapted to the more realistic comedy or problem plays written for Goodyear by Paddy Chayefsky and others. This genre might be described as the old Broadway " problem play" freed of its didactic tendencies and exploring present-day moral and social problems with a refreshing lack of pseudo-scientific theory. That is, if one of these writers - who have obviously assimilated their Freud and Marx - wants to present a domineering mother, he can do so without making her a stock villain. He will present both sides, or many sides: a whole rich social content is often sketched in with remarkable economy of means. In fact, there have been many interesting reversals of Freudian cliches - like the chronically guilty, alcoholic parent (movingly portrayed by James Dunn) intimidated by his enlightened, domineering son. Or the wife (in Chayefsky's *Sixth Year*) who is so afraid of being a " domineering wife" that she fails to give her husband the support he needs. Not all the Philco-Goodyear plays start from these social-science premises; many of them are based on traditional or Christian values. Yet it is precisely the effort to translate Freudian or other scientific insights into traditional terms of drama which makes the Chayefsky kind of play so relevant and interesting.

Since this *Playhouse* manages to show off both actors and writers at their best, the dialogue will have its full effect whether it is spoken by Rod Steiger, by some movie-veteran like Albert, or by one of the talented newcomers (like Eileen Heckart) who turn up every week. Since Chayefsky's lines (for example) are carefully flat and repetitious, reflecting the banalities of everyday speech, it is easy to imagine how these would sound in a mediocre performance. Suppose they were made " spirited" and cute, as in a Frank Wisbar production for *Fireside Theatre*, or hammily eloquent like the soap operas of Kraft or Ford, or given the portentous timing of *Dragnet* - actually they need the precise handling they get.

And like the occasional eloquence of most of us, which must be heard and not seen, they don't sound like much on paper or quoted out of context.

Earlier we mentioned that " true illusion of spontaneity" which the best of these live shows generate. Where they altogether fail to do so, this is probably the result of not exploiting T V 's unique possibilities for teamwork. As one director said, such failures are the rule in studios where the cameramen are kept rigidly to their cues and not encouraged to " look for anything." And of course some of the smaller studios are simply too haphazard and disorganized for any disciplined teamwork; they're doing well if they can follow a cue-sheet. Here television's greatest single talent, for putting across a visual idea, would have no meaning or existence.

We must speak now of television's other great talent which, as we saw in the two political campaigns, lies in capturing the backstage quality of events and giving us an illusion of real-life. Where the formal drama must strive carefully for a disciplined expression of " spontaneity" and avoid the mere dishevelment of amateurs, the dramatic presentation of a news event gains authenticity from any unstaged accidents which increase the illusion of reality. Unfortunately the usual newsreel director, who seems to think he is staging *East Lynne*, manages to avoid any illusion of reality whatever. How much better if Ike would drop his glasses, if one of those bear cubs would bite one of the bathing beauties!

Such accidents would be grotesquely out of place in a Coronation Ceremony, of course, which is formidable drama of the and highest kind - the father of all theatre. But in the American political rites, we must be assured that this is a real man, chosen by ourselves - a man just like ourselves, in fact - and not one of the unreal gods of drama, like a movie queen or Queen Elizabeth or one of the cardboard characters in a newsreel. Though we might be awed, in our American style, by the spectacle of Queen Elizabeth abasing herself, kneeling to her people, being anointed, being dressed and undressed like a witch's doll, forced to wear the stigmata of kings and bowing her head at the last to receive a thorny crown -- most of us would prefer our own more joyful occasions which show us choosing our gods, not nailing them to the cross of office. For many viewers, the high point of dramatic, if not political, satisfactions came on election night.

While waiting for the General, we were treated to a wonderfully accidental shot of Fred Waring, prim as a schoolteacher, rehearsing the audience in their cues. And next the whole fevered sequence - Ike's breathless progress accompanied by the hoarse thumpings of democracy, as the announcer kept announcing " Here he comes! Here he comes! Here he comes!" Here we really saw the underside of history; saw the awkward camera tangling itself so candidly in its cables, tripping over its moving parts, jostling the actors and falling into the orchestra pit, elbowing its way into the audience - stealing the show like an amateur child among the star performers. Here was an art-form representing - really representing - life in all its backstage chaos.

In its very inclusion of the cables, spotlights and microphones which accompany a latter-day Caesar in his triumph, television was exhibiting the nation's life in all its naked sprawl as fact, as history. There are probably few stage or movie directors who would not have tried to give our history more dignity and order, as a religious spectacle or modern Coronation. To match this actuality, we think not of the artful movie camera nor of church aesthetics but of art - secular art, classical art, Greek art romanticized by the Renaissance. We think of Breughel's Wedding or his Fall of Icarus; of Shakespeare's Caesar, and all the sodden tears and pratfalls which surround the great events of history.

What television showed us was no mere Republican victory; it was a democratic Triumph in the Roman sense, a triumph of the *demos, vulgus, hoi polloi*: the people's Caesar returning from the wars. No ordered hierarchy of the Magna Carta here; no monarchic Christian-French Republicanism of the Bill of Rights: the Romans were exulting in their anarchic, ancient rights as patriarchs and tribal chiefs, proclaiming the true communism of the village *gens*, the true democracy of the town, preserved from all the neolithic tribes of Latium and Etruria.

Perhaps we might conclude that it is some kind of dramatized history at which television excels, and excels particularly at catching real contemporary history in her moments of undress. Such a moment was that brief glimpse of Nixon on his way to the throne, catching sight of his image on a T V set - obviously a surprise, both images raising their eyebrows, looking surprised, multiplying surprise on a million screens throughout the nation. Then, as though he were seeing himself for the first time served 'up on a platter of Fame, Nixon actually made a quick gesture of pushing it all away - something like Christ on the Mount, declining the Devil's offer. This drama took only a second of playing time before Nixon resumed his nonchalance as young vice-consul, modest prince.

Meanwhile the microphones, left open in the climax of excitement, were catching all that substratum of engineering strain - technicians gossiping like foot-soldiers under Caesar's chariot. We overheard the whole machinery creaking, watched the individual get trapped in a mess of wires, saw the whole mass of science-born techniques ensnaring his volition in the 1950's; we saw the whole thing. A good show? " It was better than a play." And because of all the accidents, which only confirmed the real urgency of events, we saw television pounding away at a single idea, and the idea expanding as a sense, an experience, of history.

Comic

Joseph Kostolefsky

Like the shapes of denial,
Ringing and changing, billowing
Bell-like, stretched by longing,
Or stunted by the seasons' change,
All changes rung on the lost bird's tune,
The question is the same; What hope?
And now the answer comes: The pie.
Not in the sky, but in the face agape
Lost your hope? The cream puff's arc.
Lost your wit? The seltzer's charge.
Charge it up to experience, son.
Put it down to knowledge, know
That there are stars and stooges. So
The glowing eye gives its answer, winks
And dims to blindness, chuckling in its sleep.

The Bard on T V
Television Comes Of Age

Joseph Kostolefsky

I T SEEMS strange now, looking at our television sets, dormant at night or winking alive with the signs and wonders of clowns and cookery, that we could ever have seen in this box only a plaything, a billboard, or a gadget for transporting wrestlers, still heaving, into our quiet living rooms. For now everything has been changed. Television has "come of age." Maurice Evans has "done" *Hamlet*, and now, we're told, things will we different. Hallmark cards have spent a great deal of money, columns and columns have been given over to the unfamiliar sight of unanimous accord, and a new era has been ushered into being. While one can agree that the production's implications go far beyond its brief life-span, agreement stops there. But even agreement or disagreement seems beside the point, for it's hard to believe, after reading some of the critical comments, that the critics who came, saw, and were conquered were even watching the same program.

In fact, most of what's been said about this T.V. Hamlet, both before and after the event, seems beside the point. That the camera work, the sets, the fluid movement from scene to scene, were brilliant, is certainly irrelevant. If it's split-second timing and impeccable production you're looking for, you can find them every week on *Your Hit Parade*, where such ingenuity is needed to convert the sows' ears of popular songs into the silk purses the sponsor puts his money into. Handsome and resourceful sets are a commonplace on such

programs as *Suspense* and *Studio One*. The difference is that here they're often needed to flesh out a wobbly story and provide, on their own, some of the excitement the writers have left out of the script. But when you have a play like *Hamlet*, you don't need brilliance or fluency or dazzling camera work. What you do need, and what Mr. Evans didn't give us, is Hamlet himself. In fact, the distracting Victorian costumes and the overlay of gentility that coated these passionate people we know so well, made me wonder if I wasn't seeing *Where's Hamlet?* But alas, Ray Bolger never turned up. The grave digger, that coarse fellow, was left on T.V.'s equivalent of the cutting-room floor. And Hamlet, poor Hamlet, for whom the study guides were printed, Hamlet, for whom the network cleared two hours of valuable time, tragic Hamlet for whom we should weep, never showed up at all. That seems to me to be the point; not that Hamlet was done at all, but that he was done poorly.

Many people, I know, think highly of Mr. Evans' Hamlet, and a personal opinion on that score needn't carry such weight. But what is disturbing and should be brought into question, is some of the reasons it was liked. I got the impression, reading the reviews, that we're *supposed* to like Mr. Evans. Why? Because he's a distinguished actor, a legitimate actor, making his television debut and bringing to millions of viewers whose sensibilities have been blunted by corner-of-the-mouth gangster dramas, the glories of the spoken word. And yet it seemed that Mr. Evans was so busy being distinguished, casting off high-priced pearls of perfect diction, that he couldn't be bothered with anything as mundane as acting. I can't divine Mr. Evans' attitude as he went through his carefully planned paces. Probably there was nothing condescending in his approach. He was obviously doing his best. He'd learned his lines and gave every evidence of loving them. What stopped me was that he seemed to love them because they provided him with a vehicle for declamation. Hamlet's instructions to the players, cut from this version, really weren't missed, because they were implicit in Mr. Evans' performance. The lines went " trippingly on the tongue," but seldom slipped down to get to the heart, either of Hamlet or of the viewer.

If Mr. Evans did his work without condescension, some of the reactions to it seem more suspect. Many of them began by pointing the finger of scorn at television in general, strongly implying that it needs more of this sort of thing if it's ever going to grow up. The implication is distressing, for it assumes that television is usually so inept, so· infantile, and so lacking in value that even a good intention indifferently fulfilled is enough to raise its standards. If the critics really wanted television to stand on its own adult feet, they'd insist on applying the same standards they'd use for the legitimate theatre or any other medium. It's easy enough to say, and prove, that Shakespeare is a better writer than William Saroyan, Hamlet a character of more stature than My Friend Irma, and the play a better one than any of the hundreds seen week after week on the Kraft Television Theatre. What's more difficult, and more important, is to insist that when something with *Hamlet*'s potential for moving and shaking us is given, it be done movingly, as a play, possibly the best ever written, and not as a museum piece for the further prestige of

N.B.C. and Hallmark.

For that's what it comes down to. Mr. Evans wasn't moving. Since cuts had to be made, the adapters were sensible in focusing attention on Hamlet, to the inevitable detriment of other characters. Fair enough. But when that's done, it's not too much to ask that the actor playing Hamlet be up to carrying the play, and carrying the audience with him. Mr. Evans wasn't, and so Barry Jones' really wonderful Polonius and Sarah Curchill's af - fecting performance of what was left of Ophelia, were lost in the shuffle. That Joseph Schildkraut played Claudius as a standard-brand villain and Ruth Chatterton followed the conventional grande dame interpretation of Gertrude really don't have much to do with it, either. Elsinore was handsome, Rosenkrantz and Guildenstern, for a change, tolerable, Mr. Evans witty, even charming, and Albert McCleery's direction first-rate, at least technically. But none of this makes any difference when the man on whom the play depends brings less to the role than it needs and less than is in it.

What effect all of this has had on the standards of television drama is debatable. So far no one, except *Omnibus*, has done any other of Shakespeare's plays at such length, nor have any sponsors come breaking down the studio doors, checkbooks in hand, begging to be allowed to underwrite Sophocles. Perhaps, to be blunt about it, it's just as well. For television has shown, the demands of commercial broadcasting being what they are, and pressure groups for everything from the pharmaceutical trade to Evangelical sects being as vocal as they are, that it can do more by starting with less. Certainly none of the plays presented on last season's much-missed *Celanese Theatre* was on a par with *Hamlet*, but time and again its producers, its adapters, and its brilliant director, Alex Segal, showed that by treating the plays as if they were about human beings who mattered and by mastering limitations of time and taboo, intelligent drama is possible on television. And possible as a continuing, self-supporting production, rather than a much-hooplaed one-shot, safely shielded from crass commercial considerations. The same understanding was evident on Worthington Miner's *Curtain Call*, also of last season, and currently, though not regularly, on *Studio One, Robert Montgomery Presents, Television Playhouse,* and even, limited as it is, *Dragnet.* These programs have shown that television, limited not by any technical shortcomings, but by the nature of any advertising medium aimed at a mass audience, fares best when working with material that isn't, in itself, quite first-rate. By using second-rate novels by Booth Tarkington and Robert Carson, *Studio One*

was able to come up with two delightful productions, in *The Show Piece* and *The Magic Lantern.* And on the same day *Hamlet* was being given such short shrift, *Television Playhouse,* in an insignificant story called *Printer's Measure,* presented performances by Peg Hillias, Martin Newman, and Pat O'Malley, that were more touching and more skillful than anything Mr. Evans, for all the advantage he had with the lines at his disposal, was able to accomplish. Of course television needs more boldness, more time, and more respect for a good script, but it's highly doubtful that indifferently-acted, overly cautious, awestruck productions like Evans' *Hamlet* will do anything to bring them about.

Picture Trouble

Joseph Kostolefsky

In fifty-seven seconds I'll tell my love,
More quickly than the flickering box,
With a brightness beyond the dial's control.
Not in that snowy land of gentle flakes
Touching us, rapt, on snowshoes, wrapped in furs,
Nor streaked with light, or leaping, flopping over,
But here, in the moment of whiteness, pure,
No cigarettes to crowd the frame,
No cars to crash it, spacemen soaring through,
But while we live, in that instant, mute,
Free of the jingles, far from the saxaphones,
Statesmen and wrestlers grappling somewhere else,
I'll tell my love, unshadowed, bright, no ghosts
Trailing the image with error's old dim prints.
We'll see each other plain, in that blank between,
And know who we are, till the puppets come again.

The Revolt Against

Reuel Denny

There are a number of good reasons for looking more closely at the " social realism" of the comic strips, comic books and popular children's books. One of them is that while the " content" of the strips has been much studied, a good deal less attention has been paid to the artistic conventions of various kinds employed by their creators. Thus, while many observers prefer to think of the comic strips and books as being generally " fantastic," they fail to observe how much the comics have accepted, in recent years, the conventions and traditions once associated with the literary and artistic movement known as Naturalism.

True, the Naturalistic movement, and its high period, are not easy to define. To use an almost overworked bench mark, let us simply say that some of the tendencies present in the work of Zola have re-emerged in the popular arts. Some people define Naturalism in literature as a tendency

In Pogoland the threat of leisure is everpresent.

Naturalism in Our Comic Strips

toward the stenographic and documentary; in painting as rivalry with the photograph; and in both literature and graphic art as a willingness to take for granted a materialistic social psychology which expresses itself in terms of a theory of "interests." Surveying the impact of this convention, it is noticeable that Naturalistic influences in certain of the popular media and in children's books are the result of a socially downward distribution of fashions. In this sense, much of modern popular culture contains the diffused, reorganized, and to some extent, simplified viewpoints of a now-aged artistic movement. (It would be unfair, of course, to say that this is all there is to popular culture.) The shift toward social realism in children's books was also, in part, a result of the Popular Front of the 1930's. Moreover, the shift toward representationalism in the comic strip was largely a result of the impact upon both the artists and their

audiences of the motion picture. The 1920's, the period in which the film made its initial impact, happens to be the period during which the older, cruder cartoonist began to lose ground and the new art-school-trained cartoonist began to come into favor. Soon after the early 1920's, as we know, the film had further increased the social realism of the comic strip by encouraging it to adopt such movie techniques as serialization, continued episodic action, and rapid cutting from scene to scene. Today's comic-viewing eye is an eye trained in part by movie "Naturalism." Let us look more closely at the history of these changes.

There is no single realistic revolution of the "comic" in the years 1900 to 1950 in the United States. There are, on the other hand, a number of changes which perhaps can be viewed from some unifying historical perspective. Some of the major developments are as follows:

...a world of clearcut class and power structure where the energetic neurotics run everybody else by dint of brass, guile, crime, and paranoia.

1. The emphasis upon skilled draftsmanship in the comics following the
appearance of the illustrator and advertising artist. The major effect of
their conquest of the field, which
began in the 1920's and was consoli-
dated in the 1930's, was to put a
premium on representational draftsmanship. Some of the cartoonists who
started earlier, like Bud Fisher, the
creator of *Mutt and Jeff*, might not
have been accepted after competence
in draftsmanship was firmly established as a prime requisite in car-
tooning.

2. The continued-story method of
narration.

3. The shift of child-centering in
comics from an almost universal
emphasis on the 6-10 year old to new
emphases on both adolescence and baby-
hood. The shift to adolescent themes
was roughly coordinate with the great
increase in the number of high school
students in the U.S. and the resultant
rise in normal age at which the young
people enter the labor market.

4. The introduction of current history, as reported in the news page,
as background to strip action. This
change was engineered by Milton Caniff,
who began *Terry and the Pirates* in
1934, five years after the beginning
of illustrative realism. *Terry and
the Pirates* did not begin as a China
War background strip, but soon became
one. It is significant that the
current history theme was introduced
by the star of all the illustrator-
trained comic artists.

5. The tendency of some strips to
provide familial and sociological
continuity through action - as in
Gasoline Alley.

6. The merging of illustrator standards with cinematic standards of
drawing and narration.

7. The development of some intensive
regional and cultural realism - the
Li'l Abner of the first year, 1935.

8. The rising status of women portrayed in the comics, their increased
individualism, and increased ambivalence of portraiture.

9. Changes in the specifications of
social class and class mobility.

It appears that draftsmanlike realism
in the American comic strip was the result
in part of a rationalization of the industry. In the late 1920's, one of the
syndicates became interested in exploiting
the popularity of the Tarzan books in the
comic strip. An advertising artist named
Harold Foster was engaged to draw the con-

tinuity. The very conditions of the public
acceptance of Tarzan made it necessary to
have the strip drawn by someone who could
handle the jungle and animal scenery with
some cinematic accuracy of representation.
Foster, and his successor, Rex Maxon, turned
out a strip which soon became the envy of
the syndicate world and encouraged other
illustrators and advertising artists to
consider the possibilities of combining
their draftsmanship with someone else's
talents for fiction. The success of the
Tarzan strip appears to have broken a previous myth of the profession - that the
successful cartoonist had to be a popular
cultural " genius" of some kind.

The *Tarzan* strip's glamourously realistic portrait of Tarzan and his world hit
the public in early 1929; and the first
more or less realistically-drawn feminine
heroine appeared in the fall of that year.
This was also the result of a team collaboration (continuity by J.P. McEvoy and
drawing by Striebl) in a strip known as
Show Girl - based in part on musical comedy
sources. It is now known as *Dixie Dugan*.
In this strip there was far less passion
for documentation of special locale than
in *Tarzan* or in the later *Terry and the
Pirates,* but the important thing is that
portrayal was dominated by the realism of
illustration and advertising. Dixie Dugan,
appropriately enough, was one of the first
career girls in the American comic strip.

In succeeding years there were numerous
attempts to compete with the illustrative
realism of these strips. In 1952, *Wash
Tubbs and Captain Easy* appeared in a strip
in which Buz Sawyer went beyond the Tarzan
cinematic perspective and actually manipulated the drawing's viewpoint so that it
resembled the viewpoint of the camera eye.
Such tendencies had been forecast in the
Minute Movies of Ed Whelan (1921-1950) in
the late 1920's, but their possibilities
had never been fully realized. *Wash Tubbs,*
like its Tarzan predecessor and some of the
the following draftsmanlike strips, was a
continued story, with cliffhanger appeal,

and thus broke with deep comic traditions on still another score. *Li'l Abner* began as draftsmanlike realism in 1935, and only shifted to semi-caricature later; and *Terry and the Pirates* began as draftsman-like realism in 1939. The attempts to manipulate the same formula have been legion since the 1930's.

Looking backward, it appears that the influence of the illustrator-adman on the comic strips generally had the effect of introducing three-dimensional shading into an art which previously had been one of conventionalized line and contour. The best guess is that the influence of the ad and illustration men expressed a growing skill and realism in illustration in the first two decades of the century. Part of this influence was owed, at great distance, to illustrators like Winslow Homer and Frederic Remington, who livened the pages of American magazines in the days before photo-mechanical processes made their full impact. Some of the skills and the manners of the illustrators were developed under the influence of French poster art, and all the illustrators were influenced by the photograph and later by the movie. In part, their realism in representation was a return to the middle-class tradition of Charles Dana Gibson, whose drawings purported to be a social history of the American upper-middle class at the turn of the century.

The appearance of such realism in the comics is probably less interesting than its effects. We can say with some as-surance that the growth in the draftsman's competence immediately introduced some correlate changes in content. Thus, in the case of *Tarzan*, the draftsmanlike competence made possible a near-realistic presentation of the jungle and veldt, and this travel-ogue exoticism was repeated in *Terry and the Pirates* and the later, and much cruder, *Smilin Jack*. This demanded hours and hours of research into the *realia* and props of the scenes to be portrayed. Thus the comic became social-research minded as a consequence of its adventure into illus-trative realism. This research-mindedness in both *Tarzan* and *Terry and the Pirates*, despite being used to bolster science fiction or picaresque fantasy, had its consequences for the psychological and social portraiture of the Americans in the strips. Thrown into semi-realistic con-trast with primitives or orientals, Amer-icans fictionalized in the strips began to develop certain more specific traits of the American - they acquired regional accents, definite social psychologies, and so on.

At the same time, standards of drawing derived from advertising art meant that the artists depended more than before on the folklore of advertising for their char-acters. Dixie Dugan was an illustrator's idea of a standard young American chorus girl of the late 1920's, and was equipped with Ipana teeth, Realsilk gams, and all the rest of the show. The comics began to pick up some of the social realism of the advertisements, and to betray some of the same concerns as the advertisements. Since the advertisement is always a message about social mobility, the treatment of social mobility in the comics began to develop at a similar pace. In place of the old comics that established a fabulously naive class position for the characters, and then held them to it (*Polly and Her Pals, Abie the Agent, Jiggs*), the new comic began to treat social mobility dynam-ically, and in terms of recognized social variables such as income, ethnicity, and sexual role. Compare this with the prim-itive handling of the social climber theme in George McManus' *Jiggs*.

Doubtless the acceptance of the social realism of the new comic strip was hastened by the fact that the 1930's was a period of anxiety about the bases of society in the United States. Each class felt itself threatened, and each member of each class felt the whole class structure threatened. The comics began to represent in a much more complete way the different phases in the standard social life cycle of the model American and to some extent, the documentary ethos of the strip became for its readers, especially among children, a guarantee of its validity as social reportage. Thus, while one effect of the shift was to disclose in a more detailed way the class structure of American society, still another effect was to throw Naturalistic draftsmanship into the support of *any* picture of the mobility-system that was provided in the strip. Belief in the comic strip as a fictional reporter of the society's demands on the individual became more widespread. The comic stopped being a fantastic escape valve for hurried readers; it became a textbook for oppressed social climbers. In Romance Comic Books it became a series of studies in the folkway of American dating, and thus, in the final analysis, a rhetoric of approved social beliefs.

One way to dramatize the contrast between the Naturalistic tendency and the fantastic tendency in our comics is to compare two strips possessing some similarity in content and theme, but varying widely in the artistic formula employed. Let us take two strips that deal, in different artistic conventions, with poor rural life in the South. One is *Li'l Abner*, a product of early New Deal days, in which a certain amount of Naturalism was employed as the basis for caricature, social satire, parody, burlesque. The other is *Pogo*, a fantastic product of later New Deal, in which the highly developed fantasy of an animal community is employed as the basis for social satire expressed largely in terms of the fable or parable. *Li'l Abner* is punitive satire on the social politics of the United States. Both make ultimate reference to social fact of a community of poor folk in the South. Let us compare their symbolic content and examine the ways in which the similarities in content and the differences in artistic convention influence the expectations of the audience and enables this audience to ascribe a determinate meaning to the content.

Who is *Pogo*, what produces him, who are his readers, and what does he mean to them? The strip, as everyone knows, is a nationally syndicated comic that dramatizes the lives of a group of talking animals who have deeply distinctive characteristics and concerns. Perhaps the most important characteristic that they share is that they are a rural group. If it should be objected that most animals in stories tend to be rural because the country is where animals live, the objection can be met easily. The cat, the mouse, and the bulldog in *Krazy Kat*, although they were projected against a south-western locale, were metropolitan characters. The bulldog was a city cop who leaned against city lampposts, and the desert of the locale was surrealistically equipped with fire hydrants. It is important that the characters of Pogo are fully rural folk.

The characters of *Pogo* are the inhabitants of the Okefenokee land. It is important that they are southern, because the image of the rural Southerner has become the standard American image for the rural man in America in the 20th century. It is important that these animals live in swampy land and that one of the major characters, Albert the alligator, is a reptile, because this creates a generalized image of a primal world scene - the world of the watery margins from which life came. The swamp locale also serves the purpose of creating a scene of roadless hinterland, backwater seclusion. There is a direct reference from the animals to human beings who are uncitified folk, whose vices and virtues are an aspect of their isolation from the urbanism and urbanity of those who like most to read about them. The rural sociology of *Pogo* is rhythmically dramatized by the appearance and reappearance of a slicker with a different set of values - particularly Mr. Bridgeport, the confidence man and promoter bear.

The economics of Pogoland does not entirely correspond to stereotypes of rural poverty. In *Li'l Abner*, for example, we are asked to believe in the existence of a community whose standard of living is so dangerously low that the failure of a turnip crop or the loss of a ham may mean starvation. *Li'l Abner* is a report on rural life which was much influenced by the rural disasters of the 1930's - one of its powerful early themes of brickbat satire was the relationship between the migrant picker and his labor bosses. By contrast, in Pogoland we see little work being done to sustain a standard of living which is generally adequate for all. The appropriateness of this arises, of course, from the character of the animals themselves; they are all able little beasts who evidently spend part of their time collecting stores of food, and they can do this at all times of the year, since they never have to contend with winter. Of course, the struggle for survival in Pogoland is not quite so simple as such a description makes it out to be. The fact is that while Pogo and some of his friends are herbivorous creatures by zoological definition, some of the others, including the bear, the tiger and the alligator, are also carnivorous. We shall want to look more closely later at the way in which the economic motivations of these meat-eaters are handled in the story line.

Nevertheless, it is important that these animals are described as living a life in which they possess a certain surplus of goods and leisure time. Otherwise, they would not be able to devote themselves so fully to the activities they engage in: celebrating holidays, having poetry contests, looking for lost children, playing baseball, getting involved in civic controversies over the loyalty of postmen, and running elections for president. Few of the realities that they face are the Aesopian difficulties of getting a living - jumping for grapes, dividing cheese, trapping chickens. The question of economic distribution, it is true, is not absent from their moral struggles with the gold-bricking cowbirds, who have a zest for using other people's property, along with

an aggressive share-the-wealth philosophy. The cowbirds, however, are no great threat to the economic system of Pogoland, even though they do make away with the canned goods now and then. Pogo and his compeers live in a land of decent surplus, which frees their energies for the greater tasks of furious involvement with each other in the task of finding the right answers to questions of politics, art, science, medicine and recreation. The threat of leisure is everpresent. One of the sequences, *Slightly Holidazed*, begins with Bun Rabbit's assertion that he is going to say to the president: "Put down that piano! An'fix our holiday situation. Every time a man wants to work he got a vacation staring him in the face." One feels that this is not the enforced idleness of a rural community lacking capital and enterprise, like Dogpatch, but the enforced idleness of an economic system that works pretty well.

It is this assumption, we see, that makes it possible for the artist of Pogo to achieve his second major reversal of meanings. His first major reversal, the traditional one, is to ask us to believe that animals can act like men; his second one, the one that creates the true Pogo world, is to ask us to believe that these rural animals, in these circumstances, can act like the people of a small town, a suburb, a city neighborhood. Given the simplicity of the basic scene, there is subtlety in social behavior in our urban and impersonalized society that the artist does not exploit. In the collected version of some of the strips called *I Go Pogo*, the issues range from loyalty checks to the subtleties of political slander, from esthetic standards to rent-control picketing. In general, the people of Pogoland face these issues with a good deal of naivete and it often appears that they are going to be exploited by Bridgeport the bear, or Tammany the Tiger, or by the Deacon Muskrat, or by the cowbirds. In the end, the simple people prevail, and the manipulators and exploiters are discomfited.

Enough has been said here to suggest

that the basic political theme of the strip is that the people shall judge, and that the people are competent to judge. The threats to liberty and happiness in Pogoland are recognizable in terms of a general American politico-economic mythology. Bridgeport the bear, the Barnumesque figure, is a modern rendition of the confidence man who appeared in America before Herman Melville and Mark Twain wrote books about him. Wearing the garb and using the language of a 19th century swindler, Bridgeport the bear depends heavily on the profile of the late W.C. Fields, but displays some knowledge of modern forms of public relations dishonesty. The deacon Muskrat is, of course, the blue-nosed Puritan who was reintroduced to the American public as a symbolic figure when he was employed to symbolize Prohibition in the Rollin Kirby cartoons of the 1920's and 1930's. He is the Paul Pry, the investigator. the self-righteous slander monger; his Pharisaical character is symbolized by the fact that his speech-balloons speak the typeface of an old Bible. The cowbirds, fairly clearly, are Stalinoid birds who make a mock of Marxism by treating larceny as if it were an exemplification of the dictum: " From each what he can, to each what he deserves. " It is against such classic menaces to their political decency that the people of Pogoland are forced to struggle at least half of their waking time.

This suggests strongly that the political ethos which informs the Pogo strip is the optimistic ethos of, say, a Lincoln Steffens. We are invited to consider the probability that people are confused by democratic politics, and vulnerable to a variety of ills: corruption, authoritarianism, influence-mongering, patronage and boodling. Forced to organize against these ills, people find it difficult to do so. There is a tendency for every group of men in a democracy to form a splinter party of its own. Crusaders against the same evil, but operating on different principles, trample each other down in confusion, while the pols steal the cupboard bare. Nevertheless,

after a crisis of cross-purposes, the steadfast honesty of the people has more staying power than the forces of evil. There is much to suggest, in *Pogo*, that the portrait of the ultimate collaboration of these various beasts is imagined somewhat in terms of the collaboration of disparate forces in the American Democratic Party. Perhaps this chaos of strange bedfellows represents in some mythical way the vagaries and subtleties and inner contradictions of the Democratic " Caucus" during the New Deal years.

However, such emphasis on the topical political meanings of Pogo is quite likely to make us ignore other ranges of meaning that can be found in the strip. One way to evoke those meanings is to remind ourselves that if the political stance of the strip is Democratic and Steffens-like, the literary stance is post-Joycean, and the psychological stance is post-Freudian. These influences deserve to be bracketed together, because they both lead us to the evidence that the artist who draws the strip shares with his devoted readers a common cultural concern with the psychology of the unconscious, and, thereby, with the presence of systematic ambiguity in social life.

It is no accident that Joyce, in his anthropological and linguistic search for the sources of myth, found Mutt and Jeff quite as interesting as Romulus and Remus or Isis and Osiris. In his later work, he writes as if he believed that the fantasy of the comic strip is another form of the fantasy of the folk-tale or the myth. Joyce himself was well-steeped in American popular culture and kept written records of the development of American slang, not only in its oral appearances, but also in its recognitions by the media. It is only natural that some sophisticated American cartoonist should exploit, in turn, some of the artistic devices employed by Joyce to represent the world of myth. The maj verbal device in Pogo is polyglottism.

The artificial dialect American speech

invented by the artist for general use in
Pogo is a comic version of rural Southern
syntax, vocabulary, and pronunciation.
" They sure built that capitol awful far
up the creek...Figger them folks up there
outen touch with us ol' mortal critters
here at the headwaters?" True, there is
no attempt at phonetic accuracy, particularly, for example, in the handling of the
vowel values. One guesses that the artist
felt that this would be overdoing regional-
ism. It would certainly make it more
difficult for his characters to depart from
their basic speech, as they often do, to
speak in foreign languages, and to speak
in a variety of crypto-languages which can
only be called Pogo-Latin, or Okefenokese.
The artist's general aim is to introduce
every type of semantic and phonetic confusion, but perhaps especially punning and
malapropism, into the speech of his characters, and to employ the lack of communication that results from all these private
languages as evidence of their neurotically
unstable relations with each other. Ar-
tistically, the confusion and ambiguity of
the language of the animals is offered to
the reader somewhat in the same terms that
polyglottism is offered to the reader by
Joyce: as the representation of a stream
of individual and group consciousness - a
consciousness whose confused fantasy cannot
be adequately represented by conventionally-
ordered speech in one language, but only by
dipping into a muttered dream language.

It is true, to be sure, that the emphasis
on problems of verbal communication in Pogo
bespeaks a semantic slant in the way in
which the artist interprets the ills of
mankind. One gets the idea that the artist
has been influenced by a variety of studies
of communication leading up to the claim
that a purification of the world of words
would lead to an improvement in the world
of things. As Albert says to Pogo during
the poetry content: " I made it up. I
made it rhyme, Now I gotta make it mean
somethin'?" While Albert is almost self-
consciously taking a Dadist artistic position during this interchange, it is also

true that his anti-semantic tendencies are
constantly with him. In the strip, he
stands as one of the greatest of the
sophists, over the straight-faced Socrates
of Pogo. This is not to say that the artist
is a faddist for semantics. It is to
suggest that in a general framework of
animal fable, the reduction of communication
by way of the zoological probabilities such
as gestures, cries, scent, and so on, along
with the corresponding shift of communication to human language, does much to
suggest the predicament of a media-minded
culture in which words are expected to do
more and more.

To speak of the influence of Joyce on
Pogo is perhaps to go too far along what
some might consider Jungean lines, placing
too much emphasis on the problems of some
collective unconscious in Pogoland. That,
however, is merely the result of looking
at the Pogo comedy in terms of the employment of certain linguistic devices supplied
by the artist. If we turn for a moment
from dictional texture to plot, character,
and motivation, we see post-Freudian psychology at work in a way that invites us to
regard human existence as a series of
problems posed to individuals in the psy-
chopathology of everyday life. The prime
exemplar of this formula is probably Albert
the Alligator. Consider what he is and
what he does. Zoologically, Albert is a
meat-eating predator, situated among a
group of animals who, in real swamp life,
would be considered his potential prey. It
is true that civilization and its dis-
contents bear more heavily on Albert than
they do on many of the others, because
while Pogo and the Rabbit and many others
have only to forswear fighting with and
stealing from their neighbors, Albert has
to forswear eating them. His suppressed
cannibalism, the capsheaf of all the can-
nibalistic themes that run throughout the
Pogo script, is one of the reasons that he
often seems maladjusted in the society of
Pogoland. True, he has the substitute
gratification of a cigar, which he chews
as vigorously in place of flesh as a cig-

arette-smoker chews gum when he is trying to give up the butts. However, the suppressed tendency to want to eat everyone emerges in Albert's daily life as a proneness toward the accident of swallowing people. The small creatures of the Pogo world have to be careful what trees they fall out of because, by some mischance as powerful as the fate motif in the novels of Hardy, Albert usually, by happenstance, is underneath them with his mouth open. Albert, of course, remains quite unconscious of the older tendencies and when he has actually swallowed something or someone, he resents the event as an invasion of his privacy. This sort of parataxis, or fantasied reversal of his basic unconscious relationship to his friends, even convinces some of his friends and swallowees.

The emphasis on problems of oral aggression, as Freud would call them in his references to zone development and fixation, seems appropriate enough to a society of animals who live largely by their teeth. On first glance, this might suggest that the symbolic world of Pogoland is rather a limited one, or that oral aggression is made to substitute for all types of strongly-motivated human desire for gratification of physical impulse. We recognize that themes of cannibalism tend to be the stock in trade of any animated cartoons - despite Anna Freud's cautionary comment that all small children, at some time in their young lives, play with the fancy that they may get eaten by their parents. However, unless this be too eager a reading of some of the episodes, it seems pretty clear that the artist talks the language of Freudian theories of sexuality in some of the episodes that link Churchy La Femme the turtle, with Mamselle Hepzibah, the skunk Chloe of swampland. The turtle is a classic figure of anxiety in myth and fable, and the reader is invited to examine what the artist has made of this possibility in some of his sequences.

This brief inventory of some of the themes suspended and resolved in Pogo -

themes that the followers of the comic strip have certainly recognized from the beginning - is meant to suggest that the thematic development of Pogo is made possible, essentially, by the fabular formula employed by the artist. It is impossible to imagine Li'l Abner, for example, developing the same low-pressure mode of narration on the same subtleties of social life. The very drawing of Li'l Abner, in spite of its qualities of caricature, has the Naturalistic heaviness of a Sherwood Anderson or a Dreiser, and under its guffaws there is a nervous pressure of social seriousness and solemnity. The characters of Li'l Abner live in a world of clear-cut class and power-structure, in which the energetic neurotics run everybody else by dint of brass, guile, crime, and paranoia. The strip has never lost its hurt, serious tone of concern with inequality of social opportunity, no matter how much the poor and the sick are made to triumph in the end. Compare the dourness with which Capp pursues and makes fun of radio and the media and the lightness with which Kelley seeks out the same satirical prey.

It seems clear, from the interest taken in a Life article through which Capp explained to his readers why he married off Li'l Abner to Daisy Mae, that his strip enjoys a massive popularity. Since he specializes in irritable criticisms of both the uppermost and the lowest levels of society, one gets a feeling of class-defensiveness in his work, as if he were speaking for a middle class jammed between extremes of delinquency below and irresponsibility above. His punitive satire expresses itself in camp-style beffes about sanitation, feed habits, the battle between the sexes, and the constant clashing of etiquettes. All this suggests that it appeals to those elements in us that are in uneasy flight from lower-middle class cultural definitions, from ruralism, from any and all connections with the other side of the tracks. While the actual scene is a hill-billy village, there is reason to guess that one of the actual social scenes he has in mind is the lower middle class suburb.

By contrast, Pogo is certainly the darling of the intellectuals, their La Fontaine of the comic strip. His readers appear to be the kind of people who take a positive enjoyment in being able to read and interpret an " animal" comic strip that even their own sophisticated children cannot understand. The mock-pastoral genre of *Pogo* certainly represents, for its readers, a tacit claim that the culturally primitive and the psychologically basic patterns of human affairs are not only very fascinating - but also, *within the scope of reader control*. Thus, the strip appears to employ whimsy as a means of releasing the recognition of, and then exercising the power of, the irrational. One might add that while in *Li'l Abner*, the individual is threatened generally by social disorganization of some sort (turnip famine, idiotic intervention by urban or bureaucratic forces), in *Pogo* the individual tends to be threatened by the runaway character of his own group's originating impulses towards organization. The class locus, the content of challenge, and the artistic convention employed in each of the strips appear to interrelate.

There is a residue of cuteness and sententiousness in Kelly's manner, part of it the result of the same topical forces that reduce the universality of other animal fables and tales such as Chaucer's *Parlement of Foules, Wind in the Willows, Animal Farm*, and so on. Part of it is just cuteness - an undivested habit closely related, probably, to Kelly's training with Disney. This is sometimes accompanied by a kind of egghead self-consciousness. At the end of a sequence, when one of his small friends asks Pogo if he has been elected President, Pogo says: " Well, I dunno...I'll go 'long an' vote for EVERYBODY

in sight...that way we'll get a good one... y' know, chile, CRITTERS is nice, but human beans still makes the BEST people." One might be tempted to take this subtle continuity of thought as limp satire of liberal-labor optimism and soft-headedness, if one were not sure, on the basis of context, that there is a serious ideological pressure behind the statement and re-statement of this hopeful commonplace. Kelly's book publishers, in recent months, have gone far in dressing him up commercially as a " folksinger" type, a Kin Hubbard of the media-conscious, college-educated set.

Such reservations aside, it remains clear that Kelly's portrait of the social and political gamesmanship of the middle class, as filtered through his swamp scene, is made possible by outright revolt against the habits of illustrator realism in the comic strip. It is the artistic convention, Kelly's quasi-symbolism versus the Naturalism of, say, *Li'l Abner*, that makes the crucial difference in the appeal of this strip from most others. The sweep of that appeal defines an audience whose revolt against the sociologese of many of the illustrator strips is in part a matter of class stance. For more than fifty years now, Naturalistic devices have been passed down the social scale to the less-powerful sectors of society, while the self-identified elites have turned away from it. Comic strip changes in style in the period 1920 to 1950 recapitulate, in part, the previous history of literary and artistic style-wars. *Pogo* is a stylistic reaction against the *Li'l Abner* vein in much the same way that Flaubert's whimsical *Bouvard and Pecuchet* provided a counterstatement to his earlier Naturalism, and in much the same way that the " child's eye" 20th century painting supplanted the " camera eye" of the late 19th century. As crucial as the shift in " content" is the shift in genre.

Fon Yun

美國華人

Lilah Kan

Along Grant Avenue, the Main Street of the capital of the Chinese in the Western Hemisphere, there are modern self-service markets and there are stores that sell Hundred-Year Eggs. If you are ailing, you have your choice of going to the drug store for aspirin or the herbalist for Tiger Balm. And while the jewelers sell 17 jewel watches and Ronson lighters, they also carry jade adorned with the soft Chinese gold.

In San Francisco's Chinatown there are six newspapers printed in Chinese, English or both. Four theatres show the latest films produced in Hong Kong and occasionally the Great China Theatre houses the Chinese Opera Company.

On the news stands next to Mickey Spillane novels are racks of the most recent publications from Southeast Asia and every night you can turn the radio to KSAN and listen to an hour of Chinese music, news and commercials.

On the surface, the Fusion of East and West seems entirely successful. The merchants are prosperous, the tourists are delighted and the Chinese population produces exemplary citizens.

There is, however, a curious fact about the relationship of this Main Street and its inhabitants which is unknown to the tourists and, for that matter, to most Caucasian San Franciscans. Among the Chinese, Grant Avenue is still called "du Pont gai" although the name was officially changed from du Pont street nearly 50 years ago.

In this careless yet adamant resistance to casual change is found a hint of the width and depth of the cultural and psychological dichotomy which, for the Chinese, is always behind the "Chinese modern" facade of economic and social adjustment.

These are some of my experiences as I struggled to sew together in my own life the wound of this split.

I was born in Chicago and brought up in a Caucasian neighborhood on the South Side near the University of Chicago. My parents had come to America when they were adults and lived with my uncle who was an interpreter for the Immigration Bureau of the Department of Justice. My father learned to speak, read and write English fluently, but my mother to this day knows very little English.

Shortly after I started school, I calmly announced to the horror of my relatives that I was an American living in America and would no longer speak Chinese. I pointed out that my playmates were all Americans and that I didn't want to be different from them. Since we were not living among Chinese people, my family didn't press the issue too much. They were saving that for later.

It was our family's habit to visit Chinatown every Sunday. While Chicago's Chinatown was (and still is) very small, the people retained all the old customs and ways they had followed in China. The Chinese are the most difficult group for any other collective to assimilate. My family's friends would cluck their tongues and shake their heads over me. What kind of Chinese was I, anyway, who couldn't (or wouldn't) speak Chinese. I was turning into a regular " fon yun" (i.e., American). I remember vague and ominous rumblings of my having to attend Chinese school when we moved to San Francisco where we would live in the largest and best Chinatown of all. I was going to HAVE to speak Chinese if we were going to live among Chinese. In other words, things were going to be different in San Francisco.

When we moved to San Francisco I was thirteen. It was in 1944 and living quarters were scarce and crowded. Our " apartment" was typical of most of the dwellings in Chinatown...small rooms, community bathrooms and community kitchens. Fleas, cockroaches and mice shared our quarters. Ours was the only family in the building; the other tenants being bachelors, widowers or men whose families were still in China. Scarcely any of them spoke any English. I didn't think I was going to be very happy.

The first day we were in San Francisco my father took me with him to do some grocery shopping. The owner of the store was a friend of my father's and he started to talk to me in Chinese. I didn't answer and my father hastily explained that I had been living in a " fon yun" neighborhood in Chicago and couldn't speak Chinese. But now that we were living in San Francisco, he was going to send my brother and me to Chinese school. I can still remember how enthusiastic the man became over the idea. The next day we started.

We were enrolled in the Yeung Wo Academy on Sacramento Street between Grant and Kearny, and placed in the first grade. We were certainly novelties to our classmates...Chinese who couldn't speak Chinese. I was an even bigger novelty, being five to seven years older than anyone else in the class. It was hard for me to adjust to the fact that I was in a class with

my seven-year-old brother and that my classmates were little children. I was generally regarded as a freak and really became quite paranoid. The more defensive I got the more stubborn I became about learning Chinese...I just wasn't going to. Nevertheless, I am constantly amazed at the number of Chinese characters I recognize on sight. It is a wonder I know any.

Chinese school lasted three hours a day...from four to seven after regular school and two hours on Saturday morning. The academic year ran from August through June. We paid a tuition fee of $2.75 a a month and were responsible for getting our own supplies such as readers, note books, brush pens and ink boxes.

The first hour of school we spent reading; that is, the teacher read aloud from her reader while we looked at ours. Then we would read aloud in unison after her. Following this was the explanation of the story and the definition of words we didn't know. We were then individually called upon to stand up and read parts of the lesson. When this was done to the teacher's satisfaction, we would all read aloud again...only without her help.

Those of us not blessed with retentive photographic memories resorted to writing English phonetically next to the Chinese character. Of course this practice was discouraged as we were supposed to rely on our memories. At any rate it was not a very successful method of cheating as we often forgot whether a certain vowel was long or short or which intonation a word should have, and the sounds and meanings arrived at were often absurd. A change in inflection can easily change the meaning of a word, some words having as many as three or more intonations and therefore three or more definitions.

During the second period we learned to write Chinese characters. We had books made of a heavy tissue paper of double thickness between which we slipped a master sheet containing characters printed in one-inch square blocks. In tracing these words with our brush pens we were to duplicate the master sheet as closely as possible, and it was on how well we traced that we were graded. We were also taught the proper order in which a Chinese character is written...left to right, top to bottom.

Our last period was devoted to copying our reading lesson with brush pens. We wrote in books in which the pages were ruled with red ink into half-inch squares, each square to contain one character. We were graded for our accuracy in copying and general neatness of writing. One can see from this schedule that beginning Chinese consists entirely of memorizing and copying.

On Saturdays we went to the school auditorium to hear speeches. The principal and his guests sat on the stage which had an American flag on one side and a Chinese flag on the other. When the assembly was called to order we stood up to sing the Chinese anthem and recite the Chinese constitution, afterwards bowing three times before the picture of Sun Yat Sen on the wall. Most of us found these Saturday proceedings very boring and we would pass notes back and forth (written in English, of course). If we were caught the girls would have to copy a lesson several times and the boys would be hit on the palm of the hand with a switch.

At the end of the semester we had a " dai how" or big examination. For a week we were examined on each phase of our studies. We were tested on our reading, brush writing and ability to write word for word our reading lessons from memory. In my first semester I placed first, which made my parents inordinately proud. I was very embarrassed. It only seemed to emphasize the difference in age between my classmates and me.

There is no doubt about it; I hated Chinese school. I particularly hated one of the teachers who used to preach to us about how superior the Chinese were to any other race. His smug attitude infuriated me. I would think " It's not the fon yun who are prejudiced, it's the Chinese." This is when I began to realize that I might never have close contact with the people of my own race.

It was with anticipation that I looked for the opening of regular school. Though I was at an age where climbing trees, roller skating were " kid stuff" and I didn't have time for these things, anyway, with Chinese school on my schedule, I did long for friends and companions of my own age with whom I didn't have to speak Chinese. I missed the Caucasian friends I had in Chicago. The first day that I went to Francisco Junior High in North Beach, I couldn't get used to there being so many Chinese students in American school. I had never seen so many Chinese before. Where were the " fon yun" ?

One of the strongest first impressions I had of my classmates was that they spoke English with a decided " Chinatown accent." I was told that I " talked different" and this was generally attributed to a midwestern drawl. Many Occidentals today comment on my accentless English...to which I reply, " Why not? I can't speak Chinese.''

I found that for the most part, my Chinese classmates could express themselves much better in Chinese than in English and, when speaking among themselves they spoke Chinese. The teachers tried to discourage this as much as possible, and it was not uncommon to see signs in the classrooms saying " You are an American. Speak English." (Every time I saw one of these signs I would mutter under my breath, " That's what I say." Just as the use of English was discouraged in Chinese school, Chinese was forbidden in American school.

I had been at Francisco for about a month when I had a very upsetting discussion with a group of girls. We were on the subject of nationalities when I said that I considered myself an American.

The majority of the group rose up in arms. How could I say I was an American when I was Chinese? I wasn't white...I would never be accepted by them. They looked down on us. Could the Chinese in San Francisco live any place else but in Chinatown? Did I think I would ever be socially accepted by whites? When I told them what my background had been in Chicago they were amazed. That sort of thing didn't exist in San Francisco. Chinese students were not included in Caucasian groups and a Chinese girl going out with a Caucasian boy was unheard of, unthinkable, unpardonable in Chinatown.

Later, while I was in high school, an incident occurred that represented to me the epitome of the older Chinese people's attitude in regard to Western society. The Hearst newspapers annually sponsor an American History contest. I decided to participate, and the day before the exam I told my father that I had entered. Expecting encouragement and wishes of good luck, I received neither. Instead, the response I got was stunning. " You won't have a chance. They'll look at your name and see that you are Chinese. They'll say your skin is yellow and, no matter how well you do, you won't get anything!"

I immediately flared up. " What do you mean? This exam is conducted like a Civil Service test; your name and address are sealed in an envelope and your paper is graded before they even see your name. If I don't get anything it will be because I didn't do well enough." I stalked out of the room holding back tears of impotent rage. He represented to me the Chinese who were unwilling to change, to try anything new for fear of failure (for Chinatown is very prestige-conscious and face-saving), who clung to protective tradition and the past. By showing him I'd be showing " them." I had to do it.

That year I placed fifteenth locally and the following year I went on to place second both locally and nationally. I received a total of $1250 in bonds but what was more important was that I had shown " him," I had shown " them" and most important of all I had shown myself.

As I grew older I made many other adjustments. Still, my essential problem of being alienated from both cultures is no nearer solution. It seems to ramify continually, so that an adjustment in one area brings up fresh confusion in another.

For example, until recently I had been feeling, rather placidly, that I was identifying in a satisfactory way with the whole American milieu. I remembered that it was the Chinese who made me feel different as a child, not the Caucasians. They were the ones who jeered at me because I couldn't speak Chinese, and mentally I had mocked their accented English. Then, one day, reading of the bloody uprisings against the English in Kenya, I found to my utter horror that I, who detest violence and violent measures, was siding with the Mau-Maus.

It was a painful experience, but it forced me to realize my identification with non-whites.

So my too-facile identification with my American side has been shattered and I can not replace it with an equally facile identification with modern China. The frustrations inherent in a situation where one is emotionally proud to see a unified China and intellectually and morally revolted by the philosophy that unites it, are too obvious to dwell upon.

Of course I realize that I must stop trying to identify too exclusively with either of the two cultures that have formed me. I think that my best chance is to concentrate on what is best in the traditional cultures of the East and the West. It's a pretentious idea, and the more easily said than done, but it seems the only approach that offers hope.

It will at least be a positive approach, because Western culture represents more to me than materialistic imperialism. I still remember how my first reading of the poetry òf Keats gave me an intimation of the beauty and idealism that this culture can produce.

As for the other side of the problem, I have always rebelled at the concentrated materialism of most of the Chinese in America who have paid lip service to an older, superior "Chinese culture" which they actually know and care nothing about. But this culture can become real for me if I can learn the history of the Chinese people, their literature and art. Perhaps with understanding will come tolerance and acceptance. Perhaps, some day, I may even learn to speak Chinese.

A Daffodil

Tokihiko Suyehiro

Son is in Korea
A daffodil blossoms
On the breakfast table.

I'm a Big Red-Haired Man

A Story

Jay Thomas Caldwell

I 'M A BIG, red-haired man. My name is Larry Stone and I'm writing this just to see if I can write it. Fifteen years ago I was old man Rude's best salesman. He ran Rude Rags, Inc., in east Los Angeles. I was a driver-salesman for him. I was the best one he had. I knew it and he knew it and everybody knew it. I sold more shop towels and whites and onion sacks for him and picked up more for him than any five other drivers. I used to wear a black leather jacket and blue jeans and a felt hat when I worked the truck. And then one day I asked him for a raise after I'd worked for him for over five years and he said, "If you want more money, you'll have to go someplace else." Sure, now that I had all the accounts lined up for him, he didn't need me anymore.

I started stealing from him then. Plenty. I'd take the rags from the truck and sell them myself. I used to come into the plant with more money in my left pocket than old Rude had in the bank.

I stole enough to start my own rag laundry on Hoover Street. It was a small plant and then the war came and I began to make real dough. I married Laura. Of all the broads I knew, I picked her because she could help me with the business. She wasn't a play girl or a glamor type, though there's more than meets the eye when she takes her clothes off, even now. No. Those flashy broads train at the Mocambo and the Troc. That's okay for awhile, then they get fat. Phooey. I don't care who it is, fighter,

businessman, actress. You go home. You don't train at the Troc. You go to places like Apple Valley or Palm Springs where it's quiet, time to think, get things all straightened out. You don't do anything that's bad for you. Your head goes, your ass goes with it. I know. You go hunting and fishing and things like that. That's nice stuff out there in the mountains. I want to take the kids next vacation time. Lance is 13, and Betty's 11.

The best place for booze is in the bottle. I know. After I started making all that loot during the war, I drank as much as a fifth of Haig and Haig for breakfast with a quart of milk. People would call the house and want to know where I was and Laura would tell them I was on a business trip to San Francisco. I'd be right there at the kitchen table, drunk. Why, I even joined a snake ranch out in Downey. There was a bunch of us business guys drinking up all the profits at this guy's place we called the snake ranch. It was a real Roman orgy out there all the time, broads walking in and out. When we'd get through drinking from a glass, we'd throw it in the fireplace. The fireplace was full of broken glasses. I remember walking in there one morning and seeing George--he's an Adolph Menjou type, well-dressed, neat when he's sober. George was asleep in one of the beds. He was dressed in a tuxedo and one of those silk dressing gowns. Vomit was all over the sheets. Dry spit and juice was caked on his mouth. He was dressed in a tuxedo

and dressing gown. I woke him up and said
hello. George looked up and said, "Hello,
Uncle Larry." "Ya wanna drink, George?" I
asked him. "Yes, Uncle Larry," he said. I
got the bottle of Scotch. He started shaking, but I managed to get the bottle to his
mouth. As soon as the stuff hit his lips,
he shuddered like a guy in the electric
chair when the juice is switched on. Just
like a burnt corpse, he shook, stiffened
out straight and fell back stiff as a plank
into the bed.

One night I got tanked up in the Beverly
Wilshire Hotel Bar. I used to pay guys a
hundred dollars a night just to drive me
around from bar to bar. In the Beverly
Wilshire I leaked right there on the bar
stool and nobody even saw me. There was
some good looking broad with a millionaire
that night and I followed them outside and
made a crack to the broad and started a
fight with the man. It was in the alley
and the man's chauffer came around the
corner and got into the fight. I guess
when he saw I was going to kill his boss,
he got indignant. He drew out a pistol and
told me to stop. I had kicked the mans'
ribs in and he was laying there on the
ground and I went for the chauffeur. He
told me to stop, but I didn't and he shot
me in the chest. Well, I woke up the next
morning in the General Hospital. I had
three ribs broken. I was shot. I had a
hangover that was the granddaddy of all
hangovers. The bullet went in just above
my heart. They put me in an oxygen tent
and had to wait for three days to operate.
When they finally did they didn't know
whether I was going to live or die. I
didn't either. But I guess the thing that
kept me going was that I kept saying to
myself that I could do better than this. I
kept thinking about my kids and about Laura
and I knew I could go out a better way than
this. To top everything off, when I got a
little better they told me that there was
a charge of attempted murder against me. I
didn't remember, but they told me I was

choking the millionaire when I was shot.
But I got a lawyer to beat the rap. I tried
to talk the lawyer into suing the man for
shooting me, but he said to forget it and
thank God I was alive.

I think the way things are. Not what
they're supposed to be. Heads is heads and
tails is tails for me. I quit drinking. I
had to or lose my business, my family,
everything. But about six months after that
the factory burned down. I think that the
place burning down was the luckiest thing
that ever happened to me. Sometimes you
think a thing is bad when it's really good.
I took the eight hundred dollars insurance
money from the fire and pushed until I built
another plant on the east side. That's
where I am now. Hasn't been a year when I
didn't make more money than the year before - and that's been going on since before
the war. Just bought a Jew Hot Rod - Cad-
illac convertible to you - and Laura's got
a Packard. She lives her own life, hangs
around with that Del Mar crowd. Has her
own life. I have mine. Somebody asked me
the other day if I loved my wife and I said,
she's been good to me, but how can you love
your keeper? That's just how I feel about
Laura. I'm not interested in the stuff anymore. When you're 38 the same things don't
interest you that did when you were 28.
Met Ruth about five years ago. She's got a
good-looking daughter about 17. Can't walk
in the door but Ruth's got her hands on me.
When I get through with her and then go home
and take care of Laura, I feel like a eunuch.
But then's when I can really settle down here
behind this desk and turn out the work.
You're relaxed then. Relaxed.

I give talks before Alcoholics Anonymous
now and in schools too. One of the Anonymous members took me down to a Jesuit
monastery a year or so ago. Those guys
don't think the way anybody else does.
Serenity. It's all over their faces. They
do nothing but contemplate. That's all they
have to do. They don't even talk to each
other. The things of this world mean nothing

to them. It's good to go down there. I want to visit them again sometime this year for a day or two. The monastery is down by Palomar, near San Diego, back from the ocean about twenty five miles in those rolling, green hills. The whole thing gives off that peace and reflection you never have time for anyplace else.

Gets awful busy around the plant. Especially on Friday - payday. I pay them all a good wage, but the other day Jack Garcia and Al out in the wash room got all canned up on beer and came into the office and said they wanted a raise. I know how to handle those guys. They're just like the Armenian and Jew rag-peddlers that come around and try to sell me their shoddy for eight cents a pound. You've got to outtalk them, let them know that you don't waste your time on the small fry. You've got to fish where the fish are if you expect to get anywhere. I talk to Jack and Al for half an hour or so, let them have their say about wanting more money. I know the beer's going to wear off pretty soon and they'll go back to the washer and be glad they're getting that buck-twenty an hour. I've got a dozen people on the payroll now. Jack and Al and four other men work the washer and the bailer and I've got three drivers. The rest are women on the cutters and sorting tables. They're just working stiffs. None of them ever figured out that you get paid for what's above your shoulders. From the neck down you're worth a buck-twenty an hour, no better than a horse.

I sometimes think that getting shot and having the old plant burn down on me were the luckiest things that ever happened. Those two things got me straightened out. I go around some of the old spots I used to make when I was boozing and just watch them spending their money. I don't get any thrill out of sitting there and not drinking, but I like to watch that cash register. Everything goes into that middle drawer and nothing comes out.

The other night somebody showed me how to play chess. I like that game. You move and move. Then it's check. Then it's checkmate if you don't watch out. That's just like life, like business. You move, you check. Bang, just like that. Looking back I can see each one of my moves. It could have been checkmate for me when I was shot or when I was boozing. But you've got to think, you've got to plan your moves if you're going to win.

You sit here at this desk and sign checks and sell over the phone. I just got an order for three tons of shop towels from American Can. And I made a contract with the Navy last month. You tend to business, make your moves. Then in summer I can take the kids and Laura to Laguna Beach or go to the mountains. Move, check. Move, check. That's it.

And I'm going to find time soon to make another move and go down to that Jesuit monastery. Those guys have got something all figured out that the average business man never thinks about. I think maybe that they've really got a contact with God. They've got the current coming through. They're hooked up. They see things the way they really are. A lot of business men I know believe in God. They've got that current coming through and they use it. I'm going to take a week off soon and go down there and just sit around and contemplate. It's good. It's even better than Apple Valley or Palm Springs.

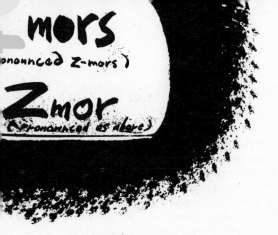

mors
(pronounced Z-mors)

Zmor
(pronounced as above)

I wish I had curly hair →

you can tell he's an entirely different
←

I feel uneasy in crowds →

I've felt sort of hemmed in lately

Preston Sturges:

Success In The Movies

Manny Farber & W. S. Poster

WHILE Hollywood, in its post-silent period, has produced many directors of unusual skill and competence, it has only developed a handful with enough temperamental and intellectual endowment to establish themselves as individual artists. To be successful and strongly individual in the present-day industry is only possible to artists of a peculiar, cross-grained character, who combine instinctive resistance to fashions with a personality that is naturally prominent and popular. As the result of such a combination, about thirty or forty Hollywood players· (stars and minor actors) have been most responsible for keeping movies alive, for preventing the industry from disintegrating through sheer slavery to its own conventions. By virtue of their skill and because of the peculiar tensions and ambivalences of their situation, they have also managed to project more of contemporary life than is delineated in nearly any other art, more of the violence, morbidity and confusion than can be evoked in genres dominated by traditional moral goals.

It is a different matter when one comes to consider the situation of Hollywood directors. They are, by and large, subjected to such crushing, box-office generated pressures that it is nearly impossible for them to survive as individuals except through an almost psychotic integrity, some deep-rooted idiosyncrasy of character which cannot be eradicated. By all odds, the most outstanding example of a successful director

with a flamboyant, unkillable personality to emerge in Hollywood during the last two decades, has been that of Preston Sturges, who flashed into the cinema capital in 1939, wrote, produced and directed an unprecedented series of hits and now seems to be lapsing into relative obscurity. Hollywood destiny has caught up with Sturges in a left-handed fashion; most whiz-bang directors of the Sturges type remain successes while their individuality wanes. Sturges seems to have been so riddled by the complexities, conflicts and opposed ambitions that came together to enrich his early work that he could not be forced into a mold. Instead of succumbing to successful conformity, Sturges has all but ceased to operate in the high-powered, smash-hit manner expected of him.

It is a peculiarly ironic fate, because Sturges is the last person in the world it is possible to think of as a failure. Skeptical and cynical, Sturges, whose hobbies include running restaurants and marketing profitable Rube Goldberg inventions, has never publicly acknowledged any other goal but success. He believes it is easily and quickly achieved in America, particularly by persons of his own domoniac energy, mercurial brain and gimmick-a-minute inventiveness. During the time it takes the average American to figure out how to save $3.00 on his income tax, Sturges is liable to have invented " a vibrationless Diesel engine," a " home exerciser," the " first non-smear lipstick," opened up a new-style eatery, written a Broadway musical, given one of his discouraged actors his special lecture on happiness, and figured out a new way to increase his own superhuman productiveness and efficiency.

In fact, Sturges can best be understood as an extreme embodiment of the American success dream, an expression of it as a pure idea in his person, an instance of it in his career, and its generalizer in his films. In Sturges and his work, the concept of success operates with such purity, such freedom from the hypocrisy that usually clogs the ideology of ambition that it becomes an aesthetic credo, backfiring on itself, baffling critics and creeping in as a point of view in pictures which are supposed to have none. The image of success stalks every Sturges movie like an unlaid ghost, coloring the plots and supplying the fillip to his funniest scenes. His madly confused lovers, idealists and outraged fathers appear to neglect it but it invariably turns up dumping pots of money on their unsuspecting heads or snatching away million-dollar prizes. Even in a picture like *The Miracle of Morgan's Creek* which deals with small-town, humble people, it is inevitable that bouncing Betty Hutton should end up with sextuplets and become a national institution. The very names of Sturges' best-known movies seem to evoke a hashish-eater's vision of beatific American splendor: *The Great McGinty, The Power and the Glory, The Miracle of Morgan's Creek, Hail the Conquering Hero, The Great Moment, Christmas in July* reveal the facets of a single preoccupation.

Nearly everyone who has written about Sturges expresses great admiration for his intelligence and talent, total confusion about his pictures and an absolute certainty that Sturges should be almost anything but what he nakedly and palpably is - an inventive American who believes that good picture-making consists in grinding out ten thousand feet of undiluted, chaos-producing energy. It is not too difficult to perceive

that even Sturges' most appreciative critics were fundamentally unsympathetic toward him. Throughout his career, in one way or another, Sturges has been pilloried for refusing to conform to fixed prescriptions for artists. Thus, according to Rene Clair, " Preston is like a man from the Italian Renaissance: he wants to do everything at once. If he could slow down, he would be great; he has an enormous gift and he should be one of our leading creators. I wish he would be a little more selfish and worry about his reputation."

What Clair is suggesting is that Sturges would be considerably improved if he annihilated himself. Similarly, Siegfried Kracauer has scolded him for not being the consistent, socially-minded satirist of the rich, defender of the poor and portrayer of the evils of modern life which he regards as the qualifying characteristics of all movie-makers admissible to his private pantheon. The more popular critics have condemned Sturges for not liking America enough; the advanced critics for liking it too much. He has also been accused of espousing a snob point of view and sentimentally favoring the common man.

Essentially Sturges, probably the most spectacular manipulator of sheer humor since Mark Twain, is a very modern artist or entertainer, difficult to classify because of the intense effort he has made to keep his work outside conventional categories. The high-muzzle velocity of his films is due to the anarchic energy generated as they constantly shake themselves free of attitudes that threaten to slow them down. Sturges' pictures maintain this freedom from ideology through his sophisticated assumption of the role of the ruthless showman deliberately rejecting all notions of aesthetic weight and responsibility. It is most easy to explain Sturges' highly self-conscious philosophy of the hack as a kind of cynical morality functioning in reverse. Since there is so much self-inflation, false piety and artiness in the arts, it was, he probably felt, less morally confusing to jumble slapstick and genuine humor, the original and the derivative together, and express oneself through the audacity and skill by which they are combined. It is also probable that he found the consistency of serious art, its demand that everything be resolved in terms of a logic of a single mood, repugnant to his temperament and false to life.

"There is nothing like a deep-dish movie to drive you out in the open," a Sturges character remarks, and besides being a typical Sturges line the sentence tells you a great deal about his movie-making. His resourcefulness, intelligence, Barnum and Bailey showmanship and dislike of fixed purposes often make the typical Sturges movie seem like a uniquely irritating pastiche. A story that opens with what appears to be a bitingly satirical exposition of American life is apt to end in a jelly of cheap sentiment. In *Hail the Conquering Hero,* for example, Eddie Bracken plays an earnest, small-town boy trying to follow in the footsteps of his dead father, a World War I hero. Discharged because of hay fever, Bracken is picked up by six Marines who talk him into posing as a Guadalcanal veteran and returning home as a hero to please his mother. The pretense snowballs, the town goes wild, and Bracken's antics become more complicated and tormenting with every scene. After he has been pushed into running for Mayor, he breaks down and confesses the hoax. Instead of tarring and feathering him, the townspeople melt with admiration for his candor and courage.

This ending has been attacked by critics who claim that it reveals Sturges compromising his beliefs and dulling the edge of his satire. "At his beginning," Mr. Kracauer writes, referring to *The Great McGinty,* Sturges insisted that honesty does not pay. Now he wants us to believe that the world yields to candor." Such criticism is about as relevant as it would

be to say that Cubists were primarily interested in showing all sides of a bottle at once. To begin with, it should be obvious to anyone who has seen two Sturges pictures that he does not give a tinker's dam whether the world does or does not yield to candor. Indeed, his pictures at no time evince the slightest interest on his part as to the truth or falsity of his direct representation of society. His neat, contrived plots are unimportant *per se* and developed chiefly to provide him with the kind of movements and appearances he wants, with crowds of queer, animated individuals, with juxtapositions of unusual actions and faces. These are then organized, as items are in any art which does not boil down to mere sociology, to evoke *feelings* about society and life which cannot be reduced to doctrine or judged by flea-hopping from the work of art to society in the manner of someone checking a portrait against the features of the original.

hat little satire there is in a film is as likely to be directed at satire as it is at society. The supposedly sentimental ending of *The Conquering Hero,* for example, starts off as a tongue-in-cheek affair as much designed to bamboozle the critics as anything else. It gets out of hand and develops into a series of oddly placed shots of the six Marines, shots which are indeed so free of any kind of attitude as to create an effect of pained ambiguous humanity, frozen in a moment of time, so grimly at one with life that they seem to be utterly beyond any one human emotion, let alone sentiment. The entire picture is, indeed, remarkable for the manner in which sequences are directed away from the surface mood to create a sustained, powerful and lifelike pattern of dissonance. The most moving scene in it - Pangborn's monumentally heartfelt reactions to Bracken's confession - is the product of straight comic pantomine. The Marine with an exaggerated mother-complex sets up a hulking, ominous image as the camera prolongs a view of his casual walk down the aisle of the election-hall. The Gargantuan mugging and gesturing of the conscience-stricken Bracken provokes not only laughter but the sense that he is suffering from some mysterious muscular ailment.

Such sequences, however, though integral to Sturges' best work, do not set its tone. The delightfulness, the exhilarating quality that usually prevails is due to the fact that the relation to life of most of the characters is deliberately kept weak and weightless. The foibles of a millionaire, the ugliness of a frump are all projected by similar devices and exploited in a like manner. They exist in themselves only for a moment, and function chiefly as bits in the tumultuous design of the whole. Yet this design offers a truer equivalent of American society than can be supplied by any realism or satire that cannot cope with the tongue-in-cheek self-consciousness and irreverence towards its own fluctuating institutions that is the very hallmark of American society _ that befuddles foreign observers and makes American mores wellnigh impervious to any kind of satire.

Satire requires a stationary society, one that seriously believes in the enduring value of the features providing its identity. But what is there to satirize in a country so much at the mercy of time and commerce as to be profoundly aware that all its traits - its beauties, blemishes, wealth, poverty, prejudices and aspirations - are equally the merchandise of the moment, easily manufactured and trembling on the verge of destruction from the moment of production? The only American quality that can conceivably offer a focus for satire, as the early movie-makers and Sturges, alone among the contemporaries, have realized, is speed. Some of the great early comic films, those of Buster Keaton, for example, were scarcely comic at all but pure and very bitter satires, exhausting in endless combinations of all possible tortures produced as a consequence of the naif belief in speed. Mack Sennett was less the satirist of American speed-mania than its Diaghilev. Strip away the comic

webbing and your eye comes upon the preternatural poetic world created by an instinctive impresario of graceful accelerations. Keystone cops and bathing beauties mingle and separate in a buoyant, immensely varied ballet, conceived at the speed of mind but with camera velocity rather than the human body as its limit. Sturges was the only legitimate heir of the early American film, combining its various methods, adding new perspectives and developing the whole in a form suitable to a talking-picture.

Since Sturges thought more synoptically than his predecessors, he presented a speed-ridden society through a multiple focus rather than the single, stationary lens of the pioneers. While achieving a more intense identification of the audience with the actors than in the earlier films (but less than the current talking pictures which strive for complete audience identification with the hero), Sturges fragmented action so that each scene blends into the next before it comes to rest, and created an illusion of relative motions. Basically, a Sturges film is executed to give one the delighted sensation of a person moving on a smoothly travelling vehicle going at high speed through fields, towns, homes and even through other vehicles. The vehicle in which the spectator is travelling never stops but seems to be moving in a circle, making its journey again and again in an ascending, narrowing spiral until it diminishes into nothingness. One of his characters calls society a "cockeyed caravan" and Sturges, himself, is less a settled, bona fide resident of America than a hurried, Argus-eyed traveller through its shifting scenes, a nomad in space observing a society nomadic in time and projecting his sensations in uniquely computed terms.

his modern cinematic perspective of mobility seen by a mobile observer comes easily to Sturges because of his strange family background and broken-up youth. He was the son of a normal, sports-loving, successful father and a fantastic culture-bug mother who wanted him to be a genius and kept him in Paris from the age of eight to about fifteen. " She dragged me through every goddam museum on the continent," he has rancorously remarked. Glutted, at an early age, by an overrich diet of aesthetic dancing, high-hatted opera audiences and impressionist painting, Sturges still shows the marks of his youthful trauma. The most obvious result of his experience has been a violent reaction against all aestheticism. He has also expressed fervent admiration for his father's business ability and a desire to emulate him. The fact that he did not, however, indicates that his early training provoked more than a merely negative reaction in him, and made him a logical candidate for Hollywood, whose entire importance in the history of culture resides in its unprecedented effort to merge art and big business.

As a movie-maker, the business-man side of Sturges was superficially dominant. He seems to have begun his career with the intention of giving Hollywood a lesson in turning out quick, cheap popular pictures. He whipped together his scripts in record-breaking time, cast his pictures with unknowns, and shot them faster than anyone dreamed possible. He was enabled to do this through a native aptitude for finding brilliant technical short-cuts. Sturges tore Hollywood comedy loose from the slick gentility of pictures like *It Happened One Night* by shattering the realistic mold and the logical build-up and taking the quickest, least plausible route to the nerves of the audience. There are no preparations for the fantastic situations on which his pictures are based and no transitions between their numberless pratfalls, orgies of noise, and furniture-smashing. A Capra, Wilder, or Wellman takes half a movie to get a plot to the point where the audience accepts it and it comes to cinematic life. Sturges often accomplishes as much in the first two minutes, throwing an audience immediately into what is generally the

most climactic and revelatory moment of other films.

The opening of *Sullivan's Travels* is characteristic for its easy handling of multiple cinematic meanings. The picture opens abruptly on a struggle between a bum and a railroad employee on top of a hurtling train. After a few feet of a flight that is at once a sterling bit of action-movie and a subtle commentary on action movies, it develops that you are in a projection studio, watching a film made by Sullivan, a famous director, and that the struggle symbolizes the conflict of capital and labor. As Sullivan and the moguls discuss the film's values and box-office possibilities, Sturges makes them all sound delightfully foolish by pointing up the naive humanity of everyone involved. " Who wants to see that stuff? It gives me the creeps! " is the producer's reaction to the film. When Sullivan mentions a five-week run at the Music Hall, the producer explodes with magnificent improbability; " Who goes to the Music Hall? Communists! " Thus, in five minutes of quick-moving cinema and surprise-packed dialogue, a complex situation has been set forth and Sullivan is catapulted on his journey to learn about the moods of America in the depression.

The witty economy of his movies is maintained by his gifted exploitation of the non-sequitur and the perversely unexpected. In nearly every case, he manages to bring out some hidden appropriateness from what seems like wilfull irrelevance. In *The Miracle of Morgan's Creek*, a plug-ugly sergeant mouths heavy psychiatric phrases in an unbelievable way that ends by sinking him doubly-deep into the realm of the psychotic. With nihilistic sophistication, Sturges makes a Hollywood director keep wondering " Who is Lubitsch?" till you are not sure if it is simply fun or a weird way of expressing pretentiousness and ignorance. Similarly, in *The Conquering Hero* the small-town citizens are given a happy ending and a hero to worship but they are paraded through the streets and photographed in such a way that they resemble a lynch mob - a device which flattens out success and failure with more gruesome immediacy than Babbitt-like satires.

What made Sturges a viciously alive artist capable of discovering new means of expressiveness in a convention-ridden medium was the frenetic, split sensibility that kept him reacting to and away from the opposite sides of his heredity. These two sides are, in fact, the magnetic poles of American society. Accepting, in exaggerated fashion, the businessman approach to films, he nevertheless brought to his work intelligence, taste, and a careful study of the more estimable movies of the past. He also took care to disappoint rigid-minded aesthetes and reviewers. Although it has been axiomatic among advanced movie students that the modern film talks too much and moves too little, Sturges perversely thought up a new type of dialogue by which the audience is fairly showered with words. The result was paradoxically to speed up his movies rather than to slow them down, because he concocted a special, jerky, spluttering form of talk that is the analogue of the old, silent-picture firecracker tempo. Partly this was accomplished by a wholesale use of " hooks" - spoken lines cast as questions, absurd statements or explosive criticisms which yank immediate responses from the listener.

Sturges' free-wheeling dialogue is his most original contribution to films and accomplishes, among other things, the destruction of the common image of Americans as tight-lipped Hemingwayan creatures who converse in grating monosyllables and chopped sentences. Sturges tries to create the equally American image of a wrangle of conflicting, over-emotional citizens who talk as though they were forever arguing or testifying before a small-town jury. They speak as if to a vast, intent audience rather than to each other, but the main thing is that they unburden themselves passionately and without difficulty - even during siesta moments on the front porch:

" I'm perfectly calm. I'm as--as cool as ice, then I start to figure maybe they won't take me and some cold sweat runs down the middle of my back and my head begins to buzz and everything in the middle of the room begins to swim--and I get black spots in front of my eyes and they say I've got high blood pressure..."

As the words sluice out of the actors' mouths, the impression is that they teeter on the edge of a social, economic or psychological cliff and that they are under some wild compulsion to set the record straight before plunging out of the picture. Their speech is common in language and phrasing but Sturges makes it effervesce with trick words (" whackos" for " whack"), by pumping it full of outraged energy or inserting a daft idea like the Music Hall gag. All of this liberated talk turns a picture into a kind of open forum where everyone down to the cross-eyed bit player gets a chance to try out his oratorical ability. A nice word festival, very democratic, totally unlike the tight, gagged-up speech that movies inherited from vaudeville, radio and the hard-boiled novel.

Paradoxically, too, his showman's approach enabled Sturges to be the only Hollywood talking-picture director to apply to films the key principles of the " modern" revolutions in poetry, painting and music: namely, beginning a work of art at the climax and continuing from there. Just as the modern painter eschews narrative and representational elements to make his canvas a continuum of the keenest excitement natural to painting, or the poet minimizes whatever takes his poem out of the realm of purely verbal values, so Sturges eliminated from his movies the sedulous realism that has kept talking pictures essentially anchored to a rotting nineteenth-century aesthetic. In this and other ways, Sturges revealed that his youth spent " caroming around in High-Bohemian Europe" had not been without a positive effect on his work. Its basic textures, forms and methods ultimately derive from post-Impressionist painting, Russian ballet and the early scores of Stravinsky, Hindemith, et al. The presence of Dada and Surrealism is continuously alive in its subsurface attitudes, or obvious in the handling of specific scenes. Sturges' fat Moon-Mullins-type female, playing a hot tailgate trombone at a village dance, is the exact equivalent in distortion of one of Picasso's lymphatic women posed as Greek statues.

Sturges' cinematic transpositions of American life reveal the outsider's ability to seize salient aspects of our national existence plus the insider's knowledge of their real meaning. But the two are erratically fused by the sensibility of the nostalgic, dislocated semi-exile that Sturges essentially remains. The first impression one gets from a Sturges movie is that of the inside of a Ford assembly line smashed together and operating during a total war crisis. The characters, all exuding jaundice, cynicism, and anxiety, work feverishly as every moment brings them the fear that their lives are going to pieces, that they are going to be fired, murdered, emasculated or trapped in such ridiculous situations that headlines will scream about them to a hooting nation for the rest of their lives. They seem to be haunted by the specters of such nationally famous boneheads as Wrong-way Corrigan, Roy Riegels who ran backwards in a Rose Bowl game, or Fred Merkle who forgot to touch second base in a crucial play-off game, living incarnations of the great American nightmare that some monstrous error can drive individuals clean out of society into a forlorn no man's land, to be the lonely objects of an eternity of scorn, derision and self-humiliation. This nightmare is of course the reverse side of the uncontrolled American success impulse which would set individuals apart in an apparently different but really similar and equally frightening manner.

Nearly all the Sturges comedies were centered with a sure instinct on this basic drive with all its complex concomitants. Using a stock company of players,(all of a queer, unstandard and almost aboriginal Americanism), Sturges managed to give his harrowing fables of success-failure an intimate, small-town setting that captured both the moony desire of every American to return to the small world of his youth, and that innocent world itself as it is ravaged by a rampant, high-speed industrialism. The resultant events are used to obtain the comic release that is, indeed, almost the only kind possible in American life: the savage humor of absolute failure or success. Sturges' funniest scenes result from exploding booby-traps which set free bonanzas of unsuspected wealth. In one episode, for example, two automat employees fight and trip open all the levers behind the windows; the spouts pour, the windows open, and a fantastic, illicit treasure-trove of food spills out upon a rioting, delightfully greedy mob of bums, dowagers and clerks. In *The Palm Beach Story*, members of the "Ale and Quail" club - a drunken, good-humored bunch of eccentric millionaires - shoot up a train and lead yapping hounds through Pullmans in a privileged orgy of destruction. This would seem the deeply desired, much-fantasied reward of a people that endures the unbelievably tormented existence Sturges depicts elsewhere - a people whose semi-comic suffering arises from the disparity between the wild lusts generated by American society and the severity of its repressions.

turges' faults are legion and have been pretty well gone over during his most successful period. Masterful with noisy crowds, he is liable to let a quiet spot in the script provoke him to burden the screen with "slapstick the size of a whale bone." A good business man believes that any article can be sold if presented with eardrum-smashing loudness and brain-numbing certitude. From a similar approach, Sturges will represent hilarity by activating a crew of convicts as though he were trying to get Siberia to witness their gleeful shrieks. To communicate the bawdy wit of a fast blond, he will show the tough owner of a lunch wagon doubled up like a suburban teen-ager hearing his first dirty joke. The comic chaos of a small-town reception must be evoked by the use of no less than four discordant bands. Sturges has been accused of writing down to his audience but it is more probable that there is too much of the business-man actually in his make-up to expect him to function in any other way. The best of his humor must come in a brash flurry of effects, all more or less oversold because there is nothing in his background that points to a more quiet, reasonable approach to life.

But even these vices are mitigated somewhat by the fact that they provide an escape from the plight of many intelligent, sensibility-ridden artists or entertainers of his period whose very intelligence and taste has turned against them, choking off their vitality and driving them into silence or reduced productivity. The result is that artistic ebullience and spontaneity have all but drained down to the very lowest levels of American entertainment. Even in the movies these days, one is confronted by slow-moving, premeditated affairs not so much works of art or entertainments aimed by the intelligence at the glands, blood and viscera of the audience, as exercises in mutual criticism and good taste. The nervous tantrums of slapstick in a Sturges movie, the thoughtless, attention-getting antics combined with their genuine cleverness give them an improvised, blatant immediacy that is preferable to excesses of calculation and is, in the long run, healthier for the artists themselves.

As a maker of pictures in the primary sense of the term, Sturges shows little of the daring and variety that characterize him as a writer and, on the whole, as a director. He runs to middle shots, symmetrical groupings, and an evenly lit screen either of the bright modern variety or with a deliberately aged, grey period finish. His composition rarely takes on definite form because he is constantly shooting a scene for ambivalent effects. The love scenes in *Lady Eve*, for example, are shot, grouped and lit in such a way as to throw a moderate infusion of sex and sentiment into a fast-moving, brittle comedy without slowing it down. The average director is compelled to use more dramatic composition because the moods are episodic, a completely comic sequence alternating with a completely sentimental scene. Sturges' treatment is fundamentally more cinematic but he has not found a technique equal to it. Fluent as a whole, his pictures are often clumsy and static in detail, and he has not learned how to get people to use their bodies so that there is excitement merely in watching them move. In a picture like *My Girl Friday*, Cary Grant uses legs, arms, trick hat and facial muscles to create a pixyish ballet that would do credit to a Massine. Even when Sturges selects an equally gifted exponent of stylized movement, Henry Fonda, he is unable to extract comparable values from a series of falls, chases, listings to portside and shuddering comas. Stray items - Demarest's spikey hair, Stanwyck's quasi-Roman nose - clutter up his foreground like blocks of wood. Even dogs, horses and lions seem to turn into stuffed props when the Sturges camera focusses on them.

The discrepancies in Sturges' films are due largely to the peculiar discontinuities that afflict his sensibility, although such affliction is also a general phenomenon in a country where whole eras and cultures in different stages of development exist side by side, where history along one route seems to skip over decades only to fly backwards over another route and begin over again in still a different period. What Sturges presents with nervous simultaneity is the skyrocketing modern world of high-speed pleasures and actions (money-making, vote-getting, barroom sex, and deluxe transportation) in conflict with a whole

Victorian world of sentiment, glamor, baroque appearance and static individuality in a state of advanced decay. In all probability his years spent abroad prevented his finding a bridge between the two worlds or even a slim principle of relating them in any other way than through dissonance. A whole era of American life with its accompaniment of visual styles is skimped in his work, the essential problems thus created being neatly bypassed rather than solved.

ut his very deficiencies enabled Sturges to present, as no one else has, the final decay of the bloated Victorian world which, though seemingly attached to nothing modern and destined to vanish with scarcely a trace, has nevertheless its place in the human heart if only for its visual splendors, its luxurious, impractical graces, and all-too-human excesses. From McGinty to Harold Diddlebock, Sturges gives us a crowded parade of courtly, pompous speech-ifying, queerly-dressed personages caught as they slowly dissolve with an era. His young millionaires - Hickenlooper III (Rudy Vallee), Pike (Henry Fonda), and rich movie director Sullivan (a similar mode of being) - are like heavily ornamented bugs, born out of an Oliver Twist world into a sadfaced, senile youth as moldy with leisure and tradition as an old cheese. Incapable of action, his obsolete multimillionaires gaze out into a world that has passed them by, but to which they are firmly anchored by their wealth.

A pathetic creature in the last stages of futility, Vallee's sole occupation consists of recording, in a little black book, minute expenditures which are never totaled - as though he were the gently demented statistician of an era that has fallen to pieces for no special reason and has therefore escaped attention. Fonda as Pike, the heir of a brewery fortune, (*The Ale that Won for Yale*), is the last word in marooned uselessness. A wistful, vague, young, scholarly ophiologist nicknamed "Hoppsey," Pike's sole business in life

consists of feeding four flies, a glass of milk, and one piece of white bread to a rare, pampered snake. In between, he can be seen glumly staring at a horde of predatory females, uncooperatively being seduced, getting in and out of suits too modern for him, sadly doing the oldest card-trick in the world and pathetically apologizing for not liking beer or ale. Oddly enough, his supposed opposite, a fast, upperclass card-sharp (Barbara Stanwyck) is no less Victorian, issuing as she does from a group of obsolete card Houdinis with an old-fashioned code of honor among thieves and courtly old-world manners and titles.

If Sturges has accomplished nothing else, he has brought to consciousness the fact that we are still living among the last convulsions of the Victorian world, that, indeed, our entire emotional life is still heavily involved in its death. These final agonies (though they have gone on so long as to make them almost painless) which only Sturges has recorded, can be glimpsed daily, in the strange, gentle expiration of figures like Shaw, Hearst, Jolson, Ford; the somewhat sad explosion of fervor over MacArthur's return (a Sturges picture by itself, with, if the fading hero had been made baseball czar, a pat Sturges ending); and the Old World pomp, unctuous-ness, and rural religiosity of the American political scene.

owhere did Sturges reveal his Victorian affinities more than by his use, belief in and love of a horde of broken, warped, walked-over, rejected, seamy old character actors. Some of these crafty bit players like Walburn, Bridge, Tannen, made up his stock company, while others like Coburn, Pangborn, Kennedy and Blore appear only in single pictures. They were never questioned by critics although they seemed as out of place in a film about modern times as a bevy of Floradora girls. They appear as monstrously funny people who have gone through a period of maniacal adjustment to capitalist society by exaggerating a single feature of their character: meekness, excessive guile, splenetic aggressiveness, bureaucratic windiness or venal pessimism. They seem inordinately toughened by experience but they are, one is aware, not really tough at all, because they are complete fakers. Sturges rarely subjects them to savage lampooning because it is obvious that they did not want to be fakers - life made it inevitable. They are very much part of the world of Micawber and Scrooge but later developments - weaker, more perfect, bloated and subtle caricatures - giving off a fantastic odor of rotten purity and the embalmed cheerfulness of puppets.

They all appear to be too perfectly adjusted to life to require minds and in place of hearts they seem to contain an old scratch sheet, a glob of tobacco juice or a brown banana. The reason their faces - each of which is a succulent worm's festival, bulbous with sheer living - seem to have nothing in common with the rest of the human race, is precisely because they are so eternally, agelessly human, over-socialized to the point where any normal animal component has vanished. They seem to be made up not of features but a *collage* of spare parts, most of them as useless as the vermiform appendix.

Merely gazing at them gives the audience a tremendous lift as if they were witnessing all the drudgery of daily life undergoing a reckless transmutation. It is as if human nature, beaten to the ground by necessity, out of sheer defiance had decided to produce utterly useless extravaganzas like Pangborn's bobbling cheeks, Bridge's scrounging, scraping voice, or Walburn's evil beetle eyes and mustache like a Fuller brush that has decided to live an independent life. It is all one can do to repress a manic shriek at the mere sight of Harold Lloyd's companion in *Mad Wednesday*. His body looks like that of a desiccated 200 year-old locust weighed down by an enormous copper hat. Or Pat Moran's wrecked jeep of a face, and his voice that sounds as if its owner

had just been smashed in the Adam's apple by Joe Louis. These aged, senile rejects from the human race are put through a routine that has, in one minute, the effect of a long, sad tone-poem and after an hour gives a movie a peculiar, hallucinatory quality as if reality had been slightly tilted and robbed of significant pieces.

No one has delineated sheer indolence as Sturges has with these characters. When one appears on the screen it looks as if he had wandered into the film by mistake and once there had been abandoned by the makers. When a second one of these *lumpen* shows up the audience begins to sit on the edge of its seat and to feel that the picture is going to pieces, that the director has stopped working or the producer is making a monkey out of it. After a few minutes of lacerated nothingness, it becomes obvious that the two creatures are fated to meet; considerable tension is generated as the audience wonder what buildup will be used to enable them to make each other's acquaintance. To everybody's horror there is no buildup at all; the creatures link arms as the result of some gruesome asocial understanding and simply walk off. In *Mad Wednesday*, this technique yields a kind of ultimate in grisly, dilapidated humor, particularly in the long episode which begins with Harold Lloyd meeting the locust-like creature on the greasiest looking sidewalk ever photographed. The two repair to a bar presided over by Edgar Kennedy, who slowly and insanely mixes for Lloyd his first alcoholic potion. This entire, elaborate ritual is a weirder cinematic version of the kind of " study in decrepit life" for which E.E. Cummings is famed; certainly it is at least comparable in merit and effectiveness.

Sturges may not be the greatest director of the last two decades; in fact, it can be argued that a certain thinness in his work - his lack of a fully-formed, solid, orthodox movie-maker's technique - prevents him from being included among the first few. He is, however, the most original movie talent produced in recent years: the most complex and puzzling. The emotional and intellectual structure of his work has so little in common with the work of other artists of our time that it seems to be the result of a unique development. Yet it is sufficiently logical and coherent to give it a special relevance to the contemporary American psyche - of precisely the kind that is found in some modern American poetry and painting, and almost nowhere else. Nothing is more indicative of the ineptitude of present-day Hollywood than its failure to keep Sturges producing at his former clip. Bogged down by poorly-selected and poorly-digested importations from the other arts, stultified by shoddy concepts expensively pruned from the orchards of fifth-rate thinkers, Hollywood's recent output shows no formal development with a fraction of the merit and rightness of Sturges' work. Nor has any other of its artists achieved even Sturges' limited success at solving the complex problems of mass-entertainment talking pictures. And this is a key genre in the development of that democratic art which in America, thus far, is conspicuous by its obstinate refusal to come wholly into being.

A Wake For Thomas

Lawrence Ferling

> *" I build my bellowing ark*
> *To the best of my love"*
> *-Prologue to*
> THE COLLECTED POEMS
> OF DYLAN THOMAS

What wonder of chirming
        what dindled dithyramb
(to tind the fother of town-tied tongues)
in these twenty years of " seathumbed leaves"
in this sea-shaken ark of a book
all tackled with waterbirds
all cawing and keening
listing to fish some leprechaun sun!

No sainted Thomas he
        no pulpit-poet almost in heaven
yet dowsing for gods
        wherever curlews cry their wingdom come
this sea-beach roarer (all stour and stound)
                pimps for Noah now as new floods flower
his body buried but his book undrowned.

The Farm As A Fragment
Of The Southern California Culture

Curtis Zahn

In this sparkling, odd, damned
Southern California country
The farm as a fragment
Is a figment
Of a segment
In the imagination of farms

A phase, a phrase of tutored horses
Unknown to the plow
Of detonating lawnmowers mechanically navigated
On trim, prim seas of inedible grass
And from barbecue spit to flagstone pit
The classified rhododendrons are vaccinated, indoctrinated
And vicariously baited, mated, feted.
And the prized cow
In its scientific cage
Is a hobby-horse; the intercourse
Of airborne semen from South America.

Who are the men, then
The men
Who hire the men
The landed men
Who've moved counter-clockwise toward the soil?
Dirtclutching old lawyers they are
And Doctors, and factory-to-you analysts,
Agents, actors; wheelmoving executives
And the big, anonymous prosperous Boys
With slack faces, morals, trousers, torso's
Bulging sexless equatorial girth under Stetsons
Or squashed, expensive felts
And hand-forged neckties
And boots for the brutalizing of throttles.
Beating their buicks through the tundra
And leaping saddle
To unlock gates
While the chromed stallion waits
Rustling, panting, leaking, squeaking
With idling heart.

These are the boys, men, the boys;
The gifted life-sized operators
Who bluffed, blustered
And blundered asunder in the paperworld
And came away with signed ranches; mortgaged cattle,
Taxed and insured into financing the earth itself;
Purchasing trees on the installment plan --
Leaned against; borrowed from --
Unavailable, unassailable,
Reigning with collateral, raining artificially
With stocks and stock, and paper
And rollingstock
And home-made lakes with man-made trout
And the thin arms of T.V.
Yielded unto the tampered sky.

These, then who have moved gently back to the soil
In personal helicopters; hauling their horses
In cushioned cars
Over mile upon mile of subsidized, fertilized earth
To grind their own coffee by electricity
Among the buttonplanted oranges;
The plums pruned by syndicates
In an avacado avocation; an avo-cultured agriculture
With a precise device for horse collateral.

Tonight, the figment is a fragment
Of the new imagined west;
Vicarious chrome burns into the grand old silent nothing
And in the moonlight, moored upon broken ground
Softly turned young coyotes
Bark darkness in their furclasped veins.
From a million miles away
Noon stabs this Rancho Romantico; its fourcar barn,
And the antenna sees the countryside without hearing it
And the neat, papery march of Papayoes,
The bedpanned Navels
Stand at subsidized, captured, enraptured attention
Their life and times clinically cradled
In the wise mathematics of distant comptometers.

The Prize Nut of Oakland

A Story

Boris Sobelman

Dear Hermie,
After being five days now in San Francisco Dago Frank and me are running the short end and have not been able to get any part of the money rolling around up here. Dago has hit every poolroom in town and says he has never seen a place like this before. All they do is play a little sociable snooker and then go down to the Chinese lottery if they feel like laying a bet. Dago is completely disgusted and says we ought to go to Reno or Las Vegas where a guy can still clean up hustling pool. "The Chinks got this town sewed up" he says, "and we ought to get out to some good spot before the war is all over." Then he began saying he was practically out of money and we'd have to do something or we'd even wind up on the wrong end eating.

All we had left between us was twelve bucks and the rent coming due. Finally I figured out the thing to do was to go to work for maybe a week and I told him I would go out on a job and he could see what was doing in the meantime. "That's a smart idea," Dago says when I was finished, "that's the smartest idea I heard in a long time. And if I don't do no good I'll work the week after and you can have a chance to circulate yourself."

Well, we went over to the hotel and started asking here and there about jobs. Wherever we asked we were told to go to the shipyards and everybody said we could make big money in any one of them and doing almost anything. Everybody we talked to kept saying the shipyards, so we decided the shipyards, and I would be working there right now except I ran into a guy the next morning and had the whole day wasted.

What happened was not knowing anything about how to get around in this town I got on the wrong bus and was taken to Oakland across the bridge instead of out to the yards.

While I was waiting in the station wondering what to do next I got to talking to a fellow who was hanging around the magazine stand looking at the racing forms. He was a short guy, dressed in a pair of coveralls and wearing a steel hat with the word "RIGGER" painted across the front, and he had a lunch pail under one arm. I figured he must be a shipyard worker and could give me some directions so I tapped him on the shoulder and started asking a few questions.

He turned out to be a shipyard worker all right, and had just quit and was going home.

I mean he had just quit the shipyards altogether. He was a Scotchman named Shorty MacLeish and when I told him I wanted to get out to the yards, he explained the reason he had quit and said he was headed back to the jewelry business even if his wife didn't like it and would have the Draft Board put him in the army. He said it was dangerous work and he had got to actual brooding, thinking about all the fellows who had dropped off the hulls and got killed. He said all he could do was wonder when his turn to fall off and get mashed up would come, and he said he had just about had enough risking his life for a bunch of English aristocrats and Wall Street millionaires.

"We'll all be bloatin the worms yet," he says, "sacrificing our lives away in England's wars."

Then he says to me, "You're a Yehudi, ain't you?" and when I said I was, he began bawling me out for ever even thinking about going to a shipyard. He said how could a Jew whose people the Lord Jehovah had kept from backbreaking labor since the days of Egypt, renegade on his faith by becoming a shipyard stiff.

I tried to explain to him I was just going out there for a fast couple of days to keep from being hungry but he wouldn't listen. He wouldn't stop talking either and bit by bit started walking me down the street with him, and began telling me all about himself.

His real name was Donald MacLeish and when he was a young fellow in Scotland just after the last war he had come down from Glasgow to see if he could do anything in London. The first thing that happened to him was he got to hating the English with their 'ear 'ears and the buck teeth on their women, and if it hadn't been for them he might have married a decent girl and had a good family life. Instead of that he had to give his prime years to a treacherous bitch who would poison him one of these days as sure as seventy nickles.

This wife of his was a Welshwoman, and when he first came to London all the English kept warning him to stay away from the Welsh saying they were worse than the Irish and were sly and crafty and treacherous. Well, this Shorty MacLeish, because he had begun to hate the English so much wouldn't believe a word they said. Further, he even started haging around with some

Welsh people instead and being a young man wanting to be married, he married one of them. This woman was his wife.

After he was married a while and they had the first baby, he began to find out that the English were right all the way, in what they said about the Welsh. Now he hated the English worse than any time before because he said they were a people so bad you had to take the truth to be a lie if it came from them.

"When you see my wife," he says, "you'll understand the magnitude of the crime."

He then started describing her to me saying she was a little, shrivelled-up, shrunken blueprint of a woman, with a thin crooked mouth containing enough venom to launch a ship. And he kept saying, wait till I saw her, and finally I told him I didn't want to go out and see her or anything like that and from what he told me there would only be a big fight.

"There's no enjoyment in that," I says, "and besides I have to get signed up on a job." But before I could say any more he said to quit worrying and that I could go to work for him. He said he had a little jewelry store and sold watches and rings on credit and he had been running it all alone and doing fine until his wife had made him become a rigger in the yards while she ran it instead. He said his brains must of turned to oatmeal when he listened to all her talk about making more money and staying out of the draft. But now he had quit and he was going to throw her out and she could go work in the shipyards herself, and he would break me into the business and show me how to make an easy buck.

Well, I still didn't want to go out there with him and I kept on telling him so and finally, he stopped in the street and says to me, "I'll tell you the straight and candid truth. I need a little moral support facing that female anti-Christ and if you'll just come out there and sort of stand around I'll give you two bucks for your trouble. You can't refuse that," he says. " Being a man of commercial blood, you can see it's not a bad deal."

Even the two bucks didn't sound good enough but then he began saying he'd do more than that for me and he would introduce me to the prize nut of Oakland. He said in walking down the street with him we had nearly come up to this fellow's house.

This nut he was talking about was a philosopher named Caeser Krebinski who used to be a professional wrestler but now was a slabman on the graveyard shift in the shipyards. He stood about six feet or seven and weighed around three hundred pounds and before we went into his house Shorty warned me not to crack off with any smiles or things like that but to act as if nothing was going on any different than ordinary life. But he started smiling to himself and he says, "If I couldn't see Caeser at least twice a week I'd go chasing after twelve year old girls or figure the Chinese lottery in my spare time."

When we came into the house this Caeser was stretched out on a daybed with his eyes closed, and a small, old man in a green bathrobe was playing to him on a violin. Caeser had a black beard that hung at least a foot and there were pictures of other guys all wearing beards on the walls. I started to ask Shorty about them and he whispered for me to keep quiet and then said in a low voice they were all philosophers.

Caeser Krebinski was about forty years old and was not married or anything and was supposed to have killed a man once who made fun of him. He had run into a little trouble at first in the shipyards where he worked but one night he was up on one of the hulls when a leadman began putting the rib on him. Caeser just lifted this fellow up and held him over the side of the boat, and what happened to the leadman's life was whatever Caeser

felt like doing and nobody ever bothered him around there again.

Well, we waited there a few minutes till this old man finished playing, and then Caeser opened his eyes and Shorty introduced me as a young philosopher up from Los Angeles who was interested in having a discussion. Shorty was smiling to himself and the first thing told Caeser I was in complete disagreement with everything Caeser believed and he had brought me up here to see who was right. Caeser sat up and when he heard I didn't agree with him he got out of the daybed and began walking around the room looking three times as big as he was.

He walked around awhile, keeping his head bent down a little and turned in my direction every once in a while and gave me a worried look. All this time Shorty MacLeish was smiling into his hand or looking up at the ceiling or giving me the wink until finally Caeser sat down on the daybed and began to talk. " No man," he says, " has ever been able to break down my ideas and I will tell them to you now so you can also make the try."

Then he began telling his philosophy which was about God being a wheel. He said things never moved yet at the same time were always moving and the answer was that everything was a wheel. Then he says, " Time itself is a wheel and there is no Zero and no number One." He said number One and Zero were part of the same thing holding different places on the same wheel. They were both together in time and Time was a wheel and the wheel was God.

Caeser finished and leaned back on the daybed looking worried and he asked me if I thought I could disprove what he had said. Well, while I was wondering what to say Shorty MacLeish spoke up and said, " No, he can't. " Shorty said he had had a long talk with me and he was sure I had nothing to break it down with. " It sounds perfect to me," I said, " and there's nothing I can do against it."

Caeser began smiling even more when he heard what I had to say and he grabbed Shorty MacLeish's hands and shook them and said I was the fifth philosopher Shorty had brought around who had been forced to give up before Caeser's ideas. Shorty began to smile and laugh with him, giving me the wink now and then when Caeser wasn't looking, and the old man picked up his fiddle and made a bow and said, " The Bumble-Bee by Rimsky and Korsakoff," and started playing something fast. Me and Shorty walked out of the place a little later laughing and smiling and feeling good.

After that we got on a streetcar and rode out to Shorty's jewelry store and he began to talk about his wife saying as long as I was around he would know what to do. He said for me not to say a word but just stand around because his wife liked to act refined and aristocratic in front of strangers.

The store was a small place with two short counters, one on each side, full of watches and bracelets and there were shelves on the walls with radios and cameras on them. Shorty's wife looked something like he had described her only a lot darker. She smiled when she saw us coming in and said, " How do you do," to me and was about to kiss Shorty but he wouldn't let her. He put his lunch pail on one of the counters and began talking.

" I've quit, woman," he says, " and you can call the bloody draft board if you like and sling me in the Army. I'm through taking my life in my hands so you can sit here glutting yourself on sweets and running my business into a bankruptcy. I've had enough of you and your treacherous Welsh ways and if I was ten years younger I wouldn't have two thirds of you around five minutes. And now you can meet my friend, Mr. Isidore Needles, a son of Israel and a man who is going to help me in my business from now on."

Well, this Mrs. MacLeish turned around and looked at me and her mouth had gotten thin and her eyes burned and she beg. saying for me to get out. I starte moving for the door and then she bega screaming at Shorty and crying and sh picked up the lunch pail and began slappin him on his steel helmet with it. A minut later Shorty and me were out on the stree and walking fast and Mrs. MacLeish wa screaming from the doorway of the stor and people were beginning to stand aroun and gawk.

" Well, son of Abraham," Shorty says when we were down the street a ways, " you let me down all right and I'll have to face her alone now. You're no good in a crisis and I needed a man who could stand steadfast. But never mind," he says, " she won't do a thing as long as I stay in the shipyards. I guess it's back to the grind again but she won't do a thing as long as I bring in the bloody buck.

Then he went on to say, wasn't he right about her and how could a man be content with an ugly, treacherous witch like that for a wife. He said if he was ten years younger and not afraid to be alone, he would pitch her out headfirst and would live a good life with only a friend or two around. " I would even be willing to go live with Caeser Krebinski right now," he says, " except some day Caeser would catch me laughing."

He said maybe now I could understand why he hated the English and what they had done to him. " A rotten country," he says and then he says, " and the States are going bad too," and he walked along with me about three blocks and then left saying he was going home and fix things up with the old woman.

Well, Hermie, it was nearly dark when I got back to the hotel and I guess the whole day was wasted. But tomorrow I'm going out to the yards again and I hope this time I make it.

Your friend,
Itchy Needles

The Live Dog

Art As Magic and As Entertainment

Marjorie Farber

Part I of THE LIVE DOG defined *craft* as the " body" of art, and *aesthetics* as the science of art's craft - much as medicine is the science of man's body. What goes beyond craft, then, is not aesthetics but metaphysics. Whereas the sportswriter, like the " New Critic" of poetry or painting, criticizes his subject in terms of its own craft, the popular arts are seldom approached in any relevant terms of craft. The usual movie-criticism is either psychology, which ignores movie-craft, or a Fine-arts approach which interprets movie-craft as painting, literature or theatre.

To go beyond the craft of art is to deal with those non-aesthetic or metaphysical values which *define the human*. If we distinguish *myth* and *knowledge* as the two broad non-aesthetic purposes of art, the *magical arts* would be those which celebrate the myth, the *entertainment arts* would be those which provide knowledge (of people and history). Myth was defined in Part I as " the ruling values of a culture, from its cosmology to its social-political institutions." Magic is " the ritual in service to the myth."

The magical arts include folk art, religious art and much social propaganda. But high art - " Art" in the modern sense - derives from the upper-class entertainments of the Renaissance and Baroque periods. The purpose of the entertainment-arts is to provide a " catharsis" or " aesthetic experience" (Euripides, Moliere, Defoe, Austen, Proust, Joyce, Chaplin, Cezanne). The purpose of the magical arts is to arouse practical emotions (social or religious) meant to be carried over into life (Aeschylus, Dante, Dostoievsky, Whitman, Kipling, Harriet Beecher Stowe, Auden, D.H. Lawrence, Diego Rivera).

Today the popular arts, though traditionally magical, include much of " entertainment" in the classical sense. The best comedies, like the more serious B movies and television plays, provide knowledge of people with a minimum of social-political propaganda. The distinction between magic and entertainment has been obscured, however, by the 19th-century exclusion of magical-religious purposes from its aesthetic definitions. And obscured further by the highbrow's habit of calling his own entertainments " Art" and those of other people " entertainment."

As in the 18th Century, when the live contemporary magic of the rural
masses was wiped out as " mediaeval superstition" - although an older
magic was preserved as " art" - so today " Art" includes chiefly dead
magic or religion along with imitations of past art.   Whatever live
magic there may be in movies, television, pocket books and comic
strips is despised as mass commercialism, childish dreams, or " entertainment"; as bourgeois myth and superstition.   " Art" means the
educated entertainments of the few.   But so, in one sense, does the
word " culture." Many educated people, equating art and culture with
museums, are thus forced to conclude that presentday American culture
is no real culture at all.   But this is nothing new.   For many generations a " cultured" few have enjoyed America's political and industrial advantages while refusing to participate in her culture.
From this long expatriation of the few - fleeing to Europe, to the
past, into private family life or various political Utopias - there
has come about that much talked-of " alienation" of the American
intellectual from his culture.

Contemporary Magic

Since it is easier to become nostalgic
for the magic of the past than to accept
the myth and magic of our own day, let's
take a closer look first at magic, then at
myth, in their contemporary forms. In the
arts there have been at least two revivals
of magic since the 1870's, together with at
least two reactions toward " pure art" --
whether of a romantic or an Aristotelian
kind. While Kipling was celebrating the
glories of Empire in the '80's, poets such
as Wilde, Swinburne and Baudelaire were
upholding various forms of a strict romantic " Art for Art's sake." Again in the
1930's, poets and painters of " social
protest" were celebrating Brotherhood and
the Rights of Man, while others were upholding the strict craft-aesthetic of non-
representational painting, or textual
analysis of poetry.

In each case the magical artists were
attacked as anti-aesthetic, while the craft
artists were attacked as " Ivory Tower."
The chief dispute was over the question:
does the subject-matter of an art-work
have intrinsic interest, apart from the
artist's handling of it? The poets of
social protest had, like Kipling, to claim
that the subject does have interest, and
that the emotions aroused by this interesting subject are meant to be carried over
into life. The proponents of the " pure"
on the other hand (whether of pure romantic
feeling or of pure aesthetic craft) have

generally insisted that art has nothing to
do with social messages or propaganda
of any kind.

But since magic has all to do with
messages and " propaganda" in some sense --
and since even the purest arts of entertainment bring us much instruction of a
non-aesthetic kind -- this confusion can
be resolved by saying that only craft is
" pure." Art itself is a most impure
mixture of aesthetic and non-aesthetic
values. A more interesting question would
be: what kind of values are the magical
arts celebrating? Are they a celebration
of God and the mythic past of men, or a
celebration of Brotherhood, Empire and the
newer Rights of Man? And when we ask that
question, we can see that every art is
magical to some degree; at least there is
no art which celebrates nothing.

But magic can be " black" or " white,"
of course, depending on what myth it serves.
The ruling values of the group determine
whether magic will be the murderous voodoo
or the beneficient harvest dance; the magic
of totalitarian propaganda or the magic of
the democracies. We have even suggested
that magic may, in secular times, take the
form of a celebration of the human itself.
On the other hand, much so-called " magic"
in the arts -- as in a Shakespeare song or
Mozart sonata -- may have more to do with
the pure aesthetics of craft than with
magic proper. For in common usage " magic"

has two opposing meanings, reflecting its history as black and white. It suggests "pure poetry" on one hand, and pure "myth and superstition" on the other.

As Collingwood defines magic we have had, in addition to the Fine Arts, " two other vigorous streams...of artistic tradition since the Renaissance," both unmistakably magical. First there is the folk "art" or magic of an agricultural people. "Secondly, there are the traditional low-brow arts of the upper classes:

> such things as the prose of the pulpit, the verse of hymns, the..military band and the dance band, the decoration of drawing rooms...

Just as every religion must have its magical arts and rites, so every social institution needs its "patriotic poem," its "school song"...

> statues of statesmen, the war-memorial, the pictures or plays recalling historic events, military music, and all the innumerable forms of pageantry procession and ceremonial whose purpose is to stimulate loyalty towards country or city or party or class or family...All these are magical in so far as they are meant to arouse emotions not discharged there and then, in the experience that evokes them, but canalized into the activities of everyday life.

Among the "low-brow arts or rituals of the upper classes" in England, Collingwood includes sports. "Fox hunting and amateur football are primarily not amusements nor means of physical training." They are "ritual activities"

> undertaken as social duties and surrounded by all the well-known marks and trappings of magic: the ritual costume, the ritual vocabulary, the ritual instruments, and above all the sense of electedness, or superiority.. which always distinguishes the initiate and the hierophant.

In this country, too, the sports undertaken chiefly for reasons of magic range from the native baseball to the ritual education of Boy Scouts in the early lore of frontiersmen, and from lowbrow prize fights to the more British or upper class rites preserved in golf, duck hunting, fly fishing, riding, tennis, skiing, bowling, boating, chess. It would be interesting if some historian of sport would trace these rit-

uals to their proper source, whether in Elizabethan England, feudal Europe, or in more primeval festivals and games. Offhand we might suppose that wrestling and prizefighting had a more ancient chivalric history than games which depend on "ritual instruments" : bats and balls, sticks, clubs, rackets, pucks and baskets, guns, wickets, rods and mallets.

In addition to ritual sports there are the ceremonies of social life. These are commonly described as magic, but nearly always as a joke:

> weddings, funerals, dinner-parties, dances; forms of pageantry(and therefore, potentially...of art)...They all involve dressing up...not for amusement...but according to a prescribed pattern...often uncomfortable...designed to emphasize the solemnity of the occasion. They all involve prescribed forms of speech...ritual instruments: a ring, a hearse, a...complicated outfit of knives and forks... flowers of prescribed kinds...a ritual gaiety or a ritual gloom.

From a rationalist point of view, "magic" is equated with unreason and superstition, and its rites appear tiresome, comical or horrifying. This stems from the scientific rationalism of early anthropologists (including Freud, as well as Frazer), who thought all primitive magic was a naive imitation of science: an effort to control the course of Nature. If we believe that a primitive magician is trying scientifically to make rain fall, when he may be only consoling or preparing himself psychologically for drought, magic will of course appear unscientific and hence irrational. Any "magical" practices among ourselves will be taken either as a joke or as a case for psychotherapy. But while savages, as Collingwood reminds us, may have their superstitious "scientism" too, their magic resembles ours in its chief purpose, which is to consolidate group loyalty, celebrate group values, and generally improve morale.

In this country, as in England, we have many lowbrow rites existing at various levels of income or prestige. For example, Americans do not admittedly read comic books above a certain social "class" or

level. Above that level we enjoy comic
strips, cartoons or movies. Or we may
find the same lowbrow magic in sports,
cocktail parties and other drinking rites;
in *LIFE* magazine, detective stories,
science-fiction and, of course, much
science too. There is magic, not of an
ancient but of a newly respectable kind, in
much self-doctoring, self-analysis, hypo-
chondria, visiting the medicine man -- a
magic derived neither from Jungian antiquity nor from Freudian neurosis, but from
a faith in Science itself.

Even the "magic of poetry" need not be
a vague term of praise. It can be anal-
yzed in terms of rhetoric and the ancient
usage of words, as the textual or "New"
critics have done. Or it can be defined in
terms of history, as Robert Graves and some
of the anthropologists have done. "Magic"
may in fact represent the oldest tradition
there is in poetry, dating back to some
very down-to-earth affairs of ancient
matriarchies. Certain words or images
evoke a primitive antiquity reaching back
of knowledge, and so call forth that "surprise of recognition" which is, perhaps,
our way of recognizing unfamiliar truth.

All evocations of antiquity are close
to the "uncanny" and are, of course,
confusingly associated with aesthetic
recognitions. They have to do with that
"tingling" or "scalp-prickling" sensation which many of us take to be the real
romantic thing in art. Called "feeling"
or "emotion," these tinglings and prick-
lings are often used as our sole aesthetic
guide. Now such sensations, I submit, may
be our way of recognizing magic. Since we
get them equally from a ghost story or a
political parade -- a glimpse of the flag
or of a lachrymose heroine -- they are
clearly sub-intellectual and non-aesthetic.
If we are not careful to use all our moral
and intellectual standards in judging art,
we shall have to call every viable or
effective bit of magic -- every parade
or horror story -- art.

Some magic found in Yeats or Eliot is
of that ancient kind which does, perhaps,

make our scalps tingle and does contribute
to the total art. Other magic, as in
Eliot, may concern a more conscious intellectual plea for magic: almost a prop-
agandizing for the religious magic of the
Christian centuries, as opposed to the
modern magic of the cocktail party, the
political rally or the scientific explanation of the Universe. Science, we
must remember, has its own mythos, *ethos*,
cosmology and metaphysic which is anything
but simple, verifiable truth. The axioms
of Naturalism, on which the social sciences
are founded, cannot be verified by anyone's
experience and must be accepted on faith.
Even the verifiable truth of physics has
its mythic Absolute (inherited from religion) as the One "real" Truth about
reality. And just as politics has elaborate ritual trappings and traditions,
Science also has its strictly prescribed
forms and celebrations. Certainly we
speak of the white-robed "priesthood"
and complain of the unbreakable rites of
hospitals. Much senseless red tape, of
bureaucracy or Science, has its origin in
contemporary magic.

But since magic is vital to our culture,
and doubtless to our existence as well, it
is meaningless to denounce or praise a
thing by merely describing it as "magical." Unless we know what kind of magic
it is -- what myth it serves -- we are
scarcely in a position to judge its value
to us.

Contemporary Myth

It is only in very late stages of a
civilization, perhaps like the declining
Roman Empire, that educated men imagine
themselves to be motivated by no faith, no
ruling myths of any kind. Since they no
longer believe naively in the particular
"Faith" of their ancestors, they feel that
no faith is required for their own beliefs.
They feel themselves to be guided by
nothing but an educated reason or enlightened science -- plus, of course, their

" animal" appetites and passions.

Yet we know how much of life knowledge and reason are powerless to explain. We know, too, that what explains the inexplicable is not knowledge but something equally valuable which is usually called "truth," "poetic truth" or "wisdom."

Knowledge, if it tries to explain too much, will be neither truth nor wisdom but a useless kind of myth. And it is the myth of Science, not its knowledge, which is so often held with the passionate, unshakable conviction more appropriate to religion than to science. But again, it is not enough to denounce or praise a belief by merely calling it a myth. We want to know what kind of myth it is: how useful are its values. Since myth concerns the unknowable and cannot be judged as fact, it can only be judged by its usefulness; what is humanly useful will in the long run be called "truth." In particular, we want to know what myths are being celebrated in the arts.

If we turn to the "serious" novel today for knowledge of people, we are apt to find a great deal of old and useless scientific myth. Even that romantic self-pity, by which the hero blames all his troubles either on his mother or on Society in general, derives not only from romantic literature but from the equally romantic myths of determinism underlying the sciences. Man is seen as a helpless plaything of Fate, of Nature, of History: a victim of all-powerful Forces, biological, economic or political. Most outraged cries against "Society" are not self-pity so much as outmoded scientism.

Nor do we find much knowledge of people in the Dore Schary, Arthur Miller problem play -- that "adult entertainment" which is neither adult nor entertaining. Insofar as both the highbrow and the "popular" forms contain the same educated myths, the same social-political exhortations and the same accusations against "Society" or one's mother, they are not entertainment-arts at all, but pseudo-arts of magic. The values celebrated by this magic are the values which our century has deduced from 19th-Century Science -- all founded on the positivist belief that Science could explain everything.

We cannot trace here the complicated history by which the romantic wish to merge oneself with Nature became the positivist conviction that one already was merged with Nature -- or that physical-science explanations could explain the human being. Suffice it to say that the medical and psychological sciences took over a terminology useful to the physical sciences, and dangerous only when applied to people. So applied, these terms provided a new metaphysic defining Man, a new ethic, and a new mythology: something to live by. This mythology, called knowledge, defined Man as a natural object, an animal, a "human machine" and a neuter organism referred to as "it."

Now even when we read the social scientists with care, it is not easy to separate their valuable knowledge of men from this inhuman theory of Man. But as disseminated by the more "progressive" plays or novels, it is the theory of Man, not the knowledge of men, which is imbibed in its purest form as myth. For this reason the old-fashioned intuitions of an experienced Hollywood producer can sometimes be a sounder guide to what is art, and what is truth, than the more educated myths of a Mankiewicz or Dore Schary.

What these educated myths enforce is a museum-approach to culture on the one hand, and a social-political approach on the other, both derived from 19th-Century theory. Of the two, it would be hard to say which is more stultifying to the living arts. The social-minded Thirties managed to combine them both, as a kind of arty "culture" with a social consciousness. "Art" included everything from the alien magic of African sculpture to the latest magic of social propaganda, taking in the self-expression of finger-painting children on the way, and adding as many new "folk-arts" of dead, remote or primitive peoples as these socially-conscious missionaries could discover. In fact the whole atmosphere of the Thirties was a new Romantic Movement, with the same emphasis on " pure" feeling and self-expression -- the same rebellious anarchy and revolution, the same fascination for the " natural," the exotic and remote -- in the 1930's as in the 1830's.

As practised twenty years ago, this magic had its very real counterpart in political and economic reform, as well as in the arts. Even as armchair rites and incantations, it was at least relevant to the times. As practised today, however, by a large mass of educated people, it has become a dangerously irrelevant magic which has almost no relation to real politics or to any real society on earth. In its approach to culture, this magic shows the same conservative clinging to the past as in its politics.The " highbrow magic" of yesterday, with its romantic art-worship, has become the social snobbery of today. Its busy rites include opera, ballet, theatre, symphony, the *SATURDAY REVIEW*, social science lectures, symposia of housewives on Aquinas, folk songs, work songs, " listener-sponsored" broadcasts, Shakespeare, Chekhov, Van- Gogh, Matisse; now Eliot and Joyce -- in fact, this educated magic swallows every Cocteau, Pollock, Kafka, as fast as the package can be labelled " art." It's not the packaging or labelling that's wrong, it's the motive. The art-work is seen not as the human work of creating and enjoying art, but as artifact and idol, end in itself: the work of art is valued above the work of being human.

The 19th-Century, setting up its **painting** and statuary as though they were **idols** to be worshipped, created a vast **institution** -- an army of people,from **symphony** musicians to piano teachers, from **art** dealers and musicologists to the **curators** of museums -- all of whom have a **vested** interest in the cultural past, **defined** as art. This huge institution **known** **as** " culture" creates almost nothing **of** **its** **own** but distributes artifacts --

other people's art -- as a commodity.

The uncultured media of radio, television and Hollywood create, on the other hand, new arts. And whatever we may think of these, the debasement of ''human values" they reflect is an accurate portrait of the 20th-Century; the popular arts are the mirror of our age. "Culture" reflects only our dissatisfaction with the present, and is too often a vain, self-satisfied pretense at living in a better age. Whatever the faults of Hollywood, it did not originate nor even greatly contribute to the general debasement of the " human." Indeed it has preserved or revived far better values, in its comedy at least, than any of the educated problem plays of Broadway.

Even now with things at their educated worst, with everyone complaining that art is dead, culture is dead, it seems that magic is as lively and mysterious as ever. If we look around us at the spectacle of people enjoying their ''debased" but useful mass pursuits -- people who never read a history earlier than last year's Book Selection, and derive their knowledge more from television than from Science; who celebrate old rites in formalistic dances, murder trials or football games; preserve old values in jokes defining the comic limitations of the *human*, cultivate charity and justice in their families, keep language fresh and changing in their comic strips and movies, get more out of Michelangelo or a statue of Abraham Lincoln than all the paintings of Matisse, prefer Groucho to Karl Marx and Disney to Cocteau; who never enter a museum or church except for some non-aesthetic humanitarian or social purpose -- well, no two prophets of gloom can agree on what, exactly, is most gloomy in this spectacle, nor what the remedy might be.

The remedies proposed have ranged from political revolutions of the Left to Agrarian rebellions on the Right, from anarchy or Communism to a modified caste-system modelled on the 13th or 16th Century. Folk dancing, peasant arts pottery, weaving, creative writing courses, creative cooking, Oriental mysticism, more progressive nursery schools -- all these are recommended for our cultural improvement. Above all, we have tried to "bring art to the masses": first it was Van Gogh, then it was Picasso, now it is Matisse and Klee and the UPA cartoons. Meanwhile new fields of real spontaneous peasant art are sought as desperately as the old imperialists looked for markets.

And are the "masses" being elevated -- would they be elevated even if they were offered Purcell and Euripides? "The aristocratic amusements of a past age," said Collingwood in 1938, are "for all their genius...less amusing than Mickey Mouse or jazz except to people laboriously trained to enjoy them." Nor will the "masses of cinema goers and magazine readers" be edified by the folk song and dance. "English folk-art was a magical art whose value lay not in its aesthetic merits" but in specific connections with "the works and days of the calendar."... connections lost and broken, useless to us. Those who are now deploring the loss of art have, in general, been those most active in destroying the cultural mainspring of that art.

In aesthetic terms, certainly, we have nothing comparable to the entertainment-arts of the Baroque age. Even in terms of magic, we can hardly compare the best educated propaganda of "adult entertainment" to the religious magic of a Dante or a Giotto, nor to the folk-magic of Elizabethan times. But what is the remedy for that? Should we merely revive and imitate the older art forms, or should we criticize the educated values by which the educated reformer puts forth such deathly entertainments?

About the only remedy left to us, short of criticizing our own enlightenment, is that the lowbrow masses might elevate us, educated citizens and highbrows, by lending us a little of their magic. Even now we turn (though not with a very good conscience) to a pulp story if we want a plot and to the lowbrow arts of comedy when we want a rest from our adult education. But already television, which had provided brand new opportunities for magic and entertainment, is in the hands of that New Yorkerish or Broadway sophistication, so often mistaken for wit and intellect. This gives us Freudianesque or Marxist drama, Freudianesque or Marxist ballet interspersed with arias from modern operas, arty settings, cute formats, "classical" production numbers, "intelligent" quiz shows, "adult" skits, dramatic ballads with a social message, French torch-singers, Negro torch-singers imitating jazz, ditto male quartets imitating bop, and occasionally -- if we are lucky -- some big "name" comedian.

Fortunately comedy is the great leveller, where high meets low and low meets middle. No comedian worthy of the name can be altogether bad -- possibly because we have as yet no college courses, no round-table symposia or research grants, nothing but tradition to help the comedian learn his craft. Behind his fine tradition of circus clowns and Renaissance wit and mediaeval farce, lies the whole ancestral dignity of *humor* itself as a guide, sometimes our only guide, to what is human. * So the popular comedian is preserved from those educated stereotypes which disfigure the arts of drama. Just as the highest art eludes such topical distinctions as "liberal" or "reactionary," so do the popular arts of comedy.

---

* Listening to two scholars explain "humor" to each other is very much like listening to two scientists explain to each other what "a human being" is. Such attempts to speak from a non-human point of view will either seem "humorless," and therefore funny, or they may seem "inhuman." If anyone is in doubt on this point, I can recommend a recent discussion among Gregory Bateson, Margaret Mead and other social scientists (reported in the *Ninth Conference on Cybernetics,* Jos. Macy Foundation, 1953). This is entitled "The Position of Humor in Human Communication" and begins: "Consider a message of a very simple kind, such as 'The Cat is on the mat.'"

An artist guided only by the question "What is funny?" is really asking the metaphysical question "What is human?" -- What is comically "human" as opposed to a superhuman: what is comically sub-human or inhuman as opposed to an ideal or "fully" human?

Thus the comic arts, like the tragic arts, relate to the larger question: What is Man? -- while the more civilized arts of drama, history and the novel provide (or used to provide) our most explicit knowledge of people and of human history. Unfortunately we tend more and more to look to doctrinaire psychology for our "knowledge of people," and to doctrin - aire politics for our notions of history and morality. Whatever is psychologically or politically "sound" is considered more improving than what is not. The educated *kitsch* inflicted on that talented comedian Sid Caesar, is considered better than the lowbrow schmaltz of Molly Goldberg or the high technical proficiency of such old masters as Hope and Crosby. The most boring and offensively snobbish UPA cartoon, whose drawing resembles Vertes out of Dufy, is considered better than a Disney or Warner Bros. cartoon, whose drawing tells us nothing about modern painting but a great deal about animals and people.

Now without denying the "aesthetic" value of the UPA -- at least as an imit- ation of easel-painting -- attractive line and color is one thing: art is another. Even in modern painting, a narrowly aesthetic approach is always in danger of sacrificing the non-aesthetic values of art -- such as knowledge or humor -- to the pure craft of line and color. Because of this, the mysterious and instructive charm of Disney's cats and dogs, who act so much like cats and dogs -- or Warner's rabbits, cats, and tweety birds, who act so much like people -- will be ignored in favor of the imitation art and predictable class-humor of the UPA cartoons. And yet it is only where UPA has been willing to compromise -- Jim Backus' voice in Mr.

Magoo competing, for example, with Mel Blanc's voices for Bugs Bunny, Sylvester the cat and Tweety Bird -- that its humor compares at all with that of traditional cartoons.

By ignoring all this "mere entertain- ment" in favor of imitation-art, we are ignoring many kinds of undefined magic which may be vital to our culture. It could be argued that the trend of violence, developed in the movie cartoon around the end of World War II, was a form of ther- apeutic magic which showed all its victims to be immortal, or at least unhurt, after every imaginable kind of death. Since many new kinds of death were invented, unknown to Science, these cartoons may have done what literary critics believed impossible: namely, to represent, assim- ilate and surpass the real-life horrors of our time. Perhaps this should be de- scribed not as magic but as the Aristo- telian "catharsis" of those entertainment arts we call "Art" itself. And since it was comedy, of this lowest kind, which provided such catharsis -- not through pity and terror but through laughter -- there is all the more reason for exam- ining our categories. Should this be called the catharsis of amusement, of "escape," of psychotherapy, or of art?

It seems to be the function of comedy, in particular, to console and humanize: to invest the frightening present with some human status and proportion. And this, at best, would be the function of all the popular or present arts as contrasted with the function of the Fine Arts. We cannot say which is better -- past or present, live dog or dead unicorn -- any more than we can say that mind is better than the body. But we can see that past arts serve to measure the present: they provide a fully human standard by which to measure and define ourselves. And we can see that present arts define the present *in re- lation to the past.* By using some fam- iliar terms of craft, they make the pre- sent comprehensible to us: give it "human" meaning. What the word "human" stands for in such cases is an older definition of the human, older than our social-political, biological and other scientific theories.

Thus if we deprive ourselves of all participation in the popular arts -- as they exist today, not yesterday -- we deprive ourselves of much present meaning. And without participation or enjoyment, what knowledge can we have of present culture? We are reduced to explaining it in terms of social-political, biological-psychological and other theories. Now it it is a truism, but a rather significant one, that such a theoretical approach is the exact opposite of what we mean by a " human" approach. Not only because it lacks warmth, but more literally because social-science theory is expressed largely in a physical-science language: a language for dealing with un-human things.

So far we have suggested, first, that present arts be studied in terms of craft. Such knowledge leads in itself to participation and enjoyment: if not to an " aesthetic" experience, at least to an experience. Secondly we were concerned to show that " entertainment" is as much the purpose of the Fine Arts as of the " mass" or present arts, and that if we find our present entertainments low in value, the fault lies not with the artist but with the myth-makers who supply us with our educated values. If we are to have a better magic and a more instructively " human" kind of entertainment, we should need a better definition of *the human*.

It may be that Man doesn't need to define himself according to whatever cosmology his science or religion has given him, but the fact is that Western men have always done so. Even when a scientific Universe has nothing human in it anywhere, " human values" will be deduced from it nevertheless. And the most mathematical Universe will be peopled with gods and goddesses of a surprisingly unscientific kind. Sportive gods, natural goddesses, blind Fate, material " spirits," omni-

scient Minds -- much the same mythologies, vulgarized or re-invented from the old religions, can be found in Science as in Science Fiction; in Cybernetics as in Christian Science; in materialist philosophy as in spiritualist seances. Over all broods that supreme deification of Reason: that Cartesian God as Mind, Super-Mind, Master Mechanic of a clockwork Universe. The science-fictioneer who calls us " stupid earthlings" and finds our human life " improbable" is speaking from the same point of view as the scientist who calls us "plausible." It is the omniscient point of view of the supreme Mechanic, Mathematician, Physicist or Engineer Himself.

The interesting fact here is not that the scientist identifies himself with God in order to speak thus; many poets and mystics have done the same. The question is: which God, what kind of a god -- Whose Omniscience is he speaking from? In the sciences, the omniscient point of view is either that of Nature herself, or that of one Supreme Scientist or another. In Science Fiction we find, in addition to these, many explicit mythologies of an interestingly pagan or even Christian variety. For example, here is the plot of a current Pocket Book called *PLANET OF THE DREAMERS* by John D. MacDonald:

The earth and two other planets were colonized some 12,000 years ago by a race of super-rational humanoids of advanced technology. (The fact of our space-ship origin is attested by old legends of fiery comets, Apollo in his chariot, sun-gods and by the remains of Aztec science which may have included space travel.) Since our ancestors were super-rational, they were of course super-moral too: they had every intention of controlling us benevolently from afar, with the aid of telepathic machines. Unfortunately their descendants, forgetting the old Science, fell into religious superstitions concerning us: they thought we were merely dreams, concocted with unusual clarity by their dreaming machines. So, dreaming away at their machines, these sportive cousins of ours have caused untold mischief on the earth--everything from the destruction of Aztec science to modern epileptic fits, wars, psychosis and unmotivated crimes of violence. The

earth will not be saved until the year
1972, when a rebel scientist on that
distant star will study the forbidden
texts and, throwing off the shackles
of religion, teach us how to build our
space-ships and get rid of human evil.
At first only a few prophets will acknowledge his real (telepathic) presence among us, and so prepare the way
for earth's redemption.   But when
finally the heavens open and the dreamer steps from his rocket ship in glorious human form, the whole earth re-
joices at his coming.

Well, I'm afraid I haven't done justice to
this sad little tale of the Messiah; it
is really a very exciting adventure story
in disguise. Much more exciting than
similar extrapolations from physical-
science data to be found in the Cybernetics literature, or in the physics-
minded psychiatric journals. In these the
mythology, more Darwinian than Christian,
is not frankly expressed in the concrete
language of fiction, but is buried deep in
a syntax borrowed from quantum physics and
electronics engineering. Otherwise it is
much the same. Men appear to these social
scientists not as " earthlings" but as
" complex aggregates of objects and
events, imperfectly isolated from other
aggregates" and " located" (I quote) " in
space and time.'' They appear not as
" humanoids" but as anthropoids: upright
mammals and ineffectual " machines" with
(I quote again) " a merely human brain.''
These objects-and-events are to be redeemed, if ever, only by the Science of
the future -- say 1972 or 2053.

But these are no doubt extreme examples
of a science mis-applied. If we can
extract the knowledge from the myth, the
social sciences offer certain values which
might protect us from the more dismal
possibilities of the future. In particular, it is our new self-consciousness
toward myth itself which can protect us

from the myths of Science, and may even
give us some clear advantage over earlier
centuries. We could, for example, change
our arts and social institutions not by
the slow, self-defeating, bloody means of
revolution, but by criticizing our culture
directly at its source, in myth.

Today we need help from Freud as well
as anthropology to recover such ancient
meanings as even a fairy tale may possess.
But if we cannot recapture the original
innocence with which our fathers believed
in their religion and practised its rites
unthinkingly, we can at least understand--
better than they, perhaps -- what the
purpose of a religion is. There is some
encouragement in this. First, we are
given a measure of choice in deciding what
myths we may believe in and what rites we
are to practise. And secondly we find
that we are not qualitatively different
from all our religious forbears, as
scientists of the last two centuries were
led to' suppose, but that on the contrary,
we merely believe -- with much the same
faith -- in a different pantheon of values,
practise a different magic.

But this is only to say that every
culture is founded on, and motivated by,
a religion; when the religion loses force,
the culture dies. At least all cultures
before us have died with their religions.
I am not convinced that this must necessarily be so. There is a special balm of
reason -- self-consciousness -- supplied
to men in the transition age between one
culture and the next. This self-consciousness is a *critical* consciousness: the
ability to criticize old values in the
light of reason and so create the new
values which become new myths -- become,
in a sense, new gods.

A Long Way From Home
Some Film Nightmares from the 40's

Barbara Deming

A Long Way From Home is a detailed and carefully documented study of the films of the Forties. Chapter II, which is concluded here, analyzes a number of the war movies from that long decade. Chapter III, 'I've Got to Bring Him Back Home Where He Belongs (A Hollywood Ariadne)' will be published in the next issue of *City Lights.* *(Copyright, 1951, 1953, by Barbara Deming.)*

II. *I Stick My Neck Out for Nobody* (War Hero)

Here is, for instance, another Humphrey Bogart film: *PASSAGE TO MARSEILLE* (1944). This is one of a number of such films which tag the hero, comfortably, a Frenchman. His precise identity is again withheld from us for a while—hid, this time, to be thorough, within not one flashback but an elaborate succession of them. A glum mask is again our starting point, the question: what lies behind this mask?—the question that sets the drama in motion. A war correspondent visiting a Free French unit at a British airfield, singles out the hero and asks about this strange grim man ('I have never seen a stronger face, nor a stranger!"). The commanding officer (Claude Rains again) nods darkly. Off the record, he could a tale unfold. So he unfolds the tale of his own attempt to puzzle out the man. He, Rains, had been first mate on a French ship ordered back to Marseille during the defense of France, when a little raft had been sighted, a bunch of ragged half starved men taken aboard, Bogart—Matraux—one of them. The men had declared themselves goldminers from an out of the way place, set forth to join the fight for their country; but this story had not

seemed convincing. Finding Rains sympathetic, the men had opened up to him, one after another (in one flashback after another) giving him their true backgrounds—all, that is, but Matraux, who had sat in brooding silence throughout. But in a further flashback which unfolds within one of these flashbacks within a flashback, the identity of Matraux is finally revealed to us. And Matraux is no disappointed lover this time. The betrayal *he* has suffered is Munich. Matraux is a newspaper man, and in his paper he savagely assails the pact. We see his place stoned in retaliation. We see him making his escape in his car, Michele Morgan by his side. And watch this figure blur now with the figure of Rick in *CASABLANCA*: on his face as he drives away is the same grimace that Rick wore that terrible day Ilse left him waiting in the rain. But France is the beloved, this time, who has betrayed him. He and Michele themselves talk of the betrayal in these terms; the parallel is none I am forcing. When he proposes to her, she tells him that she had thought France, her rival, would always stand between them. But " that is all ancient history now, " he tells her grimly. And so they do get married. But "a sigh is still a sigh, as time goes by." This broken love has even its musical leitmotif, a little song that runs through this film much as the song, "As Time Goes By" ran through *CASABLANCA*. "Some day I'll meet you again," it moans, as Matraux glooms (even on his honeymoon).

Soon those whom Matraux has outraged by his criticism of the pact, have him sent off to Devil's Island on trumped up charges. There we see him grimly pacing a solitary cell; and the scene again could almost be from *CASABLANCA*, that scene where Ilse walks in on Rick, and he strikes out at her. But here Matraux strikes out at France: "Beautiful decadent France! Rotten France!" I hate France!" Matraux has *his* "date with the heebyjeebies."

Just as in CASABLANCA, the question of whether or not he really does mean these baleful words he speaks is raised many times before the answer is given. He manages an escape from the island, with a small group of convicts of various backgrounds—eager, in spite of all they feel they have suffered there from their country to return and fight for it. They look to Matraux as to their natural leader in such a venture. And he does lead them in the escape. But all the while the question hovers for us: are his intentions in escaping really, as they think, to fight for his country? Back on shipboard, as the film begins to reel in some of its flashbacks, this question is very much the concern of Rains. In mid-ocean the Vichy armistice is announced. The camera moves among weeping faces, then hesitates before Matraux's face as before a code. A ghost of a smile distorts it. Rains and an officer who are watching him argue the meaning of this smile. The officer would give it a dark reading. But Rains is willing to stake his life that Matraux is "more of a Frenchman than any of us." He goes to him now and asks his help in seizing the ship for deGaulle. As in *CASABLANCA*, here just before that moment which will prove the hero indeed such a

Frenchman, the disquieting image at the heart of the dream stands forth in sharp relief. "I don't care anything about my country anymore!" cries Matraux; "Her death is complete! I'm trying to get back to my wife. I have never intended to join the fight!" His words are promptly annulled—more promptly than in *CASABLANCA*. (The very beginning of the film has told us in advance the outcome, but we tend rather to forget this.) When certain villains on board try to hold the ship for Vichy, the first man to the guns to keep them at bay—is Matraux. When a Nazi plane, in answer to a wireless message from these villains, dive bombs the ship, the one to bring it down—is Matraux. The film now returns us to the British airfield—and to that familiar image of the fighting group that is one happy ardent family. Rains, concluding his story to the correspondent, had remarked not merely upon the strangeness of Matraux but upon the strangeness of that French unit as a whole. The men had seemed to him, all of them, so silent, so grim. Where was that gay banter he remembered from the last war? But here this impression is forgotten. The dream has again brought us quite clear.

It is not only when Humphrey Bogart takes the role that other figures tend to blur with the figure of Rick in *CASABLANCA*. In *APPOINTMENT IN BERLIN* (1943), George Sanders is cast. This time the hero is tagged an Englishman. Again the great hurt he suffers is Munich. Listening with his father to Chamberlain's broadcast, he cannot help from crying out, "Ethiopia, Spain, China—now Munich!" He is ashamed of being English! "How dare you, sir!" exclaims his father, and puts his son out of the house. Again a scene is included in which the hero gives himself up altogether to bitterness. This hero, though, finds—out on the streets—one sympathetic soul: a little cockney newspaper hawker, who has lost an arm in the first world war. "Don't you ever wonder why?" cries the hero. And the two go off together to drink their misery down. They make an evening of it, end up scrawling sarcastic swastikas on Nelson's column. And the morning after brings summary courtmartial for Sanders.

In *PASSAGE TO MARSEILLE*, no moment is included which parallels Ilse's explanation to Rick of why she had to hurt him as she did. We are merely led from the start to question whether the hero's love for his country really is "ancient history," and when the crucial moment arrives, the doubt implanted is happily confirmed. This suffices. The focus is all on *how* he will act. We do not ponder the why's. We have time merely, as it were, to place our bets. *APPOINTMENT IN BERLIN* reduces to a minimum this guessing game (it concentrates on elaborating the hero's sufferings) but it includes a parallel to Ilse's loving explanation. Suddenly—it turns out that he has misunderstood. All in spite of herself, England *had* to hurt him. An old friend looks him up, tests him briefly in conversation, cries, "Then what happens to England does matter to you?" "What do you think?" cries the hero. "I think more than anyone I know!" cries the friend—the familiar gambit reduced to this short exchange. And now the friend, who turns out to be in Intelligence, reveals to him why it was that England had to do to him what she did on that fateful day. He shows him comparative statistics on English and German forces: Germany 40,000 planes, England 900.. "That's fantastic!" gulps the hero— and understands now. They are of course working day and night to arm, the friend tells him, and he invites him to work for him, in counterespionage. The hero is in a particularly good position to be helpful to the Cause, for with the visa of his disgrace he can enter the enemy camp, there to broadcast back to England what are ostensibly treasonable broadcasts but are in reality vital messages in special code. This hero proves a crucial figure indeed for the dream to have enlisted: he is able to save England from an entire invasion fleet!

If the figure of the disappointed liberal, in these two films, may be said to blur at moments into the figure of the sad lover of *CASABLANCA*, the reverse is also so. Before he is "unveiled" to us as love's victim, Rick might well be supposed to be suffering from the sad shocks suffered by Matraux and Sanders—Rick who, when he is reminded of his activities in Spain and Ethiopia, comments, "I found that a very expensive hobby." Before the appearance of Ilse on the scene, Rick stands before us in a variety of possible guises. For it is not only from one film to another that this image I am tracing tends to extend itself; it assumes new forms, often, even within the same film. A half—joking exchange, for example, for a tenuous moment materialises Rick as a criminal figure. Renault, recall, probing the reasons for his exile from America, asks did he abscond with church funds, run off with the President's wife, kill a man? All three, Rick lightly replies. Maltraux in PASSAGE TO MARSEILLE also flickers before us in this guise: he is introduced to us in the company of criminals, and it is the length of several flashbacks before he is clearly distinguished from them. In certain other films, the hero is tagged specifically a criminal, this his carefully given very special exile. One of these films is *THE IMPOSTOR* (1944), featuring Jean Gabin.

At the start of this film, the hero (a Frenchman again) is about to give up his life for his country, but not willingly: he is about to be executed; and on his lips are curses for France. He is saved from death by an air raid, which. crumbles the jail and allows him to make his escape—and allows the film to unwind its dream reversal of this disturbing image.

This reversal is a more difficult one than in the preceding cases, and the dream work is managed with the special assistance of one character, the dream's apprentice, as it were, who in all his attitudes anticipates for us the final magical effect, through the power of suggestion fools us into seeing what is not really there to be seen. This man, from the start, refuses to recognise the hero's behavior for what it would all too clearly seem to be. He is Gabin's commanding officer—for Gabin makes good his escape by donning the uniform, papers, ostensible identity of a French soldier he finds dead on the road. Petain has just broadcast his surrender; so once in uniform, he is immediately involved in all the decisions facing soldiers at this point, as to whether or not they will try somehow to continue the fight. Abstracted on paper, there seems little even of the ambiguous in this hero's behavior. · The men with whom he finds himself—a gathering from various disrupted outfits—are all for shipping out for Africa, to join deGaulle. He embarks on a ship *with* them—just as Matraux joined those others in escape from Devil's Island. But as a fugitive, this is the practical move for him to make. At Point Noire where the others rush to join the Free French, he promptly declares his intentions of becoming a civilian. Then he joins up with them after all. But he does so after learning that whoever signs up can ask for advance pay. Collecting the advance pay, he enters a shop to price civilian clothes, and to inquire about job opportunities across the river. He decides not to buy the clothes, but only after the shopkeeper tells him that six month's army pay would buy a rubber plantation. He never follows up this tip, either, but he doesn't get a chance; the group is suddenly moved up the Congo.

At the new post, he sulks about, holding himself aloof from the others. The others are always talking about their beloved country, and bringing out photos, reviving memories. He snarls at them, "The past is dead and buried! Let it stay there!" All of which would seem to read plainly enough—if it were not for the eye of the lieutenant upon the scene. All through this the lieutenant is watching him, as Rains watched Bogart in *PASSAGE TO MARSEILLE*, laying bets, with

himself, that this man is "more of a Frenchman than any of" them. He is promoting him steadily, to force on him the test which will *prove* him the reverse of what he seems.

The test arrives. The lieutenant falls sick and in the delirium of fever, runs about shooting off his gun, setting the lives of the men in danger. The hero, at the risk of his own life, disarms him. Soon after, the group goes off into battle in Libya, and the hero with a handful of men takes an entire enemy garrison. On the return to camp the familiar image is rendered us. His comrades gather round him, singing his praises. "We all fought together," he cries; and arm in arm, they drink to one another; and to Britain; and to Russia; and to America, too, "who's sending lots of things" —one big family.

In this film, a certain admission should be noted, that an about-face has been effected. We witness many touching little efforts on the part of the men to make Gabin feel less "out of things;" and he also speaks, later on, of the strange effect upon him of the assumption of the identity of another man. At one point, he says right out that a great change has come over him—like the change that comes over a man when he falls in love. ("A beautiful woman, our France," nods the lieutenant.) Yet, though these words are spoken, the impression that is left with us in the end is that such a love has lived in his breast always. This instinct of the dream to drown out any admission that a translation has occurred—this instinct, served in advance by the lieutenant's attitude of expectation, is further served by the fact that Gabin, like Rick, this one lapse excepted, continues to the end cynical in utterances. On the very eve of battle he comments, "I have just my own skin, and it's not worth fighting for." Thus in our minds two images are intimately linked, as if the one were to be deduced from the other: the glooming, the seeming-faithless gesture—and the decisive blow for the Cause. Near the end

of the film, one of the soldiers is talking
of Gabin to a stranger. His words refer
not to Gabin's eventual behavior but to
his behavior from the very start. " We
were driven from our homes, " he says,
" into a cruel killing world. We would
have died if it had not been for him. He
was more of a man, stronger than any of
us. " The sullen mask is again recognized
as the sign of strength, the mark of one
to be relied upon before all others—a
mark the lieutenant, a connoisseur, could
read right off.

It is through the eyes of the lieutenant
that one can see this hero, too, like Rick,
flicker before us in a number of guises
other than his own. At one point the hero
tries to decline a promotion the lieutenant
is offering, and the lieutenant suddenly
challenges him: " I know plenty about you.
Back in France they had to practically
shoot you to make you fall back. " It
appears that the lieutenant all this time,
knowing the record of the man whose name
Gabin has adopted, has taken Gabin to be
one like Matraux or Sanders. And the one
figure, at his words, does easily dissolve
into the other. The cries of Gabin—" The
past is dead and buried! " —are easily
confounded with the cries of Matraux—
" I don't care anything about my country
any more. Her death is complete! " the
cries of Sanders—" I am ashamed to be an
Englishman! " This figure dissolves even,
in a tenuous fashion, with the sad lover
of *CASABLANCA*, after he has recovered those
happy days he thought were lost. When
Gabin confides to the lieutenant his new-
found love for France, the latter nods,
" A beautiful woman, our France; give her
an even break, she'll never let you down. "

But there is still another identity
which, in stealth, is borrowed by this
" impostor. " The film continues a while
longer, after the return from battle. And
in the course of events, the hero's real
origins are discovered. The lieutenant
takes it upon himself to defend him against
official protests. He defends him in this
fashion: Many unsung heroes rallied to

France in her hour of need. They weren't
forced to take up arms, and there was " no
hope of profit" in it for them. " Simple
everyday people" they were. The hero was
" one of that number. " He took the other
soldier's name and honored it. Here is a
rather remarkable defense, if one reviews
the facts of the case. And yet, as the
lieutenant speaks, the hero does merge
somehow in our minds with those " everyday
people" —his criminal background dissolves
into simply a humble one, and he stands
there before us just a guy who had to come
up the hard way. (" Nobody ever gave me
anything, " has been his motto.)

This sudden translation of the criminal
figure into the figure of the everyday guy
is not an isolated instance. In an earlier
film than *THE IMPOSTOR*—*MR. LUCKY* (1943)—
the one figure dissolves more completely
still into the other.

MR. LUCKY provides also an example even
more pronounced of the film's ability to
outface the facts it arrays before us.
This dream has more to outface, for it
dares to make its hero an American, and
the setting the States. The time set is, of
course, to ease things, pre-Pearl Harbor,
and the hero is no everyday citizen at
first glance, but a boss gambler. A light
touch is also added. This hero enters
whistling. Mr. Lucky (Cary Grant) confronts us not with glooming sour stare but,
eyes propped wide, with the comic double-
take (Grant adept at this face as Bogart
at the other); crying not, in dark accent,
" I'm the only Cause I'm interested in! "
But, when the draft call comes, " They
can't do this to me; I'm a civilian! "
In front of the recruiting poster—finger-
levelled Uncle Sam: " I WANT YOU! " — he
performs a wonderful pantomine: uneasiness
he can't place, start of recognition,
nimble sidestep. The key is a different
one, but the tune is the same: " This
isn't my war! " " My war, " says Mr. Lucky,
" was crawling up out of the gutter. The
hard way. I won that war. I don't recognize any other. " So he ducks the draft,
by assuming the identity of a **4F** member of

his gang, one Boskopolis, who has just
died. Then—he needs money to launch his
gambling ship—he sets out to try and milch
some thousands of dollars off a certain
war relief organisation. His plan is to
run the gambling concession at their charity ball—all the machines to be conven-
iently equipped with false bottoms.

In this film, too, one can isolate the
clear lines of an about-face. Again the
new identity the hero has assumed plays
its part. A letter arrives from Boskopolis'
mother, back in Greece, describing the
futile valiant defense of that homeland,
and Mr. Lucky is impressed. He also falls
in love with Larraine Day, active in War
Relief Inc. Like the hero of THE IMPOSTOR,
he speaks right out about the change that
has come over him. " I woke up," he says
one day. And he doesn't run off with " the
take" from the gambling machines. In fact
he decides to convert his gambling ship
into a transport to deliver medical supplies for War Relief Inc. And at the end
of that trip he himself joins the Merchant
Marine.

But though the film lines up these
facts for us in clear array, a synopsis in
terms of them is less than inadequate.
Here is the more pertinent synopsis: This
is the drama of a man misunderstood, a man
whose girl, to her shame, mistrusts his
motives. In the end, this girl wakes up
and recognizes the hero for the hero he is.
" You're right always," she comes, at last,
to say.

The dream accomplishes its ends by
simple distraction. It carefully lines up
alongside the one set of facts, another:
one episode after another in which the
hero is attacked not on the score of his
very real guilt, but where he is blameless.
The fact of that real guilt, in all this,
goes barely noticed—and the fact later of
his change of heart.

When " Joe Boskopolis" goes to Larraine
Day with his plan, she tells him bluntly,
" I don't trust your motives," and sends
him away. This is our starting point: she
knows better than to trust him; so do we.

Next day he turns up again to volunteer as
a simple recruit—saucily, big-eyed, " I'd
do anything to help the Cause, anything!"
Larraine calls his bluff: she sets him to
knitting. But Joe sticks. And he soon
has this " iceberg" thawing. He thinks up
a fast one, confides in her that he has
relatives over in Greece. If he's 4F and
can't enlist, the least he can do is help
" those poor people " Larraine falls for
it and, ashamed of herself, she relieves
him of the knitting. So far so clear to
us, if not to Larraine. But from here on,
the subtle confusion begins. She continues throughout the film to suffer these
moments of shame at having belittled him,
but from here on we begin to share in her
blushes.

Joe has a rip in his coat and Larraine
takes him home with her to mend it. Joe
interprets her action as well he might,
and tries to kiss her. She protests.
(Already we sympathise with Joe.) Meanwhile she has spotted a trick coin in his
possession. She has seen Joe put this coin
to use for War Relief Inc. A certain
Scotchman has tried to overcharge them for
some blankets; Joe has flipped the Scotchman for double or nothing and, of course,
won. Larraine, who has just put that two
and two together, challenges Joe: " Suppose
we settle it with the game you played with
MacDougall. " The game is a matter of
guessing which hand, and the coin has a
little gadget to hook it to the back of
Joe's coat. Larraine cries, " Neither
hand!" but—this time he hasn't cheated.
He rebukes her, " Never give a sucker an
even break, but don't cheat a friend—I
live by it." " I lost, but I didn't know
the rules of the game, " she protests.
Poor girl, we feel—no, she doesn't at all
know the rules; it is *he* who plays by the
rules. He quietly asks for his hat. Blushing again, she suddenly cries out, " Joe,
will you run the gambling concession at
the ball?" Now she knows she can trust
him.

We know perfectly well that she can't.
In fact, he tells us so himself, promptly

reports to the boys, " She laid it right in my lap! '' And yet: we are blushing still for having doubted his morality in this other instance. Our distraction has begun. It deepens. Larraine's grandfather rages upon the scene, wanting to know what's all this about gambling. And now Larraine must blush for *him*, for he in turn attacks Joe on grounds entirely unjust. He first attacks him on the outrageous grounds of the name he bears: "Get that greasy black head out of here!" Then he looks up Boskopolis' record and begins to attack him on the basis of this. Larraine won't believe what he says about him. And she is, of course, right. For Joe is *not* Boskopolis. Nor does he know of the record, which isn't a nice one.

But Larraine now, in quick counterattack against her grandfather, proceeds to misuse Joe again, herself, most sorely. She drives him off to the home of the other side of her family, in Maryland; and there, by phone, she blackmails her grandfather:unless he permits the gambling concession to stand, she will marry this man. It works. " Yeah, why wouldn't it work?" Joe comments, and this time rebukes her at some length. In the drama of *her* conversion,this is the major scene. " Anything for the Cause!" he taunts. He tells her, " I know where I stand with you once you've cashed in on me. " And, he implies, she fails to recognise whom it is she is scorning.

The moment is worth dwelling over, for it is here that the figure of the criminal suffers complete translation into the figure of the everyday American guy. " You think the worst thing that could happen to you is to marry me," he says. He turns to the family portraits on the walls. She has led him among these, telling him of each, and one after another has been a man of inherited wealth—except for the last one in the line, the earliest ancestor. Joe triumphantly indicates this portrait. Go back far enough and somebody " made all that dough" for the others. The moral looms: in scorning Joe she is in effect scorning that first of her ancestors. Larraine, herself, has prepared the ground for the equation quietly effected here. To her grandfather, another self-made man, she has remarked that he and Joe have a lot in common. " You're both tough, " she sums it up. " I know *you* are in a highly moral civilized way," she has thrown in—trippingly off her tongue, this distinction—" but it's fundamentally the same thing: character. " " How long since anybody ever had control over you?" she has asked Joe. " Nobody ever had, or will. " Character. Under the power of this heading, a remarkable series of items now coalesce into one. Her grandfather's hot temper, Joe's scorn for traffic signals, and his tendency to flashy ties, a longago eccentric act of that remoter ancestor—what but the same sort of thing, we dimly feel. Her ancestors " never seemed to behave the way people expected, " Larraine has boasted. His descendants " had quite a time living down" this first of the line: he, a slave owner, was killed at Harper's Ferry, fighting side by side with John Brown. Now, as Joe chides her, here they stand, side by side—her grandfather, this remoter ancestor, Joe—marked by the dream with the identical sign: rugged in - dividuals. Out of some perverse snobbery, at odds with all most brave in her own background, she has been scorning this man. She doesn't know what to say. So she does the appropriate: she embraces him.

The further drama we now look forward to is the drama of Larraine's definitive awakening.   Yet look where literally we are: the hero at this point is still frankly intending to run off with the take from the gambling concession. It is soon after this very scene that we see him give the boys their instructions, cautioning " No slip-ups!" Perfectly clearly we hear him give these orders. Perfectly clearly we next witness his about-face; we see him receive the letter from Boskopolis' mother; we hear him, arrived at the ball, blurt out to Larraine, " I woke up! " But we are blissfully confused. The further thrill we stubbornly anticipate is some final act to that drama of her conversion—which is of course what we are given: the final misunderstanding, most cruel of all, and the final total " recognition. "

Joe tells the boys that the plan is off: " Our take is nothing." The boys will not have it. They force him, at pistol point, to make the grab.   In on this Larraine walks.   She doesn't see the pistols, just Joe there with his hands full of the money that was never turned over to her. " Oh Joe! " she groans. He even has to knock her out, so that she won't get hurt. " Now I recognize you, Joe boy, " says one of the gang. And there he stands, indeed, for recognition—the disturbing figure dominant in all these dreams. But for one in the audience he has been subtly altered beyond all recognition: he is the one, simply, always cruelly misunderstood. Such he now proves himself. At the risk of his life, he tackles these villains single-handed; is shot, sorely wounded, but drags himself bleeding off, the money clutched to his breast; then sends the money back by messenger to Larraine —who sees how wrong again she was to doubt him. Further confirmation: her grandfather's agents hand her the proof of that nasty record he has spoken of—and the photograph attached is not of Joe at all! The film ends as Larraine works out her contrition.   Joe, sufficiently recovered, has set sail to deliver those medical supplies, Unable to learn his whereabouts, she has managed to get to the dock only in time to see the ship pull out, and to cry across the widening gap, " Oh take me with you, please! " We see her now, waiting at the pier. Day after day, we gather, she waits there, patiently. One would not know the once haughty girl. At the last, her humility is rewarded: out of the fog walks Joe.

All of which, set down on paper, sounds like ineffective magic. Set down on paper, certain stubborn facts tend to obtrude— like the fact that if Joe is not this Boskopolis of unsavory record, he has, after

all, assumed Boskopolis' name for questionable purposes of his own; he remains a draft dodger (until he joins the Merchant Marine, in which uniform he emerges, at last, out of the fog.) For the reader these facts may stand out. For one sitting out front, the distractions are, to say the least, more lively.

I have not even done full justice to the bravado of this film. Here is an incident I have omitted: Joe has pulled off a bit of fraud on the side. He has bullied some creditor, a Mr. Hargrave, into letting him tear up a check from War Relief Inc.— deftly substituting a blank check at the crucial moment, cashing the real check then himself. At the charity ball, Larraine announces to Joe that her grandfather is out of town looking for Hargrave. We see Joe take this in, add two and two; see him proceed upstairs, collect the necessary cash, stick it in an envelope addressed to Hargrave and stroll downstairs again. When Hargrave and the grandfather storm in and confront him, he blithely takes this envelope from his pocket and hands it across, remarking that he hasn't been able to reach Hargrave, because he has been out of town. Hargrave is disarmed, and the grandfather is disarmed, and we have been disarmed long ago. Here is measure of the film's powers of distraction: in spite of ourselves, we comfortably nod: You see!

There are some films, more simpleminded than any I have detailed so far, in which the magic of the dream is abbreviated crudely. A particular moment from such a film will exhibit the essential nature of all these dreams in what amounts to caricature. This is true of *CHINA* (1943). The hero of this film is another American on his way up—one Jones, played by Alan Ladd.   While Mr. Lucky was surreptitiously identified for us as an everyday figure, Jones can be established as one openly, for this setting is a remote one, and the time is again pre Pearl Harbor. He is a salesman for a big American oil company operating in the Far East. When a Chinese Intelligence chief chides him for selling to the Japanese, and delivers an impassioned speech on the issues at stake, he interrupts him: "Going to give me more of that tripe? War's your business, oil is mine." On the road to Shanghai where Jones has a business appointment, he encounters Loretta Young (also American) in charge of a pretty little group of Chinese co-eds. They, too, have an appointment—"With the destiny of China." They are bound for a university in a distant city; and they ask Mr. Jones to take them there. Jones consents to give them a lift; but for a long while he insists that he will not go out of his way. One of the co-eds decides to stay behind at the farm of her parents, when the truck makes a stop there; and her parents also take into their keeping the orphaned baby, little "Donald Duck," Jones' pal (William Bendix) has picked up along the way. Just as the truck is nearing the crossroad at which Jones has said he must put them all down, word comes that the Japanese are approaching that farm. Loretta says that Jones must turn back. But if he turned back, he would be late for his appointment. He refuses. At which Bendix challenges him to a fight: he'll have to knock him down first, if he wants to drive on. The two have a violent scuffle. Mr. Jones does knock Bendix down. But instead of proceeding on about his business, he here declares in gruff tones: "I was going back anyway!" Off he goes to the rescue—for which he is too late; and from here on, he is definitely in the fight. He was going to all along! Here, in this moment, is the substance of all these dreams, in crude shorthand: the faithless gesture given vent, and then denied.

A similar gambit could be recalled in CASABLANCA—there but one sleight of hand among many. There, too, it was the cynicism of "business is business" that the dream was concerned to wish away. For among the various guises flickeringly assumed by Rick is also this one—of the man out for what he can make. "I got well paid for it," he has said of his past adventures. When he promises Lazslo the letters of transit, he demands a high price. Skip the thanks, he tells him, "this is strictly a matter of business." Then when Lazslo tries to pay him, "Keep it; you'll need it," he grunts, just a touch reproachfully.

There is a comparable moment in TO HAVE AND HAVE NOT (1944), another film to feature Humphrey Bogart. Morgan, an American settled in Martinique, makes his living as a guide, and with the boat he runs he could be very useful to the Free French. (Again this is pre Pearl Harbor.). But "You save France, I'll save my boat," he declares. His sympathies? "Minding my own business." He agrees, finally, to run one errand for the underground, but he'll do it, he says, just because he needs the money. When they beg him later to look after one of their wounded, he answers "Not a chance." His landlady proposes a bargain: if he'll help them, she'll cancel his bill. "Will you throw in her bill, too?" he inquires, indicating Lauren Bacall (another American wandered far from home.) She will. At which he declares in bitter tones, "You almost had me figured out right—except for one thing: I still owe you that bill."

The isolationism of Mr. Jones in CHINA is specifically established as that of one obsessed with making money. But this is not strictly so of Morgan in TO HAVE AND HAVE NOT. In the Hemingway novel on which the film is "based," the hero was, of course, a figure politically disillusioned. But in the film his background is left quite blank. As in CASABLANCA, we are diverted from doing too much guessing about him by the suggestion that he is the victim of an unhappy love affair. Lauren Bacall offers this diagnosis. "Who was the girl, Steve?" And though this leaves things a bit less definite than they were made in CASABLANCA, it serves to distract us; and, as in that film, the dream then leans heavily on the heroine's success in breaking down his resistance to her. He succumbs to the Free French and succumbs to her vigorous wooing at a significantly parallel rate, and says his definitive " yes" to each simultaneously. Off they go, in fact, together into battle. Their honeymoon is to be the risky attempt to free an underground leader from Devil's Island.

But there are other films besides CHINA in which it is specifically the obsession with making one's way that constitutes the hero's grievous isolation. Another is REUNION IN FRANCE (1942). In this film an about-face need not be obscured; it is avoided altogether. The drama framed is one of literal misunderstanding. The hero is a French industrialist, and when France falls, he continues to run his factory, at the service of the Vichy. So he is abandoned by all he loves. But in the end they learn that all the time he has been working within the enemy camp, turning out defective mechanisms. " How terribly lonely he must be! " wails his fiancee (Joan Crawford), who deserted him with all the rest. And she hurries back to face with him the death he must inevitably suffer when his work is discovered. (The only question this film braves is: why such a fantasy at all?)

But one could go on duplicating, triplicating these figures, duplicating, triplicating the sleights of hand, subtle or simple, with which the dream persuades us how wrong we have been—to be disturbed by a cynicism we only thought we recognized. I have omitted not merely further examples of figures already defined, but examples of further types of figures altogether. There are a number of films, for example, that question dramatically, then dramatically affirm, the faith of one who is foreign born. One film features an expatriate in the role. To detail more would be redundant. Line up together merely those films I have detailed and see how pervasive the image is. Figures at the periphery of society, figures who are its very staple, those at the bottom of the ladder, those at the top, some mourning a faith they never had, some a faith they once had, which is fled—that bitter light, telling

of exile, which swept the room in which Rick sat, catches them all in its circuit. From film to film, the image takes to itself new forms. And even, in many an instance, within a single film, through any of a dozen casual ways—through a half-joking exchange (CASABLANCA), or a friend's oratory (THE IMPOSTOR), a misunderstanding (THE IMPOSTOR) or a bitter masquerade (CASABLANCA, TO HAVE AND HAVE NOT)—it dissolves one figure into some other, thus extending itself.

It is obvious, of course, that some of the forms this image takes are illusive in a sense that others are not. The guise of the Frenchman, of the Englishman—these are transparencies. The guise of the sulking lover is only less transparent than these—also the guise of the one marked out a criminal, or of one set down in a foreign land, or stranger to this country, and for that reason stranger to the general faith. The disappointed liberal, and the one obsessed with making his way—these are figures of substance, cast their own shadows. These figures are illusive only in that they are not definitive. The vagueness of a figure like Morgan in TO HAVE AND HAVE NOT is, after all, apt (one does not assume on the part of the movie audience generally a knowledge of the original novel, which would correct that vagueness); and when in CASABLANCA someone demands of Rick, " What is your nationality?" and he quips " Drunkard" and Renault comments, " That makes him an international figure"—this, too, is peculiarly apt; the remark finds natural utterance. Behind all these figures looms a figure more general.

If the image is curiously pervasive, it is also more instractable than I have suggested. It is well to take a more complete look at the endings to all these films.

Look again at the ending of CASABLANCA. Stout words Rick utters to Ingrid—about the Cause, about the job he has to do. And off he goes, arm in arm with comrade—" the beginning of a beautiful friendship, " he observes. Off he goes into the fight.

But—off goes the plane, too, to America, his country, to which he can never return; bearing Ingrid, whom he loves, and whom he will never see again. Nor has the music let us forget that "man must have his mate." And "how long was it (they) had?" A stoic exit, Rick's. One may breathe: he *needs* to be "stronger than any of us." *

One may breathe this at the end of all these films. For though in each case brightly tagged now the warrier who will win for us, there, if one look twice, is one whose condition closely resembles that of the lonely figure who so discomfited us at the start. The dream has been able to confront us with no translation too total— lest, it seems, we wake.

Certain of the heroes, recall, must step into battle greviously misunderstood. Here by the very sleight of hand with which the dream chooses to deny his acquaintance with the one bitterness, it hands the hero a new bitterness. The actor need hardly change his expression—seldom does. This is true of Mr. Lucky, and of the heroes of *CHINA*, *TO HAVE AND HAVE NOT*, and even *CASABLANCA* briefly. And some of the films labor the point exquisitely. For in some the plot so arranges itself that to work most effec- tively for the Cause, the hero *must* be misunderstood, that he may work his way into the enemy's midst. I have but hinted the sufferings stoically endured by the heroes of *REUNION IN FRANCE* and *APPOINTMENT IN BERLIN*. In the latter film, the hero's ardent statement of faith is extracted early in the game. The Intelligence De- partment helps him frame himself, so as to appear a serious traitor. And then even his old friend Smitty will have nothing to do with him. "You too, eh Smitty?" he cries in his anguish. And the German girl he's ordered to court (her brother can get

him the crucial radio job), she, too, scorns him; for it turns out that she's anti-Nazi. And of course he has fallen in love with her. It is a lonely lonely fight these heroes must fight. *THE IMPOSTOR* too first arranges its hero arm in arm with his comrades but, having achieved this, it too, in still another fashion, incon- spicuously takes it all back. When the hero's real identity is discovered, the lieutenant defends him vigorously, but military form must be observed: he is stripped of his rank, before all the others, and he is told that he can no longer bear that borrowed name. The lieutenant tells him to choose in its place whatever name he will, but he chooses to step off into battle bearing no name at all.

It is relevant to note, too, that *MR. LUCKY* is the only film of all those I have detailed which ventures at the end to bring its hero home. Even in *MR. LUCKY* an alternate note has been sounded. A man down at the docks where Larraine waits for Joe day after day informs an observer that Joe's ship has been sunk: he never will return. We thrill appropriately to this news, and only at the very last moment of the film is the news disproved. In other films, such news is final. *THE IMPOSTOR* kills off its hero by having him volunteer for a particularly dangerous battlefront. In the last moments of *PASSAGE TO MARSEILLE* a plane returns from a bombing mission and Matraux is lifted out dead. And here as in *CASABLANCA*, that happiness he will now never know has first been carefully evoked for us. Matraux, it seems, had a way of taking little detours on the way home from bombing missions, to drop greet- ings over the farm house in occupied France where Michele lives, and his baby son whom he has never seen. This day we see Michele

---

* One popular and lively group of war films that I have not mentioned so far is here worth noting. The genre borrows from the documentary manner, and dramatizes a group battle situation. *GUADAL- CANAL DIARY* (1943), *A WING AND A PRAYER* (1944), *OBJECTIVE BURMA* (1945) are a few examples. Almost invariably in these films the drama is of some stoic stint, some mission the raison d'etre of which the fighters' cannot be told until the mission is completed. They must fight on grimly, not knowing whether they lay down their lives for some real purpose or not. Here is, to be sure, of- ten literally enough, the nature of battle. And yet there are other battle situations the makers of those films might have chosen. The one image does compulsively take shape, wherever one turns in the films of these years.

and the boy waiting for a note in vain. Often the dream rather strains itself to kill the hero off. It might seem only realistic in the case, say, of *APPOINTMENT IN BERLIN*, to have the hero discovered at last by the enemy and put to death. But here are a few details of that ending: When the Nazis discover what Sanders has been up to, the dream does allow him to make a getaway. It even contrives for him to steal a plane. Aloft in it, he radios that last crucial message to England, that a Nazi invasion fleet is ready to strike. At this point it would not have to stretch things much to fly the hero home. But the hero feels it necessary to show the way for the British forces by diving his plane into the Nazi fleet. "Look for a big light!" he cries deliriously. Then: "All the way down, Smitty!" Nor can the hero's death in *CHINA* be said to have been inserted in the interests of realism. The Chinese have planned to dynamite a mountain pass through which a Japanese division is to file. When the division gets there before it has been expected, the hero takes it upon himself to delay them while the charge is laid. This he does by jumping onto the road and blithely requesting of the commanding officer some gas for a stalled car. The officer, amused by his audacity, takes time out to bum from him an American cigarette, and then to inform him that Pearl Harbor has just been attacked. The hero replies with a speech about how millions of "little guys" like himself will see to it that Japan is beaten. He then sees to it that he himself gets a bullet in the stomach, by tossing his own cigarette into the off-

icer's face. And the pass explodes over them all, as Loretta on the mountain above proudly weeps.

There is a touch of the suicidal to be discerned in the final gestures of these heroes, a shadow of that impulse in which we have seen them indulge in their hours of bitterness. Dying for their country is the name given this gesture now. Yet the echo of an earlier despair does remain.

At the end of *TO HAVE AND HAVE NOT*, the hero sets out to storm Devil's Island, arm in arm with Lauren Bacall. Jaunty smiles sit on both faces. Those smiles may be read as the smiles of the valorous—and of those who, besides, are rather pleased with each other; but they easily waver, too, into the smiles of those who walk into death with a certain reckless pleasure. When this hero said "yes" to the heroine, he had warned her that if she came with him it might be a long long time before she would get home. "Maybe never," she had countered gayly. This phrase echoes in the air at the end. She might have meant simply that she intends to stick with Bogart; or she might equally have meant that they would undoubtedly, she and he, be killed.

The gesture with which the hero in one of these films steps off at last into battle, is not definitively suicidal. The note is sometimes a wavering one, as here. And Rick in *CASABLANCA*, one may say, enters the fight doubtful indeed of a homecoming, yet determined to fight on for the love, as it were, of what he has not. Here is the range, however, of this final gesture: it wavers between the suicidal and the rather bleakly stoical.

AVANT-GARDE MAGAZINES

AN ARNO PRESS REPRINT COLLECTION

Circle, 1944-1948
George Leite and Bern Porter, editors
Ten issues (all published) in two volumes

City Lights, 1952-1955
Peter Martin, editor
Five issues (all published) in one volume

Joglars, 1964-1966
Clark Coolidge, editor
Three issues (all published) in one volume

White Dove Review, 1959-1960
Ron Padgett, editor
Five issues (all published) in one volume

Work *and* Whe're, 1965-1966
John Sinclair and Ron Caplan, editors
Four issues of *Work* and one issue of *Whe're*
   (all published) in one volume

Zero, 1949-1956
Albert Benveniste
   and Themistocles Hoetis, editors
Seven issues (all published) in one volume